Each volume of this series of companions to major philosophers contains specially commissioned essays by an international team of scholars, together with a substantial bibliography, and will serve as a reference work for students and nonspecialists. One aim of the series is to dispel the intimidation such readers often feel when faced with the work of a difficult and challenging thinker.

John Locke, the founder of British empiricism, was also the seventeenth century's staunchest defender of reason in religion and politics. His *Essay concerning Human Understanding* influenced eighteenth-century thought more profoundly than any book save the Bible; his *Two Treatises of Government* helped inspire the American and French revolutions; and much of his work is pertinent to current intellectual and social problems. The essays in this volume provide a systematic survey of Locke's philosophy, informed by the most recent scholarship. They cover Locke's theory of ideas, his philosophies of body, mind, language, and religion, his theory of knowledge, his ethics, and his political philosophy. There are also chapters on Locke's life and times and subsequent influence.

New readers and nonspecialists will find this the most convenient and accessible guide to Locke currently available. Advanced students and specialists will find a conspectus of recent developments in the interpretation of Locke's philosophy.

THE CAMBRIDGE COMPANION TO
LOCKE

OTHER VOLUMES IN THE SERIES OF CAMBRIDGE
COMPANIONS:

AQUINAS *Edited by* NORMAN KRETZMANN *and*
ELEANORE STUMP (published)
ARISTOTLE *Edited by* JONATHAN BARNES
BACON *Edited by* MARKKU PELTONEN
BERKELEY *Edited by* KENNETH WINKLER
DESCARTES *Edited by* JOHN COTTINGHAM
(published)
EARLY GREEK PHILOSOPHY *Edited by*
A. A. LONG
FICHTE *Edited by* GUENTER ZOELLER
FOUCAULT *Edited by* GARY GUTTING
FREGE *Edited by* TOM RICKETTS
FREUD *Edited by* JEROME NEU (published)
HABERMAS *Edited by* STEPHEN K. WHITE
HEGEL *Edited by* FREDRICK BEISER (published)
HEIDEGGER *Edited by* CHARLES GUIGNON
HOBBES *Edited by* TOM SORELL
HUME *Edited by* DAVID FATE NORTON (published)
HUSSERL *Edited by* BARRY SMITH *and* DAVID
WOODRUFF SMITH
WILLIAM JAMES *Edited by* RUTH ANNA PUTNAM
KANT *Edited by* PAUL GUYER (published)
KIERKEGAARD *Edited by* ALASTAIR HANNEY *and*
GORDON MARINO
LEIBNIZ *Edited by* NICHOLAS JOLLEY
MARX *Edited by* TERRELL CARVER (published)
MILL *Edited by* JOHN SKORUPSKI
NIETZSCHE *Edited by* BERND MAGNUS *and*
KATHLEEN HIGGINS
PEIRCE *Edited by* CHRISTOPHER HOOKWAY
PLATO *Edited by* RICHARD KRAUT (published)
PLOTINUS *Edited by* LLOYD P. GERSON
SARTRE *Edited by* CHRISTINA HOWELLS (published)
SPINOZA *Edited by* DON GARRETT
WITTGENSTEIN *Edited by* HANS SLUGA *and*
DAVID STERN

The Cambridge Companion to
LOCKE

Edited by Vere Chappell

CAMBRIDGE
UNIVERSITY PRESS

PUBLISHED BY THE PRESS SYNDICATE OF THE UNIVERSITY OF CAMBRIDGE
The Pitt Building, Trumpington Street, Cambridge CB2 1RP, United Kingdom

CAMBRIDGE UNIVERSITY PRESS
The Edinburgh Building, Cambridge CB2 2RU, United Kingdom
40 West 20th Street, New York, NY 10011-4211, USA
10 Stamford Road, Oakleigh, Melbourne 3166, Australia

First published 1994
Reprinted 1995 (twice), 1997

Printed in the United States of America

Typeset in Trump Mediaeval

A catalogue record for this book is available from the British Library

Library of Congess Cataloguing-in-Publication Data is available

ISBN 0-521-38371-4 hardback
ISBN 0-521-38772-8 paperback

CONTENTS

List of contributors   *page* vii

Note on citations   ix

Introduction   I
VERE CHAPPELL

1 Locke's life and times   5
   J. R. MILTON

2 Locke's theory of ideas   26
   VERE CHAPPELL

3 Locke's philosophy of body   56
   EDWIN McCANN

4 Locke's philosophy of mind   89
   JONATHAN BENNETT

5 Locke's philosophy of language   115
   PAUL GUYER

6 Locke's theory of knowledge   146
   ROGER WOOLHOUSE

7 Locke's philosophy of religion   172
   NICHOLAS WOLTERSTORFF

8 Locke's moral philosophy   199
   J. B. SCHNEEWIND

9 Locke's political philosophy   226
   RICHARD ASHCRAFT

v

vi   Contents

10 Locke's influence   252
    HANS AARSLEFF

    Bibliography   290

    Index of names and subjects   316

    Index of passages cited   324

CONTRIBUTORS

HANS AARSLEFF is Professor of English at Princeton University. He is the author of *The Study of Language in England 1780–1860* (1967) and of *From Locke to Saussure: Essays on the Study of Language and Intellectual History* (1982).

RICHARD ASHCRAFT is Professor of Political Science at the University of California, Los Angeles. He is the author of *Revolutionary Politics and Locke's* Two Treatises of Government (1986) and of *Locke's* Two Treatises of Government (1987); and has recently edited the four-volume *John Locke: Critical Assessments* for Routledge.

JONATHAN BENNETT is Professor of Philosophy of Syracuse University, Fellow of the American Academy of the Arts and Sciences, and a Corresponding Fellow of the British Academy. He is the author of, inter alia, *Kant's Analytic* (1966), *Kant's Dialectic* (1974), *Locke, Berkeley, Hume: Central Themes* (1971), and *A Study of Spinoza's Ethics* (1984). He has also, with Peter Remnant, edited and translated Leibniz's *New Essays on Human Understanding* (1981).

VERE CHAPPELL is Professor of Philosophy at the University of Massachusetts. He is the coauthor, with Willis Doney, of *Twenty-Five Years of Descartes Scholarship* (1987), and editor of the 12-volume *Essays on Early Modern Philosophers* (1992). He also edited the Modern Library *Hume*, as well as the Hume volume in the Anchor Collections of Critical Essays series.

PAUL GUYER is the Florence R. C. Murray Professor in the Humanities at the University of Pennsylvania. He is the author of *Kant and the Claims of Taste* (1979), *Kant and the Claims of Knowledge*

vii

(1987), and *Kant and the Experience of Freedom* (1993), and the editor of *The Cambridge Companion to Kant* (1992). He is also general coeditor of the Cambridge Edition of the Works of Immanuel Kant, now in progress.

EDWIN McCANN is Associate Professor in the School of Philosophy at the University of Southern California. He has published a number of articles on early modern philosophy, emphasizing Locke.

J. R. MILTON is Lecturer in the Department of Philosophy, King's College, London. He has published several articles, and is currently working on an intellectual biography of Locke.

J. B. SCHNEEWIND is Professor of Philosophy at the Johns Hopkins University. He is the author of *Sidgwick's Ethics and Victorian Moral Philosphy* (1977), and editor of the two-volume *Moral Philosphy from Montaigne to Kant* (1990). He also edited the Mill volume in the Anchor Collections of Critical Essays series.

NICHOLAS WOLTERSTORFF is Noah Porter Professor of Philosophical Theology at Yale University, and has been appointed Wilde Lecturer at Oxford University for 1993 and Gifford Lecturer at St. Andrews University for 1995. He is the author of, inter alia, *On Universals* (1970), *Reason within the Bounds of Religion* (1976), *Art in Action* (1980), and *Works and Worlds of Art* (1980). His latest book, *When Tradition Fractures: The Epistemology of John Locke and the Origins of Modern Philosophy*, is due to be published shortly.

ROGER WOOLHOUSE is Reader in Philosophy at the University of York. He is the author of *Locke's Philosophy of Science and Knowledge* (1971) and *Locke* (1983), and coauthor, with Roland Hall, of *80 Years of Locke Scholarship: A Bibliographical Guide* (1983). He is also editing the Leibniz volumes in the Routledge Critical Assessments series.

NOTE ON CITATIONS

References to Locke's works are made parenthetically, using an abbreviated title of the work or its source.

The editions of or sources for Locke's works that are cited, with abbreviations given in brackets, are the following:

[B]   Manuscripts in the Bodleian Library.
[C]   *The Correspondence of John Locke*, ed. E. S. de Beer. 9 vols. (1976–).
[D]   *Drafts for the* Essay concerning Human Understanding, *and Other Philosophical Writings*, ed. Peter H. Nidditch and G. A. J. Rogers. 3 vols. (1990–).
[E]   *An Essay concerning Human Understanding*, ed. Peter H. Nidditch (1975).
[EL] *Essays on the Law of Nature*, ed. W. von Leyden (1954).
[L]   *The Life of John Locke*, by Peter, Lord King, new ed. 2 vols. (1830).
[QL] *Questions concerning the Law of Nature*, ed. and tr. Robert Horwitz, Jenny Strauss Clay, and Diskin Clay (1990).
[T]   *Two Treatises of Government*, ed. Peter Laslett, 2nd ed. (1967).
[TE] *Some Thoughts concerning Education*, ed. John W. Yolton and Jean S. Yolton (1989).
[W]   *The Works of John Locke*, new ed., corrected. 10 vols. (1823; repr. 1964).

In the case of major works and collections, the abbreviated title is followed by an array of numerals designating internal divisions – volumes, books, parts, chapters, sections, and so forth – and then a page number, preceded by a colon. Thus a reference to Book II, Chapter xxi, Section 47, page 263 of the *Essay concerning Human Understanding* is made as follows: E II.xxi.47: 263. A reference to Volume VII, page 140 of Locke's *Works* (which is a reference to *The Reasonableness of Christianity*) is made thus: W VII: 140.

Letters written by and to Locke are cited using the numbers assigned to them in the de Beer edition of Locke's correspondence, followed by "C" and the volume and page number of that edition, thus: Letter 2320: C VI: 215.

Manuscript material in the Bodleian Library, which includes nearly all of the surviving Locke *Nachlass*, sometimes is cited by title (if there is one), followed by "B" and the Bodleian catalogue designation for the manuscript in question, and then a section, folio, or page number, thus: Journal 1677: B MS Locke f.2: 46.

Some of this manuscript material, however, has been published, and it is often the published version that is cited. One major source is Lord King's biography: a citation of something in it includes a title (if there is one), followed by "L" and the volume and page number of the 1830 edition of King's work, thus: Deus: L II: 133–39.

Other material from Locke's manuscripts has been published in separate books and journal articles. Of special importance are an early work in Latin on the law of nature, and two early drafts – designated *Draft A* and *Draft B* by Locke scholars – of the *Essay concerning Human Understanding*. Two versions of the former have been published (with different English titles), one by von Leyden, the other by Horwitz et al.: these are cited using "EL" and "QL," respectively. There are also two published versions of each of the drafts: in this *Companion* it is the Clarendon edition of both drafts, edited by Nidditch and Rogers, that is cited, using "D," thus: Draft A 43: D I: 75.

Other published versions of material from Locke's manuscripts are cited using Locke's name as author, followed by the date of publication, and then a page number preceded by a colon. A reference to an early paper by Locke on infallibility, for example, that was published in 1977 by John Biddle in the *Journal of Church and State*, appears thus: Locke 1977: 301.

Works by authors other than Locke (and his correspondents) are also referred to parenthetically, using the name of the author, the publication date of the work or edition cited (followed by "a," "b," "c," etc. to distinguish publications in the same year), and a page number preceded by a colon. A reference to page 86 of John Yolton's *John Locke and the Way of Ideas*, published in 1956, is made thus: Yolton 1956: 86.

Full information about cited works and sources is given in the Bibliography.

THE CAMBRIDGE COMPANION TO

LOCKE

Introduction

The main subject of this book is Locke's philosophy, in the current academic sense of that term. So construed, philosophy is a special field of inquiry, marked off, even if not very clearly, from other fields and in particular from the various empirical sciences. Locke certainly practiced philosophy understood in this way. But he did not think of himself as any kind of intellectual specialist. He rarely even used the word "philosophy," as many seventeenth-century thinkers did, to signify the whole domain of intellectual endeavor: his favorite word for that was "science." And in addition to his work in philosophy, he pursued substantial inquiries in other disciplines: chemistry, medicine, economics, public policy, education, and theology. Still, there is no doubt that Locke's most significant as well as his most influential achievements were in philosophy; and it is as a philosopher that he is chiefly interesting to scholars today.

Philosophy, in our current view of it, is divided into various more or less distinguishable subfields, yielding, at the first level of division, logic, epistemology, metaphysics, and moral philosophy, and then, by subdividing these, such specializations as the philosophies of language, science, mind, and religion, ethical theory, and political philosophy. Locke worked actively in nearly all of these areas. It is true that the overall subject of his two most important books, the *Essay concerning Human Understanding* and the *Two Treatises of Government*, is, in the one case, epistemology and, in the other, political philosophy. But there are also significant excursions, in the *Two Treatises*, into general moral philosophy, and in the *Essay*, into ethical theory and the philosophies of language, science, and religion, and especially into what we call metaphysics, though Locke

I

would have been uneasy with that label, reeking as it did to his nose of the stale hallways of medieval schools.

In this book, separate chapters are devoted to Locke's work in each of several subfields of philosophy: metaphysics, subdivided into philosophy of body and philosophy of mind (Chapters 3 and 4, respectively); philosophy of language (Chapter 5); theory of knowledge, which covers a portion of epistemology (Chapter 6); philosophy of religion, which normally includes topics in metaphysics as well as epistemology, though it is mainly the latter that are treated here (Chapter 7); general moral philosophy (Chapter 8); and political philosophy (Chapter 9). There is also a chapter dealing with Locke's theory of ideas (Chapter 2), designed to provide some background for the discussions of the chapters following it. The issues addressed in this chapter are taken nowadays to fall within epistemology and philosophy of logic. But for Locke they would have been assigned to "Semiotics" or "the Doctrine of Signs," which is one of the three main divisions of "Science" he specifies in the last chapter of the *Essay* (E IV.xxi.4: 720–21). (Locke's other two divisions are "Practics" or "Ethicks" and "Physics, or natural Philosophy," albeit "in a little more enlarged Sense of the Word" which allows it to apply to "Spirits" as well as bodies [E IV.xxi.2–3: 720].)

It is not, however, any systematic arrangement of these various subfields within philosophy that has dictated the order of these chapters. The first six of them, Chapters 2 through 7, are placed in the order (more or less) in which the subjects they cover are treated by Locke in the *Essay*. Chapter 2 deals with issues discussed in Book I and in parts of Book II, and Chapters 3 and 4 with matters considered in other parts of Book II; Chapter 5 corresponds to Book III and Chapter 6 to the earlier portions of Book IV; and the bulk of Chapter 7 is concerned with questions that Locke takes up in the later portions of Book IV. The subject of Chapter 8, moral philosophy, is discussed by Locke at several places in the *Essay*, and also in other works: notably, the early *Essays on the Law of Nature*, the *Two Treatises*, and *The Reasonableness of Christianity*. Chapter 9, finally, on Locke's political philosophy, is devoted to the central argument of the *Second Treatise*.

Not every currently recognized subfield of philosophy is such that Locke significantly contributed to it. Formal logic and aesthetics are two to which he did not. He also avoided explicit discussion of questions of general ontology, which is another branch of metaphysics in addition to the philosophies of mind and of body – although many answers to these questions are implicit in his discussions of other topics, so that quite a rich theory of "being in general" could perhaps be constructed from them. A further branch of metaphysics is (natural) theology, the philosophy of the gods or God. To this Locke did give considerable attention, not only passim in both the *Essay* and *Two Treatises* but in several other works, including two specifically dedicated to it: *The Reasonableness of Christianity* and *A Paraphrase and Notes on the Epistles of St. Paul.* But Locke's work in this area was not very original, a lot of it is more apologetical than philosophical, and after a few decades even Christian theologians stopped being very interested in it. A few aspects of this work are mentioned in Chapter 7 of this *Companion,* but no separate chapter has been assigned to it.

In addition to the eight central chapters on Locke's philosophy, this volume contains an opening chapter on his life and intellectual context, and a closing one (Chapter 10) on the influence of his thought upon subsequent thinkers.

Although Locke's work in fields other than philosophy is not specifically examined in this book, there are brief descriptions of some of it in Chapter 1. Furthermore, some excellent extended studies of it have been produced by scholars in recent years. Locke's work in chemistry and natural philosophy (in the unenlarged sense) is reviewed by Frank 1980, that in medicine by Dewhurst 1963 (but see J. R. Milton's "Note on Sources" in Chapter 1). The best account of Locke's contribution to economics is Kelly 1991; and Tarcov 1984 and Yolton and Yolton 1989 are illuminating on his views on education. Valuable discussions of (some aspects of) Locke's theology are provided by Wainwright 1987, Spellman 1988, and Marshall 1990. Locke's treatment of religious and political toleration, which constitutes his most extensive venture in the field of what would now be called public policy, is fully examined in Horton and Mendus 1991.

The current state of Locke scholarship, in philosophy no less than in these other fields, is one of robust good health. The study of Locke has certainly shared in the growth of the whole scholarly industry in the twentieth century, and particularly in the past thirty years or so. And the intellectual habits of scholars in general have changed for the better. Students of work such as Locke's are now more astute philosophically than their predecessors were; they read texts more carefully; and they are more interested in the historical circumstances, material as well as intellectual, in which their subjects did their thinking.

But there are special factors that seem to have boosted Locke's popularity as a target of scholarly interest. Of prime importance has been the coming to light of the rich trove of unpublished material in the Lovelace Collection. Among other things, this has prompted a new critical edition of Locke's works, the Oxford Clarendon Edition, several volumes of which have now been published – most notably, Peter Nidditch's *Essay* and E. S. de Beer's eight-volume collection of Locke's whole (known) correspondence. These new editions have in turn encouraged new efforts of interpretation and historical research: progress builds upon progress.

Locke scholarship has also benefited from the industry and dedication of Roland Hall, founder and editor of the *Locke Newsletter* (Hall 1970a), coauthor (with Roger Woolhouse) of a comprehensive bibliography of twentieth-century work on Locke (Hall and Woolhouse 1983), and maintainer of the annual list of "Recent Publications" on Locke (Hall 1970b). Two further bibliographies, covering different ground, have been published recently by John Attig and by Jean and John Yolton: the one lists Locke's own writings (Attig 1985), the other secondary writings produced between 1689 and 1982 (Yolton and Yolton 1985). All in all, the research tool needs of Locke scholars have been unusually well provided for.

The editor trusts that the vitality and quality of current Locke scholarship are amply demonstrated by the essays that make up this volume.

1   Locke's life and times

John Locke was born on August 28, 1632, into a family of very minor Somerset gentry. His father, John Locke senior, owned some houses and land in and around Pensford, a small town some seven miles south of Bristol. He supplemented his income from this by practicing as an attorney and by taking a series of minor administrative posts in local government.

Locke's family seems to have had puritan sympathies, and after the outbreak of the Civil War his father served as a captain in one of the parliamentary armies, in a cavalry regiment commanded by a very much more substantial figure among the Somerset gentry, Alexander Popham. Popham's regiment served under Waller, was defeated at the Battle of Devizes in July 1643, and subsequently dispersed.

Locke's father's association with Popham, whom he continued to serve in his professional capacity and from whom he leased part of his land, had one consequence of enormous benefit to his son. Popham, since 1645 the member of Parliament for Bath, had sufficient influence to recommend boys for places at Westminster School, at that time the foremost school in England. Locke entered Westminster in 1647. The education there was centered almost entirely around the ancient languages, first Latin, then Greek, and finally, for the most academically proficient pupils, Hebrew. Locke made sufficient progress with the last of these to be able to compose an oration in Hebrew shortly before he left the school.

Westminster had a long-established connection with Christ Church, Oxford, whereby at least three studentships at the College were filled every year from among those boys who held scholarships at the school. These studentships, which were approximately the

5

equivalent of fellowships in the other colleges, were tenable for life, though they could be forfeited on a number of grounds, notably marriage. Locke was elected in May 1652; he took up residence in Christ Church in the autumn of the same year.

The curriculum that Locke was required to follow differed hardly at all from that which had irritated and bored the young Thomas Hobbes fifty years before, and Locke reacted to it in the same way. He acquired an intense dislike of the scholastic method of disputation and of the logical and metaphysical subtleties with which it concerned itself. Locke made sure that he fulfilled the not very exacting requirements for his degrees (B.A. February 1656, M.A. June 1658), but otherwise he seems to have spent much of his time reading lighter literature – plays, romances, and literary letters, much of it translated from French.

It is unclear whether at this stage in his life Locke had any definite intentions as to what career to pursue. He was admitted to Gray's Inn in December 1656, but nothing seems to have come of this; Locke's later thought is strikingly uninfluenced by any apparent knowledge of the common law. Most undergraduates intended a career in the church. There is some evidence that Locke's father had some such aim in mind, and Locke himself may have contemplated this as late as 1663, but in the end he rejected the idea of ordination.

Another possibility was medicine. Several of Locke's notebooks show that in the late 1650s he started taking detailed notes from a large number of medical works. The quantity and character of this material indicates something more than casual interest. In 1658–59 Locke may not have decided firmly on a medical career, but he was clearly investigating it as a possibility.

The study of medicine inevitably led to natural philosophy. Locke read Harvey's *Exercitationes de Generatione Animalium* in about 1658, and began exploring the problems of chemistry, taking detailed notes from the writings of Daniel Sennert. At about this time, probably early in 1660, he first met Robert Boyle.

Exactly when Locke first became acquainted with the ideas of the mechanical philosophy cannot now be determined. There is no evidence that he had any links with the group of innovators associated with John Wilkins at Wadham – unlike his precocious contemporary at both Westminster and Christ Church, Robert Hooke. If he had read anything by Descartes, there is no trace of it among his surviving papers. From 1660 onward, however, Locke augmented his medical studies with a thorough course of reading in the new mechanical philosophy, starting with Boyle's recently published *New Essays Physico-Mechanical touching the Spring of Air.* He read widely among Descartes's works, concentrating especially on the *Dioptrics* and the *Meteors* (in Latin translation) and the *Principia Philosophiae,* especially Parts III and IV; he also read at least some of Gassendi's *Syntagma Philosophicum,* though probably not very much.

Locke's attention at this time was not however held solely by medicine and natural philosophy. The rather precarious political stability achieved by Cromwell had disappeared with his death in September 1658. Locke welcomed the Restoration of Charles II and the reestablishment of strong – indeed authoritarian – government in church and state. Between November and December 1660 he wrote a short treatise, intended as a reply to a work by another student of Christ Church, Edward Bagshaw, in which he affirmed the power of the civil magistrate to determine the form of religious worship (Locke 1967: 117–75). This was followed in 1661–62 by two further works, each written in Latin and set out in the form of a scholastic disputation. One gave a more general and abstract defense of the thesis already argued against Bagshaw (Locke 1967: 185–241); the other rejected the Catholic position that it is necessary that the Bible should have an infallible interpreter (Locke 1977). Locke was at this time reading much Anglican theology, and was following the classical Anglican tradition of engaging in polemics on two fronts, against both the church of Rome and the Protestant dissenters.

At this stage of his life Locke's religious opinions were probably still broadly orthodox. He survived the post-Restoration visitation of the university, apparently without difficulty, and it is hardly likely that anyone would have advocated a policy requiring the imposition of a religious orthodoxy that he did not himself accept. In contrast with the situation twenty years later, he was clearly well thought of by the dean and chapter. In the early 1660s he was appointed to a succession of college offices: praelector in Greek (1661–62), praelector in rhetoric (1663), and finally censor of moral philosophy (1664). In the spring of 1661 he became a college tutor; he was responsible for the general welfare of his pupils, and helped impart to them the same kind of education that he had himself been given a decade earlier. He also conducted scholastic disputations of a strictly traditional kind: one set of these survive and have been published with the title *Essays on the Law of Nature.*

During this time Locke continued to read widely in medicine and natural philosophy. He took detailed notes at the lectures on medicine given in 1661–62 by Thomas Willis (Willis 1980) and in 1663 attended a class in chemistry given, under Boyle's auspices, by the German chemist, Peter Stahl. There was at this time much interest in physiological problems. Locke was a friend of Richard Lower, who, in conjunction with Boyle, Hooke, and Willis, was engaged in trying to understand the nature of respiration. Locke followed these investigations closely and recorded notes and queries about them in his commonplace books.

Locke's life at this time would seem to have been well occupied, if a little humdrum. In 1665 an opportunity for something quite new came up, and Locke promptly seized it. Sir Walter Vane was being sent to Cleves on a diplomatic mission to the elector of Brandenburg, and Locke was offered the post of secretary. The mission left England in November and returned the following February. As an act of diplomacy it proved futile, but it is clear from his letters home that Locke greatly enjoyed his first journey abroad, and the experience of staying in a community in which the members of different churches lived together without disorder may have helped him change his mind about the practicability of religious toleration.

Once back in Oxford, Locke resumed his studies in chemistry and in physiology; it is probably at about this time that he drafted a short work in the form of a scholastic disputation on the purpose of respiration.[1] In the summer of 1666, however, he met someone who was to change the entire course of his life.

Anthony Ashley Cooper, then Lord Ashley but from 1672 earl of Shaftesbury, had been chancellor of the exchequer since 1661. He was not in good health, and had come to Oxford to drink the water, conveyed there by cart, from a remote but newly fashionable rural spring. Ashley's physician in Oxford was David Thomas, Locke's chief collaborator in his chemical experiments, and it was probably through Thomas that the two men were introduced. Each was favorably impressed by the other, and by the time that Ashley left Oxford, the beginnings of a firm friendship had been established.

In the late spring of 1667 Locke left Oxford for London, to become a member of Ashley's household at Exeter House in the Strand. This was to be his place of permanent residence for the next eight years.

Locke's activities in London remained as diverse as they had been in Oxford. He continued to read extensively in medicine, but he was now able to supplement this theoretical education with clinical experience. Shortly after arriving in London he made the acquaintance of the physician Thomas Sydenham. Locke accompanied Sydenham on his rounds and made records of his advice and recommendations in various of his notebooks. The two men collaborated closely: Locke's papers contain a large number of drafts and fragmentary essays on various medical topics. The most interesting of these from a philosophical point of view is a short tract, "De Arte Medica." When first discovered in the nineteenth century this work was supposed to have been written by Locke, primarily because the manuscript is in his hand; more recently it has been ascribed to Sydenham. There are at present no decisive grounds in favor of either alternative.

"De Arte Medica" expresses a profound skepticism about all hypotheses concerning the nature of disease, and consequently advocates a purely empirical approach to medical practice. Nothing in it is incompatible with the known medical philosophies of either Sydenham or Locke. Sydenham had never been an admirer of the mechanical philosophy, or of the kind of corpuscularian explanations so indefatigably advocated by Boyle and his colleagues in the Royal Society. Locke's general approach remained close to that of Boyle, but he became much more skeptical about the prospects of our ever being able in practice to use corpuscularian principles to give a satisfactory explanation of the properties of particular bodies.

Locke's medical skills were put to a severe test in the summer of 1668. Lord Ashley's generally poor health had been growing worse, and Locke advocated and on June 12 superintended (though did not of course actually perform) an operation to drain an abscess on his liver. Ashley made a good recovery and thereafter saw Locke as the person who had saved his life.

Locke continued to pursue his scientific as well as his medical interests. It was fashionable to dabble in chemistry, and Lord Ashley maintained a laboratory in Exeter House. In November 1668 Locke was elected a fellow of the Royal Society, but though he was quickly appointed to a committee for experiments and twice served on the council (1669–70, 1672–73), he seems to have attended few meetings and to have contributed little to the work of the society.

Just as Locke's hitherto largely theoretical approach to medicine had been broadened by his association with Sydenham, so his rather academic, quasi-scholastic interest in politics was inevitably modified by his entry into the household of one of England's ablest politicians. Within a year of coming to London, Locke had written a short *Essay concerning Toleration*,[2] which expressed views very different from those put forward in the *Two Tracts* of 1660–62. He also developed an interest, hitherto absent, in economic questions. The outcome was a treatise with the title *Some of the Consequences that are like to follow upon Lessening of Interest to 4 Per Cent*, begun in 1668, and further added to in 1674. Nothing was published at this time, but Locke kept the manuscript and put it to use in the economic controversies of the 1690s.

In 1669 Ashley involved Locke in the affairs of the recently founded colony of Carolina. In August of that year the first group of settlers to leave from England took with them an elaborate constitutional document, the Fundamental Constitutions of Carolina. It is extremely unlikely that Locke was the author of this, but it is possible that he had a hand in the original drafting, and he was certainly involved in suggesting alterations and improvements (Milton 1990). Locke continued to serve the lords proprietors of the colony in a secretarial capacity until he left England for France in 1675.

At least since the autumn of 1668 Ashley had been paying Locke an annual allowance of £80. In the autumn of 1670 an opportunity arose to shift the burden to the public revenue. Locke was appointed a registrar to the commissioners of excise, at an annual salary of £175. Of this, £60 was needed to pay a clerk, who presumably performed whatever duties were required. Locke lost this useful source of income in the spring of 1675. It was replaced by an annuity of £100, which he purchased from Shaftesbury.

In the light of his later publications it is remarkable that in the 1660s Locke seems to have spent very little time reading anything on epistemology or metaphysics. It is of course unlikely that he made notes on every book that he read, and it is certain that at least some of the commonplace books in which he did record his notes have not survived; nevertheless the disparity between the extremely copious notes taken from books on medicine, natural science, travel and theology, and the almost total absence of anything on philosophical topics is very marked. In 1670 Locke was not yet a philosopher, as we would understand that term. He was however shortly to become one.

The origins of the *Essay concerning Human Understanding* are described by Locke with tantalizing brevity and a kind of studied vagueness in a well-known passage in the "Epistle to the Reader." Locke describes there how, at an unspecified but evidently fairly distant time in the past, he and a group of five or six friends had met in Locke's chamber to discuss some other quite remote topic, and had found themselves becoming entangled in a mass of wholly unanticipated perplexities. It then occurred to Locke that they should inquire instead into the capabilities of the human understanding itself. He therefore set down "some hasty and undigested thoughts on a subject I had never before considered," which he took to the next meeting.

Two surviving works dealing with epistemological topics show that this meeting cannot have taken place after 1671. The shorter, given the Latin title "Intellectus humanus cum cognitionis certitudine, et assensus firmitate" but written in English, is now generally known as *Draft A*. A reference within the work shows that Locke was in the middle of writing it on July 11, 1671. Its first few pages may well correspond to the hasty and undigested thoughts taken by Locke to the meeting with his friends. The longer work, entitled "An Essay concerning the Understanding, Knowledge, Opinion and Assent" but now known as *Draft B*, contains no dates other than the year 1671 on the title page, but is certainly later than *Draft A*. Both works were left unfinished, and both clearly leave unsolved some of the main problems that led to their being written.

During the years 1672–75 much of Locke's time was occupied by administrative activities of various kinds. In March 1672 Ashley was created earl of Shaftesbury, and in November of the same year he was appointed lord chancellor. The administration of the considerable quantity of ecclesiastical patronage that came with this office was devolved upon Locke, who was given the post of secretary for presentations; he held it until Shaftesbury was dismissed in November 1673. As if in anticipation of this, Locke had in the previous month become secretary to the Council for Trade and Plantations. In December he was made treasurer as well. He held these posts, which involved a considerable quantity of work, until the council was itself dissolved in December 1674. The combined salary of £600 per annum was never paid.

In November 1675, his administrative responsibilities at an end, Locke crossed over to France for a stay that was in the end to last nearly three and a half years. It was not his first visit to that country. In the autumn of 1672 he had spent a few weeks in Paris, but though he presumably acquired some ability to communicate in French, he was not yet able to read that language with any ease. There are no citations from any works written in French among Locke's papers before November 1675.

On arriving in France Locke began, apparently for the first time, to keep a journal, a practice he was to continue until the end of his life. In later years the number of entries grew smaller, especially after 1689, but the very well-filled volumes covering the years in France make it possible, for the first time in Locke's life, to construct an almost day-by-day account of his movements and activities.

On January 4, 1676 (N.S.), Locke arrived at Montpellier, where he was to stay for a little over a year. He made several acquaintances, notably two eminent Protestant physicians, Charles Barbeyrac and Pierre Magnol, and the Cartesian Pierre Sylvain Régis; he also engaged a tutor to teach him French for one hour a day, and began reading books written in that language.

While at Montpellier Locke resumed his philosophical inquiries. His journals contain a substantial number of entries on philosophical matters, these being especially frequent for the period from June until September 1676, when Locke had retired to Celleneuve, a village some three miles west of Montpellier.

In February 1677 Locke left Montpellier, and traveled in a leisurely manner to Paris, by way of Toulouse and Bordeaux, arriving there at the beginning of June. He was to remain in Paris, apart from a second journey through provincial France in the late summer and autumn of 1678, until his return to England.

In Paris Locke continued, at least intermittently, to work on philosophy, drawing up a list of French versions of Descartes's works, and copying into his journal a long memorandum containing critical comments on the writings of Descartes's various followers. He also became acquainted with two Gassendists, François Bernier and

Gilles de Launay, though there is little evidence that he ever had much interest in the details of Gassendi's own philosophy.

It is also clear that Locke was working on the *Essay* during this period. One of the items that he left behind in Paris in July 1678 was a folio volume described as "Essay de Intellectu." This cannot be either *Draft A* or *Draft B*. References to this volume appear elsewhere among Locke's papers: it is with him in England in 1679 and 1680, and in Holland in 1684 and 1685.

The England to which Locke returned in May 1679 was in a state of acute political crisis. The revelation of the Popish Plot, a conspiracy to assassinate Charles II and replace him with his Catholic brother, James, had burst upon an already discontented nation in the August of the previous year. The plot was itself a pure fabrication, but few of Locke's contemporaries were prepared to discount entirely the detailed mendacities devised by Titus Oates and his associates, especially after the discovery of the genuinely treasonable correspondence of James's secretary, Edward Coleman, and the murder – still unsolved – of the magistrate charged with investigating the whole matter, Sir Edmund Berry Godfrey. Charles had dissolved the old Cavalier Parliament, elected in 1660; its replacement was due to meet for the first time in May, the month of Locke's return. For the next four years, until his flight to Holland as a political refugee, Locke was to be concerned primarily, though never exclusively, with politics.

The events of the years 1679–83 fall into two phases. At first Shaftesbury and his associates attempted to use constitutional means to exclude James from the throne. Exclusion bills were passed by the House of Commons in May 1679 and November 1680, but Charles extinguished the first by dissolving Parliament, and allowed the second to be defeated in the House of Lords. The turning point came in March 1681. The new Parliament met in Oxford, but was dissolved within a week, before a third exclusion bill had time even to complete its course through the Commons. As it slowly became apparent that Charles had no intention of ever summoning Parliament again, the Whig party split; the moderates became inactive or crossed over to the other side; the radicals, led by Shaftesbury, began to think with increasing seriousness about the possibilities of insurrection.

Charles rightly saw Shaftesbury as his most dangerous opponent, and was now determined to crush him. He was charged with treason, but the prosecution failed when the Whig-nominated grand jury threw out the charge. In June 1682 however the government secured the return of two Tories as sheriffs for London, and Shaftesbury knew that once they took office he would no longer be safe. In September he went into hiding, and two months later, after a planned insurrection had fizzled out, fled to Holland, where he died in January 1683.

Shaftesbury's flight and death deprived the Whigs of their ablest leader, but did not weaken their determination to continue the fight. One group of radicals formed a plot to assassinate Charles and James at the Rye House in Hertfordshire. The actual attempt was first postponed, and then betrayed to the government; the arrests began on June 21, 1683.

The extent of Locke's involvement in these events remains obscure, but he almost certainly knew enough to put him in serious danger. He slipped out of London a week before the arrests began. The next two months he spent in the West Country, putting his affairs in order and arranging for money to be sent abroad. How he left England is unknown, but on September 7 (N.S.) he was in Rotterdam.

It is now universally agreed that the *Two Treatises of Government* were not written to defend the Revolution of 1688, but were already in existence when Locke left for Holland. Some passages were certainly added in 1689, and it is possible that some material may date back to the years before 1675, but it is generally agreed that the greater part of both books was written during the period 1679–83. Any more precise dating than this is however highly controversial. It is generally agreed that the *First Treatise* was begun soon after Locke bought his copy of Filmer's *Patriarcha*, on January 22, 1680. The main dispute is whether Locke began the *Second Treatise* rather earlier, in the autumn of 1679, or whether it dates from after the dissolution of the Oxford Parliament in March 1681. The former hypothesis, first advanced by Peter Laslett in his critical edition of the *Two Treatises* (Laslett 1967), locates the *Second Treatise* among the political literature produced by the Exclusion Crisis. The latter hypothesis, advocated most forcefully by Richard Ashcraft (Ashcraft 1980; Ashcraft 1986; Ashcraft 1987), sees it as containing a theoretical justification for an altogether more radical, indeed insurrectionary, type of politics.

The *Two Treatises* were not the only works on politics Locke wrote during this period. In 1681 Edward Stillingfleet, dean of St Paul's, published *The Unreasonableness of Separation*, a vigorous attack on those English Protestants who had chosen not to conform to the Church of England. It raised the same issues as the *Two Tracts* of 1660–62, but this time Locke's sympathies were with the other side. In collaboration with James Tyrrell, an old Oxford friend and a fellow Whig, he drafted a lengthy and still unpublished reply (B MS Locke c.34). Most of it is in Tyrrell's hand, but substantial parts were written by Locke and by his servant and amanuensis, Sylvanus Brounower. These parts at least were almost certainly written on one of the occasions that Locke was staying in Tyrrell's house at Oakley in Buckinghamshire, probably between May 1681 and the spring of 1682.

Once in Holland Locke quickly made contact with several of the other English political exiles, notably with Thomas Dare, who was to be the paymaster of Monmouth's ill-fated expedition. Locke's contacts with Dare and his fellow malcontents were reported in some detail to the English government, and in November 1684 he was expelled from his studentship at Christ Church. The following May, a fortnight before Monmouth's expedition sailed, his name was included on a list of exiles who were to be arrested by the Dutch authorities; Locke went underground, and was to remain in hiding in various places and under a variety of somewhat transparent pseudonyms until May 1685.

Locke continued to pursue his medical interests while in Holland, and his reading remained as wide as ever, but his main intellectual concern was now with philosophy. He was probably working on the *Essay* in the winter of 1683–84, and was certainly at work on it between the autumn of 1684 and the spring of 1685. As the *Essay* took shape, Locke was careful to send copies to England: an unspecified portion, probably containing Book I and Book II and very close to the surviving *Draft C*, in April 1686; Book III in August of the same year, and Book IV in December. By the end of 1686 the *Essay* existed in a form very close to that in which we know it.

It seems likely that Locke interrupted his labors on the *Essay* to write another shorter work. According to both Philippus van Limborch and Jean le Clerc, the *Epistola de Tolerantia* was written during the winter of 1685–86, when Locke had returned to Amsterdam and was living inconspicuously in the house of Egbert Veen. Locke had long been concerned with the problem of toleration in the context of English politics, but the immediate impetus was probably provided by the revocation of the Edict of Nantes in October 1685. The choice of Latin for the work shows that it was intended for a European audience; it has no textual connection with the 1667 essay, all the copies of which had been left behind in England. Before he left Holland Locke entrusted the manuscript of the *Epistola* to Limborch, who saw it through the press; it was published at Gouda in May 1689, three months after Locke had returned to England, the identity of the author being concealed by the cryptic and effectively unfathomable initials P.A.P.O.I.L.A.

Locke's last two years in Holland were less eventful than their predecessors had been. In February 1687 he moved to Rotterdam to stay with Benjamin Furly, an English merchant of Quaker beliefs who had been living there since the Restoration. Locke found Furly's company agreeable and his opinions sympathetic, and he had access to the substantial library that Furly had amassed.

An acquaintance Locke had already made in Amsterdam was another refugee with unorthodox religious views, Jean le Clerc. In 1686 he began publishing a new periodical, the *Bibliothèque universelle et historique*. The second volume included a short work by Locke, written many years earlier, the "Méthode nouvelle de dresser des Receuils"; this described in careful detail the method Locke had been using since 1660 of organizing a commonplace book. It was not a publication calculated to cause much excitement in the world of learning, but at least it was hardly likely to provoke any trouble. Much more important, a later number of the same periodical (January–March 1688) contained Locke's first publication of any real significance, a substantial abridgment (ninety-two pages) of the already completed but still unpublished *Essay*. Locke arranged for the printer to produce a number of separate copies of this – in effect, offprints – and arranged for them to be circulated among his acquaintances in both England and Holland.

The success of William of Orange's expedition and the resulting flight of James II made it safe for Locke to come back to England.

He returned in February 1689 and was almost immediately offered the post of ambassador to the elector of Brandenburg. He declined primarily on grounds of poor health, but also because a successful performance of the role would require a readiness to engage in large-scale drinking. Locke no longer touched alcohol, except occasionally for medicinal purposes.

During the spring in 1689 Locke met Newton, who had been elected a member of Parliament for the University of Cambridge, and was in London for the current session of Parliament. Locke had been one of the earliest readers of the *Principia*, and had given it a laudatory if largely uncomprehending review in the *Bibliothèque universelle*. The two became friends, though Locke soon became aware of Newton's immensely difficult personality. In the year that followed they met occasionally and corresponded on a variety of topics. Their main common interest lay not in natural science but in biblical interpretation. Locke allowed Newton to insert some notes into his interleaved Bible; characteristically these were on the book of Revelation, a part of the New Testament that fascinated Newton but meant little to Locke.

In the months that followed his return to England Locke busied himself with preparing his two chief works for publication. The manuscripts containing *Two Treatises of Government* had apparently been left in England and a large part of the *First Treatise* had been either lost or deliberately destroyed. Locke made no attempt to reconstruct it. The surviving parts, augmented with new material appropriate to the changed political situation of 1689, were licensed for publication in August and appeared, with the date 1690 on the title page, in October. It was anonymous, as were the subsequent editions of 1694 and 1698.

During this period Locke was also at work on the *Essay*. The contract with the publisher, dated May 24, 1689, suggests that the work was complete by that date, but there is evidence that Locke continued to make minor changes until printing was completed at the beginning of December. Like the *Two Treatises*, the *Essay* was on sale before the beginning of its nominal year of publication.

While Locke was revising the *Essay* and the *Two Treatises*, and seeing them through the press, an English translation was being prepared of the *Epistola de Tolerantia*. This was done without Locke's authorization but not without his knowledge; indeed Locke had supplied the translator, William Popple, with a copy of the original edition. Given that he was still concerned to keep his authorship a secret, he was in no position to give any instructions to the translator, but there is no sign that he disapproved of the project. Popple's translation was licensed on October 3 and went on sale later that autumn. It sold out quickly (a second edition appeared a few months later) and immediately aroused controversy. An Oxford clergyman, Jonas Proast, published a vigorous attack in April 1690. Locke replied with *A Second Letter concerning Toleration,* which appeared later that summer. Locke chose not to reveal his identity – he used the pseudonym "Philanthropus" – and wrote as though he were a third party taking the side of the author of the original letter. The *Second Letter* is fairly short, but a further attack by Proast in February 1691 provoked Locke into elaborating a very much longer reply. A *Third Letter for Toleration* was completed in June 1692 and eventually appeared in November. For the time being Proast made no reply, and the controversy ceased.

One reason why the *Third Letter* took so long to appear, as compared with its predecessor, was that Locke was preoccupied with economic problems. His interest in these matters had been revived in the summer of 1690 by the introduction in Parliament of bills to reduce the legal rate of interest and to devalue the silver coinage by increasing its nominal value. Though it did not appear in print until December 1691, much of *Some Considerations of the Consequences of the Lowering of Interest and Raising the Value of Money* was written the previous year; some parts were taken over almost unchanged from the unpublished tract Locke had written in 1668. Locke continued to work on *Some Considerations* during 1691; it was eventually published rather hurriedly when another bill to reduce the rate of interest was placed before the House of Commons.

After his return to England, Locke settled for the time being in London. He had lost his studentship at Christ Church (and made no sustained effort to regain it), and the prospect of retiring to Pensford can have held few attractions. Early in 1691 however he was invited to stay as a permanent guest at Oates, a small moated manor house in North Essex, the home of Sir Francis Masham. Masham's wife Damaris was the daughter of Ralph Cudworth, and had been a friend and correspondent of Locke for many years. Oates was to be Locke's main place of residence for the remainder of his life, though during

the 1690s he was forced to spend substantial periods in London attending to government business.

Once the *Third Letter for Toleration* was out of the way, Locke's
thoughts turned to a less controversial work. While in Holland he
had sent his friend Edward Clarke a series of letters giving detailed
advice about the upbringing of children. *Some Thoughts concerning
Education* was based on these letters and on a few more sent after
Locke's return to England, though some new material was included,
and a certain number of changes were made. The section on natural
philosophy was revised, rather superficially, to take account of Newton's achievement in the *Principia*. *Some Thoughts* was published
in July 1693; a new edition containing additional material came out
exactly two years later. It was the first work since the *Essay* to be
published in Locke's own name, and it helped add to his growing reputation.

During the time that Locke was adding the final touches to *Some
Thoughts* and seeing to its publication, he was also thinking about
new material for a second edition of the *Essay*. John Norris, an English admirer of Malebranche, had been the first author to publish
any critical remarks about the *Essay* (Norris 1690). He was an old
friend of Lady Masham, through whom he became acquainted with
Locke. Their initially friendly relations turned sour, however, when
Locke came to suspect Norris of prying into his correspondence.
The initial result of this was a short bad-tempered fragment, entitled
"JL Answer to Mr Norris's Reflection," dated 1692. It was followed
by two rather more substantial pieces, "Remarks upon some of Mr
Norris's Books" and "An Examination of P. Malebranche's Opinion
of Seeing All Things in God," both probably dating from early 1693.
Despite its title the second of these was at least initially directed at
Norris, as passages omitted in the version published in 1706 clearly
show. At one stage Locke wondered about including some of this
material in the second edition of the *Essay*, but on further reflection
decided against doing so. A long polemic would have looked out
of place in work that seemed deliberately to avoid controversy and
disputation. Even so, some of the new material found in the second
edition appears to have its origins in Locke's reflections on Norris's
and Malebranche's philosophy.

Many of the other changes in the second edition arose out
of Locke's very much more amicable relationship with William

Molyneux. Molyneux had referred to Locke in the most fulsome terms in the preface to his *Dioptrica Nova* (1692), and Locke, who always tended to estimate someone's capacity for philosophical thinking by the closeness of his or her thought to his own ideas, was most favorably impressed. A correspondence ensued, which continued until Molyneux's untimely death in 1698.

The most obviously visible consequence of Locke's friendship with Molyneux was the insertion into the second edition of the *Essay* (E II.ix.8: 145–46) of what has since become known as Molyneux's problem: whether a man born blind and newly restored to sight would be able by sight alone to distinguish between different shapes, such as a sphere and a cube. Apart from this the most notable changes were a wholly new chapter (II.xxvii) "Of Identity and Diversity," and the replacement of the central section of the chapter "Of Power" (II.xxi) by a largely new and much longer discussion of human volition and freedom.

The second edition of the *Essay* appeared in May 1694. Just over a year later, in August 1695, Locke published the first major work wholly written since his return from Holland. This was *The Reasonableness of Christianity*. Like the *Letter on Toleration*, it was anonymous, and immediately provoked controversy. It was not the enterprise of presenting Christianity as reasonable that caused offense, but rather that to many readers Locke's conception of Christianity seemed unduly attenuated. The first and most alarming antagonist was John Edwards, himself the son of a celebrated controversialist of an earlier era. Edwards's approach was vigorous to the point of brutality, as his later description of Locke residing in "the Seraglio at Oates" evidently bears witness. Locke replied to Edwards in a brief *Vindication* published toward the end of 1695, and then later in a much longer *Second Vindication*, which appeared in the spring of 1697.

In the years after 1691 the deterioration of the silver currency and its consequent fall in value against gold grew increasingly serious. In January 1695 a committee was set up by the chancellor of the exchequer to examine proposals for reform, and in February Locke published a brief pamphlet, *Short Observations on a Printed Paper*, to influence its deliberations. During the summer the situation grew steadily worse, with the result that Locke spent much of the second half of 1695 absorbed in monetary problems. The third edition of the *Essay*, which came out around December, was almost unchanged from its predecessor. In September Locke was chosen, along with others including Newton and Wren, to supply the government with expert advice. His recommendation of recoinage without devaluation was adopted as government policy early in November, but had still to be accepted by Parliament. Locke's last publication on economics, *Further Considerations concerning Raising the Value of Money*, in defense of these proposals, appeared at the end of December. It was the first of Locke's economic writings to be issued in his own name.

Locke's modest though adequate income from his land and from the annuity purchased from Shaftesbury had been usefully augmented from May 1689 by his appointment as a commissioner of appeals. The duties involved were not very extensive; the salary was £200 per annum. In May 1696 he was appointed to the Council for Trade and Plantations, a post he held for the next four years. This entailed substantially more work, as well as requiring periods of increasingly disagreeable residence in London, but the compensations included an annual salary of £1,000. During these years Locke was earning more in each year than the entire value of the estate left by his father.

Locke spent the early months of 1696 resting at Oates after the exertions of the previous year. In June he was sufficiently recovered to attend the first meeting of the newly constituted Board of Trade. The business generated by the board occupied a substantial part of Locke's time over the next four years, involving him with such varied problems as vagrancy, linen manufacture in Ireland, the abortive Scottish colony at Darien, the suppression of piracy, and (perhaps most time-consuming of all) the affairs of the colony in Virginia. It was the climax of his distinguished if notably discontinuous career as a civil servant.

Much of the time that Locke could spare from the affairs of the Board of Trade was spent in pursuing a lengthy controversy with the bishop of Worcester, Edward Stillingfleet. Stillingfleet was a slightly younger contemporary of Locke who had published widely and acquired a considerable reputation at a time when Locke was as yet almost entirely unknown. He was generally regarded as one of the Church of England's ablest and most formidable controversialists. When Archbishop Tillotson had died in 1694 Queen Mary had wanted Stillingfleet to succeed him as archbishop of Canterbury, but she had been overruled by her husband, who saw Stillingfleet as too high a churchman. He was not a man whose criticisms could safely be ignored.

Stillingfleet had read the *Essay* soon after it first appeared and (as he later acknowledged) had not seen it as having any dangerous consequences for the doctrines of the Church of England. (He was presumably quite unaware of Locke's unpublished attack on *The Unreasonableness of Separation*.) It was the activities of John Toland that caused him to change his mind. The 1690s saw the climax of the intellectual war between the English Socinians and their orthodox opponents, and it was as a contribution to this controversy that Stillingfleet composed his *Discourse in Vindication of the Doctrine of the Trinity*. It was while he was finishing this that Toland's *Christianity not Mysterious* made its (anonymous) appearance. Toland's rationalistic approach to theology went well beyond anything Locke advocated, or indeed believed, but it was quite apparent to Stillingfleet (as to anyone else who might make the comparison) that Toland's theory of knowledge was taken over without any significant modification from Book IV of the *Essay*. It was this that led Stillingfleet to preface his attack on Toland with a criticism of Locke.

Stillingfleet's *Discourse* was published in November 1696. Locke immediately started to produce a reply: *A Letter to the Right Reverend Edward, Lord Bishop of Worcester* was finished on January 7, 1697. Stillingfleet's riposte, *An Answer to Mr Locke's Letter*, was on sale at the beginning of May. Locke again responded quickly. *Mr Locke's Reply to the Right Reverend the Lord Bishop of Worcester's Answer to his Letter* is dated June 29. Stillingfleet replied two months later with *An Answer to Mr Locke's Second Letter*, which he appears to have intended as his final contribution to the controversy. Locke prepared a massive rejoinder: *Mr Locke's Reply to the Right Reverend the Lord Bishop of Worcester's Answer to his Second Letter* was completed in May 1698, though it was not published until the end of that year. Stillingfleet was by then in no condition to reply. His health had broken down and he died on March 27, 1699.

Some of the issues raised by the controversy with Stillingfleet appear again in the material added to the fourth edition of the *Essay*, which came out in December 1699. The most immediately obvious changes were two new chapters, both concerned with the pathology of the human intellect, "Of the Association of Ideas" (II.xxxiii) and "Of Enthusiasm" (IV.xix). One of the projected additions had, like the earlier "Examination of Malebranche," grown too large and was therefore omitted. This was *The Conduct of the Understanding*, which was begun in April 1697. It is the only one of Locke's works that shows clear evidence of having been influenced by Francis Bacon, and it is significant that the only records of Locke reading the *Novum Organum* date from about this period. Locke intended that the *Conduct* should be published, though it did not in fact appear until it was included by his executors in the *Posthumous Works of Mr John Locke*, published in 1706.

A less easily datable work from around this time is *The Elements of Natural Philosophy*, a short introduction written for the use of the Mashams' son Francis. The only firm evidence for its date comes from a reference it contains to Huygens's *Cosmotheoros*, first published in 1698.

In June 1700 Locke resigned from the Board of Trade. The last four years of his life were spent quietly; his visits to London were less frequent and very much briefer than before. He published nothing after the fourth edition of the *Essay*, in December 1699, though he continued to note down minor improvements, which were incorporated in the posthumous fifth edition.

Though less busy than before, Locke was far from idle. When his health allowed it he worked steadily on his last major project, the *Paraphrase and Notes on the Epistles of St Paul*. Locke had a long-standing interest in biblical criticism, and had been recording detailed notes on individual passages since the early 1660s. He chose to write about the Pauline epistles, partly no doubt because critics like John Edwards had accused him of ignoring them, but perhaps more importantly because he had come to believe that they had been misunderstood by generations of readers who tried to understand each verse in isolation, instead of interpreting them all in the context of the epistles as a whole.

The *Paraphrase* provides detailed evidence of Locke's views on a great variety of theological questions. The anti-Trinitarianism, which critics had rightly claimed to detect in his earlier writings, is again present, though understandably in implicit rather than explicit form. Despite his wide reading in Socinian literature, he seems not to have been a pure Socinian, but rather to have adopted a position closer to Arianism.

More generally, the *Paraphrase* reveals the deeply religious character of Locke's mind. It shows, much more clearly than *The Reasonableness of Christianity*, that the Christian vocabulary of Locke's earlier works cannot be interpreted either as a pious facade or (less implausibly) as a mere residue in a mind already fundamentally secular but either reluctant or unable to acknowledge itself as such.

Locke's original intention had been to publish the complete series by installments, at three-month intervals; the first part, on Galations, was in proof by August 1704, but nothing appeared before his death. The completed parts, on Galatians, I and II Corinthians, Romans and Ephesians, were published by his executors between 1705 and 1707.

Two other short works date from Locke's last years. The *Discourse of Miracles* was written in 1702; the unfinished *Fourth Letter on Toleration* was begun in the last months of Locke's life. Both were published posthumously.

Locke's health had not been good for many years. He suffered from asthma, which had been made worse by the smoke of London. In January 1698, during a spell of bitterly cold weather, he had been summoned from Oates to Kensington Palace by William III; the journey by his own estimation nearly killed him, and according to Lady Masham his health never fully recovered.

As far as was possible Locke spent the last winters of his life indoors, by the fire, attempting to conserve his strength and waiting for the temporary improvement in his condition that the warmer weather would bring. During the spring and summer of 1704, however, the ailments of the winter continued, and Locke rightly suspected that he was unlikely to have much longer to live. In April he made his will, leaving the greater part of his estate to his second cousin, Peter King. During the summer Locke grew steadily weaker. He had previously loved to take exercise by riding, but this was now beyond him. Instead a specially designed chaise was constructed so he could be driven about. By October he was too weak even for this, and could only be carried out into the garden to sit in the autumn sun. His mind however remained both clear and active. In September he added a codicil to his will, containing the first public acknowledgment of his authorship of the *Two Treatises*; a month later he wrote to Peter King requesting him to publish the *Paraphrase* and the *Conduct of the Understanding*, and leaving to his discretion the "Examination of Malebranche" and the *Discourse of Miracles*.

By the time this letter was finished Locke had only three days to live. His legs had swollen and he was too weak to rise. On October 28 he felt slightly stronger and was dressed and carried into his study. At three o'clock in the afternoon, while Lady Masham was reading the Psalms to him, he lifted his hands to his face, closed his own eyes, and died. He was buried three days later in the churchyard of the parish church at High Laver, where his tomb still remains.

NOTE ON SOURCES

There are two large-scale biographies of Locke. Fox Bourne 1876 has largely been superseded by subsequent work, though on many particular points it is still worth consulting. Cranston 1957 is the standard biography, though it too needs replacement. It is best on the external events of Locke's life, weakest on his intellectual development. Dewhurst 1963 provides much information about Locke's medical interests, not all of it accurate. Frank 1980 is an excellent account of physiological research in Oxford, including Locke's part in it. Bill 1988 gives a good account of Christ Church; the circumstances in which Locke's earliest works were written are discussed in Abrams 1967 and von Leyden 1954. Locke's involvement with Shaftesbury is analyzed in Haley 1968, and there is a highly detailed, though controversial, account of his political activity in Ashcraft 1986. The visit to France is most fully described by Lough 1953. Locke's retirement at Oates is briefly but vividly portrayed in Harrison and Laslett 1971. Kelly's introduction to Locke's writings on economics (Kelly 1991) contains useful material on his financial affairs. There is a vast amount of biographical information in de Beer's superb edition of Locke's correspondence.

The largest body of unpublished material is the Locke MSS in the Bodleian Library. There are smaller but important collections in the British Library and among the Shaftesbury papers in the Public Record Office.

NOTES

1 The only printed edition (Locke 1960) provides an extremely inaccurate text, and should be used with great caution.
2 This piece exists in four distinct versions, only one of which has been printed (Fox Bourne 1876: 1:174–94).

2   Locke's theory of ideas

Ideas play a large role in Locke's philosophy. In Locke's view, everything existing or occurring in a mind either is or includes an idea; and all human knowledge both starts from and is founded on ideas. The very word "idea" appears more frequently in the *Essay concerning Human Understanding* than any other noun; its occurrences outnumber even those of such common words as "he," "have," and "for."

Locke's ideas have, however, perplexed readers and provoked critics from the time of the *Essay*'s first publication. His contemporary Edward Stillingfleet, the bishop of Worcester, noted the novelty of the term "idea" and charged that Locke's use of it had encouraged "ill men" to take up the "new way of ideas" and use it "to promote scepticism and infidelity, and to overthrow the mysteries of our faith" (W IV: 129–30). Stillingfleet had no objection to Locke's own use of the word, much less to ideas themselves, since he took these to differ only *nomine* from the "common notions of things, which we must make use of in our reasonings" (ibid.). But John Sergeant, another contemporary critic, found "idea," as used in the *Essay*, to be "highly Equivocal, or *Ambiguous*"; and he argued that in at least one of the meanings assigned it by Locke the word stands for nothing at all, a "meer Fancie" (Sergeant 1697: 3; Preface). This charge of ambiguity, especially, has been a staple of Locke criticism for three centuries: Thomas Reid advanced it, and so did Gilbert Ryle, who wrote, echoing Sergeant, that not only is "the term 'idea' . . . used by Locke in a number of completely different senses," but "there is one sense in which he uses the term . . . in which it must be categorically denied that there are such things as 'ideas' at all. And," Ryle continued, "had this been the only sense in which Locke used the term, then his whole *Essay* would have been, what it is not, a laboured anatomy of utter nonentities" (Ryle 1933: 17).

My aim in this chapter is to expound and explain the theory of ideas, as it is presented in Locke's writings. I shall in so doing indicate some connections between this theory and Locke's philosophies of mind, body, language, and knowledge. These connections are further explored later in this book, in the chapters individually devoted to these topics. The discussion here is intended in part to set the stage for these later chapters.

I. MIND, THOUGHT, AND PERCEPTION

Our first task is to get clear what an idea is according to Locke. He makes a point of explaining his use of the word "idea" early in the *Essay.* "It being that Term," he writes, "which, I think, serves best to stand for whatsoever is the Object of the Understanding when a Man thinks, I have used it to express whatever is meant by *Phantasm, Notion, Species,* or whatever it is, which the Mind can be employ'd about in thinking" (E I.i.8: 47). Later, in another passage in which he is self-consciously defining the word, he says that "whatsoever the Mind perceives in it self, or is the immediate object of Perception, Thought, or Understanding, that I call *Idea.*" A snowball, for instance, may "produce in us the *Ideas* of *White, Cold,* and *Round*"; and these, "as they are Sensations, or Perceptions, in our Understandings, I call them *Ideas*" (E II.viii.8: 134). And in a response to Stillingfleet, Locke again states the meaning of his term: "the thing signified by ideas, is nothing but the immediate objects of our minds in thinking" (W IV: 130).

These passages establish that an idea, for Locke, is first of all something that exists in a mind. More specifically, it is something that exists in an understanding, which is what Locke calls the mind's intellectual or cogitative part, as opposed to its volitional or appetitive part. More specifically still, ideas are the *objects* of certain mental actions or operations, namely those of thinking or perceiving. It must not be supposed that thinking and perceiving are two different actions for Locke. He hardly ever uses the word "per-

ception," by itself, to mean sense perception: when he wants to
speak of this he adds the qualifier "sense" or "sensible" or "by the
senses." For the most part, Locke uses the terms "thought" and
"perception" (and their cognates) interchangeably (but see E II.ix.1:
143). Each of them covers, generically, every exercise of the understanding. In many cases, an instance of thinking or perceiving is
merely that, an instance of being conscious or aware of something.
But sometimes one's thinking is also an instance of some more specific type of mental action, such as remembering, discerning, comparing, compounding, judging, and reasoning.

It is also Locke's view, though he does not state it explicitly in the
passages quoted, that ideas exist nowhere but in minds, and nowise
other than as the objects of perception or thought. Furthermore,
there is no thinking or perceiving that does not have an idea for its
object. It follows that for every Lockean idea there is an act or operation of perception or thought, and conversely. Neither does or can
occur without the other.

Locke does not, however, identify ideas with perceivings. Descartes had distinguished two senses of the word "idea": according
to one of these an idea is an act of thinking, according to the other
it is the object of such an act. And it is true that much of Locke's
understanding of ideas – along with his basic decision to make ideas
central to his philosophy – was taken over from Descartes. But
Locke does not make the first of these Cartesian uses of the word
"idea" – he does not sometimes mean by "idea" an act or occurrence of perception or thought, as opposed to the object of such an
act or occurrence.

Locke does occasionally equate ideas with perceptions and even
with sensations, as in the passage quoted earlier (at E II.viii.8: 134).
But the words "perception" and "sensation," like "thought" but unlike "idea," are systematically ambiguous; they have reference both
to acts and to objects of perceiving or sensing. When Locke says that
ideas are perceptions he means perceptions in the object-sense of
the word. And when he wants to speak of perception in the act-
sense, he uses, not "idea," but "having an idea" (as at E II.i.9: 108:
"To ask, *at what time a Man has first any* Ideas, is to ask, when he
begins to perceive; having *Ideas,* and Perception being the same
thing").

II. IDEAS AS OBJECTS

Locke says that ideas are objects of the mind or understanding, and also that they are objects of perception and thought. These are not two different points but two ways of putting the same point. The fundamental fact for Locke is that ideas are the objects of thoughts, that is, of actions of thinking. Since every such action must have a mind for its agent, we can also attribute its object to the mind that performs it, although we speak somewhat loosely in doing so. It must be remembered, however, that the Lockean mind, unlike the Cartesian, is not always thinking. Hence there are times when it exists without containing, or having before it, any ideas; whereas there is no thought, or thinking, without an idea.

What does it mean to say that an idea is an object of thinking or thought? The first thing to note is that it belongs to the nature of thinking to be directed toward something, to have a subject matter or target. There is no such thing as merely thinking – thinking, period – without thinking something, thinking of or about something. And the same holds for perceiving, and for all of the other more specific operations of the understanding. Locke uses the word "object" to refer to this required target or subject matter: the object of a thought is that which the thought is of or about.

But not only is it required that a particular perception or thought be about something, and thus that it have some object or other. It also is necessary that it have the very object it has, that it be a perception or thought of that very thing. For its identity is determined by this. Locke bases the identity of mental actions on other factors as well, namely, the minds performing them and the times at which they occur. But he does hold that a perception of x and a perception of y occurring in the same mind at the same time can only be one and the same perception if x and y are one and the same object, whatever x and y happen to be.

According to Locke, every idea is an object of some action of perception or thinking. But Locke does not hold that ideas are the only such objects. Ideas are all in our minds, as our perceiving is; but very often we perceive things that are outside our minds – outside not only in the sense of being separated from them in physical space but in the sense of being independent of them, not needing them in order to exist. People see stars, hear coaches, and remember Paris in the spring. These are things they perceive and hence objects of their minds, though none exists therein, and none, therefore, is an idea. Locke acknowledges this point by characterizing ideas as the *immediate* objects of our thought, thereby distinguishing them from those external beings which are not immediately perceived and which are not ideas.

Locke's doctrine is that an action of perception *may* have a nonimmediate object, not that it *must* have one. And in fact there are plenty of cases in which perception occurs and there is no external thing perceived, no object outside the mind. We think of nonexistent entities; Macbeth saw a dagger that was not there – or if he did not see any dagger, he at least "saw" something, and in any case engaged in an action of perception. So if every action of perception has an object, and some such actions do not have objects that exist outside the mind, then there must be internal objects of perception – which is precisely what Locke conceives ideas to be.

But Locke does not hold that perceptions have ideas for objects only in those cases in which no external object is available. His view is rather that every perception has an internal immediate object – that it is the perception of an idea – whether or not it has any external one. To be sure, Locke does not say that one *thinks* of an idea as well as of Vienna when she thinks of Vienna. But he does say that one *perceives* an idea in that case, besides thinking of the external thing, Vienna. The two terms, "think" and "perceive" are not perfectly interchangeable for Locke – they are not intersubstitutable in every context – even though his frequent usage is such that, whenever a mind perceives x, it thinks of x, and conversely. (Locke also would not say that one perceives Vienna when one is only thinking of it and not actually seeing it.)

This view, that every perception is of an idea, meaning that it has an immediate object existing within the mind, has been a favorite target of the critics of Locke. Exception to it has been taken both on metaphysical and on epistemological grounds. The metaphysical objection is that Locke, by making mental objects necessary ingredients of the perceptual process, has introduced superfluous entities, thus violating Ockham's rule; besides which, the entities so introduced are of a strange and elusive kind – "shadowy beings" in Reid's phrase, "queer entities" in Wittgenstein's. The epistemological objection is that the presence of such objects in perception creates an impenetrable "veil" between perceivers and the external world, making it impossible for them to know that anything exists outside their minds; and that this leads, as Reid put it, to "paradoxes [that are] shocking to common sense, and [to] a skepticism, which disgrace[s] our philosophy of the mind" (Reid 1970: 26). These objections, and especially the latter, have weighed rather heavily with Locke's readers, enough so that some commentators who count themselves his friends have simply conceded their force, and then argued that Locke did not after all hold the view so objected to. These scholars have devoted considerable effort to reinterpreting Locke's writings, so that the offensive view will no longer be seen to be stated in them.

But these objections – and at least some of the revisionary interpretations they have prompted – are based on misunderstandings of Locke's position. The metaphysical critics have misconstrued the nature of Locke's ideas, the epistemologists their function in sense perception and knowledge, according to his system. Both sorts of criticism are instructive, however, and that, plus their currency, makes them worthy of further consideration. The first or metaphysical sort of objection is discussed in the following section. The epistemological objection will be taken up briefly in Section VII, and is more fully discussed in Chapter 6 of this volume.

III. REAL VERSUS INTENTIONAL BEINGS

What kind of being is a Lockean idea: what is its "ontological status"? This is not a question that Locke himself poses, or perhaps had any interest in: to an early critic's complaint that he had not begun the *Essay* with "an account of the Nature of Ideas" (Norris 1690: 3), he responded that it sufficed for his purpose to consider ideas no farther "than as *the immediate objects of perception*" (Locke 1971: 10). But the question has been raised by the critics just referred to, who claim that Locke has a conception of the nature of ideas, even if he does not acknowledge it, and furthermore that this conception is mistaken. Locke's defenders on this issue agree that the conception in question is mistaken, but deny that it can fairly be attributed to Locke, whose true view of ideas, they argue, is something quite different.

The most prominent such defender is John Yolton; and the critic whose position Yolton is most often concerned to refute is Thomas Reid. According to Yolton, the ontological doctrine that Reid and his ilk attribute to Locke is that ideas are "real beings," "separate, distinct real entities," which stand between a perceiver and external objects and serve as "proxy, inner objects" for the latter (Yolton 1984: 89; Yolton 1975a: 162; Yolton 1990: 59). But the truth, Yolton claims, is that Lockean ideas are not "special objects," "they are not things, entities, at all" (Yolton 1990: 58; Yolton 1975b: 383). In saying that ideas are not entities, Yolton apparently means to deny that they are independent beings, able to exist on their own, apart, in particular, from any action of perceiving or thinking, and hence from any mind. Given this meaning, Yolton's claim is certainly correct: ideas *are* mind- and perception-dependent beings for Locke, as we have noted. Unfortunately, the word "entity" is not normally given this restrictive sense, either in metaphysics or in real life. The result is that Yolton's point has been missed by many readers, and some have summarily rejected it. In the ordinary sense of the word, anything capable of being referred to, anything that can be individually considered or spoken of, is an entity. That Lockean ideas are entities in this sense is as obvious as anything could be.

As for saying that ideas are not objects, this too is misleading, since the word "object" is ambiguous. It may mean, as Yolton evidently intends it to do, "external real being," or, as the dictionary says, "individual thing seen or perceived, or that may be seen or perceived; a material thing" (*Oxford English Dictionary* 1971: 1:1963). But it also has the sense of "that to which action, thought, feeling, or action is directed" (ibid.; cf. Anscombe 1965: 158–60). It is in this latter sense that ideas are objects for Locke: he not only frequently calls them so but defines them as such. (It doesn't help Yolton's case that he seems to take passages in which Locke says that ideas are objects as somehow weighing against his own claim that they are not, as if Locke's use of "object" and his were the same: see Yolton 1975a: 160; Yolton 1984: 89).

Yolton has not stopped with saying what ideas are not for Locke: he also has ventured to describe them in positive terms. But this part of his message is clouded by the fact that he has given two different characterizations of Lockean ideas. On the one hand, he calls them "perceptions," meaning thereby "acts of perception": he does this especially while maintaining the affinity of Locke with Arnauld, citing the latter's polemic against Malebranche (Yolton 1975a: 159; Yolton 1984: 93). On the other hand, Yolton identifies Lockean ideas with the "contents" of perceptual acts (Yolton 1970b: 88; Yolton 1975b: 384). The difficulty is that these two characterizations are inconsistent with one another; besides which, as we have seen, the first one is false. Ideas for Locke are not, as they are for Arnauld and on occasion Descartes, perceptions in the sense of acts of perception. There are indeed passages in the *Essay* and in his "Examination of P. Malebranche's Opinion" in which Locke says or strongly implies that ideas are perceptions (e.g., E II.i.5: 106; E II.x.2: 150; E II.xxxii.1: 384; W IX: 220; W IX: 250). But in all of these passages, the word "perception" either must or at the very least may be taken to mean "object perceived," as opposed to "act of perceiving." And this holds in particular for all the passages cited by Yolton in his effort to bolster this account of Lockean ideas (see Yolton 1975a: 159; Yolton 1984: 90).

Yolton's other characterization, however, is more promising. In his best formulation of it, he begins by observing that Locke took for granted "an act-content . . . analysis of perception" – in common, he might have added, with every other European epistemologist in the seventeenth and eighteenth centuries. He then avers that Locke "wanted to find a way of saying that an act of awareness, [e.g., one] of being aware of the sun, is a mental act but that it also has a content, a psychic, cognitive feature distinct and different from the object seen [e.g., the sun]. [He] wanted to capture the cognitive content of awareness without turning that content . . . into entities." And the way that Locke found, Yolton concludes, is the way of ideas: "idea" is simply Locke's term for "cognitive content" (Yolton 1975b: 384; cf. Yolton 1970b: 88). Yolton's point here (bating his deviant use of the word "entities") is well taken: many philosophers since Locke have found the notion of "content" to be helpful in the effort to comprehend human mentality. In current work in philosophical psychology, the term most frequently used to convey this same notion is "intentional object"; and two leading Locke scholars, while dissenting somewhat from the position of Yolton, have recently argued that Locke's ideas are best understood as intentional objects (Mackie 1985: 223; Ayers 1986: 19).

But taking ideas to be intentional objects (or cognitive contents) does not solve every problem that arises concerning their nature. Ideas so regarded are entities, *pace* Yolton, but it must be admitted that they are indeed "queer" entities, quite apart from their dependence on minds. For one thing, as intentional objects, ideas need not be fully determinate. A real or material apple has a size and a shape and a color, and it must, in addition, have some particular size, shape, and color. But the idea of an apple need not have any size, or shape, or color at all, let alone any particular one. The point is not merely that the idea of an apple is not itself, for example, round, since roundness is a physical property and no such property can intelligibly be attributed to an idea: on that ground, the idea of an apple is also not an apple. Suppose we call the idea of an apple an "intentional apple," and speak of its properties as "intentional roundness" and the like. Then the point about indeterminacy is that an intentional apple need not be intentionally round – have intentional roundness – even if the material apple of which it is the idea is round. More radically: an intentional apple need not have any intentional shape whatsoever, even though its associated material apple – its material counterpart, as we might call it – must have some shape or other.

Now this does sound bizarre; but the principle from which it follows is stated very clearly by Locke. "Let any *Idea* be as it will," he declares, "it can be no other but such as the Mind perceives it to be" (E II.xxix.5: 364). An object of perception has all and only those properties which it is perceived to have, which is to say, those which appear in the perception, or of which the perceiver is consciously aware. And not only do people sometimes perceive things to have features they don't in fact have: they often fail to perceive features they do have, even features in themselves perceptible, and features the things in question could not exist without having. (Of course we must distinguish not perceiving something to be F from perceiving it not to be F: an intentional apple could not be intentionally shapeless.) Thus the indeterminacy of intentional objects is, given their nature and the facts of human psychology, perfectly normal. Such objects only seem bizarre, no doubt because we unreflectingly tend to assimilate them to material objects, to suppose that the former are objects in the same sense of the word that the latter are.

It is worth noting that Locke does not in general use the language of predication in speaking of ideas (although in the passage just

quoted he does speak of an idea as *being* "no other but such . . .").
It would not be at all natural for him to say that the idea of an apple
is red or round, or that it has color or shape, even the idea of color
or shape (or intentional color or shape). The reason is that he does
not regard an idea such as that of an apple as a subject, or its specifications such as color and shape as properties. The idea of an apple
is rather, for Locke, a compound entity, made up of simple (or simpler) components: a "complex idea" that "includes" or "contains"
"simple ideas" of qualities such as redness and roundness. (Locke's
doctrine of complex and simple ideas will be discussed shortly.)

IV. SIMPLE AND COMPLEX IDEAS

One basis for the charge that Locke's use of the word "idea" is ambiguous is that he applies it to entities of different kinds. He himself
makes a number of divisions within the class of ideas: between
simple and complex, particular and general, concrete and abstract,
adequate and inadequate, and so forth. But the items so divided are
still all ideas, in one and the same sense of the word: several species
in a genus not only does not entail several senses in the term for the
genus, it entails the contrary (see Matthews 1972). A more substantial point is that Locke uses the one term "idea" indifferently to
refer to things that his predecessors had called by different names.
Again, he is quite explicit about this: "I have," he says, "used [this
term] to express whatever is meant by *Phantasm, Notion, Species*"
(E I.i.8: 47). But to his critics the differences among the things cus-
tomarily meant by these terms were such as to make Locke's usage
at the least misleading to readers, and beyond that, they took it as
an indication of a false opinion on his part, the opinion that these
things do not in fact differ among themselves, or do not differ in any
significant way. Thus John Sergeant says that this passage by itself
"manifests that [Locke] uses that word [sc. "idea"] very *Equivocally:*
For a *Phantasm*, and a *Notion*, differ as widely, as *Body* and *Spirit;*
the one being a *Corporeal*, the other a *Spiritual* Resemblance; or
rather, the one being a Resemblance, or a kind of *Image*, or Picture;
the other the *thing Resembled*" (Sergeant 1697: 3).

Whatever the differences between notions and phantasms as Sergeant conceived them, they are not our concern here. But we do
need to consider some of the divisions that Locke himself saw fit to

make within the class of ideas, beginning with the most fundamental: that between simple and complex ideas.

A simple idea, Locke says, is one that, "being . . . in it self uncompounded, contains in it nothing but *one uniform Appearance, or Conception in the Mind, and is not distinguishable into different Ideas*" (E II.ii.1: 119). This suggests that the defining feature of simplicity in an idea is experiential or phenomenal: an idea is simple if no variation or division is perceived within it. But in other passages, Locke proposes a semantic or logical criterion of simplicity: simple ideas are those "the *Names of* [which] *are not capable of any definitions*" (E III.iv.4: 421), which means that such ideas cannot be analyzed, or understood as entailing other ideas. These two specifications may not be equivalent: a simple idea according to one of them may not be such according to the other. But this is not a fatal difficulty for Locke, whose main purpose in marking off simple ideas is to bolster his empiricism, that is, the doctrine that "all the materials of Reason and Knowledge" are ultimately provided by experience (E II.i.1: 104). For this purpose it is sufficient that there be some clear examples of simple ideas.

Prominent among the examples Locke gives of simple ideas are those of the "sensible qualities" of physical objects: "*Yellow, White, Heat, Cold, Soft, Hard, Bitter, Sweet*," and the like (E II.i.3: 105). Locke calls such ideas "ideas of sensation" because it is by means of the bodily senses that they are "convey[ed] into the mind" (ibid.). In addition, he recognizes simple "ideas of reflection," so called because the mind gets these "by reflecting on its own Operations within it self": these include the ideas of "*Perception, Thinking, Doubting, Believing, Reasoning, Knowing, Willing,* and all the different actings of our own Minds" (E II.i.4: 105). Sensation and reflection are each modes or forms of experience for Locke, and the two together exhaust it, so that any idea we have from experience must flow from one or the other of these two "fountains." On the other hand, Locke lists several ideas that he says are simple and yet certainly are not ideas either of sensible qualities or of mental operations: those of "*Pleasure,* or *Delight,* . . . *Pain,* or *Uneasiness. Power. Existence. Unity*," to which list he later adds "the *Idea* of *Succession*" (E II.vii.1 and 9: 128 and 131). Hard put to attribute these ideas either to sensation or to reflection, Locke declares that they "convey themselves into the Mind, by all the ways [both] of

Sensation and Reflection" (E II.vii.1: 128). They do so because they always (or almost always) "join themselves to," or "are suggested . . . by," the ideas we do have by sensation and reflection (E II.vii.2 and 7: 128 and 131).

Locke holds that every simple idea that is present in a mind has its source in experience, that is, has come into the mind either by sensation or by reflection. And the mind, he says, "is wholly passive in the reception of all its simple *Ideas*" (E II.xii.1: 163). For "the Objects of our Senses . . . obtrude their particular *Ideas* upon our minds, whether we will or no: And the Operations of our minds, will not let us be without, at least some obscure Notions of them" (E II.i.25: 118). Not only is the mind unable to "refuse, alter, or obliterate" any such idea; it also cannot create any new one in itself. It is not Locke's position, however, that simple ideas are the only ones that come from experience. Many of the ideas we receive via sensation and reflection are in fact compounds consisting of two or more simple ideas joined together. It is such compounds that Locke calls "complex ideas." The idea that I have when I see an apple, for example, is a complex idea, composed of simple ideas of the apple's color, shape, size, and so forth. And the reason these simple ideas are joined together in my mind is simply that the visible qualities to which they severally correspond are really joined together in the external apple I see. So my mind is no less passive with respect to this complex idea than it is with respect to the simple ideas that compose it.

But in addition to complex ideas of this kind, which experience imposes on our minds, Locke recognizes others which the mind itself creates. It does not create them *ex nihilo*, of course. What it does, Locke claims, is join together ideas that are already in its possession separately, so as to make a single new idea out of them: the former serve as raw material or data for the latter. These prepossessed ideas may be simple, or they may themselves be complex: all that Locke's empiricism demands is that they, or their components, or their components' components, . . . , have come into the mind originally by sensation or reflection. In this process of creating new complex ideas, the mind is no longer merely passive. Instead it actively exerts itself, operating upon the ideas it has to make the new ones. Furthermore, its action is voluntary; and the products thereof may be quite out of line with any preexistent reality, external-sensible or mental-operational: ideas of fantastic voyages and fabulous monsters.

In fact the mind has, for Locke, several different ways of acting on ideas so as to generate new complex ones, and the ideas so generated are divided into different kinds accordingly. First, the mind may simply combine or put together several different (simple or complex) ideas into one. This Locke calls the action of "composition" or "compounding"; and the resulting complex ideas are either "ideas of substances" or else "modes," with modes being subdivided into simple modes and mixed ones, all this depending both on the nature of the ideas compounded and on the manner of their compounding. Second, the mind may bring two ideas together, "setting them by one another, so as to take a view of them at once, without uniting them into one" (E II.xii.1: 163); and then the result is a complex idea of the kind Locke calls "relations."

It should be noted that when Locke first treats of complex ideas in Book II of the *Essay*, he speaks of "ideas of substances," but uses the terms "mode" and "relation" to stand for what are themselves ideas. This usage comports with his official metaphysical position, according to which substances are real beings existing outside the mind, whereas relations and modes (at least the mixed ones) are "creatures of the Understanding," "having no other *reality*, but what they have in the Minds of Men" (E II.xxx.4: 373). But Locke often abandons this official position, and his usage shifts accordingly: especially in Books III and IV he regularly speaks of "ideas of modes" and "ideas of relations." From the standpoint of his theory of ideas, this shift is merely verbal – which is not to say that the difference in metaphysical doctrine it reflects is so.

Locke's discussion of these different kinds of complex idea – relations, modes, and ideas of substances – and of the realities (if any) that answer to them extends throughout the *Essay*, and includes much of what is most distinctive and valuable in his philosophy. While it is beyond the scope of this chapter to follow this discussion further, several aspects of it are considered elsewhere in this volume, especially in Chapters 3, 5, 6, and 8.

V. ABSTRACT AND GENERAL IDEAS

In addition to the actions of compounding and comparing, Locke recognizes a third kind of mental operation on ideas, abstraction.

The new ideas produced by this operation he calls "abstract ideas"; but because he holds that all and only abstract ideas are general, he often calls the products of abstraction "general ideas" as well. The two terms "abstract" and "general" do not have the same meaning for Locke; but they do serve to mark off one and the same subclass within the whole class of ideas.

In Book II of the *Essay* Locke describes abstraction as an action in which the mind takes "particular *Ideas,* received from particular Objects," and considers them "as they are in the Mind such Appearances, separate from all other Existences, and the circumstances of real Existence, as Time, Place, or any other concomitant *Ideas*" (E II.xi.9: 159). Further on in the same book he speaks of abstraction as the act of "separating" ideas already in the mind's possession "from all other *Ideas* that accompany them in their real existence" (E II.xii.1: 163). Then in Book III, in recounting how our ideas develop "from our first Infancy," Locke gives the following account of the "way of abstraction":

the *Ideas* of the Persons Children converse with . . . are like the Persons themselves, only particular. . . . Afterwards, when time and a larger Acquaintance has made them observe, that there are a great many other Things in the World, that in some common agreements of Shape, and several other Qualities, resemble . . . those Persons they have been used to, they frame an *Idea,* which they find those many Particulars do partake in; and to that they give, with others, the name *Man,* for Example. . . . Wherein they make nothing new, but only leave out of the complex *Idea* they had of *Peter* and *James, Mary* and *Jane,* that which is peculiar to each, and retain only what is common to them all. (E III.iii.7: 411)

It is clear that Locke is describing two different forms of abstraction in these passages, if not two different procedures altogether. In the case presented in Book II, the mind starts with a complex idea, say an idea of one's mother, visually perceived on a particular occasion. It then picks out one component of this complex idea, say the simple idea of brown (taking brown to be the mother's skin color), and focuses on it alone, ignoring its fellow components. In the Book III kind of case, the mind also starts with a complex idea, suppose again the idea of one's mother. Here, however, it proceeds by removing several components from this complex idea, say the simple ideas of the mother's color, shape, size, and such, while keeping its attention on the original idea, or what is left of it, which is now no more than the idea of a woman – some woman or other. In the one case, the abstract idea, the intended product of the mind's abstractive action, is one simple idea, isolated from the complex idea that originally contained it. In the other, the abstract idea is a complex idea, the same one the mind started with, deprived of some of its original content – a "partial" idea, as Locke says.

Locke does not give much attention in the *Essay* to the operation of abstraction as such: he says almost nothing more about it than is contained in the passages just quoted. But he says a great deal about the abstract ideas that are its products. The chief reason for his interest in them is that abstract ideas also are general ideas. Furthermore, general ideas are the only entities that are general for Locke, apart from the words used to signify them. For there is no generality in nature: "all things that exist are only particulars" (E III.iii.6: 410). Yet generality is fundamental to civilized human life: not only developed language and effective communication among persons but thought itself, beyond the most primitive level, depend upon it. Despite its importance, however, generality is entirely a human creation, according to Locke; and it is by the mental operation of abstraction that generality is brought into the world. Thus abstract general ideas play in Locke's philosophy the roles assigned to Universals and Forms and Essences in the theories of his predecessors – the deficiencies of which he never tires of reminding his readers.

Locke explains how general ideas are created in the same passages as those in which he describes the abstraction process. In the Book II passage he says that

the Mind makes the particular *Ideas*, received from particular Objects, to become general; which is done by ... *ABSTRACTION*, whereby *Ideas* taken from particular Beings, become general Representatives of all of the same kind; and their Names general Names, applicable to whatever exists conformable to such abstract *Ideas*. (E II.xi.9: 159)

He then cites an example:

the same Colour being observed to day in Chalk or Snow, which the Mind yesterday received from Milk, it considers that Appearance alone, makes it a representative of all of that kind; and having given it the name *Whiteness*, it by that sound signifies the same quality wheresoever to be imagin'd or met with; and thus Universals, whether *Ideas* or Terms, are made. (ibid.;

the first hiatus marked here is where the description of abstraction quoted earlier occurs)

In the Book III passage Locke says that

Ideas become general, by separating from them the circumstances of Time, and Place, and any other *Ideas,* that may determine them to this or that particular Existence. By this way of abstraction they are made capable of representing more Individuals than one; each one of which, having in it a conformity to that abstract *Idea,* is . . . of that sort. (E III.iii.6: 411)

Proceeding to describe the abstractive process "a little more distinctly" – this is the passage containing the second description quoted earlier – he writes that children's first ideas of their nurses and mothers, being "only particular,"

represent only those Individuals. The Names [the children] first give to them, are confined to these Individuals; . . . Afterwards, when time and a larger Acquaintance has made them observe, that there are a great many other Things in the World, that in some common agreements of Shape, and several other Qualities, resemble their Father and Mother, . . . they frame an *Idea,* which they find those many Particulars do partake in; and to that they give, with others, the name *Man,* for Example.

And thus, he concludes, "*they come to have a general Name,* and a general *Idea*" (E III.iii.7: 411).

Comparing these passages, one sees that Locke recognizes two different kinds of general ideas, corresponding to the two different "ways of abstraction" by which they are produced. In both cases, to be general, for an idea or for a word, means to be applicable to many distinct individual things. In the Book II case, the general idea is a simple idea of a sensible quality: whiteness. It applies to many distinct individuals – individual instances of whiteness or individual white things – because it has been separated from all the ideas accompanying it (on the occasion of its possessor's perception thereof) that serve to particularize it, that is, which serve to connect it with the individual white physical object – "Chalk or Snow" – whence it has come into the perceiver's mind. Locke's presupposition, evidently, is that such ideas are general in themselves and of their own nature, and that their application to particular individuals is determined by factors extraneous to them as such – especially by such "circumstances of real Existence, as Time, and Place," or rather by the ideas thereof.

In the case described in Book III, by contrast, the general idea is a complex idea of a material substance: man. It applies to many distinct individual men because all simple or simpler ideas of features that serve to distinguish one man from another have been removed from the idea by the abstraction process. It is the point of this kind of abstraction, Locke says, to "leave out of the complex *Idea*" one has of distinct individuals "that which is peculiar to each, and retain only what is common to them all" (E III.iii.7: 411). The features the ideas of which are left out in this way are not merely the extraneous circumstances of time and place, but include proper qualities such as color, size, and shape. Thus ideas that are general in this manner are indeterminate within themselves, unlike the general ideas of Book II, which, though simple, are fully determinate. Indeterminacy, as we have noted, is a perfectly acceptable property for ideas to have in Locke's philosophy.

In both these kinds of general idea, the idea is general in its own nature – it is itself a "general Nature," as Locke puts it. This might seem a violation of the fundamental principle of Locke's nominalistic metaphysics, the principle that all existing things are particulars. But it is not really so. For this principle applies only to the realm of real existence. This includes physical objects, and their qualities, which are outside people's minds; and it includes the actions and events that occur within minds, including acts of perception and thought. But it does not include the intentional objects of such acts, which is what ideas are according to Locke: ideas so conceived are entities, but not real entities, not entities that really exist or occur.

Of course, Locke does often speak of particular ideas, and he has more than one reason for doing so. He calls some ideas particular because in their own nature they are particular, just as some ideas are in their own nature general. These are for example the child's earliest ideas of its nurse and mother, the ones (among others) whence it eventually abstracts the general idea of man. Also particular in this way are one's primitive visual sensations of (cups of) milk and (patches of) snow, from which the general idea of whiteness is eventually abstracted.

But there is another reason for calling ideas particular, and this applies to ideas that are general in nature as well as to those that are not. To understand this, it is useful to compare ideas to words. Philosophers and linguists nowadays commonly distinguish two senses of the word "word," according to whether what is meant is a "type" or a "token": they also say that the word "word" is "type-token ambiguous." The difference between these two senses can be exhibited by asking how many words are contained in the sentence, "The cow jumped over the moon," for example. For there are obviously two correct answers to this question: "six" and "five." "Six" is the correct answer if "word-tokens" are what "words" is taken to mean, "five" if "word-types" are meant. A similar point holds for the word "idea" in Locke's use of it. When Locke says that "*Ideas are actual Perceptions in the Mind, which cease to be any thing, when there is no perception of them*" (E II.x.2: 150), he is speaking of idea-tokens. If, on the other hand, the same idea is said to occur to both you and me at the same time, you and I being different people or minds, or one of us is said to have the same idea on several different occasions, then the idea referred to is an idea-type. (Strictly speaking, it is not idea-types themselves that occur to people or exist in their minds: to "have" [loosely] an idea-type is to have [strictly] a token of that type.) The point about particularity, then, is that the phrase "particular idea" is often used to mean "idea-token," or "idea as occurring in such and such a particular context." Using the phrase in this way, we could say without contradiction that some particular ideas were nonetheless general, that is, general with respect to their own natures. For the particularity in this case would be extrinsic to the idea-type; it would be a function or consequence of the context in which that type was instantiated, just as a word-token is particular in virtue of the particular inscription or utterance in which the corresponding word-type is embodied.

Before leaving this topic of abstract and general ideas, we ought to look at a famous passage in the *Essay*, the misreading of which has caused many critics, beginning with Berkeley, to attribute an absurd doctrine of abstract general ideas to Locke (see Berkeley 1948–57: 2:33–34). The passage occurs in Book IV, where Locke is arguing that so-called maxims, such as the axioms of geometry, are not "the *Truths first known* to the Mind." For, he observes, it "require[s] some pains and skill to form the *general Idea* of a *Triangle*," for example. And the reason it does is that this idea "must be neither Oblique, nor Rectangle, neither Equilateral, Equicrural, nor

Scalenon; but all and none of these at once. In effect, it is something imperfect, that cannot exist; an *Idea* wherein some parts of several different and inconsistent *Ideas* are put together" (E IV.vii.9: 596). The implication of this passage, the critics contend, is that general ideas for Locke are self-inconsistent, because they are made up of parts that are inconsistent with one another. But this is not what the passage says. First, Locke does not state that the general idea of a triangle itself contains inconsistent parts, but that it contains parts of other ideas which are, taken as a whole, inconsistent with one another: but the parts in question are not said to be those that are responsible for that inconsistency. Second, when Locke declares (somewhat loosely, it must be admitted) that this idea is both "all and none of" Oblique, Rectangular, and so forth, what he means is (1) that the ideas of none of these determinations of triangles are explicitly contained in the general idea of a triangle, and (2) that the general idea applies to all the triangles that have these determinations. And finally, when he says that the general idea of a triangle is "something imperfect, that cannot exist," he means that it is indeterminate because incomplete or "partial" and that it cannot exist in reality: but it does not by any means follow for Locke that it cannot exist in the way that intentional objects are wont to exist, that is, as objects of perception and thought.

VI. IMAGES AND CONCEPTS

In interpreting Locke's theory of ideas, a number of commentators have appealed to a distinction between "concepts" on the one hand, and "images" (understood to include "sensations") on the other. It is admitted that Locke himself did not draw this distinction: the word "concept" does not occur in the *Essay*, and though "conception" and "image" do appear occasionally, they are only rarely applied to anything that Locke would call an idea. But some scholars have claimed that the class of things that Locke calls ideas is divided into (what they call) concepts and images (including sensations). Others have claimed, presupposing the same distinction, that all Lockean ideas are images, and that Locke provides no place in his philosophy for concepts.

It is not always clear just how the proponents of these interpretations understand the terms "concept" and "image." One point seems to be that concepts are general and abstract, whereas images are particular, in the sense of being particular in their own nature. On that understanding, it is correct to claim that for Locke some ideas are concepts and some are images (given the interpretation of Locke advanced in this chapter). Sometimes, however, the term "image" is applied to ideas that are "sensible" or have sensory features – have them intentionally, that is. In that case images include not only present sensations, both of sensible qualities and of physical objects possessing such qualities, but also the subsequent memories of such sensations. On that understanding too the claim that Lockean ideas divide into concepts and images is correct – though now the line dividing concepts from images no longer coincides with that between general and particular ideas. For some of the ideas that Locke does or would countenance are nonsensible and particular – those, for example, of God and one's own mind or soul. And some are general and sensible – the abstract idea of whiteness for one, and an idea of man that is only slightly abstract, that is, an idea of a particular man from which size, say, but not shape and color have been removed by abstraction.

The alternative claim, that all of Locke's ideas are images and none concepts, has been defended recently by Michael Ayers. Locke, according to Ayers, is "an imagist," for whom "the only thing 'which the Mind can be employ'd about in thinking' is a sensation or image" (Ayers 1991: 1:45). It is evident that Ayers takes images to be both sensory and particular, for his imagists hold that "thought is bound to particular sensations and sensory images" and that "when we think of X in its absence, X is presented in consciousness in the same general way as it is presented in sensation" (Ayers 1991: 1:249; Ayers 1986: 4). One consequence of this interpretation is that no Lockean idea is abstract or general in its own nature. Ayers not only acknowledges, he embraces this consequence, for he thinks it can be shown independently that "for Locke an abstract idea is a particular perception or image 'partially considered' . . . and given a certain function in thought"; so that "it is not possible to have the abstract idea of *two* in mind without having in mind the idea of some dual in particular, but considered barely *as* a dual" (Ayers 1991: 1:49).

It will be obvious that Ayers's reading of Locke conflicts with the one that has been presented in this chapter. But it would take us too far away from our main business to try to refute Ayers's view, which is developed with great care and subtlety. It is worth noting that Ayers himself says that the question "whether Locke's 'ideas' are all sensory images . . . has yet to be settled by modern commentators"; and he concedes the "relative unpopularity" of his way of settling it – while yet claiming that the grounds favoring his position are "conclusive" (Ayers 1991: 1:44).

There is another use of the word "concept," different from the one we have been considering, that is current among modern philosophers. According to this usage, the concept of a triangle is not the abstract, nonsensory idea that one keeps consciously in mind while proving a Euclidian theorem, for example, although that would be a concept in the other sense of the word. A concept in this sense is not something that occurs or exists in a mind at some times and not others, nor is it something that one perceives or is aware of. It is rather a potentiality or power, itself unperceived, a disposition to do or suffer certain things under certain conditions, which, once acquired, is kept and possessed even at times when it is not being manifested. Thus the concept of a triangle is the ability one has, inter alia, to understand and use the word "triangle" correctly, to recognize certain visual shapes as triangles, and to carry out proofs of theorems about triangles. In this sense there are concepts, not only of abstract nonsensible entities such as triangles, but also of sensible qualities and of physical objects – the concept of whiteness and the concept of man. Let us call concepts in this sense "dispositional concepts," to distinguish them from the concepts that are mental occurrents. The question now to be raised is whether Locke's ideas include dispositional concepts, in addition to the mental occurrents – sensations and images as well as occurrent concepts – that are most prominently called by that name.

Quite a number of commentators have answered this question affirmatively. In support of this answer they often have cited two passages about memory that Locke added to the *Essay*'s second edition. The first occurs in the context of his polemic against innate ideas in Book I. If there were any innate ideas, Locke contends, there would be "*Ideas*, in the mind, which the mind does not actually think on"; and these would have to be "lodg'd in the memory, and from thence . . . be brought into view by Remembrance." For, he continues, "whatever *Idea* is in the mind, is either an actual perception, or else having been an actual perception, is so in the mind,

that by memory it can be made an actual perception again"
(E I.iv.20: 96–97). Here Locke is granting that there are ideas that are
"lodg'd in the memory," and he contrasts them with those that are
actually present to consciousness on particular occasions. And the
distinction between these two sorts of ideas seems exactly to match
that between dispositional concepts and mental occurrents.

In the second passage, which he inserted in his discussion of the
mental operation of retention in Book II, Locke provides a gloss
upon his earlier references to memory as a storehouse or repository
in which ideas are "laid aside out of Sight."

> But our *Ideas* being nothing, but actual Perceptions in the Mind, which
> cease to be any thing, when there is no perception of them, this *laying up*
> of our *Ideas* in the Repository of the Memory, signifies no more but this,
> that the Mind has a Power, in many cases, to revive Perceptions, which it
> has once had, with this additional Perception annexed to them, that it has
> had them before. And in this Sense it is, that our *Ideas* are said to be in our
> Memories, when indeed, they are actually no where, but only there is an
> ability in the Mind, when it will, to revive them again; and as it were paint
> them anew on it self. (E II.x.2: 150)

In this passage Locke still is granting the existence of things that
reside in the mind more or less permanently, and distinguishing
them from actual perceptions, although he no longer wishes, in
strict speech, to call them ideas. And in making these things abilities or powers he is aligning them even more closely with the modern philosopher's dispositional concepts. It is true that the only
power Locke mentions here is that of producing an actual perception, as if – for example and loosely speaking – having an idea of
magenta in one's memory entirely consisted of being able to bring a
visual image of magenta before one's present consciousness. For our
philosophers this is only one of several abilities that having the concept of magenta would entail, and a minor one at that, since in their
view the most important constituents of concepts are verbal and
perceptual capacities – the capacity to use the word "magenta" correctly, for instance, and to distinguish by sight the magenta flowers
in a bouquet from those of other colors. But it turns out that Locke
too assigns different functions to (still speaking loosely) ideas stored
in the memory, over and above that of generating, or of themselves
reappearing as, consciously entertained memory images.

To confirm this, it is useful to examine some of the passages in which Locke describes the process by which children first acquire ideas. One of these occurs early in Book I of the *Essay:*

The Senses at first let in particular *Ideas,* and furnish the yet empty Cabinet: And the Mind by degrees growing familiar with some of them, they are lodged in the Memory, and Names got to them. Afterwards the Mind proceeding farther, abstracts them, and by Degrees learns the use of general Names. In this manner the Mind comes to be furnish'd with *Ideas* and Language, the Materials about which to exercise its discursive Faculty. (E I.ii.15: 55)

Another such passage is found in Book II, where Locke is considering ideas of reflection. It is, he observes,

pretty late, before most Children get *Ideas* of the Operations of their own Minds; . . . Because, though they pass there continually; yet like floating Visions, they make not deep Impressions enough, to leave in the Mind clear distinct lasting *Ideas.* (E II.i.8: 107)

In both of these passages, the ideas with which the acquisition process begins are particular occurrents, things that pass in and out of the mind. Those which the process produces, by contrast, are general and, once established, remain in the mind permanently. These latter ideas reside in the memory, since in Locke's view that is the only way that ideas other than occurrent perceptions can be in the mind. But being there they are apt to be used in ways other than that simply of being recalled to present consciousness. It is in fact these acquired ideas, the ones that the mind "comes to be furnished with," that are Locke's primary concern in the whole *Essay.* It is these that his empiricist thesis is a thesis about, and these that, as the first quoted passage indicates, make human language and reason and knowledge possible – these in which "both the Rightness of our Knowledge, and the Propriety or Intelligibleness of our Speaking consists" (E II.xxxii.8: 386). The case, therefore, for regarding ideas of this sort as concepts, in the modern dispositional sense of the word, is overwhelming.

Just how it is that acquired general ideas, which is what our words "immediately signify," make language possible according to Locke is detailed in Chapter 5 of this book. How knowledge and reason are fashioned from these ideas, which serve as their only "materials," is considered in Chapters 6 and 7, respectively. These matters need not, therefore, be further pursued in this chapter. As for the many questions that a critic might raise about Locke's treatment of memory and concept acquisition – whether his views are coherent and, if so, whether they are supported by a more exact rendition of the facts of experience than he himself was able to provide – these we may not pursue for want of space. We must, to use Locke's own frequent phrase, leave them to be considered.

VII. IDEAS AND REPRESENTATION

We have now examined the major divisions that Locke makes, or that exist, within the class of ideas: between ideas simple and complex, concrete and abstract, particular and general, between images and concepts, and between occurrent and dispositional ideas. Near the end of Book II of the *Essay*, in Chapters xxix–xxxii, Locke introduces several features of ideas that generate further divisions among them: clarity, distinctness, reality, adequacy, and truth. The first two of these need not concern us; but the others are important, not so much in themselves but because they presuppose a more fundamental property of ideas. These features belong to ideas, Locke says, "in reference to things from which they are taken, or which they may be supposed to represent" (E II.xxx.1: 372). It is this representative function of Lockean ideas, the fact that they stand or are supposed to stand for things other than themselves, that we need to examine.

Locke defines real ideas as those that "have a Foundation in Nature; [that] have a Conformity with the real Being, and Existence of Things, or with their Archetypes." These are contrasted with "fantastical" ideas, which "have no Foundation in Nature, nor have any Conformity with that reality of Being, to which they are tacitly referr'd" (ibid.). Adequate and inadequate ideas are then marked off as subclasses of real ideas. Adequate ideas are those "which perfectly represent those Archetypes, which the Mind supposes them to be taken from; which it intends them to stand for, and to which it refers them," whereas those "which are but a partial, or incomplete representation of those Archetypes to which they are referred" are inadequate (E II.xxxi.1: 375). As for truth and its contrary falsity, these are not actually properties of ideas, since it is only propositions or judgments that are in strict speech true and false for Locke.

Still, when an idea is judged or supposed to conform to something "extraneous to" itself, then in a loose or derived sense it may, he says, be "called true" (E II.xxxii.4: 385).

Locke's discussions of the reality, adequacy, and truth of ideas are divided into three sections, corresponding to the three major categories of ideas he has distinguished: simple ideas, complex ideas of (mixed) modes (and of relations), and complex ideas of substances. The conclusions he reaches are: (1) that all simple ideas are real, all are adequate, and all are true; (2) that all ideas of mixed modes (and relations) are real, adequate, and true; and (3) that some ideas of substances are real and some "fantastical," none are adequate, and some are true while others are false.

Among the several claims that Locke is making here, the most important for our purposes are those concerning the reality and the adequacy of simple ideas and ideas of substances. For not only is truth not strictly a property of ideas, but the conformity that justifies our calling an idea true is precisely that which makes it real, and perhaps also adequate, so that its being real or adequate entails its being true. As for ideas of mixed modes, their reality and adequacy (and therefore truth) are at best merely nominal. For since such ideas have "no other *reality*, but what they have in the Minds of Men," they have no archetypes, no "standing Patterns" to which they are intended to conform. This means that they "cannot differ from their Archetypes," or "want any thing" that such archetypes might possess (E II.xxx.4: 373; E II.xxxi.3: 376). But instead of concluding that the notions of reality and adequacy have no application to such ideas, and that they simply have no representative function, as he might well have done, Locke chooses to say that the ideas of modes are themselves archetypes and that they represent themselves (E II.xxxi.3: 377). By making this choice he does indeed guarantee the reality and adequacy of such ideas; but he also renders their possession of these properties quite trivial.

Locke claims that simple ideas are real because they are the "constant Effects" of "Qualities, that are really in things themselves," and thus are able to serve as "the Marks, whereby we . . . know, and distinguish Things, which we have to do with." These qualities may be no more than "Powers . . . ordained by our Maker, to produce in us" such ideas, and the ideas need not in any way resemble those qualities: indeed, Locke claims to have "shewed" that no idea of a secondary quality does resemble the quality of which it is the idea. But the ideas are nonetheless real because of "that steady correspondence, they have with the distinct Constitutions of real Beings," that correspondence consisting in the fact that the same constitutions constantly produce the same ideas (E II.xxx.2: 372–73).

The same consideration proves the adequacy of simple ideas according to Locke. Since simple ideas are "nothing but the effects of certain Powers in Things, fitted and ordained by GOD, to produce such Sensations in us, they cannot but be correspondent, and adequate to those Powers." They are adequate thereto because their function is merely to indicate the presence of the powers. They do not purport to provide information about them, about their nature or what they are like; and we do not expect them to do so (E II.xxxi.2: 375).

Complex ideas of substances, by contrast, are sometimes real, sometimes fantastical. For such ideas are "made in reference to Things existing without us, and intended to be Representations of Substances, as they really are." Hence they are real only when they are "such Combinations of simple *Ideas*, as are really united, and co-exist in Things without us" (E II.xxx.5: 374). But some of our ideas of substances are combinations that we ourselves create and whose elements are never found together in nature, as for example the idea of "a rational Creature, consisting of a Horse's Head, joined to a body of humane shape, or such as the *Centaurs* are described" (ibid.). These then are fantastical ideas.

Our (real) ideas of substances are nonetheless, Locke holds, all inadequate. For as he has argued in his chapter on substance, every such idea contains three kinds of component: (1) several ideas of observable qualities and powers; (2) the idea of an unknown essence from which such qualities and powers "flow"; and (3) "the obscure and relative *Idea* of Substance in general" (E II.xxiii.3: 296). But, first, "those Qualities and Powers of Substances, whereof we make their complex *Ideas*, are so many and various, that no Man's complex *Idea* contains them all." Not only do we "rarely put into [our] complex *Idea* of any Substance, all the simple *Ideas* [we] do know to exist in it"; but there are vast numbers of qualities and powers of substances whereof we have no knowledge and no ideas whatsoever (E II.xxxi.8: 381). Second, even "if we could have, . . . in our complex *Idea*, an exact Collection of all the secondary Qualities, or Powers of any Substance, we should not yet thereby have an *Idea* of the Essence of that Thing" (E II.xxxi.13: 383), which essence must indeed remain forever beyond our ken. And finally, "a Man has no *Idea* of Substance in general, nor knows what Substance is in it self" (ibid.).

It is not easy to extract a coherent doctrine of representation from these discussions. Locke most often seems to treat representation as a relation, whereby ideas are connected (except in the case of mixed modes) to things other than themselves. But sometimes he makes this an absolute relation, one that holds without qualification – either an idea x does represent y or else it does not – as in his discussion of the reality of ideas. And sometimes he makes its holding a matter of degree – x represents y more or less fully or accurately or faithfully – as in his discussion of the adequacy of ideas. So representation is either one relation with apparently contradictory properties, or two different relations with the same name. One way or the other, Locke has some explaining to do.

In some passages, however, Locke seems not to be thinking of representation in relational terms. It is natural enough to treat a real idea, for instance one that represents the sun, as standing in a relationship to something, because the sun is something that does really exist, and so is able, so to speak, to hold up one end of a relationship. But what of a fantastical idea, for instance that of Santa Claus, for which there is no thing for it to be related to? We might say that this idea does represent something, just not something existent. Alternatively, we might say that because there is nothing for the idea to represent, it has no representative function: the idea is not a representer at all. What Locke does say is that fantastical ideas are such as have no conformity "with that reality of Being, to which they are tacitly referr'd, as to their Archetypes" (E II.xxx.1: 372). Hence it appears that even fantastical ideas are "referred to" things other than themselves thought of as archetypes – even if no such archetypes exist. And being so referred may be all that is required for an idea to be representative. If so, then being representative could be an intrinsic property of ideas, or one that belongs to them solely in virtue of their relation to a mind – which in either case would be a property belonging to every idea, fantastical as well as real. On the alternative view, whether an idea is a representer or not would depend upon the existence of things external to itself and indeed to the mind it is in, and thus might change as such things come into and pass out of being.

Whether or not he conceives of representation relationally, Locke must have some answer to the question of how an idea acquires its representative function. Some passages suggest that ideas become representers for Locke by being caused to exist by some real thing without the mind: the idea then represents the thing that causes it. Others suggest that representing is a function imposed upon an idea by the mind to which it belongs: ideas become representers when the mind refers them to or intends them to stand for things outside themselves. It may be, however, that Locke takes both of these factors, the external-causal and the mental-referential, to figure essentially in representation. It could be his view that in order for an idea x to represent something y, not only must y have caused x, but z, the mind in which x resides, must refer x to y, that is to that, whatever it is, which x has been caused by.

Even if so, there would have to be something about x that prompts or enables z to take referential action with respect to it. Locke himself suggests that a mind takes its ideas, at least those that come from external realities (qualities or substances), to be "marks" or signs of those realities, and that that is how it is able to make the uses of them that it does – for example "to know and distinguish Things, which we have to do with" (E II.xxx.2: 373). The fact that a mind takes its ideas in this way could be attributed to that ordination by nature or God which Locke sometimes appeals to, whereby certain sorts of external realities cause certain sorts of ideas to appear in our minds, in constant and regular ways. God or nature could also ordain that ideas so appearing be labeled as signs, or rather as representers of the things that have caused them – so labeled that their text, as it were, would be intelligible to the minds that receive such ideas. Or, rather than supposing them labeled, we could imagine each such idea to have the "additional Perception annexed" to it that it has been produced by something without – in the way that memories for Locke are nothing but "Perceptions, which [the mind] has once had, with this additional Perception annexed to them, that it has had them before" (E II.x.2: 150). On this view, ideas would be "natural signs" of their representata.

If Locke did hold such a position then he would have a defense against those critics mentioned in Section II, who claim that Locke's insistence that the mind's immediate objects are always ideas condemns him to an extreme and incurable skepticism with respect to the external world. Locke could simply respond to such critics that our perception of external objects, the causes of our ideas, is altogether natural, as natural as our perception of ideas – which, after all, itself requires some special capacity on the part of the mind, a capacity that Locke regards as part of its natural endowment. There would not be any fallible or in-principle unverifiable inference involved in perceiving external objects, even though the perception would not be immediate, as it is in the case of ideas. The mind would simply be drawn or led without thought or awareness from the idea it perceives to the external object that is causally responsible for it.

To be sure, the fact that a mind is naturally moved in this way does not mean that it thereby has knowledge, or even a justified belief, that external objects exist. Skepticism is often taken to be a doctrine about the relation not between our ideas and their representata, but between our beliefs and the things they are supposed to be true of. It is in this form that Locke himself discusses skepticism in Book IV of the *Essay*; and the present defense would not by itself be conclusive against it. (Locke's response to this form of skepticism is considered in Chapter 6 of this volume.) The fact that representation is a natural process also does not mean that a person could not be misled on a matter of representation in particular cases, that she could not suppose a particular token of the idea of the sun in her mind on some occasion to represent and so to have been caused by the sun on that occasion, when in fact it was the hypnotist's suggestion, or the hallucinogenic drug she had taken, that caused it. What God or nature ordains is general; it is that some certain sort or species of substance or quality correspond to some certain type of idea, that the instances of the one constantly and steadily produce tokens of the other, and hence that such tokens be reliable indicators of instances of such sorts – reliable but not infallible.

Of course, it remains to be shown that Locke does in fact hold the position on representation that we have been sketching for him. That is likely to be a difficult task: he is not very explicit on the topic of representation – as indeed he is not on some of the other topics discussed in this chapter. It is, however, one of the attractions of Locke's work for contemporary philosopher-scholars that credible answers to philosophical questions he himself never considered can often be drawn from his texts, even when they are not obviously present there.

3   Locke's philosophy of body

I. THE CORPUSCULARIAN CONCEPTION OF BODY

Locke's treatment of such central philosophical issues as substance, qualities, identity, natural kinds, and the structure and limits of scientific explanation was fundamentally shaped by the conception of body (or as we would say it nowadays, the basic nature of material things) that he inherited from Gassendi and Boyle. This conception of body was part of what Boyle called the corpuscularian hypothesis, or corpuscularianism. This doctrine, a form of mechanistic atomism, had the following core tenets:

1. The matter of all bodies is the same in kind, namely, extended solid substance.
2. All bodies are either (a) individual atoms or corpuscles, which are physically indivisible and which have as their only qualities (in addition to extension and solidity) size, shape, location, motion or rest, and number; or (b) aggregates or collections of atoms. There are no physically real components or constituents of a body beyond its component atoms (except for the material that "glues" the atoms together, if any). Compound bodies have a further quality, their "texture," which is the arrangement of their component atoms resulting from their various sizes, shapes, relative situations, and relative motions.
3. All changes of state of bodies are due to a change in texture (note that atoms cannot change their size or shape, since they are indivisible); and all changes in texture are the result of impact or contact action of one body upon another. That

is to say, all causation involving bodies is mechanical causation.

This conception of body traces back to antiquity, specifically to the atomism of Democritus, Epicurus, and Lucretius. It was revived in the seventeenth century by Pierre Gassendi, whose version of corpuscularianism or mechanistic atomism was championed in England by Hobbes, Walter Charleton, and, most influentially, Robert Boyle. It was from Boyle that, in the first instance, Locke drew his understanding of the corpuscularian or mechanical philosophy.

It might seem odd to the modern reader that the notion of body should play such a pivotal role in Locke's philosophy. It should be remembered, however, that the nature of body was one of the most hotly contested issues in the seventeenth century. Its treatment not only defined who was a partisan of the scientific revolution and who was not, but served to distinguish different factions among the revolutionaries. The eminent historian of science E. J. Dijksterhuis has noted that at the middle of the seventeenth century there were four main competing theories about the structure of matter vying with one another: (1) the Scholastic-Aristotelian doctrine of four elements (earth, air, fire, and water), which was one component of a comprehensive metaphysical theory about the nature of individual substances; (2) spagyritic chemistry or iatrochemistry, a doctrine central to the alchemical tradition developed by Paracelsus and by his followers, the van Helmonts, according to which there are three principles or basic causal agents of matter (salt, sulfur, and mercury), of which the last (mercury) is an active or vital (and therefore more than merely material) principle; (3) the Cartesian philosophy, which is based on the identification of matter with extension; and (4) corpuscularianism or mechanistic atomism (Dijksterhuis 1961: 433–34). Although each of last two was called "the mechanical philosophy" by its friends and by its detractors, and each was genuinely a mechanistic theory, there were profound differences between them. Consequent upon the identification of matter and extension, the Cartesians held that a void is impossible, that matter is divided to infinity, and hence that there are no genuine atoms. The corpuscularians held, on the contrary, that solidity is no less a part of the essence of body than is extension, thus opening up the possibility (and, most claimed, the actuality) of void space, and were also committed to the existence of genuine atoms, that is, physically (if not conceptually and/or divinely) indivisible parts of matter that were too small to be perceived.

Where, however, Boyle had tried to downplay as far as possible the differences between the Cartesian and corpuscularian versions of the mechanical philosophy, Locke explicitly (and accurately) treated Cartesianism as a direct rival to corpuscularianism and went out of his way to urge objections to the identification of matter and extension, as well as to the general epistemological framework of Cartesianism. On the other hand, Locke was much less concerned than Boyle was to argue against spagyritic chemistry, whether because he thought Boyle's arguments had already finished it off, or because the philosophical framework for spagyritic chemistry was relatively thin and poorly worked out, or even simply because he was not a professional chemist as was Boyle. Whatever the case, Locke's neglect of spagyritic chemistry as a serious alternative was generally shared by the major scientists and philosophers working at the close of the seventeenth century.

Accordingly, we can see Locke as fighting the battle for corpuscularianism on two fronts: he wants to uphold the claims of corpuscularianism both against those of its principal mechanistic rival, Cartesianism, and also, even more so, against those of the common enemy of all versions of mechanistic natural philosophy, Scholastic Aristotelianism. It is often said by commentators that one of Locke's main aims in the *Essay* was to provide philosophical foundations for corpuscularian science. If this means only that Locke disclaimed any ambitions to make contributions to corpuscularian science as such, choosing instead to address some of the broad philosophical issues surrounding corpuscularianism, then the statement is acceptable. But if more weight than this is put on the phrase "philosophical foundations," then the claim could be seriously misleading, particularly if we use as models for such foundations the Aristotelian-Scholastic and the Cartesian grounding of natural philosophy in a priori epistemological and metaphysical doctrines set out in systematic fashion: "first philosophy," as both the Aristotelians and the Cartesians called it. Not only are Locke's aims less ambitious than this, but it is part of his purpose to cast suspicion on any such project.

With this background we can properly interpret the famous "under-labourer" passage in the *Essay*'s "Epistle to the Reader," which, while sounding a characteristic note of modesty, gives a clear indication of the goals Locke sets for his book:

The Commonwealth of Learning, is not at this time without Master-Builders, whose mighty Designs, in advancing the Sciences, will leave lasting Monuments to the Admiration of Posterity; But every one must not hope to be a *Boyle*, or a *Sydenham*; and in an Age that produces such Masters, as the Great——*Huygenius*, and the incomparable Mr. *Newton*, with some other of that Strain; 'tis Ambition enough to be employed as an Under-Labourer in clearing Ground a little, and removing some of the Rubbish, that lies in the way to Knowledge. (E Epis: 9–10)

This passage is noteworthy not only for its disclaimer about pretending to make any contribution to science, but even more for the hint it gives as to the sort of contribution Locke will try to make. He talks of clearing ground, removing the rubbish that lies in the way to knowledge; the context of the passage makes it plain that he has in mind Scholastic Aristotelianism, which had retained its stranglehold on the curricula of the universities and which was the main rival to the mechanical philosophy. But while it is one of the main tasks of the *Essay* to show up the inadequacies of the rivals to corpuscularianism, especially those of Scholasticism but also those of Cartesianism, we should not conclude that its aims in regard to the corpuscularian hypothesis are wholly negative. Locke also tries to show, even in the course of criticizing its rivals, that the corpuscularian hypothesis conforms especially well with our common-sense views about the nature of body, about the qualities and workings of bodies, and about the source and extent of our knowledge of them. In this lies Locke's distinctive contribution to the corpuscularian program; Boyle, for all of his boosterism, makes appeal only to completely undefined and unexplicated standards of "intelligibility" or plausibility in recommending his corpuscularian explanations. To show that the corpuscularian hypothesis fits well with, or even naturally grows out of, our commonsense picture of the world, and that its serious rivals are on important points flatly in conflict with this picture, is not perhaps to provide philosophical foundations for corpuscularianism, but given Locke's suspicions of any such enterprise it is the most he can hope to do, and even those who do not share Locke's suspicions of the general enterprise will have to agree that securing the result Locke seeks is, after all, not nothing.

II. PRIMARY AND SECONDARY QUALITIES

A good example of the central role played in Locke's philosophy by the notion of body is to be found in his famous distinction between primary and secondary qualities. Although Locke was not the only, or the first, philosopher to argue for the distinction, his treatment of it was, and remains, the most well known and philosophically influential one.[1]

Locke inherited this distinction from his mentor in corpuscularianism, the chemist Robert Boyle. For Locke and Boyle, the primary qualities are solidity, extension (the property of having spatial dimension), figure (shape), motion-or-rest (or mobility), number, situation, bulk, texture, and motion of parts; among the secondary qualities are colors, sounds, tastes, smells, and heat and cold.[2] Locke follows Boyle as well in the basis he gives for sorting qualities into these two lists; he characterizes the secondary qualities as being "nothing in the Objects themselves, but Powers to produce various Sensations in us by their *primary Qualities, i.e.* by the Bulk, Figure, Texture, and Motion of their insensible parts" (E II.viii.10: 135). The twin claims here – that sensible qualities such as colors, sounds, and hot and cold are nothing but powers to produce the corresponding sensations in us, and that these powers are causally based in the primary qualities of (note well for later purposes) the insensibly small parts of the object – are prominent in Boyle's various treatments of the primary-secondary quality distinction. In respect both of the content of the distinction and the basis for drawing it, Locke is simply following Boyle.

Locke's major innovation lies in the way he argues for these claims. Boyle presents the distinction between primary and secondary qualities as part of the corpuscularian hypothesis – a hypothesis that is, he claims, plausible in itself, one that goes much further in making intelligible the qualities and workings of bodies than does any of its competitors, and one that provides the means for explaining any number of interesting experimental results (mainly chemical); but still, a hypothesis that is finally to be vindicated in terms of its explanatory success. Locke, on the other hand, gives a philosophical argument for the distinction, claiming that it is the only understanding of the nature of qualities that is conformable to our commonsense, everyday, prescientific notions of body and of the causality of bodies.

This strategy is reflected in the criteria Locke gives for being a primary quality. Introducing the distinction at *Essay* II.viii.9, Locke says that primary qualities are "utterly inseparable from the Body, in what estate soever it be"; that they are "such as in all the alterations and changes it [the body] suffers, all the force can be used on it, it constantly keeps"; and that they are "such as Sense constantly finds in every particle of Matter, which has bulk enough to be perceived, and the Mind finds inseparable from every particle of Matter, though less than to make it self singly be perceived by our Senses" (E II.viii.9: 134–35). Commentators have wondered how an empiricist could license talk about the mind "finding" something inseparable from a particle of matter too small to be perceived, and the same problem arises in connection with the other criteria, given the full generality with which they are stated ("in what estate soever it be," "in all the alterations and changes it suffers"). On what basis can Locke assert these claims?

The answer has to be that it is by appeal to our commonsense idea of body, or in other words, what we mean by the word "body." Locke insists in many places that our idea of a body is that of an extended solid substance.[3] Of course, a finite extended solid substance will necessarily have some figure or other, some size or other, will be movable in space, and will, in relation to the particles making it up and/or to the particles with which it makes up a larger body, have and/or be part of a texture (an arrangement of corpuscles defined by their shapes, sizes, relative situation, and relative motion). That the body has these further qualities follows from the fact that it is an extended, solid (finite) substance.

That this is Locke's reasoning is attested by the thought-experiment he offers at *Essay* II.viii.9 to make out the claim that the mind finds the primary qualities inseparable from every particle of matter. We are asked to imagine dividing a grain of wheat, dividing the two resulting parts, and so on until we are down to insensibly small parts, which still have solidity, extension, figure, mobility, and the rest. Now how do we know this, especially as regards the insensibly small parts? Locke appeals to the character of the process of division itself, the salient feature of that process being that it begins with one body and leaves two or more bodies at the end, that is, extended solid substances which therefore must each have shape, size, figure, mobility, and so forth. It is also clear from this thought-experiment that what Locke supposes to be inseparable from body are not its particular size, shape, and so forth, but rather its having some size or other, some shape or other. (In the jargon of recent philosophy, it is the determinables of these properties, and not the particular determinates, that are inseparable from bodies.) Of course, once we get down to the level of atoms or corpuscles, which are indivisible by any physical force, the particular size or shape of these parts of matter cannot be changed, except in our imagination or by an act of God.

Locke's second main claim, that secondary qualities are nothing in bodies but powers to produce certain sensations, is also ultimately based on our commonsense conceptions of things. This time, however, it is not our conception of body but rather that of the causality of bodies that is the basis. This conception, and its consequences, are set out in Sections 11-13 of *Essay* II.viii. It is surprising, in view of the importance of these considerations in Locke's overall argument for primary and secondary qualities, that these sections have been so little commented upon. Locke's claim in Section 11 is that we cannot conceive how one body can act upon or affect another body except by impulse, that is, by contact action, and so we must hold that bodies produce ideas in us by means of contact action.[4] But since we perceive bodies at a distance from us, the proximate cause of the sensible ideas these bodies induce in us must be the contact action of imperceptibly small particles inducing motions in our sensory organs, our nerves, and, finally, our brains, which motion ultimately produces the appropriate ideas in our minds (Section 12). This causal account would hold for the ideas of secondary qualities – colors, sounds, tastes, smells, heat and cold – just as much as for the observable primary qualities of bodies (Section 13).

The conclusion Locke draws from this discussion of our commonsense view of the causality of bodies is that secondary qualities "are in truth nothing in the Objects themselves, but Powers to produce various Sensations in us, and *depend on those primary Qualities,*

viz. Bulk, Figure, Texture, and Motion of parts" (E II.viii.14: 137).
There is an important point to note about this formulation. Locke
does not say that the secondary qualities are nothing in the objects
– that is, are not in the bodies. He says they are nothing in the objects but powers to produce ideas. This implies that, considered as
powers, the qualities are in the bodies, and are not just ideas in our
minds; this is later made explicit at II.viii.23. This view of the status
of secondary qualities sharply distinguishes Locke's and Boyle's view
from those of their predecessors Galileo and Descartes, for whom
secondary qualities have no reality in the body, but are just ideas in
our minds. It also distinguishes their view from that of the "modern
philosophers" attacked in the first of Berkeley's *Three Dialogues between Hylas and Philonous* and in Sections 18ff. of Part I of the
Principles of Human Knowledge, an attack that is still widely mis-
apprehended to be effective against Locke, its intended target.

Locke draws a further conclusion from this one. In the next section he says that "the *Ideas of primary Qualities* of Bodies, *are Resemblances* of them, and their Patterns do really exist in the Bodies
themselves; but the *Ideas, produced* in us *by* these *Secondary Qualities,* have no *resemblance* of them at all" (E II.viii.15: 137). This
has been one of the most misunderstood formulations in the *Essay,*
due mainly to puzzlement over how to understand the term "resemblance" as it is used here. If we read the term in its everyday,
nontechnical sense, we run up against the problem that Berkeley
pointed out, namely, that ideas, which are states of mind, are in
their nature quite unlike states of bodies, so that if the claim has to
do with overall resemblance, ideas of primary qualities do not resemble bodies any more than do ideas of secondary qualities. (Ideas
and states of bodies are just too different in nature for there to be
any resemblance at all.) There is the further problem that we have
no access to the qualities of bodies except through our ideas, and so
no independent standpoint from which to compare ideas and qualities and thus gauge their overall resemblance. If, alternatively, we
read the resemblance claim as saying that our judgments about the
primary qualities of bodies such as their shape and size are somehow
more secure or less likely to be false than are judgments about their
colors and tastes, then, as Berkeley also insisted, the claim cannot
be upheld at all, as we are no less liable to make mistaken judgments about (macro) shape and size than about color and taste. To

understand this, we need to remind ourselves of the Aristotelian background to the discussion. The Aristotelian-Scholastic doctrine of qualities held that most, at least, of the sensible qualities of objects are real qualities, that is, that they are real entities existing or inhering in the objects, and that perception of them involves the mind taking on the form of these qualities as they exist in the object. This is facilitated by the transmission through a medium – light, for example, in the case of qualities perceived by means of vision – of an intentional species that becomes the form of the relevant perception or act of mind; this intentional species is the form that exists in the object, except that this form exists not in matter, as it does in the object, but in the mind. The idea in the mind is thus qualitatively identical with the quality in the body that initiated the whole causal process, since these two are the same in form or species; and so it can properly be said to resemble the quality as it is in the body.

With this as background we can see why it is a short step from the premise that secondary qualities are nothing but powers to the conclusion that the ideas of secondary qualities are not resemblances of them (i.e., the qualities as they are in the bodies). For our ideas of colors, sounds, heat, and so forth present these as manifest qualities in the bodies; there is nothing in these ideas of either the actual physical basis in the body that is causally responsible for the production of these ideas in perceivers, or the dispositional character of the powers to produce ideas that these bodies consequently have. On the other hand, the ideas of primary qualities are qualitatively similar to the actual causal basis in the object of the production of these (and all other) sensible ideas.

Read as directed against the Aristotelian doctrine of qualities in its own terms, however, Locke's claim makes perfect sense. The ideas of the primary qualities of bodies are caused in us by those qualities, and they are qualitatively like the qualities in the bodies that are their causes, even if only generically.

To what extent do Locke's arguments for the primary-secondary quality distinction depend on assuming that the corpuscularian hypothesis is true, or at least the best supported or otherwise most probable scientific hypothesis among the going alternatives? Some commentators have taken the distinction between primary and secondary qualities to be just a distinction between those qualities which are basic to the scientific explanation of the qualities, powers, and operations of bodies and those which are explained in terms of those qualities; the lists of which qualities count as primary and which as secondary would then shift as science progresses, and one would stay with Locke's list only as long as the corpuscularian theory was the best theory going. That Locke is not committed to any such account as this is confirmed at IV.iii.11, where he says, "The *Ideas*, that our complex ones of Substances are made up of, and about which our Knowledge, concerning Substances, is most employ'd, are those of their *secondary Qualities*; which depending all (as has been shewn) upon the primary Qualities of their minute and insensible parts; or if not upon them, upon something yet more remote from our Comprehension" (E IV.iii.11: 544). Of course, if the qualities and powers of bodies did in fact turn out to depend on something other than the corpuscularian's primary qualities (bulk, figure, motion, etc. of the solid parts of bodies), then Locke's distinction, even if it were still conceptually available, would be of no account.

But in fact Locke does not base the distinction between primary and secondary qualities on the alleged scientific superiority of corpuscularian mechanism. When he says in Section 9 that the mind finds the primary qualities "inseparable" from body no matter what state it is in, he is appealing to the commonsense meaning of the term "body." On a similar basis, Boyle had argued that any finite extended solid thing will have a determinate figure and size and will be movable in space. It will thus, according to Locke and Boyle, be a function of our ordinary concept of body that anything that is a body must have all of the qualities listed as primary in Section 9; there is no need to appeal to the corpuscularian hypothesis and its presumed scientific superiority in order to deliver this claim.

Sections 16–21 of *Essay* II.viii present a series of thought-experiments designed to bring out the fact that it is part of our ordinary commonsense picture of the world that (1) secondary qualities are not in bodies, except as powers to produce sensations, and (2) secondary qualities depend on the primary-quality constitutions of bodies. There are two basic sorts of example. The first sort, found in Sections 16 and 18, compares the secondary quality of warmth with the pain that is caused by extreme heat, or again the secondary qualities of sweetness and whiteness in manna with its power to cause sickness and pain in us. In each of these comparisons, Locke points out that we would not for a minute suppose that the pain or sickness is a real quality of the fire or the manna; the warmth of the fire, and sweetness and whiteness of the manna are in the same boat with these, powers to produce ideas that objects have in virtue of their primary-quality constitutions. The other sort of example, found in Sections 19, 20, and 21, asks us to imagine the physical basis of variations in the sensible qualities of things. Hindering light from striking porphyry takes away the red and white colors we see when it is illumined; but we do not think that the presence or absence of light makes for any physical change in the porphyry. Locke is careful to note that there is no change in the powers of the object: even in the dark, it has the power of producing ideas of red and of white in observers under suitable conditions (e.g., of illumination), and it has this power in virtue of its microphysical constitution. Pounding an almond with a pestle will change its color and its taste, but we can't imagine any other way that a pestle operates on an almond than by changing its texture, that is, the disposition of its parts. And finally, we can't imagine how it should be that the same water should appear hot to one (previously cooled) hand and cold to the other (previously heated) hand unless we imagine that the sensations of hot and cold result from differences between the motion of particles in the water and those in the respective hands.

There are two points to note about these examples. First, they are not supposed to be decisive counterexamples to the Aristotelian theory of qualities, or conclusive demonstrations of the correctness of the corpuscularian theory. (That is a good thing, since taken singly or all together they obviously fall short of either goal.) They are intended rather to remind us that given our pretheoretical conception of the causality of bodies, rough as this conception is, we find it most natural and plausible to think that the changes we observe in the sensible qualities of objects are rooted in changes in their physical structure, as these changes in turn affect our sensory organs. Second, in line with this we should note that these examples appeal to nothing beyond our commonsense view of the world; in particular, they do not rely upon a prior acceptance of the corpuscularian hypothesis. On this view of Locke's arguments, the distinction between primary and secondary qualities is not based on the scientific correctness or at least the current scientific superiority (both alleged) of corpuscularianism, nor is it backed only by a promissory note about the future development of science; it is instead a natural consequence of the ways we ordinary people think of the world, for better or worse. Granted, this is hardly a basis for a conclusive argument for the truth of corpuscularianism; but we have seen that this was not Locke's intention. He aimed to show that the corpuscularian theory meshes very well with our commonsense views of things and that, in contrast, the Aristotelian theory, given its bizarre theory of causality and its indefensible distinction between sensible qualities that actually reside in the object ("real qualities") and those which are merely imputed to it on the basis of the sensations they induce in us ("mere powers"), is one that we cannot finally make sense of.

III. THE LIMITS OF MECHANISM

Locke is unique among the seventeenth-century champions of mechanism in emphasizing the severe limitations on our ability actually to deliver mechanistic explanations of natural phenomena. In the important chapter "Of the extent of human knowledge" (Book IV, Chapter iii) he argues at length for the conclusion that "we are not capable of a philosophical *Knowledge* of the Bodies that are about us," so that "as to a perfect *Science* of natural Bodies, (not to mention spiritual Beings,) we are, I think, so far from being capable of any such thing, that I conclude it lost labour to seek after it" (E IV.iii.29: 560).

Odd words from a supposed friend of mechanism. (With friends like this, . . .) In an influential recent paper, Margaret Wilson has argued that Locke's deep pessimism about our prospects of arriving at a genuinely explanatory natural science conflicts with his professed commitment to Boylean mechanism, leaving it unclear to what extent he is really a mechanist. Wilson notes that Locke has several different reasons for being pessimistic about our prospects for achieving genuine scientific knowledge, some of which tend to cast doubt on the comprehensibility of the mechanist hypothesis itself (Wilson 1979).

The least problematic set of reasons has to do with the extremely small size of the corpuscles that make up the bodies around us, a size that puts them well beyond the limits of resolution of our senses. Locke takes this to suggest that we will probably never have detailed knowledge of the actual microphysical constitutions of bodies, and so will be unable to provide detailed mechanistic explanations of observable phenomena. This is an important limitation, but this limitation on our ability to deliver mechanistic explanations does not by itself challenge the inherent comprehensibility of mechanism.

Other reasons Locke cites for pessimism about lack of prospects of having a science of nature are much more troubling to the mechanist. Locke recites some of the leading conceptual difficulties faced by mechanists of his period, including two of the most notorious problems, that of explaining what it is that holds aggregates of particles together so that they may constitute large-scale organized bodies, and that of specifying the mechanism by which bodies transmit their motion one to another in contact action. Mechanists tried various means to account for the cohesion of bodies, including some kind of glue or cement sticking the parts together, the pressure of the ambient fluid or ether pushing and holding the parts together, and even a hook-and-eye scheme whereby the parts stick together by virtue of their shapes (sort of a microscopic Velcro). Locke points out the well-known problems with each of these suggestions – what holds together the particles making up the cement or glue, or why can you separate the polished surfaces of two pieces of marble by moving them away from each other in a line parallel to their surfaces but not in a line perpendicular to them, if you assume equal pressure of the ambient fluid on all sides? – just as Boyle had done. But where Boyle regarded these as open problems to be resolved by the developing corpuscularian science of bodies, Locke regards them as less readily remediable. Of course, Locke admits that we do know from daily experience that bodies cohere together, and that they transmit motion from one to another by impulse, but, he insists, we haven't even the beginnings of a conception of how they do these things. This is a much deeper ignorance than that of the detailed microstructures of bodies, one that goes more nearly to the heart of mechanism, and Locke is much less sanguine about the prospects of overcoming it than Boyle seems to be.

It gets worse. Not only are we ignorant of the detailed structure of particular bodies, and of some of the more general conceptual underpinnings of mechanism, such as what accounts for the cohesion of bodies and their ability to transmit motion by impulse; but we cannot even begin to conceive how it is that the sensible secondary qualities of a body are causally connected with its primary-quality constitution.

Locke is clear about the reason for this conceptual lack of ours; it has to do with the poverty of our ideas of body and of mind (or mental states). The relative lack of content of these ideas provides the basis for one of the most controversial claims of the *Essay*, the claim that it is, for all we know, possible that suitably organized systems of matter may have the power of thought. In a famous passage Locke writes:

We have the *Ideas* of *Matter* and *Thinking*, but possibly shall never be able to know, whether any mere material Being thinks, or no; it being impossible for us, by the contemplation of our own *Ideas*, without revelation, to discover, whether Omnipotency has not given to some Systems of Matter fitly disposed, a power to perceive and think, or else joined and fixed to Matter so disposed, a thinking immaterial Substance: It being, in respect of our Notions, not much more remote from our Comprehension to conceive, that GOD can, if he pleases, superadd to Matter a Faculty of Thinking, than that he should superadd to it another Substance, with a Faculty of Thinking; since we know not wherein Thinking consists, nor to what sort of Substances the Almighty has been pleased to give that Power, which cannot be in any created Being, but merely by the good pleasure and Bounty of the Creator. (E IV.iii.6: 540–41)

The incommensurability of the ideas of matter and thinking leaves us unable to conceive how there could be any causal connection between states of bodies and states of mind (supposing, what Locke clearly takes to be a mere supposition, that the latter are really distinct from the former):

What certainty of Knowledge can any one have that some perceptions, such as *v.g.* pleasure and pain, should not be in some bodies themselves, after a certain manner modified and moved, as well as that they should be in an immaterial Substance, upon the Motion of the parts of Body: Body as far as we can conceive being able only to strike and affect body; and Motion, according to the utmost reach of our *Ideas*, being able to produce nothing but Motion, so that when we allow it to produce pleasure or pain, or the *Idea* of a Colour or Sound, we are fain to quit our Reason, go beyond our *Ideas*, and attribute it wholly to the good Pleasure of our Maker. For since we must allow he has annexed Effects to Motion, which we can no way conceive

Motion able to produce, what reason have we to conclude, that he could not order them as well to be produced in a Subject we cannot conceive capable of them, as well as in a Subject we cannot conceive the motion of Matter can any way operate upon? (E IV.iii.6: 541)

Locke goes on later in the chapter to draw from these considerations a very strong conclusion regarding the explanatory connections between primary-quality constitutions of bodies and their sensible secondary qualities that are required for the success of corpuscularian science.

We are so far from knowing what figure, size, or motion of parts produce a yellow Colour, a sweet Taste, or a sharp Sound, that we can by no means conceive how any *size, figure, or motion* of any Particles, can possibly produce in us the *Idea* of any *Colour, Taste, or Sound* whatsoever; there is no conceivable *connexion* betwixt the one and the other. (E IV.iii.13: 545)

Since the secondary qualities of things are by far the greatest part of their observable qualities, it follows that we will probably never be able to arrive at genuine mechanistic explanations of most of the leading qualities of bodies, and this because we find it incomprehensible that there should be any lawlike connections between primary-quality constitutions and sensible secondary qualities. As Wilson notes, this seems to threaten Locke's claim that the sensible qualities of things "flow from" the primary-quality constitution, or real essence, of the thing (Wilson 1979: 144–47).

There is an expedient suggested in several of the relevant passages that looks like an attempted solution to the problem. In the quotation from *Essay* IV.iii.6, we saw Locke saying that we must put it down to the "good pleasure" of "our Maker," who, we are to suppose, has annexed effects to motions (of parts of bodies) that we cannot conceive them to have. Later in the chapter, returning to the issue, Locke says this:

'Tis evident that the bulk, figure, and motion of several Bodies about us, produce in us several Sensations, as of Colours, Sounds, Tastes, Smells, Pleasure and Pain, *etc.* These mechanical Affections of Bodies, having no affinity at all with those *Ideas*, they produce in us, (there being no conceivable connexion between any impulse of any sort of Body, and any perception of a Colour, or Smell, which we find in our Minds) we can have no distinct knowledge of such Operations beyond our Experience; and can reason no otherwise about them, than as effects produced by the appointment of an infinitely Wise Agent, which perfectly surpass our Comprehensions. As the *Ideas* of sensible secondary Qualities, which we have in our Minds, can, by us, be no way deduced from bodily Causes, nor any correspondence or connexion be found between them and those primary Qualities which (Experience shews us) produce them in us; so on the other side, the Operation of our Minds upon our Bodies is as unconceivable. How any thought should produce a motion in Body is as remote from the nature of our *Ideas*, as how any Body should produce any Thought in the Mind. That it is so, if Experience did not convince us, the Consideration of the Things themselves would never be able, in the least, to discover to us. These, and the like, though they have a constant and regular connexion, in the ordinary course of Things: yet that connexion being not discoverable in the *Ideas* themselves, which appearing to have no necessary dependence one on another, we can attribute their connexion to nothing else, but the arbitrary Determination of that All-wise Agent, who has made them to be, and to operate as they do, in a way wholly above our weak Understandings to conceive. (E IV.iii.28: 558–59; see also E IV.iii.29: 559–60)

This seems to provide for the requisite causal connections, although at the cost of giving up our prospects of ever coming to know these connections – that is, short of God's explicitly revealing them to us.

It might seem that the cost is even steeper than that. Wilson thinks that the arbitrariness of these God-forged connections conflicts with Locke's "official position" on body – that is, with mechanism – in several respects. First, she notes that the arbitrariness of the connections would not allow for the "a priori conceptual connection between a body's real essence and its secondary qualities" that she sees as part of the official position. Second, taking up a suggested reading that has Locke denying only a rational connection that we can conceive, and not denying in principle that there is a rational connection, Wilson argues that this runs afoul of several key Lockean claims, including the one (in his elaborate proof of the existence of an intelligent creator in Book IV, Chapter x) that matter cannot naturally produce thought, as well as his contentions that we cannot understand gravitational attraction to be among the natural powers of matter and that a man with microscopical eyes would still not be able to give a rational explanation or derivation of the sensible qualities of bodies (Wilson 1979: 147–48).

But there really is no conflict here. Locke's epistemology of scientific explanation does require that we apprehend a necessary connection between, in this case, the primary-quality constitution of a body and a sensible secondary quality, if our belief that the latter flows from the former is to count as genuine scientific knowledge (what the tradition called "scientia"); and this in turn requires that we be able to demonstrate that such a connection holds. Now, in the expedient suggested by Locke, we do suppose that God has set up a necessary connection between the primary-quality constitution in question and the effect it has on our sensation. We are supposing him to have ordained a law according to which it cannot but happen that if a body has that primary-quality constitution and is in the appropriate circumstances, it will produce the corresponding sensation in the appropriately constituted subject. Admittedly, this connection would not be a "rational" one, since its necessity would not be demonstrable independently of the fact that God had expressly (and arbitrarily) ordained that such a necessary connection obtain. But if we could somehow learn (by revelation, say) that God had ordained such a connection, we could use this information in a strict demonstration that a body constituted as this one is cannot fail to have such-and-such a sensible quality (supposing we also could come to know the detailed microphysical constitution of the body). Of course, short of revelation we could probably never come to apprehend the necessity of the connection, and so could never give the demonstration. But this is precisely Locke's point. No wonder that the man with microscopical eyes cannot rationally derive the sensible qualities of a body from his knowledge of its inner constitution: ascertaining what God has arbitrarily decreed in the way of connections is obviously not a matter of microscopy, or of reason. This does not make the decreed connection any less necessary, or any less capable of functioning in a strict demonstration, even if we and the man with microscopic eyes are unable to apprehend the necessity of the connection and thus know that there is a demonstration to hand.

The related claims about the power of thought not belonging naturally to matter, and similarly with the power of gravitational attraction, look to be more problematic, as they seem to constitute ontological claims of some sort. But a close look at the relevant passages belies this appearance. Consider the principal passage about gravity; it doesn't say that the power of bodies to attract one another over a distance is not natural to bodies, but that we can't see it as such, given our idea of body:

The gravitation of matter towards matter, by ways inconceivable to me, is not only a demonstration that God can, if he pleases, put into bodies powers and ways of operation above what can be derived from our idea of body, or can be explained by what we know of matter, but also an unquestionable and every where visible instance, that he has done so. (W IV: 467–68)

"By ways inconceivable to me"; "above what can be derived from our idea of body"; "can be explained by what we know of matter": these phrases indicate the character of Locke's claims about what is and what is not included in the "natural" powers of matter. Any estimates that we might make about what is included in or what follows from the "nature" of matter are grounded on our idea of body, or matter; on what else could they be grounded? Locke's claim about gravity is thus another instance of the by now familiar litany: given the meagerness of what follows from our idea of body as an extended solid substance, we cannot conceive how one body should attract another at a distance, that is, we cannot imagine a suitable mechanism merely in terms of the bulk, figure, and motion of bodies together with the transmission of motion by impulse or contact action that would account for the phenomena of gravitational attraction; in our conceptually impoverished circumstances, then, we are forced to put the phenomena down to "powers" and "ways of operation" superadded to the mechanical affections of bodies by an omnipotent God.

The main outlines of the case of mind-body connections are the same. We have already seen how the particular connections between the primary-quality constitutions of bodies and the sensations these constitutions regularly cause in us, the connections by virtue of which secondary qualities can be said to be based on, or to flow from, the real essences of bodies, must be conceived by us, faute de mieux, to be the results of divine acts of superaddition. This reflects the more general relation between mind and body summed up in the claim we encountered earlier, namely, that it is, for all we know, possible that God has superadded the power of thought directly to suitably organized systems of matter, in which case thinking things would be merely, and thoroughly, material. What then of the claim cited by Wilson and crucial to Locke's proof of God's existence as an intelligent thinking being, the claim that matter, however it may be shaped or moved, cannot come to have (Locke actually says, "cannot put into itself") the power of thought? The correct handling of this claim is in fact indicated by Stillingfleet, in the book that sparked the correspondence between him and Locke:

> It is said indeed elsewhere, That it is repugnant to the Idea of Senseless Matter, that it should put into it self Sense, Perception and Knowledge: But this doth not reach the present Case; which is not what Matter can do of it self, but what Matter prepared by an Omnipotent hand can do. (Stillingfleet 1697a: 242, citing E IV.x.5: 620–21)

Stillingfleet makes this point in the course of arguing that Locke cannot on his own principles demonstrate that the substance that thinks within us is a spiritual (by which Stillingfleet means immaterial) substance, a point that Locke willingly concedes. As both saw, Locke's claim that matter cannot naturally, by itself, come to have the power of thought is not inconsistent with his other claim that an omnipotent God can endow certain systems of matter with the power of thought.

Locke's appeals to God's omnipotence as enabling him to forge connections "inconceivable to us" between (1) the primary-quality constitutions of bodies and the ideas these bodies cause us to have; (2) certain configurations of systems of matter in motion and the powers of thinking and willing that those same systems of matter come to have; and (3) the basic defining qualities of matter (extension and solidity) and the propensity of matter to attract other matter over a distance (gravity) – to mention just the instances of otherwise incomprehensible phenomena that he explicitly puts down to divine acts of "superaddition" – might seem to be nothing more than desperate, and perhaps finally empty, appeals to a deus ex machina. (Given that it is a mechanistic world that this God is being called in to salvage, the phrase is particularly apt.) This overlooks two important features of Locke's appeal, however. First, even though he emphasizes that our appeal to God's arbitrary annexations is an appeal of last resort, for want of any better way, or any way at all, of conceiving how the connections hold, he is quite clear about the particular content of that appeal. We suppose that God superadds these various powers to matter by decreeing that certain laws hold, connecting the mechanical affections of matter with the powers that result from them. This is absolutely crucial for mechanism, for it means that the superadded powers and ways of operating are not due to any real, nonmechanical component or constituent of the body; the only causally active qualities of the body are its mechanical affections. It is just that, given the laws God has established, these affections are capable of producing the effects in question. Furthermore, since God ordains these laws as necessary connections (E IV.iii.29: 560), they could function in proper demonstrations of the sort strict scientific knowledge (scientia) demands – could we but come to know them.

To a modern reader, this way of salvaging mechanism in the face of the severe strictures Locke finds on our knowledge will seem ad hoc, given its essential appeal to the inscrutable actions of an omnipotent God. What seems to us a crippling defect in the theory, however, was, in the intellectual context in which Locke and Boyle worked, a positive advantage. One of the main orders of business for the seventeenth-century inheritors of the ancient atomist tradition was to remove the taint of atheism that clung to the view. As its opponents were fond of pointing out, Democritus, Lucretius, and other ancient atomists held such theologically unacceptable views as that matter was eternal and uncreated, that the world was a result simply of chance motions of unguided matter, and so forth. Gassendi on the Continent, and Boyle in England, were very much concerned to show that atomism could be pruned of these troubling excrescences, and Boyle ventured much further in trying to argue that the role God plays in the new conception of mechanistic atomism provides a new basis for establishing God's existence, attributes, and providence. Locke's making God and his action an ineliminable part of the mechanistic world-picture is thus entirely in line with the Gassendi-Boyle program, if something of an extension of it.

We can now appreciate how complex and multilayered was Locke's understanding of mechanism, and concomitantly his notion of body. We have seen that there is finally no conflict between Locke's extreme pessimism about our prospects for achieving true scientific knowledge and his commitment to corpuscularianism as the best view of nature that we can arrive at. What is perhaps most important, we have seen that Locke bases his argument for the latter commitment not on any claim that corpuscularianism now is, or soon will prove to be, the correct or at least the best-established scientific theory of the world, but instead on an analysis of our ordinary, prescientific notions of body and of the causality of bodies.

IV. SUBSTANCE AND SUBSTRATUM

Since the first round of critical response to Locke's *Essay* its doctrine of substance has been a focus of controversy; the only other Lockean doctrines to draw such intense criticism were the denial of innate knowledge and the assertion of the possibility of thinking matter. For Berkeley, Locke's notion of substance was merely the despised *materia prima* of the Scholastics got up in modern dress; for Leibniz, Locke's impoverished (as it appeared to him) conception of substance was a basic cause of the latter's supposed inability to accommodate the necessary truths of metaphysics; and for Edward Stillingfleet, bishop of Worcester, Locke's dismissive treatment (as it appeared to him) of substance was part of an attack on the traditional theological doctrine of the Trinity. According to many of these critics, Locke offers a denatured notion of substance, on which the substance of a thing is nothing but a substratum or support to the qualities and powers (the "accidents," in Scholastic parlance); in itself it is featureless, lacking any properties or qualities of its own: a "bare particular" as it is called (or disparaged) nowadays.[5]

Understood in this way, Locke's doctrine of substance is a subject ripe for criticism. The notion of a bare particular is, it is generally agreed, shot through with confusion (it is supposed to be a thing that has no properties of its own, so it can be what "has" all of the properties of the object). More than this, the notion does not seem to have any place in the corpuscularian theory, which it was, after all, Locke's aim to advance. Indeed, if we take the substratum of a body to be something over and above the aggregate of insensibly small particles of matter (corpuscles) that make up the body, then the notion of substratum is inconsistent with corpuscularianism.

Most commentators on Locke, whether sympathetic or critical, have tended to view Locke's doctrine of substance in much the same way as did his early critics, regarding it as either the product of confusion on Locke's part, or a mindless holdover from his Oxford training in Scholastic logic. Within the past twenty years or so, however, several revisionist views have been advanced, each aimed at eliminating the apparent commitment to bare particulars. Before we consider these rival proposals, we should look at some of Locke's most important statements about substance.

There are two extended discussions of the nature of substance in the *Essay*, one in Chapter xxiii of Book II ("Of our Complex Ideas of Substances"), the other in Sections 17–20 of Book II, Chapter xiii, the chapter on space. As is indicated by its title, Chapter xxiii is officially concerned with the notion of substance, and its treatment of the notion of substratum has been taken to be canonical. Reading through this chapter, especially the beginning sections, one can see why the traditional interpretation should have been so widely shared. Locke begins with an analysis of the ideas we have of the various sorts of substances (e.g., human beings, horses, gold, water): these are complex ideas, which collect together and unite into one idea (1) the ideas of the various sensible qualities we perceive the individual substances that are the members of the sort to agree in (in the case of gold, e.g., such qualities as yellowness, heaviness, malleability, solubility in aqua regia, etc.), together with (2) the idea of substance in general, said at *Essay* II.xii.6 to be "the first and chief" of the ideas collected together in any of the ideas of the sorts of substances. Locke emphasizes that the idea of substance in general is not one among the ideas of the sensible qualities, and hence that it is not directly derived from experience; instead, it is supposed or constructed by us: "not imagining how these simple *Ideas* [the ideas of the sensible qualities] can subsist by themselves, we accustom our selves, to suppose some *Substratum*, wherein they do subsist, and from which they do result, which therefore we call *Substance*" (E II.xxiii.1: 295). The resulting idea is said in the next section to be "nothing, but the supposed, but unknown support of those Qualities, we find existing" (E II.xxiii.2: 296), and this looks very much like the formula for bare particulars.[6]

The other extended discussion in the *Essay* of the idea of substance in general, in the chapter on space, complicates the picture. There Locke discusses the idea of substance in general in terms so sharp and sarcastic as to raise the question whether he thinks there could be anything to the idea at all. Jonathan Bennett points to these passages in support of his claim that "Locke's treatment of 'substance in general' is mainly skeptical in content and ironical in form" (Bennett 1971: 61).[7] Bennett is certainly right about the irony:

in these passages we find Locke retelling the story of the Indian philosopher who supports the world by an elephant, and the elephant by a tortoise. If that philosopher had only thought of "the word Substance," Locke says, he could have used that to support the earth, without troubling with the menagerie. For it's just as good an answer to the question what supports the earth

as we take it for a sufficient Answer, and good Doctrine, from our *European* Philosophers, That *Substance* without knowing what it is, is that which supports *Accidents*. So that of *Substance*, we have no *Idea* of what it is, but only a confused obscure one of what it does. (E II.xiii.19: 175; cf. E II.xxiii.2: 295–96)

Locke concludes the discussion with this:

But were the Latin words *Inhaerentia* and *Substantia*, put into the plain English ones that answer them, and were called *Sticking on*, and *Underpropping*, they would better discover to us the very great clearness there is in the Doctrine of *Substance and Accidents*, and shew of what use they are in deciding of Questions in Philosophy. (E II.xiii.20: 175)

The sarcasm fairly drips from the page here, but in case any reader were to mistake the tone, Locke spells out the message in his marginal summary for Sections 19 and 20: "Substance and Accidents of little use in Philosophy."

The two main discussions of substance in the *Essay* thus appear to point in opposite directions. It seems that the notion of substance, which was invoked in the chapter on substance to explain what it is for different qualities and powers to be jointly instantiated in one thing, and at the same time how it is that any one of these powers and qualities exists, is in the chapter on space being rejected as a hopelessly obscure notion that is of little use in philosophy. One last set of passages, however, this time from Locke's defense of the *Essay*'s main doctrines against criticisms published by Edward Stillingfleet, bishop of Worcester, seems to settle the issue.[8]

One of the main charges in the book that initiated the correspondence was that Locke had "almost discarded substance out of the reasonable part of the world" (Stillingfleet 1697a: 234). Locke's reply to this charge in his first letter to Stillingfleet ran as follows:

The other thing laid to my charge, is as if I took the being of substance to be doubtful, or rendered it so by the imperfect and ill-grounded idea I have given of it. To which I beg leave to say, that I ground not the being, but the idea of substance, on our accustoming ourselves to suppose some substratum; for it is of the idea alone I speak there [referring to *Essay* II.xxiii.1 and 4], and not of the being of substance. And having every-where affirmed and built upon it, that a man is a substance; I cannot be supposed to question or doubt of the being of substance, till I can question or doubt of my own being. (W IV: 18)

Locke is even more explicit in his third letter to Stillingfleet. Here he takes up Stillingfleet's criticism that in saying, for example at *Essay* II.xxiii.1, that we "accustom ourselves to suppose" a substratum underlying a thing's sensible qualities, Locke was demoting a "Consequence of Reason" or "Deduction of Reason" to a mere usage of custom (Stillingfleet 1698: 12). "Your lordship goes on to insist mightily upon my supposing," Locke says in reply, and continues:

Your lordship . . . concludes that there is substance, "because it is a repugnancy to our conceptions of things . . . that modes or accidents should subsist by themselves;" and I conclude the same thing, because we cannot conceive how sensible qualities should subsist by themselves. Now what the difference of certainty is from a repugnancy to our conceptions, and from our not being able to conceive; I confess, my lord, I am not acute enough to discern. And therefore it seems to me, that I have laid down the same certainty of the being of substance, that your lordship has done. (W IV: 445–46)

Locke finishes off this discussion by affirming that he holds that "there must certainly be substance in the world, and upon the very same grounds that your lordship takes it to be certain" (W IV: 446). These passages seem to settle the question in favor of the positive construal of the notion of substratum suggested in the chapter on the idea of substance, and they certainly settle the question whether Locke ever meant to deny that there is such a thing as substratum.[9]

Thus the relevant passages seem on the whole to support the orthodox view of Locke's doctrine of substance, although the negative-seeming passages from the *Essay*'s chapter on space still need to be explained. Now let us turn to the leading recent alternative construals of Locke's doctrine.

Peter Alexander's recent, and very ingenious, interpretation sees Locke as denying that there is any wholly general notion of substance, one that could be common to body and spirit. Instead the notion of substance is, as it were, absorbed into the notions of the two basic and fundamentally different kinds of (finite) substance, spirit and matter or body. Thus the essential characteristic of body, solidity, and the essential characteristic of spirit, "perceptivity" or the power of perception and thinking, are not to be thought of as qualities inhering in some featureless substratum, but instead define each of the two irreducibly different kinds of substance (Alexander 1985: 224, 233–34).

Alexander's interpretation has two great virtues: it gets rid of substrata as bare particulars, and it brings Locke's notion of substance squarely into line with corpuscularianism. But there are problems. In the first place, the claim that solidity (or thinking) is not a quality runs afoul of a number of passages in which solidity (or thinking) is classified as a primary quality, hence a quality, hence something that must exist in a substratum if it is to exist at all.[10] Second, Alexander's interpretation conflicts with one of Locke's central doctrines, that of the possibility of thinking matter. (More exactly, this is the doctrine that it is possible, for all we know, for God to give thinking things the power of thought by superadding this power directly to suitably organized parcels of matter.) If one and the same individual object had both the quality of solidity and the power of thought (or perceptivity), which is what would happen if God superadded the power of thought to a body, then on Alexander's model that object would have two distinct natures, and would belong to each of the two general kinds of substance.

There is also some textual evidence against Alexander's interpretation. In Locke's first letter to Stillingfleet, for example, he writes:

your lordship will argue, that by what I have said of the possibility that God may, if he pleases, superadd to matter a faculty of thinking, it can never be proved that there is a spiritual substance in us, because upon that supposition it is possible it may be a material substance that thinks in us. I grant it; but add, that the general idea of substance being the same every where, the modification of thinking, or the power of thinking joined to it, makes it a spirit, without considering what other modifications it has, as whether it has the modification of solidity or no. As on the other side, substance, that has the modification of solidity, is matter, whether it has the modification of thinking or no. (W IV: 33)[11]

This passage says at least that there is a single idea of substance in general that is a component of both the idea of a body and that of a spirit; and given Locke's general carelessness about observing the distinction between ideas and the things they are ideas of, he may be read as saying that substance or substratum is the same in bodies and in spirits. (This reading is encouraged both by the context and by the fact that he refers to "Spirit" and "Matter" in the quoted passage, and not to the ideas thereof.) Alexander is aware of this passage, and attempts to explain it away, saying that Locke is for the moment falling in with Stillingfleet's (mis)interpretation of his views (Alexander 1985: 228). But there is nothing in the context to suggest that Locke is speaking other than in propria persona, and the claims made here are perfectly in line with everything he says later in the correspondence.[12] It seems then that Alexander's interpretation, ingenious and attractive as it is, cannot finally be accepted.

The other recent rival to the traditional interpretation telescopes the substance or substratum of a thing into its real essence.[13] It thus shares the main virtues of Alexander's interpretation – it does away with the commitment to bare particulars, and it renders the notion of substance in terms conformable to the basic framework of corpuscularianism – and is probably the currently most widely accepted interpretation of Locke's doctrine of substance. We should be careful to note that this interpretation does not claim that the concept of a substratum (support to qualities) is the same as the concept of a real essence (the causal basis of the powers and qualities of an object), but instead that these different concepts pick out the same thing, that is, that the real essence of an individual substance also functions as the substratum to the properties and qualities of that individual substance.

The reasoning behind this interpretation is quite plausible. It begins from the fact that, according to Locke, neither the substratum of a thing nor its real essence is observable; each is defined in terms of its relation to the sensible qualities or powers of a thing that we do observe. In the case of the substratum, the defining relation is that the substratum supports the powers and qualities in existence, or in other words, the qualities inhere in the substratum; in the case of the real essence, it is that the real essence is the causal basis in the object for its having the powers and qualities that it does in fact have. Why not then take it that the real essence performs both of these functions, eliminating any need for a mysterious undifferentiated entity entirely lacking in qualities? Maurice Mandelbaum, the originator of this interpretation, accordingly says that the idea of a substratum functions as "a surrogate for what in the object is material and exists independently of us . . . an indeterminate and general notion standing for something in the object which makes that object a self-subsisting thing," and notes that "it is the atomic constitutions of objects, not 'pure substance in general,' which cause the ideas of them which we actually have, and which also cause the effects, whether perceived or unperceived, which objects have upon one another" (Mandelbaum 1964: 39). In a similar vein, Ayers says: "The concept of 'substance,' 'substratum,' or 'thing (having such and such properties)' is thus a concept by means of which we refer to what is unobserved and unknown – or known only through its effects and relatively to the level of observation. In other words, *substance* is a 'dummy' concept like *power*" (Ayers 1975: 9). Again, "what underlies 'the powers or qualities that are observable by us' in anything is *a substance constituted* (or modified or determined) *in certain ways*. There are not two underlying levels, *first* the real essence, *then*, beneath it, the substance" (Ayers 1975: 17). Any progress that would be made in coming to know more about the detailed internal constitutions, or real essences, of things would at the same time give us more insight into the nature of the substratum of the thing.

This line of reasoning is appealing, but there is no textual evidence that supports it. Even in such propitious places as the long and involved discussion of real and nominal essences in Chapters iii and vi of *Essay* Book III, and the controversy with Stillingfleet, Locke refrains from any suggestion that substance and essence are to be identified. (Indeed, he argues at length against Stillingfleet's identification of these two concepts, in connection with both the doctrine of substance and the possibility of thinking matter.) This is not surprising in view of the fact that the notions of substratum and of real essence are quite different, each with different theoretical work to do. The real essence of a thing, both as traditionally conceived (as substantial form) and as thought of by Locke (as the microphysical internal constitution of a thing), is the causal basis of that thing's powers and qualities. On the other hand, substance – the traditional notion of which Locke claims is identical in content with his notion (W IV: 8 and 449) – supports the powers and qualities in being, that is, the powers and qualities inhere in the substratum.

Now while it is not in general impossible that there should be both causal and logical relations between one set of things and another, in this particular case there are difficulties in identifying substratum and real essence. For the logical tradition that gave rise to the notion of substance as substratum takes it that all of the accidents of a thing have the same relation (that of inhering in) to the substratum, whereas the powers and qualities of a thing may be quite differently related to the real essence (changes in the microphysical constitution of a thing will in general change some of the powers and qualities of that thing but leave others intact). In the absence of any text of Locke's in which he identifies, or even implies the identification, of substratum and real essence, the only support proponents can claim for this interpretation is that it does not obviously conflict with any texts, and it does do away with the embarrassment of bare particulars. But on the whole, it leaves entirely unexplained large and central stretches of both the *Essay* and the Stillingfleet correspondence in which the notion of substance is discussed.

Turning back to these passages, we see two themes figuring centrally in the discussion of substance in both the *Essay* and the Stillingfleet letters. The first is that the core of the notion of substance in general (indeed, the only content we can give it) is that substance or substratum is the support to powers and qualities. The second is that the notion is obscure and confused: when talking of substance we talk like children, or like those who try to support the earth on an elephant resting on a tortoise; the doctrine of substance and accidents is of no use in philosophy; and so forth. Now it is the first theme, as set out in such central passages as *Essay* II.xxiii.1–4 (and especially in Sections 2 and 3) that has encouraged commentators to attribute the bare-particulars construal of substratum to Locke. But if we read those passages carefully, we find Locke saying only that our idea of substance has nothing more in it than that it supports qualities. It does not follow from this that whatever answers to the idea of substance (if anything does) can have no other properties or features than that it supports qualities, which is what the bare-particulars doctrine requires. So there is no need to attribute the doctrine of bare particulars to Locke.

The other difficulty faced by the standard interpretation of Locke's theory of substance is to account for the apparent "two-faced" character of Locke's treatment of substance. He apparently invokes the notion in a positive way to explain the existence and coinstantiation of observable qualities in the early sections of the *Essay's* chapter on our ideas of substances; but in those same sections, and especially in the chapter on space, he emphasizes the unclarity and obscurity of the notion, even to the point of declaring it of little use to philosophy. Again, a careful reading of those opening sections of the chapter on our ideas of substances, as well as the relevant passages in the Stillingfleet correspondence, will show that Locke never claims to explain anything, including the existence of sensible qualities, in terms of substance. All he says is that we come up with ("suppose") the notion of substance when we find that we cannot imagine that the qualities are able to exist of themselves, or one in another. This is not to claim that we are explaining anything by invoking the notion; rather, especially in view of its sparse content – "So that of *Substance*, we have no *Idea* of what it is, but only a confused obscure one of what it does" (E II.xiii.19: 175) – we should say that the idea does no more than mark our inability to give a satisfying explanation here.

This may seem a rather limited result, and it may legitimately be wondered why Locke bothered to give, and defend, a theory of substance if this is all that comes of it. In response to this we should note, first, that it was one of the central aims of the *Essay*, and especially of Book II, to catalogue the important ideas we have and to show how they can each of them be derived from sensation and reflection; and Locke certainly agrees with the tradition that we have an idea of substance as a support to qualities. It would have been quite a gap in this project if Locke were not able to show how we can derive the idea of substance from sensation and reflection.

Much more important than this, however, is the subversive use to which Locke puts his account of the idea of substance. To appreciate this, we need to recall that the doctrine of substance and accidents had already had a long history by Locke's time, stretching back to Aristotle's *Categories*. For Aristotle, the category of substance was the first and most important of all the logical categories; the items in the other categories (quality, quantity, relation, and so on) can exist only by existing in, or being predicated of, substances. Substances, on the other hand, can exist on their own, without having to exist in anything else. Aristotle's pronouncements about substance left it unclear, however, what the relations were between the substance or substratum, the form or essence of the thing, and the matter out of which the thing is composed. During the long heyday of Scholasticism, just about every combination and permutation of possible relations among these entities (or putative entities) was represented by some position or school, so that by Locke's time the doctrine of substance and accidents was indeed a perplexed one. The doctrine of substance and accidents is also to be found doing important work in Descartes. The cogito argument, with its implicit reliance on the principle that "Nothing has no properties" (contrapositive: "Anything that has properties is something") to show that any thought must have a thinker, that is, must be thought by someone; the consequent analysis of the nature of mind and body, and the argument for the real distinction between mind and body; and the claim that the essence of material things can be clearly and distinctly perceived by the intellect – all rest on some version of the traditional Scholastic doctrine of substance and accidents. We have seen that one of Locke's main aims in the *Essay* was to promote the corpuscularian version of mechanism over the Cartesian one, and to eliminate the Aristotelian-Scholastic obstacles to the acceptance of mechanism. We have also noted how each of these rival views makes central use of the doctrine of substance. Now we have Locke arguing that this notion is irredeemably obscure and confused, and of little use in philosophy, even as he is affirming that we do indeed have such an idea and that its content is the same as had traditionally been asserted. If this pulls the rug out from under Aristotelianism and Cartesianism, then so much the worse for these views and so much the better for mechanistic corpuscularianism.

Viewed in this way, Locke's treatment of substance does better than cohere with the rest of his brief for corpuscularianism; it becomes an important part of that brief. Careful attention to all of the relevant passages, then, coupled with due regard for the historical circumstances of the *Essay*, enables us to arrive at a reading of Locke's treatment of the notion of substance that fits well with all the texts (even those which at first sight seem to cut in opposite directions), is coherent in its own terms, and contributes to the overall project of the *Essay*, that of establishing the philosophical superiority of mechanistic corpuscularianism. Properly interpreted, the treatment of substance in the *Essay* thus comes to seem less like a host of confusions perpetrated by a philosophical bungler than a subtle exercise in philosophical criticism by a philosopher of genius. It is fortunate that the state of Locke commentary has advanced far enough that this can be counted a point in favor of the interpretation rather than one against it.

V. CONCLUSION

Several major themes have emerged in this discussion of Locke on body. First, we have seen that the corpuscularian conception of the nature of body adopted by Locke plays a central role in his treatment of such basic philosophical issues as that of substance, the status of sensible qualities, and the structure of scientific explanations. Further, we have seen that although it is the corpuscularian hypothesis as put forward by natural philosophers that plays this central role, the basis for putting this hypothesis to philosophical use is not that it is the best current scientific hypothesis or that it promises to give us detailed knowledge of the workings and qualities of bodies. The basis rather is its conformity with the commonsense picture of the nature of body and of the causation of bodies. Locke's leading claims, therefore, are not backed by a promissory note of future scientific success; they are put forward simply as accounts of the world as it must appear to us, given our (good, bad, or indifferent) commonsense views of things. Finally, we should hark back to our starting point, and recall that the corpuscularian conception of body was one of several competing conceptions, the main competition being the Aristotelian and the Cartesian theories. Not long after Locke wrote, Newton, who worked largely in the corpuscularian tradition, put paid to the competitors. As Ayers has remarked in this connection, "His [Locke's] capacity for winning, in metaphysics as in politics, should not be despised."

NOTES

1 It was indeed virtually a badge of being a mechanist to draw this distinction, in some version or other. Galileo, Descartes, Gassendi, Hobbes, Charleton, and Boyle all did so.
2 This is a composite of various lists given by Locke. I am taking it, as is usual to do, that these lists are all lists of primary qualities, and that there is no deep significance to the fact that in some lists Locke omits

certain of these, and in others others. For a contrary view, see Alexander 1985: 131–49.

3 Actually, at *Essay* III.x.15 Locke distinguishes the idea of body, which is that of an extended solid figured thing, from the "partial and more confused" idea of matter as simply solid substance. Everywhere else, however, he gives the idea of body as simply that of extended solid substance; and even in this passage he goes on to note that this is merely a notional distinction, "since Solidity cannot exist without Extension, and Figure" (E III.x.15: 498).

4 This is one of the few passages in the *Essay* to undergo significant change as the result of Stillingfleet's objections to Locke. Where the first three editions of the *Essay* had said flatly that bodies operate on each other "*by impulse,* and nothing else," this is emended in the fourth edition to say only that we cannot conceive them to operate in any other way (E II.-viii.11: 135–36).

5 This is not, however, the position of Berkeley. His complaint is the opposite one, that Locke's notion of substance as substratum (as this figures in the idea of material substance) is too robust.

6 In the correspondence with Stillingfleet, Locke describes the idea of substance in general as "a complex idea, made up of the general idea of something, or being, with the relation of a support to accidents." He then goes on to give the most detailed account he gives anywhere of the process by which the idea of substance is derived, albeit indirectly, from ideas given in sensation and reflection (W IV: 19).

7 In a subsequent paper, Bennett retracts the claim that in these passages Locke means to deny that there is such a thing as the substratum of an object (Bennett 1987). Bennett's current position is much closer to the one I defend here, although there still are some important differences between us.

8 We need to be clear about what the correspondence with Stillingfleet was. It was not a private exchange of letters; each "letter" was a published book, offered to the public at the same time it was sent to the addressee. Stillingfleet was an important figure of the time, who enjoyed a solid reputation as an intellectual and as a friend of the new science, and who had a high position in the Church of England (he was bishop of Worcester). The charge to which Locke was responding was a grave one, to wit that he was at least a fellow traveler of the Socinian heresy.

9 Locke tells Stillingfleet that the passages about the elephant and the tortoise

were not intended to ridicule the notion of substance, or those who asserted it, whatever that "it" signifies: but to show, that though substance did support accidents, yet philosophers, who had found such a support necessary, had no more a clear idea of what that support was, than the

Indian had of that which supported his tortoise, though sure he was it was something. (W IV: 448)

10 See, e.g., E II.viii.9: 135; E II.viii.22: 140; E II.xxiii.17: 306; and E II. xxiii.30: 313. The last of these passages brings out the parallelism Locke asserts between the relation of solidity and extension to the substance of body and that of thought and willing to the substance of spirit.

11 Note that in this passage Locke calls both thinking and solidity "modifications of substance."

12 Consider, e.g., Locke's argument in his third letter to Stillingfleet to the effect that Stillingfleet's admission that it is within God's power to change a body into an immaterial substance actually commits him to the possibility that God may give the power of thought to a merely material being (W IV: 470–71). Alexander attempts to dismiss this passage in the same way he did the earlier one (Alexander 1985: 231–32). But again, there is nothing in the context to suggest that Locke is only going along with Stillingfleet's misconceptions.

13 This interpretation was first put forward by Maurice Mandelbaum in his essay, "Locke's Realism" (Mandelbaum 1964). It is also advanced by John Yolton (Yolton 1970a) and by Martha Brandt Bolton (Bolton 1976b). M. R. Ayers, in his essay "The Ideas of Power and Substance in Locke's Philosophy" (Ayers 1975), is widely taken to have identified substance (substratum) with real essence; but Ayers has informed me in correspondence that he never in fact intended to do this. His arguments against the view that Locke is committed to substratum as an actual entity distinct from the real essence (and from the individual object) are, some of them, similar to arguments given by Mandelbaum et al.; this similarity may have contributed to the misconstrual of Ayers's position. Since Ayers's essay does contain a forceful and influential presentation of some of these arguments, I shall sometimes cite it as a source for them, even if Ayers does not take them to yield the conclusions that others have drawn from them. As I understand Ayers's explanation (in correspondence) of his position, his interpretation of Locke may not be very different from the one I present here.

4 Locke's philosophy of mind

The topics to be covered in this chapter are as follows: (I) Locke's acceptance of Descartes's view that there is a radical separation, a perhaps unbridgeable gap, between the world's mental and its physical aspects; Locke's view of (II) the cognitive aspects and (III) the conative aspects of the mind; (IV) what Locke said about the possibility that "matter thinks," that is, that the things that take up space are also the ones that have mental states; (V) the question whether all thought could be entirely caused by changes in the physical world; (VI and VII) what it is for a single mind to last through time; and (VIII) what it is for a mind to exist at a time when it is not doing anything.

I. PROPERTY DUALISM

Descartes held a position that is sometimes called "property dualism." According to it, the properties that things can have fall into two classes – those pertaining to materiality and those pertaining to mentality – with no overlap between them. This is best understood as involving also a dualism of concepts: the concepts that can be applied to things fall into two classes, with no concept in either class being reducible to or explainable through any belonging to the other class.

This property dualism can be felt all through Locke's *Essay*. He does not announce it as a thesis, any more than Descartes does, apparently accepting it as an unchallenged and unexamined axiom. While using facts about bodily behavior as evidence for conclusions about states of mind, Locke never asks *why* they are evidence (the "other minds" problem seems to have begun with Berkeley); nor does he ever suggest that any cognitive concept might be analyzable in terms of behavioral dispositions or that sensations or feelings or "ideas" might be physiological states.

Locke also accepts Descartes's view that minds must be transparent to themselves, for example, in his polemic against innately possessed ideas and knowledge, where he says that we aren't aware of any such possessions and couldn't have them without being aware of them: "To imprint any thing on the Mind without the Mind's perceiving it, seems to me hardly intelligible" (E I.ii.5: 49; see also E II.i.11: 109–10). But unlike Descartes he does not use this to define the realm of the mental, and it is not clear that he defines it at all. If he does, it is by saying that the idea of "spirit" – which is one of his words for "thing that has mentalistic properties" – is "the *Idea* of Thinking, and moving a Body" (E II.xxiii.15: 305). The second of those may seem odd: cannot bodies also move bodies? Not really, Locke thinks, because

when by impulse [a billiard ball] sets another Ball in motion, that lay in its way, it only communicates the motion it had received from another, and loses in it self so much, as the other received; . . . [This] reaches not the Production of the Action, but the Continuation of the Passion. . . . The *Idea* of the beginning of motion, we have only from reflection on what passes in our selves, where we find by Experience, that barely by willing it, barely by a thought of the Mind, we can move the parts of our Bodies, which were before at rest. (E II.xxi.4: 235; but see the conflicting story in E II.vii.8: 131)

Unlike Descartes and his followers, Locke held no views about causation that posed any special problem for the idea of causal interaction between the material and mental realms, despite the categorial difference between the two kinds of property. We shall see that he allows not only that minds act upon bodies but also that bodies act upon minds.

The link between "spirit" and "mental" on the one hand and "thinking" on the other does not help us much to grasp Locke's concept of mentality, because he gives no systematic account of what thinking is. In this respect, he does no better than Descartes, though also, to be fair, no worse.

II. COGNITION

"Thinking" and "moving a body" – Locke's focus on these two fits with his statement elsewhere that "The two great and principal

Actions of the Mind ... are these two: *Perception*, or *Thinking*, and *Volition*, or *Willing*" (E II.vi.2: 128; see also E II.xxi.5–6: 236). Locke's use of "perception," and especially his relating of perceiving to having ideas, is chaotic. In one place, for example, he says that ideas are "actual Perceptions in the Mind, which cease to be any thing, when there is no perception of them" (E II.x.2: 150). Nor does he say, carefully and consistently, what he means by "thinking." Still, in those formulations we can see him as expressing the view – held by many before and since – that mental doings fall into two large categories, the cognitive and the conative, or the intellectual and the volitional. This has been accepted and given a structural role by many philosophers in recent decades who have sought to base a theory of mentality on the concepts of belief and desire.

At a quick glance, one would say that this leaves out two large mental matters: (1) emotions, feelings, and passions, and (2) sensory states, sense-data, qualia, phenomenal states, and the like. The nearest Locke gets to a treatment of (1) is in the chapter "Of Modes of Pleasure and Pain," in which he says that "*Pleasure* and *Pain* ... are the hinges on which our *Passions* turn" (E II.xx.3: 229). This chapter has its interest, but it does not contribute much to our picture of Locke's picture of the mind; and I shall not discuss it. As for (2), these appear in Locke's work as the having of "ideas," which are treated in Chapter 2 of this volume and can be dealt with quickly here. The main point is that Locke uses the term "idea" not only for these sensory items but also for intellectual items that might be called "thoughts" or "concepts," these being the ingredients out of which beliefs are made. This is not an ambiguity in Locke's use of "idea"; rather, he holds as a matter of theory that the mental items that come into the mind, raw, in sense perception are – after a certain kind of processing – the very items that constitute the basic materials of thinking, believing, and the like.

Setting aside, then, emotions and sensory states, we are left with the intellectual and volitional aspects of the mind, highlighted by Locke and also by a dominant trend in the recent philosophy of mind, namely the tendency to think that a proper understanding of mentality should be based largely on *belief* and *desire*. Let us see how these figure in the *Essay*.

To believe something is to believe *that P* for some propositional value of P. Locke's account of the rudiments of thinking is conducted in terms of "ideas" (considered in their intellectual rather than their sensory role), and he takes these to be subpropositional: he speaks of the idea of *horse*, of *man*, of *whiteness* and so on. In his view, then, we have subpropositional thoughts that we can combine in a certain way to yield propositional ones such as the thought that there is a horse over there, or that few of the men I know own guns. We do this, he says, by "joining" ideas in our minds (E IV.v.2: 574). As Leibniz pointed out, joining in my mind the idea of *man* and the idea of *wisdom* I get the thought *wise man*, which is not the thought *The man is wise*, and the latter – which really is propositional – remains unexplained (Leibniz 1981: 396).

As though anticipating this criticism, Locke writes in Section 6 that he does not stand by the term "joining" or "putting together," and adds: "This Action of the Mind, which is so familiar to every thinking and reasoning Man, is easier to be conceived by reflecting on what passes in us . . . than to be explained by Words" (E IV.v.6: 576). He has, in short, no theory about how subpropositional items are combined to yield propositional thoughts.

What about beliefs? Like most philosophers up to about a century ago, Locke does not try to analyze the concept of belief. The only general characterization of it in the *Essay* is this:

The entertainment the Mind gives this sort of Propositions, is called *Belief, Assent,* or *Opinion,* which is the admitting or receiving any Proposition for true, upon Arguments or Proofs that are found to perswade us to receive it as true, without certain Knowledge that it is so. (E IV.xv.3: 655)

Someone trying to analyze the concept of belief would not help himself to "receive as true"; in this context Locke is merely trying to distinguish belief from knowledge. I don't doubt that if he had tried to explain more generally and deeply what belief is, Locke would have given an "entertainment plus . . ." analysis, explaining what it is *to believe that P* by saying that it is *to have in mind the thought that P* and also . . . something further which brings it about that one actually believes that P rather than merely "entertaining" the thought that P. But I cannot support this suspicion by pointing to texts.

In at least one place, Locke leaps over both of these hurdles, from subpropositional to propositional, and from entertained to believed. Early in the *Essay*, at a stage where only elementary, unprocessed, un-"joined" ideas have been introduced, and have sometimes been called "perceptions," Locke writes: "The Mind has a Power, in many cases, to revive Perceptions, which it has once had, with this additional Perception annexed to them, that it has had them before" (E II.x.2: 150). At this stage in his exposition he has not entitled himself to the form "perception that P" where P is propositional.

Although a propositional thought is, in some sense, made up of subpropositional components, it does not follow that the best way to explain what it is to have a propositional thought is through an account of some operation on subpropositional thoughts. And although propositional thought is a genus of which belief is just one species – as Locke implies when he speaks of items that "produce in the Mind such different Entertainment, as we call *Belief, Conjecture, Guess, Doubt, Wavering, Distrust, Disbelief,* etc." (E IV.xvi.9: 663) – it does not follow that the best way to explain what it is to believe that P is in terms of entertaining the thought that P and doing something further with it that marks belief off from the other species in the genus. These things that don't follow are indeed not true, according to contemporary "functionalist" theories of mind. These theories start with the notion of belief; and if they say anything about the genus "entertaining," or about subpropositional thoughts, it is on the basis of and with help from their account of what it is to believe that P. If the procedure of these theories is the best one, then Locke's two failures were inevitable: he couldn't satisfactorily go from ideas to propositions, or from those to beliefs, because in each case that is the wrong order.

The thesis that propositional items are in a certain way more basic than subpropositional ones was assumed by Kant, when he derived his list of twelve privileged concepts from a list of twelve privileged kinds of proposition. It was first explicitly declared and employed by Frege, and has had some currency ever since. The primacy of belief in the philosophy of mind became current much more recently, through the "functionalist" view that an account of the contentful or that-P-involving aspects of the mind should start with the role that the concepts of belief and desire play in explaining behavior. It is an essential part of this position that belief and desire must be introduced and explained together: there is no chance of starting with either one and then later introducing the other. Nothing remotely like this seems to have occurred to Locke or to any of his contemporaries. Of course, he knew that beliefs and desires jointly lead to action (see E II.xxi.58–70: 272–82); what did not occur to him, or to anyone until about a century ago, is that one might use that fact as a point of entry into an explanation of what belief and desire are.

III. VOLITION

Locke's treatment of desire is one theme in the longest chapter in the *Essay*, entitled "Of Power." Its dominant theme is the issue about whether and in what sense the will is free. This is a seminal document in the literature of compatibilism: Locke argues at great length that the truth of determinism is consistent with everything that we reasonably believe about ourselves: the crucial question is whether "the man is free" and that can be answered yes consistently with determinism. Briefly, a person is free if there is no impediment both to his doing what he wants or chooses to do and to his not doing that; and, Locke says, there is no further problem about whether the person is free *in* his wants or choices. Many people have thought that there is such a further problem, and Locke offers several suggestions about what they might have in mind and dispatches each of them briskly. For example, he says, they may think that the needs of morality and human dignity are not met unless *the will* is free, to which Locke replies that, since the will is a faculty and not a thing, it makes no sense to say or to deny that it is free.[1] Nested within this discussion are twenty pages of a different kind, in which Locke advances a theory about how, or by what, the will is determined. This is an all-purpose theory about what prompts people to act voluntarily. Of course, people have all sorts of reasons for their actions, but Locke thinks that all the motivating circumstances have something nontrivial in common, and that he knows what it is: all voluntary actions proceed from some "uneasiness" that the person is trying to relieve.

It is pretty clear that Locke thought that this was an almost obvious truth. The underlying thought is this: when I act I am trying to bring about some state of affairs S, and my trying to do that is unintelligible unless I am dissatisfied with my present non-S condition. My awareness that the nonobtaining of S is unsatisfactory to me is my uneasiness – it's my sense of something wrong – and my action is an attempt to cure it by making S obtain. For example, if I walk to the other side of the room, that must be because I prefer being there to being here; so my present location is less than ideal from my point of view; in Locke's terminology, that means that my present location makes me "uneasy," and so I try to relieve the uneasiness by moving.

Leibniz saw that there must be something wrong with this (Leibniz 1981: 188–89). If voluntary action must always be an attempt to cure an unsatisfactoriness in one's present condition, the peak of satisfactoriness would involve perfect inactivity; but we all know that inactivity is a great source of misery. As his own rival theory shows, however, Leibniz did not get to the root of the trouble, which is this. Granted that voluntary actions must reflect a preference for some possible future over x, the relevant value of x is not *the present* but *some other possible future*. Sometimes, for example, one acts so as to bring about a future that will be just like the present in some satisfactory respect.

Locke evidently attached importance to his "uneasiness" theory of action. Why? What did he think it does for him? Well, in the first edition of the *Essay* he advanced a different theory, namely that volitions proceed from perceptions of what is good or, rather, of what would be good if it happened.[2] By the second edition he had permanently changed his mind about this, and had come to think that a mere perception of or belief about what is good cannot of itself rouse a person to volition or action. His first-edition handling of "the greater good" made the determinant of volition and action purely cognitive, and Locke seems to have come to think that this can't be right and that something specifically conative – something motivational – must be added. This motivational item is *uneasiness:*

To return then to the Enquiry, *what is it that determines the Will in regard to our Actions?* And that upon second thoughts I am apt to imagine is not, as is generally supposed, the greater good in view: But some (and for the most part the most pressing) *uneasiness* a Man is at present under. This is that which successively determines the *Will,* and sets us upon those Actions we perform. This *Uneasiness* we may call, as it is, *Desire;* which is an *uneasiness* of the Mind for want of some absent good. All pain of the body of what sort soever, and disquiet of the mind, is *uneasiness.* (E II.xxi.31: 250–51)

Locke seems to regard his original story not as wrong but rather as incomplete: it omitted the vital link between beliefs about good and volition. Thus: "Good and Evil, present and absent, 'tis true, work upon the mind: But that which immediately determines the *Will*, from time to time, to every voluntary Action is the *uneasiness* of *desire*, fixed on some absent good" (E II.xxi.33: 252; see also E II.xxi.35: 252–54). Note the word "immediately." Notice also that when Locke is arguing that his account of freedom gives us everything we can reasonably want (especially in Section 48), he emphasizes thoughts about good, and not uneasiness, as a determinant of our volitions. This is evidence that he thinks of uneasiness as an addition to his previous theory, not a replacement of it.

Locke has some empirical reasons for rejecting the first-edition theory. In particular, he thinks that it is contradicted by the facts about how people will do things that they believe will prevent them from attaining infinitely great goods (see Sections 56–70). But he also thinks that the theory virtually stands to reason, as I have explained.

Where does desire fit into all this? Locke sometimes identifies it with uneasiness (E II.xx.6: 230–31; E II.xxi.31–32: 250–51), but that seems not to be his considered, confident opinion. He writes: "All pain of the body . . . and disquiet of the mind, is *uneasiness*: And with this is always join'd Desire, equal to the pain or *uneasiness* felt; and is scarce distinguishable from it" (E II.xxi.31: 251). The expressions "joined" and "scarce distinguishable" rule out an identification, although Locke goes straight on to muddy the waters by saying: "For *desire* being nothing but an *uneasiness* in the want of an absent good . . ." (ibid.).

In just one place Locke clearly implies that uneasiness causes desire: "Where-ever there is *uneasiness* there is *desire*: For we constantly desire happiness; and whatever we feel of *uneasiness*, so much, 'tis certain, we want [= lack] of happiness" (E II.xxi.39: 257). Uneasiness is unpleasant, he is implying, so one desires to be quit of it. I'm sure that this is not Locke's principal theory about how desire relates to uneasiness. If it were, he would be confronted by the question, when I want to swim half a mile and then drink capuccino and talk philosophy, how do I know that that's what I want? According to the present theory, what I most immediately want is to rid myself of a state of uneasiness, but I count as wanting those other things because I know that getting them is the way to get rid of this particular uneasiness. How do I know what the cure is? There are possible answers to this, but no plausible ones.

Locke's best and probably his most considered view is that states of uneasiness are caused by desires. That is suggested but not quite asserted here: "*Envy* is an uneasiness of Mind, caused by the consideration of a Good we desire" (E II.xx.13: 231). Just what that means depends on how we take "the consideration of a Good we desire." The following passages, however, are unambiguous: "it raises desire, and that proportionably gives him *uneasiness*, which determines his *will*" (E II.xxi.56: 270). "*Good*, the *greater good*, though apprehended and acknowledged to be so, does not determine the *will*, until our desire, raised proportionably to it, makes us *uneasy* in the want of it" (E II.xxi.35: 253).

I believe that Locke wants to say not merely that unsatisfied desires cause uneasiness but further that that is how they cause acts of the will and thus actions. He seems to make no real distinction between desire and beliefs about what would be good; and he is saying that it/they can be effective in causing volitions only through the mediation of states of uneasiness. If there were desires (or beliefs about what would be good) that somehow failed to generate uneasiness, those desires would have no effect on action.

We should applaud Locke's seeing that he had a problem here – the problem, namely, of explaining how a mental representation of a future state of affairs can have effective power over a person's behavior. It is typical of the depth and thoroughness of much of his thought that he doesn't rely complacently on the idea that *of course* desires contain propositions and *of course* they generate action, and instead tries to explain how these two facts are connected. He cannot be said to have succeeded, though. To do so, I believe, he would need to start again in the spirit of twentieth-century functionalism, mentioned at the end of the preceding section. That would involve starting with the idea of beliefs as explainers of behavior, and thus as collaborators with desires; there would be no notion of static belief, of something merely believed and having no bearing on conduct, except as derivative from beliefs that have a role in guiding behavior. Although this approach was not fully developed until the past couple of decades, it was clearly adumbrated in F. P. Ramsey's suggestion that a belief is "a map . . . by which we steer" (see Armstrong 1973: 3).

It must be stressed, however, that this fruitful approach in which belief and desire are run in a single harness is hardly workable in the context of Lockean property- and concept-dualism. It is hard to put functionalism to work except as a form of materialism, namely the thesis that mentalistic facts are a subset of physicalistic facts – for example, to have a belief is to have a complex behavioral disposition of a certain kind. Locke was nowhere near to accepting that.

IV. THINKING MATTER

Although he follows Descartes in his dualism of properties, Locke does not confidently accept a dualism of substances. That is, he holds that there is a radical separation between properties having to do with mentality and ones having to do with materiality, but unlike Descartes he thinks that a single thing *could* have properties of both kinds. As for whether any single thing *does* have both kinds of property: Locke offers "Do any material things think?" as a prime example of a question to which we probably cannot ever know the answer. He ignores Descartes's arguments for answering no.

In *Essay* II.xxiii.15–18 and 22–32 Locke defends the notion of an *immaterial* thinking substance, but this does not seriously conflict with his later defense of the possibility of material thinking substances. In the Book II discussion, Locke is not taking it for granted that there are thinking things and asking whether they are extended or not. Rather, he is facing up to the radical materialist – Hobbes, perhaps – who questions the entire category of thought, and is arguing that there are indeed thinking things. He does not and need not argue that the thinking things are immaterial. He does often say that they are immaterial, using that adjective fourteen times; but twelve of those occurrences were added in the fourth edition of the *Essay* (1700). Michael Ayers has suggested to me that they may have been a nervous response to Bishop Stillingfleet's accusation, a year earlier, that Locke was a materialist. They muddy the waters and should be ignored.

It is in one long section in Book IV that Locke does, taking for granted that there are thinking things, confront the question of whether or not they are extended (E IV.iii.6: 539–43). The notion of matter that thinks is hard to swallow, hc admits, but the notion of a real thing that has no extension is equally difficult to choke down, so that the reasonable stance is that of the agnostic:

He that considers how hardly Sensation is, in our Thoughts, reconcilable to extended Matter; or Existence to any thing that hath no Extension at all, will confess, that he is very far from certainly knowing what his Soul is. . . . he who will . . . look into the dark and intricate part of each Hypothesis, will scarce find his Reason able to determine him fixedly for, or against the Soul's Materiality. (E IV.iii.6: 542)

We are not told what the difficulty is about real unextended things. Let us focus on the other side of the dilemma. Locke says that thought – or anyway sensation – is "hardly reconcilable to extended Matter," suggesting that there is almost a contradiction in the notion of thinking matter. But his property or concept dualism implies that there are no entailments or contradictions between mentalistic and materialistic concepts or properties, so that any description of a substance *qua* extended substance must leave logical room for the addition of mentalistic items to the description.

Sometimes, Locke virtually says as much, as in his remark that solidity and thought are "both but simple *Ideas*, independent from one another" (E II.xxiii.32: 314). He shouldn't have said that the ideas of thought and solidity are "simple" in his sense: on his own showing, solidity is a "mode," which means that it is logically complex. Still, his dualist foundation implies that they are logically non-overlapping and thus simple relative to one another, as one might put it. It follows that there cannot be conceptual trouble in the idea of a thinking solid thing; and in his correspondence with Still-ingfleet Locke comes close to arguing like that.

When Locke says that it is hard to "reconcile" thought with matter, he probably means only that it is hard to see how a thing's thinking could be connected with its physical properties. Even with a severe logical separation between the mental and the physical, there still remains the question of whether an animal's material nature has some causal, less than absolutely necessitating, connection with its thought. Locke doubted that: he speaks of our "finding not *Cogitation* within the natural Powers of Matter" (E IV.iii.6: 542). But he does not infer that matter does not think, because he holds that it might think through divine intervention rather than through its own natural powers (see, e.g., E IV.iii.6: 540–41).

V. DEPENDENCE OF MIND ON MATTER

The issue about thought and the "natural powers" of matter is the question of whether mental facts depend on physical ones, that is, whether all mental changes are matched and causally explained by corresponding physical changes. Locke has no post-Cartesian scruples about causal interaction between mind and matter. We have seen him allowing that mind acts upon matter, and he has no objection in principle to allowing causal flow the other way. But how far if at all bodily changes *do* change minds is something he prefers not to go into.[3] Early in the *Essay* he says that he won't "meddle" with such questions as

by what Motions of our Spirits, or Alterations of our Bodies, we come to have any Sensation by our Organs, or any *Ideas* in our Understandings; and whether those *Ideas* do in their Formation, any, or all of them, depend on Matter or no. (E I.i.2: 43)

He seems not really to be agnostic about whether ideas of sensation depend purely on bodily states. He writes: "*Ideas* in the Understanding, are coeval with *Sensation;* which is such an Impression or Motion, made in some part of the Body, as produces some Perception in the Understanding" (E II.i.23: 117). He says that we can't know whether my perceptions are like yours "because one Man's Mind could not pass into another Man's Body, to perceive, what Appearances were produced by those Organs" (E II.xxxii.15: 389). And he says that I cannot perceive an external thing except through some spatial contact with my body, because all material causation is through impact – a line of argument that presupposes that I can't perceive anything unless I am caused to do so by some change in my body (E IV.ii.11: 536).

Still, none of that implies a complete dependence of the mental on the physical; and Locke really does hold off from assenting to that. He says (and how could he deny it?) that there is probably a partial dependence in mental areas other than that of ideas of sensation:

whether the Temper of the Brain make this difference [to memory], that in some it retains the Characters drawn on it like Marble, in others like Free-stone, and in others little better than Sand, I shall not here enquire, though it may seem probable, that the Constitution of the Body does sometimes influence the Memory; since we oftentimes find a Disease quite strip the Mind of all its *Ideas*. (E II.x.5: 152; see also E II.xxvii.27: 347)

But this carefully stops short of complete dependence, and it is clear that Locke meant to do so. The thesis of complete dependence was a matter of anxious debate in the seventeenth century. Leibniz famously denied that mental events could be causally explained in terms of events in the brain:

perception . . . cannot be explained on mechanical principles, i. e. by shapes and movements. If we pretend that there is a machine whose structure makes it think, sense, and have perception, then we can conceive it enlarged, but keeping to the same proportions, so that we might go inside it as into a mill. Suppose that we do: then if we inspect the interior we shall find there nothing but parts which push one another, and never anything which would explain a perception. (Leibniz 1875–90: 6:609 [my translation]; see also Leibniz 1981: 66–67)

This relies on the assumption that all physical causation is through impact, that the small differs from the large only in size, and that impact alone could not suffice to explain thought. These are tendentious assumptions. It is especially regrettable that Leibniz does not explain or defend the third.

Locke reached the same conclusion through a more interesting argument than Leibniz's. Sometimes he treats his view about this as obvious (see, e.g., E IV.x.10: 623–24), but in one of the places where he asserts that mentality couldn't be caused to come into existence in a nonmental world purely through a change in the material arrangements, he claims to "have proved" this (E IV.iii.6: 541). Actually, the "proof" occurs seven chapters later (at E IV.x.1–19: 619–30), where Locke discusses the existence and nature of God.

Having argued that there has from all eternity been a thinking being that is the source of all other thought in the universe, Locke then considers whether that being could be material. After rejecting certain versions of that idea, he comes at last to this: "it only remains, that it is *some certain System of Matter* duly put together, that is this *thinking eternal Being*" (E IV.x.16: 627). He means this as the thesis that the universe contains thought because, and only because, a certain material system has a structure and mode of operation that cause it to be a thinking thing. The operations of this structure must be purely mechanistic, with no help from a thinking interferer; this is because we are discussing a theory about the origin of *all* mentality in the universe: if there are any designers or guardians, that must be as a result of the workings of the material system we are now discussing, and so they cannot help the system to work in the first place.

Locke argues that no system of matter could pull off this feat. His argument bears not only on whether God is a material thing, but also on what for many of us is a more interesting question, namely whether mentality could completely depend on the behavior of unaided matter. The argument is a reductio, starting from the hypothesis that a certain material system causes itself to have thought, which is the source of all other thought. In that case, says Locke:

If it be the motion of its parts, on which its Thinking depends, all the Thoughts there must be unavoidably accidental, and limited; since all the Particles that by Motion cause Thought, being each of them in it self without any Thought, cannot regulate its own Motions, much less be regulated by the Thought of the whole; since that Thought is not the cause of Motion (for then it must be antecedent to it, and so without it,) but the consequence of it, whereby Freedom, Power, Choice, and all rational and wise thinking or acting will be quite taken away: So that such a thinking Being will be no better nor wiser, than pure blind Matter; since to resolve all into the accidental unguided motions of blind Matter, or into Thought depending on unguided motions of blind Matter, is the same thing; not to mention the narrowness of such Thoughts and Knowledge, that must depend on the motion of such parts. (E IV.x.17: 627)

This argument, whatever it is doing, patently does not assume that seventeenth-century impact mechanics must be the final truth in physics, or that the laws governing the very small must be the same as those governing the large; so it has two advantages over Leibniz's argument. But how does it work?

The argument can be seen as saying that there is some kind of regularity or orderliness such that: (1) thought that is worthy of the name must have it, (2) something that has it cannot be caused by something that lacks it, and (3) no movements of bits of matter can have it unless they are under the guidance of thought.

To evaluate the argument, we have to know what kind of regularity Locke has in mind. It cannot be merely: regularity. Locke knew perfectly well that there are regular, orderly systems of matter that are not guided by minds – clocks, for example. Nor can it be: a very high degree of ordered complexity, or anything like that. Locke must have known that the ordered complexity of a material system's behavior depends purely on the ordered complexity of its structure, and Locke seems not to believe there is any principled upper limit on that: he implies only that it is not "*probable* . . . that a blind fortuitous concourse of Atoms, not guided by an understanding Agent, should *frequently* constitute the Bodies of any Species of Animals" (E IV.xx.15: 716; my emphases). The possibility of one such occurrence would be enough to kill the God argument on this interpretation of it.

If the argument is to survive, Locke must have in mind some *kind* of regularity. The only plausible candidate I can discover is the kind *teleological*. Then the argument would run as follows. (1) Mentality essentially involves teleology: it is because the mind reaches out to possible futures that it leads people to do things so as to bring about various upshots, thus endowing them with "Freedom, Power, Choice"; the teleological nature of mentality is the source of the possibility of "rational and wise thinking [and] acting." (2) There cannot be anything goal-oriented about the movements of matter that is not guided by thoughts, the "accidental unguided motions of blind Matter." Therefore (3) no such movements could be a sufficient cause for mentality.

That argument is valid, and many philosophers today would endorse its first premise: the kind of mentality that is in question here rests on belief and desire; belief alone cannot do the job; and desire is essentially teleological. But it now seems that the second premise is false: although work remains to be done on this, it is widely and rightly believed that there can be goal-pursuing, teleological behavior that is mechanistically explainable (see, e.g., Dennett 1978; Bennett 1976).

I do not claim that Locke presented his argument against dependence in full consciousness of what he was up to. When he explains that all animals have perception while no plants do, he comes close to saying that the apparent teleology of plants is not genuine, but he does not quite say it explicitly, as one would expect if he consciously held that teleology suffices for mentality (see E II.ix.11: 147–48). As for its being necessary for mentality: we have seen that Locke expends a lot of energy on a theory of volition that seems to aim at reducing the role of teleology, or at least of teleological effectiveness, in his account of the human condition.

Still, the God argument seems to have been guided by the subliminal thought that matter cannot cause teleological patterns that are necessary for thought. If not, I do not know how the argument is supposed to work.

VI. MINDS AND SUBSTANCES

Locke's famous account of personal identity (E II.xxvii.9–29: 335–48) is really an account of what it is for a single mind to last through time, or for two mental events to be episodes in the life of a single mind. His brilliant account of "same plant" is extended to "same animal," which he takes to cover also "same man." Or, rather, that is how he understands "man" at the start of II.xxvii.8; at the end of the section he seems to allow "man" to involve mental as well as animal identity, this probably being a carry-over from the account of "same man" that he gave in the first edition of the *Essay*; and there are further complexities in Sections 21–25 (for details and discussion, see Curley 1982).

His treatment of sameness of "person," on the other hand, is conducted entirely in mentalistic terms. For Locke, a man is not the same as a person. Is the man now walking past my door the man I talked to at noon yesterday? That depends on – and only on – whether there is the right kind of animal continuity linking yesterday's man and today's. But, according to Locke, whether the person now walking past my door is the person I talked to at noon yesterday depends on a mental link that has no conceptual tie to animal continuity. Even if it was just one man, it might have been two persons, and it is also not absolutely impossible that it should have been different men and the same person. Because of the way it centers on mental linkage, Locke's treatment of personal identity is really an account of what it is for the mind that has thought x at t_2 to be the mind that had thought y at t_1.

Locke prefaces his treatment of personal identity with a discussion of the identity of atoms, plants, and animals. For each kind K of item, he starts with a synchronic account of what a K is – one that omits to say what it is for a K to last through time, that being a diachronic account of what a K is. In each case, he purports to infer the diachronic account from the synchronic one; the inferences are not rigorously valid, but perhaps they were not meant to be. The discussion of personal identity starts in the same way, with a synchronic statement about what a person is: it

is a thinking intelligent Being, that has reason and reflection, and can consider it self as it self, the same thinking thing in different times and places; which it does only by that consciousness, which is inseparable from thinking, and as it seems to me essential to it: It being impossible for any one to perceive, without perceiving, that he does perceive. (E II.xxvii.9: 335)

Having emphasized the essentialness of thought to personhood and of self-consciousness to thought, Locke goes on to imply that unity of consciousness is necessary and sufficient for personal identity through time:

Since consciousness always accompanies thinking, and 'tis that, that makes every one to be, what he calls *self*; and thereby distinguishes himself from all other thinking things, in this alone consists *personal Identity*, *i.e.* the sameness of a rational Being: And as far as this consciousness can be extended backwards to any past Action or Thought, so far reaches the Identity of that *Person*. (ibid.)

This is another attempt to get the diachronic account out of the synchronic one; it doesn't work very well, but Locke has more than that to say in defense of his diachronic account of personal identity.

The diachronic account, in effect, treats an enduring person as a special kind of aggregate of person-stages (not that Locke uses that terminology). Unlike Hume, Locke does not treat each person-stage as a special kind of aggregate of subpersonal items. Hume conceptually builds up a mind that lasts through time first by assembling mind-stages out of "perceptions" and then assembling minds out of mind-stages. The former step is omitted by Locke, whose account of what a person is starts with "a thinking intelligent Being," with no suggestion that such an item might be built up out of subpersonal items and no attempt to say what it is for two synchronous thoughts to belong to the same person.

The most powerful reworking that anyone has done of Locke's account of personal identity is more radical than Locke in just this respect. I allude to H. P. Grice's "Personal Identity," which is broadly Lockean in what it says about what makes two "total temporary states" count as differently dated states of a single person, but unLockean in that it tries to say what it is for two states to be synchronous states of a single person (Grice 1941). Locke, in contrast, seems to regard the unity and singleness of a person at a time as a primitive, not as an upshot of how certain subpersonal components relate to one another.

He does, however, treat an enduring person as an aggregate of person-stages. He devotes twenty sections to two things: a barrage of arguments against basing sameness of person on sameness of thinking substance; and the development of a positive view about what does make the different temporal stages hang together as stages of a single person.

In denying that sameness of person requires sameness of substance, Locke implies that persons are not substances. Yet his basic meaning for "substance" is just that of "thing," and he says firmly that a person is a thinking thing. This, as Thomas Reid pointed out, seems to be a contradiction. The trouble spreads further. The diachronic identity of an oak tree does not involve sameness of substance, Locke says, because one oak can have atoms flowing into and out of it throughout its lifetime; but it is clear that in other contexts he would classify a tree as a substance (see, e.g., E II.xxiii.3: 296 and E II.xxiii.6: 298).

Evidently, in this context an atom is a substance and a tree is not. It seems that here, though not elsewhere in the *Essay*, a "substance" is a *basic* kind of thing. The general basic-nonbasic distinction has several species, of which the one that is most likely to be relevant here is the simple-composite distinction: trees are not substances for the reason that Leibniz said they are not, namely that they are composite, or have parts.[4] Trees, we might anachronistically say, are quantified over by Locke only at a nonbasic level of his metaphysic, whereas material substances, atoms, belong on the ground floor. He is saying that whatever the basic, nonaggregate thinking things may be, there is no strong reason to believe that a single person involves just one of these. A single enduring person might consist in or result from a steady flow-through of thinking substances, as an oak tree involves a flow of atoms.

In the case of Locke's oak tree, we know what the underlying reality is that we conceptualize by saying "this is the same oak" – that is, we know what is involved in an oak's enduring – so we know that it does not involve the persistence of one or more substances. In the case of the enduring person, on the other hand, we don't know what the underlying reality is. For all we know, Locke says, it may be that each person does in fact involve a single thinking substance throughout his or her existence; and he declares that "the more probable Opinion" is that personal identity involves "one individual immaterial Substance" (E II.xxvii.25: 345). I cannot find any solid basis he could have for this opinion, and perhaps Locke cannot find one either, for he goes straight on to say, "But let Men according to their divers Hypotheses resolve of that as they please." His "more probable Opinion" may have been merely an attempt to placate the indignant conservatives among his readers.

Notice: "one individual *immaterial* Substance." Locke ought to allow – and *Essay* IV.x.15 suggests that he would allow – the possibility that personal identity should be carried instead by a single material substance, an atom of matter that remained in the person's animal body amid all the flow-through of other atoms. Locke would say that God could, if He chose, endow an atom with the ability to think, and could enable one atom to carry the mental history of a single person. But this seems not to be a possibility that engaged his attention.

As for the more plausible supposition that what thinks is (a part of) an animal: Locke sees that if this is right, then sameness of person certainly does not involve sameness of substance:

those, who place Thought in a purely material, animal, Constitution, void of an immaterial Substance . . . conceive personal Identity preserved in something else than Identity of Substance; as animal Identity is preserved in Identity of Life, and not of Substance. (E II.xxvii.12: 337)

If it is indeed animals that think, and given that Locke is right about animals, is there any such thing as a thinking substance? Consider a thinking animal at a moment – abstracting from questions about persistence through time, that is, diachronic identity – and ask: are we here confronted by a momentary stage of a thinking substance? I think that Locke would say no, on the grounds that an animal at a moment does not constitute a substance at a moment because it is an aggregate and thus is not basic. But I am not sure about this, and can find no evidence that Locke asked himself this question.

Although he seems to hold that "one person, one substance" is reasonably tenable only if the substance is immaterial, Locke firmly denies the converse conditional (E II.xxvii.12: 337). The mere hypothesis that persons essentially involve immaterial substances does not imply that each person involves just one such substance, he says, unless we can "shew why personal Identity cannot be preserved in the change of immaterial Substances, or variety of particular immaterial Substances." He is suggesting that a person might be like a monarchy in which different kings reign, one at a time, or like a committee in which the power is exercised at each moment by a number of members. Or, of course, it might be like both at once, which would perfect the comparison with how a tree relates to its constituent atoms.

VII. THE SAME MIND

So much for what personal or mental identity conceptually is not. What, according to Locke, is it? Well, he says that the identity of a person (or a mind) through time depends upon some kind of unity of consciousness. He seems to be sure that this account best fits the plain thoughtful person's intuitions on this topic. Here, for example, we are apparently expected to find the line of thought intuitively irresistible:

though the same immaterial Substance, or Soul does not alone . . . make the same Man; yet 'tis plain consciousness, as far as ever it can be extended, should it be to Ages past, unites Existences, and Actions, very remote in time, into the same Person, as well as it does the Existence and Actions of the immediately preceding moment: So that whatever has the consciousness of present and past Actions, is the same Person to whom they both belong. Had I the same consciousness, that I saw the Ark and *Noah*'s flood, as that I saw an overflowing of the *Thames* last Winter, or as that I write now, I could no more doubt that I, that write this now, that saw the *Thames* overflow'd last Winter, and that view'd the Flood at the general Deluge, was the same *self*, place that *self* in what Substance you please, than that I that write this am the same *my self* now whilst I write . . . that I was Yesterday. (E II.xxvii.16: 340–41)

What is to make this plausible, it seems, is the thought: I have recollections of such and such experiences; what grounds do I have for regarding those experiences as mine other than that I now recollect them, that is, the fact that there is a single consciousness that takes in both them and my present conscious state? "If we take wholly away all Consciousness of our Actions and Sensations, especially of Pleasure and Pain, and the concernment that accompanies it, it will be hard to know wherein to place personal Identity" (E II.i.11: 110).

In one way, Locke's analysis of personal identity is too strong, because it implies that the person who is F at t_1 is not the person who is G at t_2 unless the person who is G at t_2 does at t_2 recall having been F at t_1. (There is virtual unanimity among readers of Locke that what he calls unity of consciousness between a later time and an earlier is just episodic memory.) That makes personal identity much too tight to fit our normal ideas and intuitions about it, because we know perfectly well that people forget things that they have experienced.

As Butler and Reid saw, this feature of the analysis even interferes with the transitivity of identity: there are plenty of cases where the theory implies that x is y and y is z but x is not z. In short, identity is transitive whereas any relation such as "remembers" or "is a memory of" is nontransitive, and so the latter cannot be the whole analytic truth about the former.

One defense against this was deployed in Grice's refurbishing of Locke's theory (Grice 1941). It weakens the analysans firstly by requiring not consciousness of being F at t_1 but just consciousness of being in some state at t_1, and then further by building transitivity into it. I find it plausible to suppose that each of these was part of Locke's intent. The resultant analysis says that

If (i) the person who is G at t_2 does at t_2 recall having had some mental state s at t_1, and if (ii) s at t_1 was part of the same momentary consciousness as that which included being F at t_1, then (iii) the person who is G at t_2 is the person who was F at t_1.

Add, as part of the analysis, that identity is transitive, and the worst counterexamples disappear. To get the result that the retired general is not the person who was beaten for stealing apples as a boy, we need to hold not merely that the general now cannot recall the incident, but that he cannot recall any previous state of himself that he was in at a time when he could recall the beating, or that he was in at a time when he could remember a still earlier state he was in at a time when he remembered the beating, or . . . and so on. It would not be madly implausible to say that if the general is as cut off as that from the beating, it wasn't he who was beaten.

A second possible defense is to say only that the person who is F at t_1 is the person who is G at t_2 if the person who is G at t_2 *can* recall being F at t_1. (Or this could be added to the weakening just discussed. That is, a single analysis could involve transitivity, coconsciousness at a single time, *and* possibility.) That sometimes seems to be Locke's actual view, as evidenced here:

have a consciousness that cannot reach beyond this new State. (E II.xxvii. 14: 338)

consciousness, as far as ever as it can be extended, . . . unites Existences, and Actions . . . into the same Person . . . (E II.xxvii.16: 340)

That with which the *consciousness* of this present thinking thing can join it self, makes the same *Person* . . . (E II.xxvii.17: 341)

If there be any part of its Existence, which I cannot upon recollection join with that present consciousness . . . (E II.xxvii.24: 345)

supposing a man punish'd now, for what he had done in another Life, whereof he could be made to have no consciousness at all . . . (E II.xxvii. 26: 347)

The modals in these and other expressions suggest that the analysis is meant to depend not on actual consciousness but on the possibility of it. That might enable it to meet a range of counterexamples to which it would otherwise be subject.

Whether it does so, and how, depends upon what kind of modal is involved. It might be logical, conceptual. But the only basis I can find for that is the meaning of "recall" in which it is analytic that if I recall being F at t_1 then I was F at t_1. This would give a kind of truth to the statement that if I wasn't F at t_1 then I *cannot* recall being F at t_1, on a par with the statement that if something doesn't have three sides then it *cannot* be a triangle; and then by contraposition we get that if I can recall being F at t_1 then I was F at t_1. That reading of the analysis, however, reduces it to vicious circularity: it offers to give us leverage on "It was I who was F at t_1" through "I can recall being F at t_1," but the latter, we find, can be known to be true only through knowing that I was F at t_1.[5]

So the modality in question had better be causal: The thesis will have to be that whether the person who is F at t_1 is the one who is G at t_2 depends upon what it is causally possible for the person who is G at t_2 to recall experiencing at t_1.

This notion of what a mind can do at a given time would have to be a part of any account of mentality. It's a notion that Locke demonstrably has, with respect not only to what a given mind can do at a certain moment but also to its more durable capacities and incapacities. It is conspicuous in his polemic against innatism, where he says that "Men, barely by the Use of their natural Faculties, may attain to all the Knowledge they have" (E I.ii.1: 48), that what "the Souls of Men . . . bring into the World with them" are not ideas but only "their inherent Faculties" (E I.ii.2: 49), and that "there are natural tendencies imprinted on the Minds of Men" (E I.iii.3: 67). All of this, presumably, is to be understood in causal terms.

Locke is not well placed to tell us much about the causal powers of mind, especially about what the intrinsic features are of the mind by virtue of which it has these powers. This is one of those matters that he is resolutely unwilling to "meddle" with; and it essentially involves a question that he says we cannot answer, namely whether a mind-stage is a stage of an immaterial substance, of a material substance (an atom), or of an animal.

As well as seeming to be in one way too strong, Locke's analysans for personal identity is in another way too weak. It implies that if x has experience e at t_1, and y at t_2 is conscious of having e at t_1, then x is y. On one interpretation of this, it means that if

y later is in a state that bears all the internal marks of being a memory state, and which represents an experience just like e,

then . . . etc. That makes the thesis much too generous about personal identity, for we can make sense of the thought of my having a memory-like state containing a representation of an experience that was previously yours, not mine. On the only other interpretation, it means that if

y later genuinely remembers having experience e at t_1,

then ... etc. That makes the thesis true, but robs it of all power to elucidate personal identity; for "y genuinely remembers having e at t_1" entails that y had e at t_1, that is, that the person who had e at t_1 *was y*, so that the analysans has the entire analysandum nested within it.

   The best way of meeting this charge of undue weakness is to modify the analysis so that it says that if

y's state at t_2 includes an e-type representation whose occurrence in y's mind is an effect of the occurrence of e in x's mind,

then ... etc. That could be a first step toward a causal theory of memory, which, when added to the rest of what Locke has, generates a causal theory of personal identity.[6] This causal theory has, I think, a fair chance of being true, but I cannot find the least hint of it in Locke's pages. In any case, he could have presented it only in a sketchy and abstract fashion, because he declines to have any views about what kind of item a mind is.

VIII. THE MIND'S CONTINUITY

Descartes held that thinking is the whole essence of minds, and extension the whole essence of matter. This committed him to two biconditionals, namely: necessarily, for all values of x,

x is a mind when and only when x thinks

and

x is a portion of matter when and only when x is spatially extended.

Locke accepts one-half of each biconditional and rejects the other. Agreeing that all matter must be extended, he says that there can be extended items that are not material, namely stretches of empty space. Agreeing that whatever thinks is a mind, he denies that whatever is a mind at time t must be thinking at t, that is, that "actual thinking is as inseparable from the Soul, as actual Extension is from the Body" (E II.i.9: 108). Even if thinking is "the proper Action of the Soul," it does not follow, and is not true, that the soul is "always thinking, always in Action" (E II.i.10: 108).

That is near the start of *Essay* II.i.10–19, which is entirely devoted to arguing that "the Soul thinks not always." On this matter, Locke is content to take his stand on his own knowledge – as he thinks it to be – that last night he slept dreamlessly; during that time, he says, his soul was not thinking.

Here again we run into the question that Locke cannot answer: What kind of item is a soul or mind? When it is quiescent, or not "in Action," in what does its reality consist? As well as not answering this, I suspect that Locke did not even ask it. That is, he seems not to work with any robust idea of a soul or mind or person as a continuously existing item. In his treatment of personal identity, he uses such turns of phrase as "whether the same *self* be continued in the same, or divers Substances" (E II.xxvii.9: 335), and "continued in a succession of several Substances" (E II.xxvii.10: 336; see also E II.xxvii.25: 345–46 and E II.xxvii.29: 348). But I cannot find in this chapter, or anywhere else in the *Essay*, any working notion of mental continuity that goes beyond the mere possibility of reidentification of a single mind or soul or person at different times. The concept of a person could be such as to permit such a reidentification across an ontological gap; and, while I have no evidence that Locke believed that there are such gaps, nothing in his thought seems to reflect a solid conviction that there are not.

When the diachronic identity of other kinds of things is in question, it's a different story:

an Atom, *i.e.* a continued body under one immutable Superficies, . . . must continue, as long as its Existence is continued. (E II.xxvii.3: 330)

such an Organization of those parts, as is fit to receive, and distribute nourishment, so as to continue, and frame the Wood, Bark, and Leaves, *etc.* of an Oak . . . it continues to be the same Plant, as long as it partakes of the same Life . . . parts of the same Plant, during all the time that they exist united in that continued Organization. (E II.xxvii.4: 331)

what makes an Animal, and continues it the same. Something we have like this in Machines . . . If we would suppose this Machine one continued Body, all whose organized Parts were repair'd, . . . by a constant Addition or Separation of insensible Parts, with one Common Life, we should have something very much like the Body of an Animal. (E II.xxvii.5: 331)

For atoms, plants and animals, continuity through time is in-sisted upon. This is in contrast with Locke's treatment of the dia-chronic identity of minds, in which continuity is not mentioned and, from Locke's examples, seems not to be required. Thus, if we ask Locke to tell us how things stand with a mind when it is not thinking, for example when its owner is dreamlessly sleeping, it would be harmonious with the overall tone of his philosophy of mind for him to say: "While the man is sleeping and not dreaming, there isn't any such object as his mind or soul. The fundamental reality at that time consists in a sleeping animal which can, and when it receives certain stimuli will, start thinking again." This is a long way short of the kind of materialism that finds favor with most Anglophone philosophers today, but it is a step along the way.

It is, furthermore, a step that can be taken consistently with the dualism of properties and concepts that Locke inherited from Des-cartes. Even while maintaining that form of dualism, Locke could have taken the position that there is no such item as a mind, and that colloquial uses of "mind" are just ways of talking about the mental lives of animals.[7]

NOTES

1 It is no accident that one of the first publications by Gilbert Ryle, who popularized the notion of a "category mistake," was a monograph on Locke (Ryle 1933).

2 The first-edition version of *Essay* II.xxi.28–60 is printed with the notes at the foot of pages 248–73 in the Nidditch edition. The crux is "*the greater Good is that alone which determines the Will*" (E II.xxi.29 [1st ed]: 251n), and "the preference of the Mind [is] always determined by the appearance of Good, greater Good" (E II.xxi.33 [1st ed]: 256n).

3 The main texts are E II.x.5: 151–52, E IV.x.5–6: 620–21, E IV.x.10: 623–24, and E IV.x.16–17: 627–28. See also E II.i.15: 112–13.

4 The generic idea is explored in Alston and Bennett 1988; the simple-composite species is developed in Chappell 1990.

5 This is one of several good points made in Flew 1951.

6 For contemporary causal theories of memory and personal identity, see, respectively, Martin and Deutscher 1966 and Perry 1976.

7 For a deeper exploration of some of the issues I have discussed here, see Perry 1975.

5   Locke's philosophy of language

I

Locke's first reference to language in the "Epistle to the Reader" at the outset of his *Essay concerning Human Understanding* suggests merely a pragmatic, Baconian insistence that we must strive for clarity in language because obscurity of speech is a frequent but avoidable source of theoretical confusion: *"The greatest part of the Questions and Controversies that perplex Mankind [depend] on the doubtful and uncertain use of Words, or (which is the same)* inde-termined Ideas, *which they are made to stand for"* (E Epis: 13). Such a statement does not imply that one needs any theory about language in order to avoid such problems, but just a special degree of care in its ordinary use. Later passages might also be taken to suggest such a Baconian stance, free of any specific linguistic theory:

Some gross and confused Conceptions Men indeed ordinarily have, to which they apply the common Words of their Language, and such a loose use of their words serves them well enough in their ordinary Discourses and Affairs. But this is not sufficient for philosophical Enquiries. Knowledge and Reasoning require precise determinate *Ideas.* . . . The multiplication and obstinacy of Disputes, which has so laid waste the intellectual World, is owing to nothing more, than to this ill use of Words. (E III.x.22: 503–4)

In fact, there is much more to Locke's view of language than such comments suggest. Locke does not merely counsel care in the use of words. Instead, he proposes a theory that is intended to show that room for certain kinds of confusion is an inherent liability in the nature of language and classification themselves, and that this "imperfection" of language can be remedied only if this fact is clearly understood. Locke's theoretical discussion of the nature of language and classification and his discussion of the imperfections of language and their remedies are not two separate themes, but parts of a single argument.

Locke's discussion of the meaning of words in general is part of his attack upon Platonic ideas that were enjoying a revival in the seventeenth century. His more specific discussion of classification is an essential part of his attack upon the Aristotelian world-view, which he, along with all of the great scientists if not all of the other great philosophers of the seventeenth century, was attempting to undermine. On Locke's view of classification especially, confusion does not arise from mere sloppiness in discourse but from false assumptions about the meaning of general terms. Locke's project in Book III of the *Essay* is to replace both Platonic and Aristotelian assumptions with a more accurate account of the meaning of names, especially general terms and the classificatory concepts they connote (Chapters ii–vi).[1] On the basis of this theory, Locke then diagnoses "imperfections" in the use of language that are inherent in the way it really works (Chapter ix), only subsequently cataloguing mere "abuses" that do not depend on a particular theory of language (Chapter x), and finally prescribes strategies to limit these inevitable imperfections, although they cannot simply be avoided like mere abuses (Chapter xi). Thus, Locke's strategy is complex: he wants to undercut philosophical confusions arising from a false view of language, especially classificatory language, but he also wants to show us that a true view of this use reveals inherent liabilities in the ideal of perfect communication through language – although, of course, we have no other medium for communication.

Locke's attack upon Aristotelianism in particular proceeds on two main fronts. First, Locke attacks the underlying assumption that the qualities of objects that are most salient in our perceptual experience should also be most fundamental in scientific explanation. Aristotle's theory of the elements, for instance, placed perceptually salient properties such as the hot and cold, the moist and dry, at the basis of its explanations; on the basis of the corpuscularian hypothesis, however, Locke argues that such perceptually salient features of our ideas of objects may have no resemblance to the features of objects that cause our ideas of them. An idea like that of coldness may not represent a positive quality of objects at all, but only a privation of another quality (heat), and in general ideas such as temperature of any degree, as well as color, taste, smell, and so on, bear no resemblance to the primary qualities or aspects of shape, size, number, and motion of imperceptible particles, which are the conjectured causes of our ideas of objects (see E II.viii: 132–43). Scientific explanation, Locke argues, must at least in principle be carried out in terms of primary qualities, even if the so-called secondary qualities are most salient in our actual experience.

Second, Locke attacks the Aristotelian assumption that the classification of natural objects into kinds or species reflects the natural or objective existence of a determinate number of fixed or unchanging "substantial Forms" (E III.vi.10: 445) or a "certain number of Forms or Molds, wherein all natural Things, that exist, are cast, and do equally partake" (E III.iii.17: 418). He argues that when we use general terms to group things into kinds or species we are not attempting to discover determinate species that exist independently of our own classificatory activity, but are rather choosing from among the innumerably many similarities (as well as, of course, dissimilarities) that are to be found among the particular objects comprising nature those that will be central in our own classificatory scheme. As Locke puts it,

I would not here be thought to forget, much less to deny, that Nature in the Production of Things, makes several of them alike: there is nothing more obvious, especially in the Races of Animals, and all Things propagated by Seed. But yet, I think, we may say, the *sorting* of them under Names, *is the Workmanship of the Understanding, taking occasion from the similitude* it observes amongst them, to make abstract general *Ideas,* and set them up in the mind, with Names annexed to them, as Patterns, or Forms ... to which, as particular Things existing are found to agree, so they come to be of that Species. (E III.iii.13: 415)

Only by recognizing the role that our own choices of defining criteria play in the constitution of species, Locke concludes, can we come to realize how often scientific and philosophical disputes arise from competing definitions of the species under discussion, and how important not only due care but also agreement with others is in the definition – and therefore constitution – of species.

There may seem to be a conflict between Locke's first thrust against Aristotelianism and this second one. For while Locke's attack upon the Aristotelian conception of scientific explanation denies any privilege to perceptually salient qualities of objects, his alternative to the Aristotelian conception of scientific classification appears to insist upon the employment of perceptually salient features of objects in lieu of any substantial forms by which to classify them. He insists that "'tis their own Collections of sensible Qualities, that Men make the Essences of their several sorts of Substances" (E III.vi.24: 452), and that "we could not reasonably think, that the *ranking of things under general Names, was regulated by* [their] internal real Constitutions, or any thing else but *their obvious appearances*" (E III.vi.25: 452). We shall see that it is a consequence of Locke's conventionalist account of the relation between word and object – an account that in fact goes back to Aristotle himself – that the meanings of words must be constituted by known rather than unknown properties of objects, and thus, in a state of very imperfect scientific knowledge, by obvious features of sensible appearance rather than anything else; but we shall also see that is a consequence of Locke's account of generality that we must still decide for ourselves which properties of objects to recognize in their classification into species no matter how much we can come to know about them and no matter how much we may subsequently learn about their currently hidden properties: even if (*per impossibile*, as Locke rather pessimistically supposes) we were fully acquainted with the most minute level of the atomic constitution of things, we would still have to choose which features of this constitution to make the basis of our classifications. Locke's doctrine is thus that while our systems of classification must always be based on what we actually know about objects, no matter how much we know we will never find anything that removes the burden of choice from us in constituting these classifications. His theory of generality and classification thus remains relentlessly anti-Aristotelian.

II

Locke stresses the importance of communication among human beings in laying down the premises for his arguments about language: his most fundamental assumption is that the "Comfort, and Advantage of Society, [is] not . . . to be had without Communication of Thoughts" (E III.ii.1: 405). From this he infers that a language user requires not just the capacity to make a variety of repeatable articulate sounds, which after all a mere parrot has, but also "that he should be *able to use these Sounds, as Signs of internal Conceptions;* and to make them stand as marks for the *Ideas* within his own Mind, whereby they might be made known to others" (E III.i.2: 402). In saying this, Locke is making a point that goes back to Aristotle himself, who wrote that "spoken sounds are symbols of affections in the soul, and written marks symbols of spoken sounds" (Aristotle 1984: 1:25). But Locke's use of this traditional view is designed to undermine the easy assumption that Aristotle added to it, namely that although the "spoken sounds" "are not the same for all men," "what these are in the first place signs of – affections of the soul – are the same for all" (ibid.). What Locke will argue is that because our words are in the first instance expressions of our own conceptions of things, we cannot just assume that we automatically mean the same as other speakers of our language do, but must take considerable care to ensure that this highly desirable but equally contingent result ensues.

Locke lays the foundation for this argument in Chapter ii of Book III. First, he asserts a premise that is implicit in Aristotle's statement, and was perhaps directed against the view of Plato's *Cratylus*, namely that there is no "natural connexion" between "particular articulate Sounds and certain *Ideas*" but only a conventional, man-made, or "voluntary Imposition, whereby such a Word is made arbitrarily the Mark of such an *Idea*" (E III.ii.1: 405).[2] But Locke adds to this Aristotelian view an inference that will be of great importance in what follows: if words have no natural meanings, but only such meanings as we speakers give them, then their meaning cannot lie in anything that is unknown to us, but must be drawn from our own stock of knowledge. "Words being voluntary Signs, they cannot be voluntary Signs imposed by [a speaker] on Things he knows not" (E III.ii.2: 405).

Next, following the argument although not the terminology of Thomas Hobbes, Locke asserts that there are not just one but two uses of names: "The use Men have of these Marks, [is] either to record their own Thoughts for the Assistance of their own Memory; or as it were, to bring out their *Ideas,* and lay them before the view of others" (ibid.).[3] From this twofold claim about the purpose of the use of names, Locke then drew the inference that "*Words in their primary or immediate Signification, stand for nothing, but the* Ideas *in the Mind of him that uses them"* (ibid.). Apparently his inference is that if words are to be used either to record and remind us of our ideas or to communicate our ideas to others, then they can only do that by being signs of those ideas they are to record or communicate; and if recording and communicating are the primary functions of language, then standing for ideas must be the primary function of words, any other function being secondary to and presumably dependent upon this.

This inference has brought Locke a great deal of criticism, even derision from critics going back as far as John Stuart Mill, who argued that "When I say, 'the sun is the cause of the day,' I do not mean that my idea of the sun causes or excites in me the idea of day" (Mill 1973–74: 25). The point is that, even if we are prepared to concede that our possession of ideas is a necessary condition of the meaningful use of articulate sounds, it is certainly not normally the case that we are talking *about* these ideas or, as we now say, *referring* to them. Indeed, it can be argued that even if our purpose is to communicate our ideas to others (the recording function of words generally drops out of this discussion), it is usually our ideas *about things* that we are trying to communicate, and this purpose will best be served with words that refer to *those things*. And even in those rare cases in which we actually wish to draw the attention of others to our ideas themselves, that would seem to be best accomplished by the use of words standing for the things that our ideas are about, perhaps because others can learn about the meanings of our terms only by means of their connections with publicly accessible objects. More generally, it is argued that Locke's thesis has implausible metaphysical and epistemological consequences. First, it commits us to the idea that our meaningful use of terms must always be accompanied by a stream of ideas that, to put it kindly, introspection does not always reveal. And as far as epistemology is concerned, Locke's view seems to lead to a radical skepticism. In order to know that another speaker means anything by his words, we have to know that he has ideas, and in order to know what he means, we have to know which ideas he has. But another's ideas are "all within his own Breast, invisible, and hidden from others" (E III.ii.1: 405) – indeed, that's why we need words in the first place – and this means that we can never really know what another means or indeed that he means anything at all.

It is quite clear that Locke does not mean to say that our words refer *only* to our ideas rather than to things, and it may be the case that, in saying that our words "signify" or "stand for" our ideas, he is not actually even saying that these words *refer* to, that is, are intended to be *about*, our ideas at all. Rather, Locke is arguing that we refer to things by means of the ideas of them that we associate with our names for them. He makes this clear in a passage which is not cited as often as the notorious statement of III.ii.2:

the *ends of Language in our Discourse with others*, [are] chiefly these three: *First, To make known* one Man's Thoughts or *Ideas* to another. *Secondly,* To do it *with* as much ease and *quickness,* as is possible; and *Thirdly,* Thereby *to convey* the *Knowledge* of Things. Language is either abused, or deficient, when it fails in any of these Three. (E III.x.23: 504)

Recent commentators have suggested both philological and philosophical grounds for an interpretation of Locke's account of signification along these lines, and we will now consider some of the elements of Locke's view that make it clear that his statement is by no means as silly as some of his critics have thought. In so doing, however, we must keep in mind a point that Locke's most recent defenders have not stressed. Although Locke clearly does believe that our words refer to objects, not just ideas, and that it is a fundamental use of them, even if not their "primary signification," to convey information about such objects, it is also a central part of his thesis that the connection of words to things is indirect or secondary rather than primary. As critics have noted, this has a skeptical consequence: if our words immediately signify only our own ideas, and stand for outer objects as well as the ideas of others at best indirectly, then indeed we can never be quite sure that another means exactly the same thing we do ourselves, or is saying the same thing about an object that we are, and we had better be careful about hastily assuming that he does. But this skeptical consequence is hardly a refutation of Locke's view: instead, it is exactly the practical lesson that he wishes us to learn from his theoretical inquiry.

First, recent historical research has made it clear that Locke's term "signification" does not mean the same as our contemporary term "reference," and thus it should not be supposed that Locke means to argue that our words primarily *refer* to our own ideas. Instead, "signify" (*significare*) is a technical term from late medieval philosophy of language that means something quite general, namely representing something in some way to the cognitive faculty, and which thus includes functions like *expressing, revealing,* or *making known,* which apply to meaning as well as, if not better than, to reference (Ashworth 1981: 309–11, 314). The specific element of directedness or aboutness, the speaker's intention of drawing the hearer's attention to a specific object, which is part of our concept of reference, was not part of the general notion of signification. Scholastic authors argued that there were several possible significates for words, or things that words could make known, including the word itself, the speaker, the speaker's idea, and the object referred to by the speaker, although attention was focused on the last two, the idea and the thing that the idea is about (Ashworth 1981: 310). Different authors differed on the order of priority among these significates of words, some arguing that a speaker makes his idea known by first making a thing known to another, while others held that a speaker makes a thing known by making known his idea, in which case the idea would be the primary significate and the thing the secondary significate. By the seventeenth century, many writers preferred the latter view, although they did not always offer any arguments for it; thus, Franco Burgerdijk, an author whom Locke used, held that "Articulate utterances signify the concepts of the mind, primarily, that is, and immediately; for they also signify things, but by means of concepts" (Ashworth 1981: 324). Locke is now seen as attaching himself to this tradition. His claim would then be that words which in our sense may well *refer* to things nevertheless by so doing *make known* what ideas a speaker has, namely, ideas of the things to which the words refer, and indeed that it is only by so doing that they make known the objects which the speaker intends to refer to – thus the signification of ideas is primary and that of things secondary, in the sense that the former is the means to the latter. But Locke would not be implying either that a speaker typically means explicitly to refer to his own ideas, and certainly not that he can refer to nothing but his own ideas.

Two points about this view should be noted. First, it is not likely that Locke merely adopted a view that he found in the latest textbooks; instead, his preference for the view that words have ideas as their primary significations and things only as their secondary significations has its roots at the most fundamental level of his philosophy, in his theory of ideas itself, that is, the claim that ideas are always the immediate objects of our thought. Second, the fact that a word signifies a thing only through the mediation of an idea is no merely technical triviality, but explains why we cannot automatically assume that the ideas any one of us associates with his or her words necessarily accurately express either the ideas of others or the nature of things themselves.

The first of these points but not the second has been emphasized in recent philosophical commentary on Locke's thesis. It has thus been argued that, although Locke's argument from the purposes of communication fails to imply that our words refer only or even primarily to ideas, his representative theory of ideas does imply that ideas are always the immediate objects of our thought, yet at the same time themselves signs – indeed natural rather conventional signs – of things, through which the words that are associated with them not only can but indeed inevitably do become signs of things as well.

Locke's general claim about the representative nature of ideas comprises two theses: (1) that things are never presented to us directly, but only by means of intervening ideas, but also (2) that ideas do naturally and evidently represent things beyond themselves, although not necessarily the whole or even the most important aspects of the nature of those things. Locke says "Whatsoever the Mind perceives in it self, or is the immediate object of Perception, Thought, or Understanding, that I call *Idea*" (E II.viii.8: 134), from which he infers that "'Tis evident, the Mind knows not Things immediately, but only by the intervention of the *Ideas* it has of them" (E IV.iv.3: 563; see also E IV.xxi.4: 721). Thus, the representation of things is always at best indirect, and since we can never think of things but indirectly, obviously we cannot but also use signs to recollect them or refer others to them indirectly. Yet at the same time ideas (at least simple ideas and complex ideas accurately made from simple ones) do inherently represent things distinct from themselves: "simple *Ideas* . . . the Mind . . . can by no means make to it self, [thus] must necessarily be the product of Things operating on the Mind in a natural way, and producing therein those Perceptions, which by the Wisdom and Will of our Maker they are ordained and adapted to. From whence it follows, that . . . they represent to us Things under those appearances which they are fitted to produce in us" (E IV.iv.4: 563–64). Ideas are natural signs of things, and words that are conventional signs of ideas thus become conventional signs of natural signs of things: the ideas to which our words are connected by convention naturally suggest to us the objects that produce them.

Locke's qualification, however, that ideas represent things to us only "under those appearances which they are fitted to produce in us," is meant to remind us that our ideas do not reveal to us everything about their objects that might be revealed to better or just different kinds of observers, for instance, the details of the primary qualities of their insensible particles. Our ideas are surely effects of objects as their causes, but do not resemble their causes in all possible ways, and so convey to us limited and indirect information about the nature of their objects. The representative theory of ideas implies, therefore, that as signs of ideas words are also signs of objects but, likewise as signs of ideas, not necessarily signs of objects that reveal everything about them we might like to know. The representative theory of ideas simultaneously justifies our use of words as signs of things and admonishes us to caution in this use of them.

There can be no doubt that Locke's thesis about the signification of words is meant to imply that (1) we can say nothing about things without having ideas of them and (2) *what* we can say about things is determined by *what* ideas we can have of them. The latter implication is of great importance in his theory of general terms, as we shall shortly see, for it requires us to take great care in our interpretation of what we actually say about things in designating them by the name of a species. But more generally, his claim that our ideas are the primary signification of our words and its implied corollary that things are only secondary significates, thus that our reference to things is indirect, shows us where room for error lies. Locke makes this clear by turning directly from his thesis that ideas are the primary significations of words to two fundamental dangers or "secret references" in the use of words. As Locke puts it,

But though Words, as they are used by Men, can properly and immediately signify nothing but the *Ideas,* that are in the Mind of the Speaker; yet they in their Thoughts give them a secret reference to two other things.

First, they suppose their Words to be Marks of the Ideas *in the Minds also of other Men, with whom they communicate:* For else they should talk in vain, and could not be understood . . . But in this, Men stand not usually to examine, whether the *Idea* they, and those they discourse with have in their Minds, be the same: But think it enough, that they use the Word, as they imagine, in the common Acceptation of that Language; . . .

... *Secondly*, Because *Men* would not be thought to talk *barely* of their own Imaginations, but of Things as really they are: therefore they *often suppose their Words to stand also for the reality of Things.* (E III.ii.4–5: 406–7)

Thus Locke says that although the words of individual speakers "properly and immediately" signify only the ideas of those speakers, by a "secret reference" we also suppose that they stand for both ideas in our auditors and the reality of things as well. Some have interpreted this just to be Locke's clumsy way of saying that words indirectly but legitimately express ideas shared by a community of speakers and refer to things outside of those ideas altogether. This misses the force of Locke's claim, however, which is that although of course we can succeed in communicating our ideas to others and in referring to things as well as ideas, we open ourselves to the possibility of grievous error if we just assume that our words mean the same to others as they do to ourselves and that they express, not the existence, but the real nature of things. The indirectness of the connection between words on the one hand and things as well as the ideas of others on the other hand is the natural imperfection of language that calls for careful remedy, but we are likely to overlook these problems if we unthinkingly give words "secret reference" instead of explicitly and carefully securing their correspondence to the ideas of others and the real natures of things – as far as that is possible.

Locke's chapter "Of the Imperfection of Words" (Chapter ix of Book III) builds upon this critique of the "secret reference" of our words. The general thesis of the chapter is that "the very nature of Words, makes it almost unavoidable, for many of them to be doubtful and uncertain in their significations" (E III.ix.1: 475–76). Locke then refers back to his original twofold characterization of the uses of language and says that, while there is little room for error when an individual uses words merely to record his own thoughts, the communicative use of language is inherently liable to error precisely because words have only a conventional connection to our ideas as well as indirect connection to things:

The chief End of Language in Communication being to be understood, Words serve not well for that end, neither in civil, nor philosophical Discourse, when any Word does not excite in the Hearer, the same *Idea* which it stands for in the Mind of the Speaker. Now since Sounds have no natural connexion with our *Ideas,* but have all their signification from the arbitrary imposition of Men, the *doubtfulness* and uncertainty *of their signification,* which *is the imperfection* we here are speaking of, has its cause more in the *Ideas* they stand for, than in any incapacity there is in one Sound, more than in another, to signify any *Idea:* . . . Words having naturally no signification, the *Idea* which each stands for, must be learned and retained by those, who would exchange Thoughts, and hold intelligible Discourse with others. (E III.ix.4–5: 476–77)

Precisely because there is no natural connection between any word and the idea it signifies, a fortiori no immediate connection between any word and the thing it may refer to, we cannot simply assume that another signifies the same idea and thus means the same thing that we do even when he or she uses the same word.

That our words have no natural connections to things but signify them only through ideas on which those words are voluntarily imposed, while those ideas are hidden within the breasts of each of us, is the first reason why although language is our only instrument for the communication of ideas we can never think of it as a transparent medium: it cannot give us direct access to the ideas of others. But there is another sense in which language is a "voluntary imposition" on reality: in order to communicate with each other we must agree on a scheme of classification, but nature never dictates such a scheme to us, and we must consequently secure agreement in the use of such a scheme by our own efforts. Here too we must avoid merely giving our words a "secret reference" to the reality of things and instead recognize our own work. This is the gist of Locke's argument in his discussion of general terms.

III

Locke begins his discussion "Of General Terms" (Chapter iii of Book III) with the observation that "All Things, that exist, being Particulars, it may perhaps be thought reasonable, that Words, which ought to be conformed to Things, should be so too, I mean in their Signification" (E III.iii.1: 409). The premise that only particulars exist in nature is the basis of all of Locke's ensuing argument (see also E III.iii.11: 414). But, given his underlying account of the uses of language, he rejects the inference that our language should therefore consist of proper names alone. First, it would exceed the limits of human capacity to employ such a language even for recording one's own thoughts – a general who can remember the names of all his soldiers is already a prodigy, but even the "most capacious Understanding" could not remember proper names for every leaf or grain of sand (E III.iii.2: 409). But, much more important, the use of only proper names would defeat the communicative purpose of language: by the use of a proper name, I would not be able to communicate any idea about a particular to another person unless the other was "acquainted with all those very particular Things" that I was (E III.iii.3: 410) and, further, had given them the same names I had; moreover, by the use of such names alone one would never be able to communicate – or learn – any new information about particulars, and thus use language *"for the improvement of Knowledge"* (E III.iii.4: 410). In order to fulfill its functions of recording and communicating information, therefore, language must employ general as well as particular names.

It follows from Locke's general thesis about signification that general names or terms must signify their objects through the ideas that are associated with them; but further, if nature contains only particulars and no objects that are themselves general, general terms can only designate particulars through the mediation of an idea that can introduce generality. Such an idea is an abstract idea, and thus Locke argues that

Words become general, by being made the signs of general *Ideas:* and *Ideas* become general, by separating from them the circumstances of Time, and Place, and any other *Ideas*, that may determine them to this or that particular Existence. By this way of abstraction they are made capable of representing more Individuals than one; each of which, having in it a conformity to that abstract *Idea*, is (as we call it) of that sort. (E III.iii.6: 410–11)

As this conception of abstract ideas is the basis for Locke's argument in the remainder of Book III, but has also been controversial – Berkeley rejected it violently (Berkeley 1948–57: 2:32–33) – it is worth pausing over it. On Locke's account, an abstract idea is a conception formed by omitting from the very complex idea that is the experience of a particular object features that determine it to a particular time or place, thus leaving features it may share with other particular objects existing at other times and places. Locke illustrates by saying that a child may start off with particular ideas of its nurse and mother, named "Nurse" and "Mamma," which are indeed rather "like Pictures," and then gradually notice "agreements of Shape, and several other Qualities," which these figures have with each other, and then with other objects as well, for instance, the father, and by so doing arrive at conceptions such as those of women and then human beings more generally (E III.iii.7: 411). In order to do so, the child must abstract from, that is, leave out of his idea, such features of size and shape and color, for instance, which may distinguish his mother from his nurse, and then from further features, such as secondary sexual characteristics, which distinguish those two from his father. Locke says that in forming abstract ideas we separate from our ideas of particulars circumstances of their time and place, but obviously this must also include all sorts of features that depend on them, for instance, features of stature and hair color, which differ not only between individuals but also over the life-span of a single individual.

It must be clear that this process of abstraction is completely open-ended, with nothing to tell us in advance how many or how few similarities between particular objects to include in any given abstract idea. The process of abstraction can be taken so far as to yield a single simple idea that a variety of particulars share, such as their color or smell, or can stop short of that. But if it stops short of that, then there are any number of places it may stop. As Locke's example suggests, the process of abstraction may reveal features shared by women, or go on to separate only those features held in common by both women and men; beyond that, it may form ideas of the smaller number of properties shared by, say, humans and other primates, humans and animals more generally, or even more generally by both plants and animals under the "more comprehensive term, *Vivens*," and then it may reach to even more general notions such as body, substance, and finally being itself (E III.iii.9: 412). The process of abstraction that yields abstract ideas is an activity of the mind constrained only by the ultimate limits of irreducible simple ideas, and thus abstract ideas and therefore general terms can be created which will mark off any similitude that can be found among particulars and group them into classes of individuals manifesting those similarities. General terms thus involve a "voluntary imposition" in two senses: the connection between the word and the idea is only conventional, but, even more important, the abstract idea itself must be a reflection of our own intellectual choice of important similarities among individual objects. Nature offers us similarities, but cannot tell us which ones to mark off with our abstract ideas.

Our abstract ideas thus define classes of individual objects manifesting similarity in those properties included in the abstract idea, and designation of a particular by the name, that is, general term, associated with a given abstract idea indicates that it possesses those properties included in that abstract idea. Membership in a "sort of Things," or, as Locke says, "if the Latin word pleases better," a species (E III.iii.12: 414), just means that an individual manifests the features that have been picked out by some abstract idea designated by a general term. Thus Locke can infer that *"General and Universal, belong not to the real existence of Things; but are the Inventions and Creatures of the Understanding, made by it for its own use, and concern only Signs, whether Words, or Ideas....* When therefore we quit Particulars, the Generals that rest, are only Creatures of our own making, their general Nature being nothing but the Capacity they are put into by the Understanding, of signifying or representing many particulars" (E III.iii.11: 414). And since it is the abstract ideas associated with general terms that define the classes of things, and it is we who define the abstract ideas, it is therefore we who define the boundaries of the sorts of things there are: "the sorts of things, and consequently the sorting of Things, is the Workmanship of the Understanding, since it is the Understanding that abstracts and makes those general *Ideas*" (E III.iii.12: 415).

As Locke says in his next paragraph (quoted earlier), "nature in the Production of Things, makes several of them alike" (E III.iii.13: 415), and there is thus an objective basis for our observation of "similitudes" among things. But nature makes an indefinitely large number of similarities among things. The nurse and the mother resemble each other in a number of ways, in some of which they also resemble a little girl, who in turn in different ways resembles a little boy, who in turn in different ways resembles his father, who in turn in yet different ways resembles his wife and his nurse, all of whom in certain ways resemble gorillas, and so on, at least it seems, ad infinitum. There seems to be nothing to stop us in the proliferation of abstract ideas capturing particular resemblances among individuals – but of course we must stop, otherwise our creation of abstract ideas and general terms would become just as useless as the project of simply naming particulars. But then we must decide where to stop, and which species to recognize in our system of classification. And that means that there are natural similarities among particulars, but no natural kinds. It is we who must decide, for instance, to ignore all the differences of size, shape, color, texture and so on among adult men and women and boys and girls in defining the species of human beings, and instead choose as our criterion for membership in a single species something like the potential for fertile mating.

Locke's conclusion that species are the workmanship of the understanding is derived solely from the logic of his analysis of the force of general terms, and has nothing to do with substantive claims about the kinds of similarities that actually obtain among individuals in nature or with specific limits in our scientific knowledge of natural objects.[4] Locke's more detailed discussion of the general names of substances in Chapter vi does not make this clear, and has thus misled his contemporaries as well as more recent commentators about the logic of his claim. Before we can unravel this conclusion, however, we must introduce a concept that has so far been suppressed in this discussion, namely the concept of essence.

IV

Locke first introduces the concept of essence solely in connection with the idea of membership in a species. "Having the Essence of any Species," he stipulates, is what "makes any thing to be of that Species"; he then infers from his argument linking species membership to our abstract ideas that it is "the conformity to the *Idea*, to which the name [of the species] is annexed" which "gives a right to that name." Thus, "having the Essence" of a species and possession of properties conforming to those picked out by the abstract idea that is the signification of the name of the species are identical, and "the *Essences of* the *sorts*" are themselves equated with the abstract ideas that define the names of the sorts (E III.iii.12: 414). He soon admits, however, that there are "*several significations of the Word Essence*" itself, and he thus defines two different senses of the term. First, he claims that "*Essence* may be taken for the very being of any thing, whereby it is, what it is." This is an explanatory concept, as is obvious from the fact that "the real internal, but generally in Substances, unknown Constitution of Things, whereon their discoverable Qualities depend, may be called their *Essence*" in this sense. Locke suggests that when we speak of the essence of particular things without reference to any classification under which they fall, we are speaking of essence in this sense, although he does not explicitly say that this is the only case in which we correctly employ this sense of essence. In any case, Locke designates this sense of essence *real essence*. The second sense of essence is that on the basis of which "Things are ranked under Names into sorts or *Species*"; and it has already been argued that this is done on the basis of their agreement with or manifestation of the properties specified by "certain abstract *Ideas*, to which we have annexed those Names." Thus Locke reiterates his previous conclusion that in this sense "the *Essence* of each *Genus*, or Sort, comes to be nothing but that abstract *Idea*, which the General, or *Sortal* . . . Name stands for." Essence in this sense Locke calls *nominal essence* (E III.iii.15: 417).

Locke immediately makes two further points about this distinction between real and nominal essence. First, he observes that there are two different theories about the explanatory or real essences. One is that there is a "certain number" of such essences that are "Forms or Molds, wherein all natural Things, that exist, are cast"; thus the facts that explain the nature of individual things also determine a unique classification of them into species. The other is that the real constitutions of particulars that explain their features do not themselves uniquely determine their classification: "all natural Things . . . have a real, but unknown Constitution of their insensible Parts, from which flow those sensible Qualities, which serve us to distinguish them one from another, according as we have Occasion to rank them into sorts, under common Denominations." This is of course the "more rational Opinion" that Locke advocates (E III.iii.17: 418). On this account, although it is of course the real essence of a particular that explains – or would, if our scientific knowledge were more perfect – why it has the properties it does, it is only the agreement of some of those properties with an abstract idea or nominal essence associated with the name of a species that makes the particular a member of the species.

Next, Locke observes that the real and nominal essences of mixed modes are "*always the same*," but the real and nominal essences of substances "*always quite different.*" The interpretation of this claim has engendered considerable controversy, but a brief account will have to do here.[5] In the case of a simple idea, such as the idea of white, Locke seems to mean that it is one and the same thing that makes a thing white and entitled to be classified under the name "white." In the case of a mode, especially a mixed mode (that is, an actual or possible property of substances that is represented by a complex rather than simple idea; see E II.xii.6: 165), such as gratitude or triangularity, Locke seems to mean that the conjunction of properties that defines what it is to be of that sort, for instance, being a plane figure enclosed by three straight lines in the case of a triangle, also explains everything else that is true of a case of that mode, for instance, one supposes, having interior angles equal to three right angles. In the case of a substance, however, what explains the way it is, on Locke's corpuscularian hypothesis, is "the real Constitution of its insensible Parts," and this is not the same as the abstract idea formed out of sensible properties, such as, in the case of a piece of gold, "its Colour, Weight, Fusibility, Fixedness, *etc.*," agreement with which gives the particular "a right to that Name ['gold'], which is therefore its nominal *Essence*" (E III.iii.18: 419). Indeed these cannot be the same, for, Locke claims, we "know not" the real constitution of gold (at least in any detail) but certainly do know its nominal essence, since that is our own abstract idea.

This set of claims seems confused and misleading. The claim of identity between real and nominal essence in the case of many simple ideas seems to be undermined by Locke's own distinction between primary and secondary qualities: what explains why a particular is white is a disposition of the primary qualities of its insensible particles which has no resemblance to the perceived appearance on the basis of which we call it "white." In the case of mixed modes, while there are some cases, for instance geometrical cases like that of the triangle, where we might be willing to say that everything that is true of a triangle *qua* triangle flows from its defining characteristics, we may not want to say the same of a case like gratitude or murder (another of Locke's examples). Here we may feel that there is much that is important about, say, murders as such which does not flow from the definition of the sort but can only be empirically discovered by criminology. But, most important, Locke's emphasis on the fact that the real and nominal essences of substances cannot be identical because the former is unknown while the latter must be known might suggest that the distinction would collapse if the real essence became known, thus that we would not have to base our classification of substances on abstract ideas of our own construction if only we were better acquainted with their real essence. Yet Locke's basic analysis of the meaning of general terms implies otherwise: even if we were to become perfectly acquainted with the real constitutions of the insensible parts of individuals in nature, his argument implies, all that we would have discovered would be a great deal more similarities among the properties of these objects from among which we must select in order to construct the abstract ideas that will give sense to our general terms.

As if to emphasize this point, Locke subsequently suggests that the twofold distinction between real and nominal essence should be replaced with a threefold distinction that makes it clear that the classification of individuals into species always depends upon our own creation of abstract ideas no matter how well acquainted we are with the real constitutions of objects. He does this when he redefines real essence as "that real constitution of any Thing, which is the foundation of all those Properties, that are combined in, and are constantly found to co-exist with the *nominal Essence*," and states that "*Essence, even in this sense, relates to a Sort, and supposes a Species*" (E III.vi.6: 442). His point seems to be that while the *real constitution* of a particular is the totality of the features of its insensible particles that explains the totality of its sensible qualities (or would if we were scientifically more advanced), a *real essence* is that *aspect* of a particular's real constitution which explains its possession of those among its sensible qualities that have been singled out as comprising the *nominal essence* of the species in which it is being classified by the general term by which it is denominated. In Locke's example, "Supposing the nominal Essence of *Gold*, to be Body of such a peculiar Colour and Weight, with Malleability and Fusibility, the real Essence is that Constitution of the parts of Matter, on which these Qualities, and their Union, depend."[6] Locke thus suggests that the concept of a thing's real constitution is nonrelational, that constitution in no way depending upon our own mental activity, whereas the concept of its real essence is relative, depending upon our construction of a nominal essence. There are real constitutions but no real essences apart from our own classificatory activity, and thus similarities but no species apart from the classificatory systems we produce.

Locke's relational characterization of real essence most explicitly suggests that it is that aspect of the real constitution of particulars which explains their possession of the common *sensible* features required for their membership in a single species, for example, that aspect of the real constitution of some lumps of gold which explains their possession of the sensible features of color and weight on the basis of which we call them all "gold" but not other sensible aspects in which they may differ. It should be clear, however, that Locke's basic position on generality implies that even if we are dealing directly with the nonsensible and explanatory features of the real constitution of things, we must still make choices among them before we can speak of their classification into species. Contrary to Locke's expectations, we have now learned a great deal about the real constitution of many kinds of matter, and among their "insensible particles" we can now distinguish, among others, neutrons and protons. But what forces us to classify two lumps in the real constitutions of which there are the same numbers of protons but different numbers of neutrons as two different isotopes of the same substance rather than two different substances? Nothing but our own decision to use the number of protons rather than neutrons as the basis of our system of classification of the kinds of matter – a choice for which we (or Mendeleyev) may have had very good reason, but which nonetheless remains a product of our own intellectual activity and is not simply forced upon us by objective similarities in nature. Even when we know real constitutions, therefore, real essences still depend upon nominal essences, our own abstract ideas, and thus the boundaries of species remain the "workmanship of the understanding."

We must now consider Locke's argument in some subsequent sections of Chapter vi, where he manages to obscure this straightforward conclusion before returning to a strikingly clear illustration of it. Beginning at Section 14, Locke lays down a number of conditions that would have to be satisfied in order to justify the supposition that our system of classification reflects the existence of "certain precise *Essences* or *Forms* of Things, whereby all the Individuals existing are, by nature, distinguished into *Species*" (E III.vi.14: 448).

First, he claims, we would have to know that the products of nature objectively remain within well-defined boundaries: specifically, we would have to know "that Nature, in the production of Things, always designs them to partake of certain regulated established *Essences*" (E III.vi.15: 448), that "Nature always attains that *Essence*" (E III.vi.16: 448), and that it produces no "*Monsters*" which break down the boundaries of those species (E III.vi.17: 448–49). Second, our system of classification would have to be based on actual knowledge of the real essences that determine these well-defined boundaries of species: "The *real Essences* of those Things, which we distinguish into *Species*, and as so distinguished we name, ought to be known; *i.e.* we ought to have *Ideas* of them" (E III.vi.18: 449); further, if our classification of things on the basis of their sensible properties is to be founded upon a system of real essences, then we would also need "perfect complex *Ideas* of the *Properties* of things" on the basis of which we classify them in practice as "flowing from their different real Essences" which underlie this classification in principle (E III.vi.19: 449; see also E III.x.21: 502). But, Locke argues, neither of these conditions is met. In fact, nature does not stick to well-defined boundaries in its production of individuals, but is constantly throwing up changelings and "monstrous Productions" that break every conceivable boundary – for instance, "Naturals amongst us, that have perfectly our shape, but want Reason" (E III.vi.22: 450); "the mixture of a Bull and a Mare"; and the "Issue of a Cat and a Rat . . . wherein Nature appear'd to have followed the Pattern of neither sort alone, but to have jumbled them both together" (E III.vi.23: 451). Moreover, although the corpuscularian hypothesis may yield us a general conjecture, it certainly gives us no detailed knowledge of the real essences of things and their production of sensible qualities. And even if it did, these real essences could not possibly be the basis of our well-entrenched systems of classification, "since Languages, in all Countries, have been established long before Sciences" (E III.vi.25: 452). Thus, Locke concludes, "'tis evident, that 'tis their own Collections of sensible Qualities, that Men make the Essences of their several sorts of Substances; and that their real internal Structures, are not considered by the greatest part of Men, in the sorting them" (E III.vi.24: 452).

By these arguments Locke makes it appear that his position that species are the workmanship of the understanding rests on a

combination of factual claims (that nature is unruly) and epistemological pessimism (that we do not know much about the real basis
of sensible differences among things in nature). In his commentary
on Locke's *Essay*, his *New Essays on Human Understanding*, Leibniz responded to this appearance with objections that continue to
be made against Locke. Leibniz expresses reservations about Locke's
stories about monsters, suggesting that there may be scientific explanations of ontogenetic mishaps that are not incompatible with
the existence of generally well defined boundaries in animal and
human reproduction (Leibniz 1981: 315–17). Thus, Leibniz suggests,
objective similarities in nature between contemporary and successive members of single species are better defined than Locke recognizes. Second, Leibniz argues that our ignorance of the real constitution of things is not itself a bar to classification on the basis of real
essence: it just means that the classifications in use at any given
time are "conjectural" and "provisional" (Leibniz 1981: 311). "If we
had the acuity of some of the higher spirits," he argues, "and knew
things well enough, perhaps we could find for each species a fixed
set of attributes which were common to all the individuals of that
species and which a single living organism always retained no matter what changes or metamorphoses it might go through." We do not
have such knowledge, at least not yet, "so we avail ourselves of the
attributes which appear to us most convenient," namely sensible
qualities. But, he holds, "those attributes always have their foundation in reality," and the fact that we have only an "empiric's kind of
knowledge" of them implies only that we must recognize that "our
definitions are all merely provisional" and subject to revision in
light of improved knowledge (Leibniz 1981: 310 and 300). To Locke's
claim that our classifications cannot be based upon knowledge of
real essences because ordinary language long predates science, Leibniz confidently replies that "the people who study a subject-matter
correct popular notions" (Leibniz 1981: 319).

Leibniz's reply to Locke would be completely compelling if the
basis of Locke's argument were just his claims about the unruliness
of nature and the limits of our knowledge of it. As we have seen,
however, Locke's argument does not depend on these claims, but on
his underlying theory of the connection between general names and
abstract ideas, which implies that no matter how much objective
similarity there is between natural entities and how much we know

about them, we must still choose which similarities to make the basis of our system of classification. This holds even if we can recognize the microscopic constitutions of things, and even if things which can reproduce themselves do so truly and without any blurring of the evident boundaries among their obvious groupings.

Locke makes it plain that even perfect knowledge about the internal constitution of things does not itself automatically settle questions of classification in a "very familiar" but striking example later in Chapter vi. Taking the case of a kind of artifact like watches, he asks "what is sufficient in the inward Contrivance, to make a new *Species*?" He continues:

There are some *Watches*, that are made with four Wheels, others with five; Is this a specifick difference to the Workman? Some have Strings and Physies, and others none; some have the Balance loose, and others regulated by a spiral Spring, and others by Hogs Bristles: Are any, or all of these enough to make a specifick difference to the Workman, that knows each of these, and several other different contrivances, in the internal Constitutions of *Watches*? 'Tis certain, each of these hath a real difference from the rest: But whether it be an essential, a specifick difference or no, relates only to the complex *Idea*, to which the name *Watch* is given: as long as they all agree in the *Idea* which that name stands for, and that name does not as a generical name comprehend different *Species* under it, they are not essentially nor specifically different. But if any one will make minuter Divisions from Differences, that he knows in the internal frame of Watches; and to such precise complex *Ideas*, give Names, that shall prevail, they will then be new *Species*. (E III.vi.39: 463–64)

Locke never denies that there are objective and perfectly well defined similarities and differences among particular objects at any level of description; he merely argues that no such similarities or differences constitute the boundaries of species unless we choose to use them for that purpose. Because this point follows from the logic of general terms alone, it holds just as well for natural objects as artifacts:

No body will doubt, that the Wheels, or Springs (if I may so say) within, are different in a *rational Man*, and a *Changeling*, no more than that there is a difference in the frame between a *Drill* and a *Changeling*. But whether one, or both these differences be essential, or specifical, is only to be known to us, by their agreement, or disagreement with the complex *Idea* that the name *Man* stands for: For by that alone can it be determined, whether one, or both, or neither of those be a Man, or no. (E III.vi.39: 464)

Both Locke and Leibniz agreed that no one yet possessed knowledge of the springs and wheels that differentiate ordinary humans, defectives, and mandrills from one another, but also that there must be objective bases for these differences. But what Locke saw and Leibniz did not was that even as such knowledge improves, we must still decide where to draw the boundaries that define our conceptual scheme, that nothing can relieve us of the burden of the "voluntary imposition" of sense upon the particularity of nature.

In fact, Leibniz did not seem to recognize it but he tacitly conceded Locke's fundamental point that it is always up to us to choose the criteria for distinguishing species. As we have seen, Locke and Leibniz had a factual dispute about propagation, Locke arguing that it is not always confined to well-defined boundaries and Leibniz replying that it generally is, and therefore an objective foundation for speciation independent of any choices of ours. Even so, Leibniz could not avoid writing as if the use of propagation of like offspring to define the boundaries of animal species is itself logically speaking a matter of choice. Thus he writes: "when men settle on physical species . . . it is for them to say whether stuff which they themselves are able to restore to its previous form continues to be of the same 'species' so far as they are concerned. And . . . in the case of organic bodies – i.e. the species of plants and animals – we define species by generation, so that two similar individuals belong to the same species if they did or could have come from the same origin or seed. In the case of man we demand not only human generation but also the quality of being a rational animal" (Leibniz 1981: 309). Leibniz's language illustrates Locke's point precisely: nature may present us with all kinds of similarities, but it is *we* who define the boundaries of animal species by facts about generation and *we* who demand rationality as well as human origin in the case of the human species. No facts about nature can free us from the necessity of choosing our criteria for the differentiation of species by a "voluntary imposition" of sense on our general terms.

Locke insists that it is a fundamental difference between our use of general names for mixed modes and for substances that the former can be defined at will but that in the definition of the latter we

are attempting to capture the real regular co-occurrence of properties among actual individuals, thus that in the case of names of substances nature does set a standard for our definitions: "though these
nominal Essences of Substances are made by the Mind, they are *not
yet made so arbitrarily, as those of mixed Modes*" (E III.vi.28: 455).
But, he argues, the standard to which we try to conform our definitions of substances is set by the sensible properties of individual
objects, such as voice, shape, color, and weight, not by their hidden
features: "The *simple Ideas* that are found to *co-exist in Substances*,
being that which their Names immediately signify, these, as united
in the several Sorts of Things, *are* the proper *Standards* to which
their Names are referred, and by which their Significations may best
be rectified" (E III.ix.13: 482). He recognizes that people typically
assume that there must be a unique internal constitution in all objects manifesting a shared set of sensible qualities, and that for this
reason they are tempted to give the names of substances a "secret
reference" to the supposed real essences of species:

the Mind . . . makes [words], by a secret Supposition, to stand for a Thing,
having that real Essence, as if thereby it made some nearer approaches to it.
For though the word *Man* or *Gold,* signify nothing truly but a complex *Idea*
of Properties, united together in one sort of Substances: Yet there is scarce
any Body in the use of these Words, but often supposes each of those names
to stand for a thing having the real Essence, on which those Properties depend. (E III.x.18: 500)

Some, as it were taking up where Leibniz left off, have asked why
Locke did not accept this as an account of the meaning of names of
kinds of substances, an account on which we would use currently
recognized sensible qualities of a kind of object as a guide to naming
it but in which our intention would be to rigidly designate as members of a single species all and only those objects having the single
real constitution underlying those sensible properties, whatever
that might turn out to be (see Mackie 1976: 93–100). In Locke's view,
however, to speak with such an intention is a "plain Abuse" of language, attempting to make our words "stand for something, which
not being in our complex *Idea,* the name we use, can no ways be the
sign of" (E III.x.18: 500). In general, we are asking for trouble when
we talk about what we don't know in any detail. But more specifically, Locke's analysis of meaning implies that such an approach

would mask the kinds of decisions about classifications we must still make even as we do learn more about the real constitution of objects. Locke claims that "any one who observes their different Qualities can hardly doubt, that many of the Individuals, called by the same name, are, in their internal Constitutions, as different one from another, as several of those which are ranked under different specifick Names" (E III.x.20: 501–2). Perhaps he exaggerates the degree of discovered difference among real constitutions of members of a species that we are prepared to tolerate: when we discover that the real constitutions of two lumps of metal are as different as that of gold and iron pyrites, we may feel a very strong urge to classify them as members of distinct species regardless of how similar they may be at the macroscopic level. But although that decision may be easy, it is still our decision; and of course, in many cases, the differences in real constitution will be much less global, and the need for us to decide which differences to count as specific differences and which to ignore will be more apparent. We do not just "tolerate different isotopes of the same element" (Mackie 1976: 93), but we decide to do so, and we will always have to make such decisions even if we intend our system of classification to capture differences at the microscopic rather than macroscopic level. On Locke's account, we cannot simply intend that our system of classification rigidly designate differences of microscopic real essence, not merely because we are – or were – largely ignorant of such differences, but because there are none. Of course, there are plenty of differences in microscopic real *constitution*, but no matter how much we discover about them we must still decide which of them to count as determining the boundaries of distinct species of substances.

V

We can now return to Locke's theory of the imperfections of language. Of course, Locke believes that there are certain "abuses" of language which do not have any source much deeper than mere carelessness and do not require much more of a remedy than good care.[7] But, more important, his argument has shown that there are certain "imperfections" inherent in the very nature of language that we can to some extent remedy but cannot simply avoid. We have already seen that the fact that words signify immediately only their own speakers' ideas and signify only mediately both the ideas of others and things means that we can never simply assume that we understand each other but must take what care we can to ensure that we do. But in the use of general terms, especially names of mixed modes and substances, we necessarily face additional difficulties. In the case of names for simple ideas, our problem is that we cannot define them because we cannot analyze their signification into any complexes of further simple ideas (E III.iv.7: 422). But we can usually secure agreement about their significance by acts of ostension, drawing another's attention to "single" perceptions that are "much easier got, and more clearly retain'd, than the more complex ones" (E III.ix.18: 487). The names of mixed modes and substances, on the contrary, can be defined, but the problem here is that there are no natural standards that can automatically produce agreement in their definitions.

Since the real and nominal essences of mixed modes coincide, everything we need to know about mixed modes may in principle be learned from their definitions. But there can nevertheless be a great deal of confusion about the meanings of the names of mixed modes in practice, because the complex ideas that give sense to these names can be very complicated (E III.ix.6: 478) and because, since these ideas are made at will rather than according to any natural standard, they may be made very differently by different speakers. "They have their union and combination only from the Understanding which unites them under one Name: but uniting them without any Rule, or Pattern, it cannot be, but that the signification of the Name, that stands for such voluntary Collections, should be often various in the Minds of different Men" (E III.ix.7: 479). In the case of the names of substances, we do intend to define species on the basis of standards supplied by nature, but, even if we confine ourselves to sensible properties rather than attempting to make distinctions on the basis of properties which are hidden from us, we must still make decisions about which of the numerous sensible properties of objects to use for classificatory purposes – and here nature provides us with no rules. Thus,

Because these simple *Ideas* that co-exist, and are united in the same Subject, being very numerous, and having all an equal right to go into the complex specifick *Idea*, which the specifick Name is to stand for, Men, though they propose to themselves the very same Subject to consider, yet frame very different *Ideas* about it; and so the Name they use for it, unavoidably comes to have, in several men, very different significations. . . . Each has his Standard in nature, which he appeals to, and with Reason thinks he has the same right to put into his complex *Idea* . . . those Qualities, which upon Trial he has found united; as another, who has not so well examined, has to leave them out; or a third, who has made other Trials, has to put in others. (E III.ix.13: 482–83)

Whether we are in a position to base our classification of substances on macroscopic or microscopic features, we must still decide which features to use for this purpose. Different speakers may then decide to define the names of substances differently, and two speakers who employ different definitions may then refer to different sets of objects or say different things about the objects they are referring to without even realizing it, thereby producing great confusion in subjects from chemistry to theology.

It may sometimes seem as if Locke is advocating individualism in the use of language when he emphasizes how different speakers of the same language may define their terms, especially names of substances, differently: "And therefore *different Men* leaving out, or putting in several simple *Ideas,* which others do not, . . . *have different Essences of Gold*" (E III.vi.31: 458–59). But Locke is not advocating that we each use public words to make up private languages, or idiosyncratic definitions and classifications; he is instead arguing that this is an inevitable liability in the nature of language, which can only produce confusion unless we take steps to avoid it.

But what steps can we take to avoid such confusion? Obviously, we must try to ascertain how others define the terms of our common language and to conform our own usage to theirs. While in principle we all have the same freedom Adam had in the creation of definitions, in practice we should surrender that freedom in the interest of successful communication: "The same Liberty also, that *Adam* had of affixing any new name to any *Idea,* the same has any one still, . . . but only with this difference, that in Places, where Men in Society have already established a Language amongst them, the signification of Words are very warily and sparingly to be alter'd" (E III.vi.51: 470–71). "Words, especially of Languages already framed, being no Man's private possession, but the common measure of Commerce and Communication, 'tis not for any one, at pleasure, to change the Stamp they are current in"; instead, speakers of a common language "*must* also take care to *apply their Words, as near as may be, to such* Ideas *as common use has annexed them to*" (E III.xi.11: 514).

Yet Locke is too subtle to think that "common use" can automatically guarantee trouble-free communication of ideas. First, common use is based on past and current beliefs and knowledge, yet knowledge advances, and language must be open to modification: "because Men in the Improvement of their Knowledge, come to have *Ideas* different from the vulgar and ordinary received ones, . . . they must either make new Words . . . or else *must* use old ones, in a new Signification" (E III.xi.12: 515). Careful inquiry into the "*natural History*" of things will best "rectify and settle our complex *Idea*, belonging to each specifick Name" (E III.xi.24: 521), but will not automatically ensure that everyone agrees in its results, because they must still be communicated by language itself, typically by the modification of the signification of already current terms.

Second, there can be no noncircular determination of what common use is: common use is, after all, just a summary of what ideas others have attached to their words, and one's access to that always remains indirect. Common use cannot free us from our indirect access to the ideas of others through their words. Thus, although "'tis true, *common Use*, that is the Rule of Propriety, may be supposed here to afford some aid, to settle the signification of Language; and it cannot be denied, but that in some measure it does . . ., the rule and measure of Propriety it self being no where established, it is often matter of dispute, whether this or that way of using a Word, be propriety of Speech, or no" (E III.ix.8: 479). While of course some speakers are more careful than others, no one can be in a privileged position to discover the common use of language. Any claim about common use is a claim about what ideas others attach or have attached to their words, and in the nature of things no one can ever have direct evidence of that.

Locke's two controversial claims about language, his claim that the immediate signification of a speaker's words is always only his own ideas and his claim that species are the workmanship of the understanding, combine to ground a cautionary view of language. The purpose of language is to expand the knowledge of each of us by allowing us to communicate our ideas, and especially our general ideas, to others, and to acquire new ideas from them; but as we have no direct access to the ideas of others, and no way of determining upon a scheme of general terms without choosing criteria to define the boundaries of species ourselves, we can have no guarantees that we will all use our language to say the same things about the same objects and thus that we will succeed in the communication of ideas at which we aim. Certainly no easy appeal to "common use" can evade the imperfection of language. Yet for Locke this is no counsel of despair: "the import of . . . Discourse will, for the most part, if there be no designed fallacy, sufficiently lead candid and intelligent" speakers of a common language "into the true meaning of it" (E III.xi.27: 524). But it can only do this if we always remember that the sense of our language is our own "voluntary imposition."

NOTES

1 Locke does not actually assume that all words are names, and devotes one chapter (vii) of Book III to "particles" or syncategorematic terms instead of names. This chapter, however, does not contribute much to the main theoretical and diagnostic thrust of Book III, which might better be understood as a theory of names than as a theory of linguistic meaning in general (see Kretzmann 1968: 178–80). I will not say anything about Chapter vii in this essay.

2 The claim that the meaning of words is conventional rather than natural can be traced back to Aristotle (see Ashworth 1988: esp. 155–57). The conventionalist view of meaning was accepted throughout the Scholastic period, and the alternative view, that words have single, determinate natural meanings – sometimes called the "Adamic" theory of meaning, on the assumption that before the Fall Adam must have spoken the true natural language – was only briefly popular in the sixteenth and seventeenth centuries before Locke again returned conventionalism to the mainstream. Locke argues against the "Adamic" theory (as do Aarsleff 1982 and Brandt 1988), but this is not his main point; his main point is rather that the Aristotelian view of the conventionality of meaning itself has anti-Aristotelian implications, especially about classification.

3 Hobbes argued that we use names, first, as aids to memory, in order to recall previous thoughts to mind, and, second, as instruments of communication, in order to disclose our own thoughts to others. He called "tokens" of the first kind "marks" and those of the second kind "signs," although nonnatural or conventional rather than natural signs (smoke is a natural sign of fire; the ringing of an alarm bell, perhaps, is a nonnatural

and conventional sign of it) (Hobbes 1981: 192–97). Locke follows Hobbes
in the substance but not terminology of his doctrine, for he uses the expressions "mark" and "sign" interchangeably.

4 Many writers have suggested that Locke's theory of classification follows
from his assumption of a great chain of being at the level of phenomenal
properties, or even more directly from his acceptance as part of the corpuscularian hypothesis of the idea that there is an infinite gradation of
differences among objects at the microscopic level (see esp. Ayers 1981a).
But Locke's thesis is not that we must draw arbitrary lines between species because they naturally form a continuum; his position is rather that
just because nature contains only many particulars resembling each other
in many ways we must decide which differences between individual objects, whether grossly salient or barely noticeable, to include in our abstract ideas of them and thus in our definitions of general terms. His
position may have been motivated by the corpuscularian hypothesis or
the idea of the great chain of being or both, but it is not logically dependent on either of them.

5 For some discussion of this issue, see Woolhouse 1971: 115–49 and Bolton 1976b: 488–513.

6 Locke also tries to make the point terminologically, saying that the real
essence is "that real Constitution, on which the Properties depend, . . .
Properties belonging only to *Species*, and not to Individuals" (E III.vi.6:
442). The linguistic contrast between properties and mere qualities,
which a thing has regardless of its classification, is no longer obvious,
even if it was in Locke's time.

7 Locke enumerates these abuses in *Essay* Book III Chapter x. They are (1)
the tendency to use words without any clear idea of their significance at
all (Section 2); (2) inconstancy in the assignment of meaning to one's
words (Section 5); (3) "*affected Obscurity*" (Section 6); (4) taking words
for things, i. e. assuming that all expressions, even those like "*vegetative
Souls*" or "*intentional Species*," necessarily signify something real (Section 14); (5) using words to talk about that of which we have no ideas,
such as real essences (Sections 17–21); and (6) assuming that there must
be a necessary connection between words and their meanings so that everyone must mean the same things by the same words (Section 22). Only
the last two of these depend in any way upon Locke's theoretical arguments; the other "abuses" may be avoided by any careful speaker even
without comprehension of Locke's theory of language.

6 Locke's theory of knowledge

In the course of its considerable length the *Essay concerning Human Understanding* deals with many topics; but its main theme and concern is knowledge and the capacity of the human understanding to acquire it. "[M]y *Purpose*," Locke tells us, is "to enquire into the Original, Certainty, and Extent of humane Knowledge; together, with the Grounds and Degrees of Belief, Opinion, and Assent" (E I.i.2: 43). What is knowledge and how is it acquired? Are there any limits to what we can know and, therefore, things about which we can have only beliefs and things about which we must be ignorant? What, indeed, is the difference between knowledge and belief? As its title indicates, the *Essay* intends these as questions more about the human knower and believer rather than about what is known and believed. What can we, with our minds, know? In setting out to inquire into knowledge Locke is setting out "to take a Survey of our own Understandings, examine our own Powers, and see to what Things they were adapted" (E I.i.7: 47).

In the background to his questions was a contemporary debate that arose from a large number of arguments against the very possibility of knowledge, arguments that were found in an account of early Greek skepticism, *Outlines of Pyrrhonism*, written by Sextus Empiricus (fl. A.D. 200). Pointing out that people disagree, these arguments challenge anyone who thinks the truth can be found to say who is its proper judge or real discoverer. Pointing out that our senses are unreliable and our reasonings often mistaken, they ask by what means truth is to be discovered.

But though Locke is often dealing with questions like this, his ultimate interest is not merely academic. It has to do with the human predicament, or our place in the total scheme of things. A pervading feature of his thought as a whole is a deep concern with how we should lead our lives here and now in this world, as God's creatures and in the light of some expectation of an afterlife in another world. So, since we have been given the ability to reason and think, one aspect of this is how we stand as knowers and believers. His basic aim is to "find out those Measures, whereby a rational Creature put in that State, which Man is in, in this World, may, and ought to govern his Opinions, and Actions depending thereon" (E I.i.6: 46).

There is some disagreement as to how exactly Locke's responses to the challenges of the traditional skeptical arguments relate to those of some of his contemporaries.[1] But there can be no doubt that they, and his underlying interest in how we should arrange our lives and thoughts, are of a piece and form a coherent picture.

His response, as expounded in general terms at the beginning of the *Essay* and confirmed by all of its later detail, is that to an extent the skeptics are right. There are things we do not know, things about which we can only form beliefs and things about which we are ignorant. But some things we do know and our beliefs are often not foundationless. On this earth "we are here," as he records in his journal, "in a state of mediocritie, finite creatures, furnished with powers and facultys very well fited to some purposes, but very disproportionate to the vast and unlimited extent of things" (Journal 1677: B MS Locke f.2: 126).

The things we do know, furthermore, and the things we justifiably believe, answer to our true needs and real interests. "How short soever . . . [people's] Knowledge may come of an universal, or perfect Comprehension of whatsoever is, it yet secures their great Concernments" (E I.i.5: 45). In brief, we are not in ignorance of our duties and obligations to each other and to God; we can, that is, know what we need to know for salvation. As to the practicalities of life in this world, we can learn enough for our everyday comfort. People should be "well satisfied with what God hath thought fit for them, since he has . . . put within the reach of their Discovery the comfortable Provision for this Life and the Way that leads to a better" (ibid.).

Not only have we no need to know much of what we do not know, we also are not suited to know it. A skeptical attitude would be avoided if people would recognize "the Horizon . . . between what is, and what is not comprehensible by us" (E I.i.7: 47). If they did

they would "not be inclined . . . to . . . Despair of knowing any thing;
. . . and disclaim all Knowledge, because some Things are not to be
understood" (E I.i.6: 46). It is no wonder that people fall to thinking
that the truth as a whole lies beyond their grasp when they concern
themselves with matters to which they are not suited. "Men, ex-
tending their Enquiries beyond their Capacities, . . . 'tis no Wonder,
that they raise Questions . . . which never coming to any clear Resolution, are proper only to . . . confirm them at last in perfect
Scepticism" (E I.i.7: 47).

In Locke's picture of things, our capacities and abilities are given
us by God. So not only should we thank Him for what we have, also
we should be less greedy and "more cautious in meddling with
things exceeding [our] Comprehension" (E I.i.4: 45). There is an im-
modest ungrateful egotism in attempting to know what we are not
suited to know, and in complaining that our knowledge has bounds.
We should patiently accept our limitations.

When he says that we should not fret at the limitations and
bounds to knowledge that are set by the nature of our understandings, Locke does not mean that we should not aim to get what is
attainable by us. Rejecting any innateness of knowledge, his view is
that what God gave us was not the knowledge that is necessary and
useful, but rather the means to acquire it. He speaks of the benefit
to mankind of the invention of printing, of the mariner's compass,
and of the discovery of quinine, and stresses that he does not "dis-
esteem, or *dissuade the Study of nature,*" but only "that we should
not be too forwardly possessed with the Opinion, or Expectation of
Knowledge, where it is not to be had" (E IV.xii.12: 647).

For substantiation and illustration of this general picture, we
must turn to the detail of Locke's inquiry into the origin and extent
of human knowledge. In a word, the origin, the "Fountain of Knowledge," is experience: "In that, all our Knowledge is founded; and
from that it ultimately derives it self" (E II.i.2: 104). But this view,
that knowledge is "founded in" and "ultimately derives from" experience, presupposes a distinction between knowledge as such and
the ideas that are "the materials of Knowledge" (E II.i.25: 118).

In a draft version of the *Essay* Locke faces up to an objection,
which, he says, he has sometimes met: not all knowledge could have
come from experience; some things we know could not have been
learned "from our senses." We know that any number is either even

or odd. But "we can by noe means be assurd by our senses" of this, "because neither our senses nor thoughts have been conversant about all numbers" (Draft A 43: D I: 74–75).

His answer makes clear that his claim is not that all knowledge is "made out to us by our senses," unassisted and by themselves. This would ignore the fact that human beings have understandings; it would ignore our reason, "which I thinke by a right traceing of those Ideas which it hath received from Sense or Sensation may come to . . . knowledg . . . which our senses could never have discoverd." His claim is, rather, that all ideas, all the materials out of which knowledge is fashioned by our reason, are derived from experience. We do not learn through experience that any number is even or odd. From experience we get the ideas of numbers and of the properties of evenness and oddness; and then, by our reason, we come to know that any number is even or odd. This insistence on the point that the use of reason is in some way involved in the acquisition of knowledge is one thing that shows the need for caution about the common characterization of Locke as an empiricist.

Locke explains that, behind this mistaken objection to his claim that experience is the "Fountain of Knowledge," there lay the view that some of our knowledge is not acquired, does not come from anywhere during our lifetime, but is innate. Book I of the *Essay* is a lengthy attack on this innatist view about the origin of knowledge; and we should look at it before looking at Locke's positive account of the production of ideas by experience and, out of those materials, of knowledge by reason. "It is," he says, "an established Opinion amongst some Men, That there are in the Understanding certain *innate Principles* . . . as it were stamped upon the Mind of Man, which the Soul receives in its very first Being; and brings into the World with it" (E I.ii.1: 48). These supposed innate principles were divided into the "practical," or moral and religious (e.g., the commandment *"Parents preserve and cherish your Children"* [E I.iii.12: 73]), and the "speculative," or theoretical (e.g. *"'Tis impossible for the same thing to be, and not to be"* [E I.ii.4: 49]). The exact identity of those who believed such principles to be "stamped upon the Mind" is not completely clear.[2] Their reasons for the belief are easier to see.

One reason for believing in the innateness of speculative principles has already been mentioned. It is that their innateness explains how we can come by truths which we could not have learned from experience. Even after reading Locke's attacks, this is just how James Lowde defended an innateness of knowledge. He argues that we do have knowledge that in "no ways depends upon Observation" and so concludes that it is innate or "naturally inscribed":

Our Souls have a native power of finding or framing such Principles or Propositions, the Truth or Knowledge whereof no ways depends upon the evidence of sense or observation: thus knowing what is meant by a whole, and what by a part, hence naturally results the truth of this Proposition [the whole is greater than the parts], without being in any ways oblig'd to sense for it. (Lowde 1694: 53)

Another reason is that the hypothesis of innate knowledge provides a needed explanation why some things should seem obviously true, beyond question, and in no need of support. Some people think, Locke says, that if there are any propositions to which "all Men, even Children, as soon as they hear and understand the Terms, assent," this is "sufficient to prove them innate. For since Men never fail, after they have once understood the Words, to acknowledge them for undoubted Truths, they would inferr, That certainly these Propositions were first lodged in the Understanding . . . without any teaching" (E I.ii.17: 56). Lowde provides an example of this way of thinking too in his reply to Samuel Parker who, along with Locke, was a critic of innatism. According to Parker, there is no need of innate knowledge. Why should God imprint obvious truths on our minds? An obvious truth needs no such artificial support. Lowde's reply makes clear that there is something to explain: "these truths do in great measure, owe their clearness and evidence to their being thus imprinted . . . the needlessness of imprinting such evident Notions cannot be argued from their present clearness; because it is their being thus imprinted or thus connatural to our minds that makes them so" (Lowde 1694: 57).[3]

Since Locke agrees that some propositions (among them those picked out by the innatists) do seem obviously true to all understanding people who consider them, and since he is sure that this is not to be explained by appeal to innate "native Inscription," he is right, despite what Parker says, to acknowledge that he will need to provide an alternative explanation (E I.ii.11: 52–53).

Various arguments lie behind his conviction that innateness is not the answer (see Barnes 1972). Innateness will not, or is not the only thing that will, adequately explain what it is meant to explain. It is too liberal: that "white is not black" would be readily accepted, but no one would want so specific a proposition to be innate; and it could be so only if, implausibly, its constituent ideas, "white" and "black" are innate (E I.ii.18–21: 57–60).

Different considerations are brought against the supposed innateness of practical and moral principles. People who accept them do so without question but, unlike speculative principles, they are not accepted by everyone. Anyone who is "but moderately conversant in the History of Mankind" knows this (E I.iii.2: 66). Ready acceptance by those who do accept them cannot, therefore, be explained by innateness. For the same reason, of course, it cannot be explained by the appeal, which Locke himself makes in the case of speculative principles, to some other general feature of the human mind.

What does explain people's unquestioning adherence to their moral principles, Locke thinks, is that as children they took them on trust, and then, due to laziness, lack of time, or timidity, never examined them. Moral principles are "instil[led] into the unwary, and, as yet, unprejudiced Understanding" of infants who, "as they grow up, [have them] confirmed to them, either by the open Profession, or tacit Consent, of all they have to do with" (E I.iii.22: 81), and who, as grown people "perplexed in the necessary affairs of Life, or hot in the pursuit of Pleasures" (E I.iii.25: 82), or afraid to question what is commonly accepted in their society, continue to accept them. The coda to Locke's diagnosis is the ironic twist that people forget how they came by these principles and so suppose them innate!

Though moral principles vary from group to group, and though their being unquestioned means only that they are taken blindly on trust, Locke does not think that there is no moral truth or that we cannot find it. There are moral truths but they are not to be dictated to us. They are, we shall see later, like anything else we come to know, to be worked out by "Reasoning and Discourse, and some Exercise of the Mind" (E I.iii.1: 66).

Having argued that none of our knowledge is innate or has its origin in divine imprinting, Locke turns to give his own positive account. Since knowledge presupposes ideas, which are its materials, he first discusses them.

There is much to be said about "ideas" in seventeenth-century philosophy (see Ashworth 1972, McRae 1965, and Yolton 1975a), and Chapter 2 of this volume says much about Locke's own conception of them. Here we need only mention his major points. Having defined an idea as "whatsoever is the Object of the Understanding when a Man thinks" (E I.i.8: 47), Locke follows Descartes and uses "thinking" to cover not just reasoning but also all other mental activities such as sensing, perceiving, remembering, imagining. So ideas not only figure in thinking and the understanding of language, but are also identified with perceptions of objects and their qualities, and with sensations like pain.

We saw earlier that the origin of ideas is, without exception, "experience." So, for example, "*our Senses*, conversant about particular sensible Objects, do *convey into the Mind*, several distinct *Perceptions* of things . . . And thus we come by those *Ideas*, we have of *Yellow, White, Heat, Cold, Soft, Hard, Bitter, Sweet*" (E II.i.3: 105). Prior to experience, the mind is "white Paper, void of all Characters, without any *Ideas*" (E II.i.2: 104). All the content of our thought must, in the end, be derived from experience. "All those sublime Thoughts, which towre above the Clouds, and reach as high as Heaven it self, take their Rise and Footing here" (E II.i.24: 118). This does not necessarily mean that we can have no idea of something of which we have had no experience. But such an idea must be a complex, derived by various mental operations of "*Enlarging, Compounding,* and *Abstracting*" (E II.i.22: 117) on ideas we have had from experience.

How is knowledge produced from such materials? To suppose that knowledge itself, rather than merely ideas, is "made out to us by our senses," unassisted and by themselves is, as noted earlier, "to leave noe roome for reason at all, which I thinke by a right traceing of those Ideas . . . may come to . . . knowledg" (Draft A 43: D I: 75). How, then, does reason produce knowledge from ideas?

Knowledge is defined as "*the perception of the connexion and agreement, or disagreement and repugnancy of any of our Ideas*" (E IV.i.2: 525). The basic thought of this is that some ideas are connected with others, and various truths reflect these connections.

Knowledge of these truths consists in the "perception," the recognition by our understanding, of these connections. The angles of a triangle are equal to two right angles; and the idea of this equality is connected with the idea of the triangle's three angles. To know this truth about triangles is to "perceive" the connection between these ideas. Our knowledge consists in the "perception" "that Equality to two right ones, does necessarily agree to, and is inseparable from the three Angles of a Triangle" (ibid.).

Sometimes these connections are direct and immediate, and sometimes indirect, as in the case just now. We have intuitive knowledge when "the Mind perceives the Agreement or Disagreement of two *Ideas* immediately by themselves, without the intervention of any other"; so we can perceive directly "that *Three* are more than *Two*, and equal to *One* and *Two*" (E IV.ii.1: 530–31). This notion of an intuitive grasp of an immediate, direct connection between ideas that were originally derived from experience is, of course, Locke's promised replacement for the doctrine of innate knowledge. It is his explanation of our knowledge of propositions that "the Mind at very first Proposal, immediately closes with, and assents to" (E I.ii.17: 56).

We have demonstrative knowledge when the connection between two ideas is indirect and mediated by other ideas. "By an immediate view and comparing them" we cannot know that the angles of a triangle are equal to two right angles. A proof is needed. Our mind has to "find out some other Angles, to which the three Angles of a Triangle have an Equality; and finding those equal to two right ones, comes to know their Equality to two right ones" (E IV.ii.2: 532). A straight line across an apex of a triangle and parallel to the opposite side will produce these "other Angles." Of the three angles on that line, which together equal two right angles, one is one of the angles of the triangle, and the others together equal the other two angles of the triangle; and so the triangle's three angles equal two right angles.

Besides the two "degrees" of intuitive and demonstrative knowledge Locke notes a third, sensitive knowledge. This is knowledge of "the existence of particular external Objects, by that perception and Consciousness we have of the actual entrance of *Ideas* from them" (E IV.ii.14: 537–38). Whereas (excepting the intuitive knowledge of our own existence and the demonstrative knowledge of God's) the former concern generalities (such as that triangles have angles adding to two right angles), the latter concerns particularities (such as the reality of what is now going on before my eyes). Another, and connected, difference is that this "degree" of knowledge does not fit Locke's official definition. Sensitive knowledge is not knowledge of some connection between two ideas, but knowledge of the existence now of something in the world corresponding to our present perceptions or ideas. It will be discussed later, when Locke's account of the extent of our knowledge of general truths has been detailed.

These three "degrees" of knowledge cut across a fourfold classification of the agreement or connection between ideas, the perception of which constitutes knowledge, into "sorts" (E IV.i.3: 525): "*Identity, or Diversity*"; "*Relation*"; "*Co-existence, or necessary connexion*"; and "*Real Existence*." The four sorts of proposition these generate are, respectively and roughly, propositions such as that "white is white" or that "three is more than two" (which are intuitively known); general propositions such as those about geometrical figures (which are intuitively or demonstratively known); general propositions about the properties of substances such as gold (about which, as we will see, we have little knowledge); and, leaving aside the intuitively and demonstratively known propositions that we and God really exist, propositions sensitively known.[4]

Now it is plausible to say of our knowledge of the properties of triangles in general that it is not "made out to us by our senses" and is based on our intellectual grasp of connections between ideas. But it is not plausible to say so of our knowledge of silver in general (that, e.g., it dissolves in nitric acid) or of gold (that it does not so dissolve). In these cases there is no discoverable connection between our ideas, and we are "left only to Observation and Experiment" (E IV.iii.28: 558). In these cases it does look as though our knowledge is "made out to us by our senses" and not by our reasoning about ideas. Locke's position on this is, simply, that these are not cases of knowledge. Knowledge is the perception of connections between ideas, so where we do other than perceive such connections we do not have knowledge. What we do have is what he calls "belief" or "opinion" (E IV.xv.3: 655).

In the absence of intuitive or demonstrative knowledge we must exercise judgment about probabilities and what to believe, and Locke devotes a handful of chapters to this investigation of "the Grounds and Degrees of Belief, Opinion, and Assent" (E I.i.2: 43).

We do not find in these what hindsight might lead us to expect. In them Locke is not much interested in the extent to which "Observation and Experiment" justify general beliefs and expectations about the properties of material substances that go beyond that observation, nor is he interested in how we decide just which general beliefs we should form on its basis. There is, that is to say, little interest in what became known as Hume's problem of induction, and there is nothing of the kind of the canons of inductive logic later drawn up by John Stuart Mill. He does at one point acknowledge that his experience that this piece of gold is malleable "makes me not certain, that it is so, in all, or any other" similar thing (E IV.xii.9: 644). But his references to "common Experience" and "the ordinary course of Nature" (E IV.xvi.9: 663), and to what "our own and other Men's constant Observation has found always to be after the same manner" (E IV.xvi.6: 661), are not problematic for him in the way they would be for later philosophy. His interest, which he shares with his contemporaries, including the natural philosophers of the Royal Society, is in the rather different matter of the extent to which our own experience, the testimony of others and of written records, lend support to the probability of beliefs about the likelihood of various particular events, both ordinary and miraculous (see Shapiro 1983: Chap. 2).

There is a close relation between Locke's notion of "knowledge" and the more recent one of "a priori" or "conceptual knowledge." He says that "in some of our *Ideas* there are certain Relations, Habitudes, and Connexions, so visibly included in the Nature of the *Ideas* themselves, that we cannot conceive them separable from them, by any Power whatsoever. And in these only, we are capable of certain and universal Knowledge" (E IV.iii.29: 559), and this runs parallel to what is said in this century in explanation of knowledge of the a priori kind such as we have in mathematics and geometry.

There is an equally close relation between Locke's notion of "belief," which is based on "Observation and Experiment" because of "a want of *a discoverable Connection* between those *Ideas* which we have" (E IV.iii.28: 558), and the notion of "a posteriori knowledge" of the kind which we have in a systematic form in empirical sciences such as chemistry. But just as Locke would not call such empirical knowledge "knowledge," but rather "belief," so he would not call chemistry (and other parts of what was then known as "natural philosophy") "a science": a "science" is a body of "knowledge," not one of "belief." So though geometry and arithmetic are sciences for him, and though – so he says – morality could be one, "natural Philosophy is not capable of being made a Science" (E IV.-xii.10: 645). These facts – that Locke is not thinking in terms of two kinds of knowledge, and that he sees geometry but not natural philosophy as a science – are symptomatic of differences underlying the similarity between his knowledge-belief distinction and the more recent distinction between a priori and empirical knowledge. These will be reviewed later.

In some cases, then, our understandings grasp necessary connections between our ideas, and in others they do not. In some cases we have "knowledge," and in others we have only "belief" or "opinion." Why is this? The briefest answer is that it is because in some cases our ideas (what Locke calls nominal essences) are ideas of (what Locke calls) real essences, and in others they are not. But this needs explaining.

In claiming that all ideas come from experience, Locke distinguished between simple and complex ideas. At the same time he categorized complex ideas into (among others) substances and modes. The first of these divisions is discussed in this volume in Chapter 2, the second in Chapter 5, but something needs to be said about them here too. They are important for Locke's theory of knowledge, as is evident from the fact that geometrical figures (about which we can have "knowledge") are modes, whereas things such as gold and lead (those things whose properties interest the natural philosopher and about which he has "beliefs") are substances.

The nominal essence of something, mode or substance, is our idea of that thing. So the nominal essence of a triangle or of gold is what we mean by the word "triangle" or "gold," in the sense of being a description or set of characteristics that something must have in order for us to count it as a "triangle" or "gold." It is, Locke says, "nothing but that *abstract* Idea *to which the Name is annexed*: So that every thing contained in that *Idea*, is essential to that Sort" (E III.vi.2: 439). The real essence of something is its "very being . . . whereby it is, what it is" (E III.iii.15: 417); it is that "upon which depends this *nominal Essence*, and all the Properties of that Sort"

(E III.vi.2: 439), that "on which all the properties of the *Species* depend, and from which alone they all flow" (E III.v.14: 436–37).

The wonderfully elaborate Strasbourg Cathedral clock provides Locke with a good illustration for this distinction. In Strasbourg on market day, the "gazing Country-man" (E III.vi.3: 440) would be struck by the representation of the moving planets, the lifelike figures that moved on the hours, the mechanical cock that crowed at noon, and other such features of this famous clock. He would doubtless be inclined to accept that there must be something (probably some mechanism of some sort, he would suppose) about the clock that gives rise to all these features by which he recognizes it. But he would know nothing of the complex system of cogs and wheels, which is what the clock would be to the cathedral horologist. In effect, then, the ideas the countryman and the horologist have of the clock, their nominal essences, are importantly different. The countryman's is of some of its observable features and characteristics; the horologist's is of its real essence, of what gives rise to those observable features and characteristics, and so which explains the clock's possession of them.

To allow of something that it has a real essence is to allow that there is something which it fundamentally is and which gives rise to, or explains its having, its characteristic features and properties. If we felt that all there was to it were characteristic features and did not accept that there might be something else about the thing which is basic to it and which produces or explains those characteristic features, then the notion of a real essence would have no place there.

Locke makes a relatively easy application of these thoughts to substances such as lead or gold. On the one hand there are the familiar, observable, and discoverable properties of these things – their particular color, their malleability, their solubility in some acids and not in others. On the other hand, or so it is natural to think, there is something else that lead or gold really is, something on which these properties depend and which can be used to explain why lead and gold have them. Appealing to their latest theories chemists could provide us with detail about what lead or gold is and why these substances have the properties they do. Someone less knowledgeable but not totally ignorant of natural science might well think, somewhat vaguely, in terms of the movements of elementary particles.

Chemical theory has moved on in the three hundred years since Locke, but our thoughts about these things have a basic continuity with his. Specifically, his conception of the real essence of a substance is modeled on the workings of the Strasbourg clock. He supposes that what gold, for instance, basically is, is a collection of minute particles, "insensible Corpuscles" (E IV.iii.25: 555), which only have the so-called primary qualities of solidity, size, shape, and motion. It is in terms of the arrangement and rearrangement of these particles that the observable properties of gold, such as its malleability and solubility in certain acids, are to be explained and understood. The differences in qualities of different substances stem from differences in the shape, size, arrangement, and motion of the insensible corpuscles that make up their corpuscular "real Constitutions" (E III.ix.12: 482).

Though this is the general picture Locke provides of the real essence or inner constitution of substances, he does not think we can fill in the details (in the way chemists now think they can, or as the cathedral horologist could with the Strasbourg clock). God can certainly fill them in and possibly the angels can too (E III.vi.3: 440), but with respect to substances we humans are all "gazing Countrymen." Our nominal essences of substances, our ideas of them, are not ideas of their real essences.

Locke's picture of matter is continuous not only with ours but also with that of the classical Greek atomists, Leucippus, Democritus, and Epicurus. Their theory of the terms in which the phenomena of the material world are to be understood was revived and revitalized in the seventeenth century by Galileo, Gassendi, and Hobbes; and, in its essentials, it was accepted by Locke. But this view of what a substance's "real essence" is like, and how it gives rise to the characteristic qualities of the substance, contrasts with and replaces a quite different view that had some currency in the seventeenth century. As Locke says, "Concerning the real Essences of corporeal Substances, . . . there are . . . two Opinions." His own, the "more rational Opinion," supposes "all natural Things to have a real, but unknown Constitution of their insensible Parts, from which flow those sensible Qualities, which serve us to distinguish them one from another, according as we have Occasion to rank them into sorts, under common Denominations." The other, which he rejects, supposes "a certain number of Forms or Molds, wherein all natural Things, that exist, are cast, and do equally partake" (E III.iii.17: 417–18).

This rejected account of essences belongs to the Aristotelian hylemorphic account of material things. Whereas those in the recently revived atomic tradition thought of a material thing as a collection of corpuscles, the Aristotelians thought of it as a composite of "form" (morphe) and "matter" (hyle) by analogy with the way a human artifact such as a bronze statue is a composite of bronze matter and of a certain shape or form. It is because some naturally occurring thing has the "form" (or "essence" or "nature") that it does that it is the kind of thing it is and has its characteristic properties. On the face of it there might seem little difference between a corpuscularian real essence and a Scholastic form. After all, they both have the role of explaining and being the source of the characteristic properties of various kinds of thing. But, at least to their opponents, the Scholastics' detailed characterizations of these forms (e.g., "man is a rational animal") seemed like mere verbal definitions, rather than descriptions of what certain things really are, an appearance that was encouraged by there being strict rules for the construction of these definitions. There was a general feeling among the "new philosophers" of the seventeenth century that the Aristotelian hylemorphic theory was useless as a means of understanding the world. It has, as Locke says, "very much perplexed the Knowledge of natural Things" (E III.iii.17: 418). The structure of material things was best seen in the terms of the atomic theory, not in those of Aristotelian hylemorphism.

We saw earlier – to turn now from substances to modes – that the nominal essence of a geometrical figure such as the triangle is our idea of such a thing. Presumably, for most people, something will count as a triangle if it is "a closed figure with three straight sides." What of its real essence? Obviously this cannot be a corpuscular constitution, or arrangement of particles – for the triangle is not a material thing but rather a shape, or way in which material things may be arranged. But it is not immediately obvious what it could be. This may partially explain why some people are less than enthusiastic about the idea of modal real essences.[5] What also may partly explain this is that Locke sometimes speaks of modes as though they were something other than a united whole with a mind-independent coherence – which is, it seems, what something with a real essence should be like. Thus he sometimes speaks of them as though they are simply what we, at our convenience, make them to be: they are, he sometimes says, composed of "scattered and independent *Ideas*" connected only by the mind (E II.xxii.1, 2, 5: 288–89, 290; and E III.v.8, 10: 433, 434). It is a mistake, however, to think that modes do not really have real essences. Locke quite plainly thinks they do, and his theory of knowledge depends on their having them. Moreover considerable sense can be made of the idea.

What is required is room for a distinction between the characteristic properties of some mode, and an essence from which those properties result. Locke plainly and plausibly thinks this requirement can be met for geometrical figures. The real essence of a triangle, he says, is "a Figure including a Space between three Lines." This is "the very *Essentia*, or Being, of the thing it self, that Foundation from which all its Properties flow, and to which they are all inseparably annexed" (E III.iii.18: 418). He intends a parallel between (on the one hand) gold's having certain characteristic properties and their arising from gold's being matter with a certain corpuscular constitution, and (on the other hand) a triangle's having certain characteristic properties and their arising from a triangle's being a closed three-sided figure. The cases are different only in that while we are "gazing Country-men" with respect to gold, ignorant of what precisely its real essence is, we do have knowledge of the real essence of a triangle.

This last fact is what lies behind Locke's remark that "*in the Species of . . . Modes, they* [sc. real and nominal essences] *are always the same:* But *in Substances, always quite different*" (ibid.). This remark should not be taken as a definition, a necessary truth about substances and modes. For, as Locke allows, it is possible to be ignorant of the real essence of an ellipse – it has to do with its relation to two points, which are called its foci – and so to have a nominal essence different from it and solely in terms of some of this mode's more obvious properties (E II.xxxi.10–11: 382).

Though considerable sense can be made of the idea of modal real essences there are problems with it. Some people feel it is arbitrary to say that "closed three-sided figure" is a triangle's real essence, what a triangle is, and that having three angles which sum to two right angles is a property that results from that essence. Since all and only closed three-sided figures have angles summing to two right angles, the latter has, they feel, an equal claim to be the real essence. A further problem is that with other modes, such as "procession" (E III.v.13: 436) and "parricide" (E II.xxii.4: 290), it is not obvious how one would even attempt to distinguish between essence and dependent properties.

In summary, then, our ideas (nominal essences) of substances are not of their real essences; our ideas (nominal essences) of modes at least often are. Why does this mean that "natural Philosophy is not capable of being made a Science" (E IV.xii.10: 645), while in geometry we can make systematic deductions? Quite simply, our idea of gold not being of its real essence from which its properties flow, there is no discernible connection between our ideas of gold and of those properties. Quite the contrary would be the case if our idea of gold were of its real essence. On the other hand, our idea of a triangle is of its real essence from which its properties flow, and so those properties are deducible from our idea of a triangle (E II.xxxi.6: 378–80).

So when our ideas are ideas of real essences, we can get "certain and universal Knowledge" (E IV.iii.29: 559) by the a priori methods of intuition and demonstration. This is why Locke says that "*Morality is capable of Demonstration, as well as Mathematicks*" (E IV.xii.8: 643). For "the *Ideas* that Ethicks are conversant about" (ibid.) are, he believes, modes whose real essences we do, or could, know. By contrast, however, where, as in natural philosophy, our ideas are not of real essences, we cannot go in for demonstration and acquire real knowledge, but are dependent on beliefs formed in experience.

Substances afford Matter of very little general Knowledge; and the bare Contemplation of their abstract *Ideas*, will carry us but a very little way in the search of Truth and Certainty.... *Experience here must teach me*, what Reason cannot: and 'tis by trying alone, that I can certainly know, what other Qualities co-exist with those of my complex Idea, *v.g.* whether that *yellow, heavy, fusible* Body, I call *Gold*, be *malleable*, or no; which Experience ... makes me not certain, that it is so, in all, or any other *yellow, heavy, fusible* Bodies, but that which I have tried.... Because the other

Properties of such Bodies, depending not on these, but on that unknown real Essence, on which these also depend, we cannot by them discover the rest. (E IV.xii.9: 644)

There is a contemporary context to Locke's view, that the method appropriate to natural philosophy, and to the investigation of the properties of substances, is basically that of observation. A tangible expression of this was the Royal Society of London for the Improving of Natural Knowledge, which was founded in 1660. Besides Locke, it included amongst its fellows various people who figure in histories of the development of modern science, and whom Locke refers to as "*Master-Builders*" of the "*Commonwealth of Learning*" (E Epis: 9): Robert Boyle, Christiaan Huygens, and Isaac Newton. They advocated that natural philosophy must be based on careful observation and the compilation of so-called "natural histories," accounts of observed properties – as in Boyle's *General History of the Air.* Thus Robert Hooke, in his account of things seen under the recently invented microscope, says that what is important in natural philosophy is "the plainness and soundness of Observations on material and obvious things" (Hooke 1665: Preface).

The Royal Society was consciously anti-Scholastic and its recommendation for natural philosophy of what Locke called the "Historical, plain Method" (E I.i.2: 44) was married to its rejection of the ultimately Aristotelian idea of *scientia*. According to this doctrine, *scientia* is knowledge structured in a certain way which gives an understanding of why certain things are necessarily so. One would have "scientific understanding" of something, say gold's being malleable, if one had demonstrated the necessity of its being so by deriving it, from first principles, as the conclusion of certain syllogistic arguments that had to be constructed according to strict canons of form. Among these first principles would be things that, so it was said, have to be known if anything is to be known – "maxims" such as that it is impossible for the same thing to be and not to be. Also among these principles would be a definition, as understood according to the hylemorphic theory, of the "form" or "nature" or "real essence" of the kind of thing whose properties were under investigation. Locke and many of his contemporaries felt that, with the possible exception of geometry, no "science" as conceived in this way ever had been or could be produced. In particular the strict

syllogistic demands placed on the structure of *scientia*, and its association with an unacceptable account of "real essence," did not fit
it for use in the study of natural phenomena. It turned attention
away from things to words.[6]

We have been brought back, at this point, to the similarities between Locke's distinction between knowledge and belief and the
more recent distinction between two kinds of knowledge, a priori
or conceptual and a posteriori or empirical. Let us now look at
the differences. According to the logical positivists of this century,
all a priori knowledge is, in the end, trifling and empty of content.
Locke would deny that this is true of all that he calls knowledge
(E IV.viii.8: 614).

He would not deny it is true of some. Given an idea of gold as a
stuff that is yellow and malleable, there is a necessary connection
to be perceived between being gold and being malleable; we can be
certain that gold (what we count as gold) is malleable. But, in
Locke's view, not all necessary connections between ideas are of this
trifling sort. The necessary connection we suppose there is between
the real essence or corpuscular constitution of gold and gold's malleability, is not; nor, in his view, is that connection, which we can
actually perceive, between the real essence of a triangle as a closed
three-sided figure and the property of having angles equal to two
right angles. The certainty that a triangle has that property is – in
Locke's view – informative. It is to be contrasted with the trifling
verbal certainty that three-sided figures have three sides. Whether
we think Locke is right depends on how much sympathy we have
with his theory of real essence, a theory with which logical positivism shows some impatience.

An antipathy to real essences underlies a further difference between the Lockean and the more recent distinction. The idea that
all a priori knowledge is trifling and lacking in content has a natural
affinity with the idea that the reason why the properties of substances are not known a priori, the reason why natural philosophy
is not (in Locke's terms) a science, lies in the nature of things and
not (as for Locke) in the nature of our understandings. To the positivists' way of thinking the natural world is contingent through and
through; hence there could be no other way to acquire knowledge of
it except by observation and experiment. But to Locke's way of
thinking there are necessities in the world; for substances do have

real essences from which their characteristic properties flow. Our reliance on observation and experiment is a consequence simply of our ignorance of these essences.

> Had we such *Ideas* of Substances, as to know what real Constitutions produce those sensible Qualities we find in them, . . . we could, by the specifick *Ideas* of their real Essences in our own Minds, more certainly find out their Properties . . . than we can now by our Senses: and to know the Properties of *Gold*, it would be no more necessary, that *Gold* should exist, and that we should make Experiments upon it, than it is necessary for the knowing the Properties of a Triangle, that a Triangle should exist in any Matter, the *Idea* in our Minds would serve for the one, as well as the other. (E IV.vi.11: 585)

Besides looking forward to a more recent distinction, Locke's distinction between knowledge and belief also looks back to an older one: the Aristotelian distinction between "scientific knowledge" and "opinion." Knowledge, as defined and explained in the Aristotelian tradition, has to do with what must be so and cannot be otherwise; and, for Locke too, "knowledge" is "certain and universal" (E IV.iii.29: 559). We have seen, though, that whereas for the Aristotelian knowledge has a structure arising from its development and acquisition on the basis of syllogisms that have maxims and definitions for premises, for Locke it does not. "Science" for him is a body of deductively related knowledge, but he places no particular value on syllogistic methods and abstract maxims.

As for "opinion," it has to do with contingencies on the traditional view, with things that might have been otherwise. As we have seen, however, this is not the case for Locke. It is true that, for him, natural philosophy, that collection of "beliefs" about substances and their properties, is not a science or body of knowledge. But this is because of the nature of our understandings, and not because of the nature of things. So whereas for the Scholastic tradition "opinion" concerns contingencies, for Locke it concerns what to us seem like contingencies, but what in reality may be universal certainties.

A feature of the Scholastic tradition was that the pursuit of *scientia* was the proper use of man's reason. Man is a rational animal, and one thing that was taken to mean is that he is a syllogistic reasoner. Opinion is not worth or even capable of serious and systematic attention. Indeed, talk of "system" is out of place in its connection, for it would imply an arrangement structured by syllogistic demonstrations from first principles. But Locke thinks that "opinion" is worth systematically searching for and having. There can be a body of it, and it is "natural philosophy." Even for him, it is, of course, not a "science"; and to that extent Locke is under some influence from the older tradition. But, as in the activities of many of his colleagues in the Royal Society, it can be systematically pursued; and to that extent, and as witnessed to by his occasionally calling the beliefs of natural philosophy "experimental Knowledge" (E IV.iii.29: 560; E IV.vi.7: 582), he is throwing off that influence.

Now, though we have no knowledge in natural philosophy, geometry and mathematics are not the only areas where we do have it. Commenting that it has indeed "been generally taken for granted, that Mathematicks alone are capable of demonstrative certainty" (E IV.ii.9: 534), Locke says that this assumption is false. Because the relevant ideas are modes, whose real essences we either do or might come to know, he thinks, perhaps surprisingly, that it may be possible to "place *Morality amongst the Sciences capable of Demonstration:* wherein I doubt not, but from self-evident Propositions, by necessary Consequences, as incontestable as those in Mathematicks, the measures of right and wrong might be made out" (E IV.iii.18: 549). This moral science would be based on two ideas. First there would be the idea of God. This idea, of "a supreme Being, infinite in Power, Goodness, and Wisdom" (ibid.), is, of course, not innate but is constructed on the basis of experience (E II.xxiii.33: 314; E IV.x.1: 619). It is a foundation for ethics because moral rules are simply the dictates of such a being: "God has given a Rule whereby Men should govern themselves . . . This is the only true touchstone of *moral Rectitude*" (E II.xxviii.8: 352). The second basic idea would be that of ourselves as beings with understanding and rationality, and who are created by and dependent on God. From this it self-evidently follows both that we can understand God's will and that we should obey it: we "as certainly know that Man is to honour, fear, and obey GOD, as . . . that *Three, Four,* and *Seven,* are less than *Fifteen*" (E IV.xiii.3: 651).

We need to know too, of course, that, beyond our idea of Him, God really does exist; and He Himself has provided us with the means to do so, by creating us with the power of reason and so the ability to demonstrate His existence. Locke says in the *Essay* (E IV.x.7: 622) that the traditional ontological proof should not be used as the only argument for such an important conclusion; later he actually rejected it (Deus: L II: 133–39). His objection is that the existence of something can hardly be proved from a mere idea, but only from the existence of other things. His preferred proof is not open to this objection. Very briefly, starting from our intuitive knowledge of the fact that we exist as intelligent things, he concludes that only an eternal intelligent being could have created us (E IV.x.1–5: 619–21).

Locke recognized that no one had yet produced a demonstrative morality and, despite urging from his friend William Molyneux, did not attempt it himself. But this does not mean to Locke that human reason has failed completely in "its great and proper business of morality" (W VII: 140), for we do have some moral knowledge, acquired in this fashion (E I.iii.1, 4: 65–66, 68; E II.xxviii.8: 352). But, as he makes particularly clear in *The Reasonableness of Christianity*, this process is not easy, and moral knowledge is hard won. There is, however, another source, alternative to our reason and understanding, and one to which those who have neither the time nor the ability may fortunately have recourse. "The Gospel," Locke explains, "contains so perfect a body of Ethicks, that reason may be excused from that enquiry" (Letter 2059: C V: 595). It follows, naturally, that our relation to any moral principles arrived at in this way, from the written revelations of the Gospels and not by our reason and the perception of connections between ideas, can only be one of belief, not of knowledge.

We saw that in the background to what Locke had to say about the origin and extent of knowledge was the debate provoked by Sextus Empiricus. It is there in the background to what he says in particular about the place of reason in the discovery of moral and religious truth, and the importance of the Gospels as a source. For one particular arena where that debate took place was in the religious controversies of the Reformation. The view had been that religious truths were determined by and to be sought in the traditions of the Catholic church, and in the decrees of the pope and of church councils. Martin Luther's challenge was that they were determined by, and to be found in the Scriptures. There is some evidence that it was this specific question about the sources of religious and moral knowledge that initially led to Locke's writing the *Essay*.

In the course of his rejection of innateness Locke inveighs against people who "taking things upon trust, misimploy their power of

Assent, by lazily enslaving their Minds, to the Dictates and Dominion of others, in Doctrines, which it is their duty carefully to examine" (E I.iv.22: 99; E IV.xx.17: 718–19). So for him, the possible sources of religious and moral truth come down to two: one's own reason and the Scriptures, "the light of Nature, or the voice of Revelation" (E II.xxviii.8: 352). The central point of his discussion of the relation between these two is that reason has supremacy over revelation. But this does not mean simply that reasoned knowledge is superior to faith, or revelation-based belief. It means also that revelation is answerable to reason.

Some moral truths are discoverable both by reason and by a reading of the Gospels (E IV.xviii.4: 690–91). But the revelations of the latter cannot make us more certain of the discoveries of reason. We need to know we are faced with a genuine revelation, and we cannot be as certain of this as we are of our reason-based knowledge. "The Knowledge, we have, that this *Revelation* came at first from GOD, can never be so sure, as the Knowledge we have from the clear and distinct Perception of the Agreement, or Disagreement of our own *Ideas*" (E IV.xviii.4: 691). Similarly, in the case of some divergence, we should follow reason rather than the supposed revelation. It "would be to subvert the Principles, and Foundations of all Knowledge ... if ... what we certainly know, give way to what we may possibly be mistaken in" (E IV.xviii.5: 692).

But the human understanding does have its limits, and some supposedly revealed truths (e.g., "that the dead shall rise, and live again" [E IV.xviii.7: 694]) are "above Reason" and undiscoverable by it. This still does not mean, however, that reason has no relevance for our acceptance of them. If something is a revelation from God it is bound to be true: "But whether it be a divine Revelation, or no, *Reason* must judge" (E IV.xviii.10: 695).

A further way in which the revelation of truths that are "above Reason" places no restriction on the supremacy of reason is that belief in them is not necessary for salvation. Anything that is necessary for salvation can be reached by our natural faculties. God, Locke says, has "given all Mankind so sufficient a light of Reason, that they to whom this written Word [the Bible] never came, could not (when-ever they set themselves to search) either doubt of the Being of a GOD, or of the Obedience due to Him" (E III.ix.23: 490).

The regulation of revelation by reason distinguishes faith from what was called "enthusiasm" – a religious enthusiast being one who "laying by Reason would set up Revelation without it" (E IV.xix.3: 698). Locke's rejection of enthusiasm, and his allocation of a central role to reason in morality and religion, give him a place in the history of the development of Deism. These are topics of discussion in Chapter 7 of this volume.

Our discussion of the extent of knowledge has so far had as its focus general propositions that have to do with the first three kinds of "connexion and agreement" between ideas – "Identity, or Diversity," "Relation," and "Co-existence, or necessary connexion." Let us turn now to the fourth kind of agreement, and so to our knowledge of particular "Real Existence." We have intuitive knowledge of our own existence and demonstrative knowledge of God's, but what we have of "*the Existence* of any other thing" is sensitive knowledge (E IV.xi.1: 630). The poor fit here with Locke's official definition of knowledge was noted earlier. Sensitive knowledge of some real existence is not knowledge of a connection between two ideas but knowledge of the existence of something in reality corresponding to our perceptions or ideas.

There are, of course, traditional skeptical arguments against the possibility of any such knowledge. Locke rehearses them: though we may be sure that we have an idea in our minds we cannot "thence certainly inferr the existence of any thing without us, which corresponds to that *Idea*, . . . because Men may have such *Ideas* in their Minds, when no such Thing exists" (E IV.ii.14: 537). But he is unimpressed. Though he concedes that the certainty he has from "the Testimony of my Eyes" is not so perfect or absolute as that from intuition or demonstration, it yet "*deserves the name of Knowledge*" (E IV.xi.2–3: 631). He appeals to us to acknowledge that the ideas we have in veridical perception just are qualitatively different from those of, for example, memory. The skeptic would feel that this begs the question, for how do we know what veridical perceptions are like when the problem is to know whether we have any veridical perceptions? To say, as Locke does, that "the actual receiving of *Ideas* from without . . . makes us know, that something doth exist at that time without us, which causes that *Idea* in us" (E IV.xi.2: 630) hardly meets the worry. How do we know we are actually receiving ideas "from without" and not dreaming? But Locke's interests and intellectual concerns are quite other than those of the skeptics who put such questions. His response to them fits with what we noted at the outset, namely his concern with how we should live our lives· "no body can, in earnest, be so sceptical, as to be uncertain of the Existence of those Things which he sees and feels" (E IV.xi.3: 631). Meeting the questions with sarcasm and impatience he concludes that "we certainly finding, that Pleasure or Pain follows upon the application of certain Objects to us, whose Existence we perceive, or dream that we perceive, by our Senses, this certainty is as great as our Happiness, or Misery, beyond which, we have no concernment to know, or to be" (E IV.ii.14: 537).

In Locke's view, then, though we are fitted to know some things, we are not fitted to know everything. The most obvious and large-scale limitation is the lack of scientific knowledge in natural philosophy, but there are others that Locke cites – all of them standard and frequently cited problems in seventeenth-century philosophy. We will never know how physical changes in the body produce ideas in the mind, and we will never know how the mind acts on the body to move it – "How any thought should produce a motion in Body is as remote from the nature of our *Ideas,* as how any Body should produce any Thought in the Mind" (E IV.iii.28: 559). We will never know whether an immaterial mind is required for thought or whether thinking could be an ability "given to some Systems of Matter fitly disposed" (E IV.iii.6: 540), and we are quite in the dark as to "how the solid parts of Body are united, or cohere together to make Extension" (E II.xxiii.23: 308).

But we do not just happen to have the faculties and abilities we have. They are those which God chose to give us, and we "have Cause enough to magnify the bountiful Author of our Being, for that Portion and Degree of Knowledge, he has bestowed on us" (E I.i.5: 45). Locke does not explain why there is any need for geometry to be a science, and hence why rules of thumb such as builders use are not sufficient for practical purposes. But it plainly does not matter to him that natural philosophy will never be one. We have no need of strict knowledge of the properties and characteristics of material substances in order to acquire "whatsoever is necessary for the Conveniences of Life" (ibid.): from "Experiments and Historical Observations ... we may draw Advantages of Ease and Health, and thereby increase our stock of Conveniences for this Life" (E IV.xii.10: 645).

There is no doubt in Locke's mind that these practical matters are important. He speaks with passion of how benighted the American Indians were who lacked the use of iron (E IV.xii.11: 646). But to want to go beyond such matters of practical importance is to want something that is "of noe solid advantage to us nor help to make our lives the happyer" and is "but the uselesse imployments of idle or over curious brains which amuse them selves about things out of which they can by noe meanes draw any reall benefit" (Journal 1677: B MS Locke f.2: 46).

But our aim here in this world is not merely to live a comfortable life, to have "a quiet prosperous passage through" it. This is secondary to our real concern which is to find our way into the next world. "Heaven being our great businesse and interest the knowledg which may direct us thither is certainly soe too, soe that this is without peradventure the study which ought to take up the first and cheifest place in our thoughts" (Journal 1677: B MS Locke f.2: 92–93). Men have reason to thank God too, then, "that they have Light enough to lead them to the Knowledge of their Maker, and the sight of their own Duties" (E I.i.5: 45). So it is, says Locke, that "I think I may conclude, that *Morality* is *the proper Science, and Business of Mankind in general*" (E IV.xii.11: 646).

NOTES

1 The disagreement concerns whether Locke is to be placed in a tradition of "constructive skepticism" (see Van Leeuwen 1963: 121, 124; Woolhouse 1983: 14; and, in opposition, Ferreira 1986: 211–22).
2 Two classic discussions of this issue are Gibson 1917: 39–44 and Yolton 1956: 26–71.
3 Lowde is replying to Parker 1666.
4 Note that "co-existence" is sometimes taken to refer not only, e.g., to the universal concomitance of the properties of gold in general (about which, we shall see, we have little knowledge), but also to the coinstantiation of those of a particular piece of gold at a particular time (about which, Locke says [E IV.xii.9: 644], we do have "certain," presumably "sensitive" [E IV.iii.29: 560], knowledge).
5 See, e.g., Aronson and Lewis 1970: 195–97 and Chapter 5 of this volume. For further references, see Woolhouse 1983: 122–24.
6 Locke's attack on various parts of this doctrine can be found throughout

the *Essay* – see Woolhouse 1983: 65–80. His rejection of innate knowledge can be seen as a facet of it, for, though diverging from Aristotle in this respect, some seventeenth-century defenders of *scientia* thought of "maxims" or "speculative principles" as being innate.

7 Locke's philosophy of religion

John Locke's philosophy of religion is one of the great creative achievements in the history of philosophy of religion in the West. It has also proved powerfully influential; at least until recently, probably most modern Western intellectuals have thought about the interconnections among reason, responsibility, and religious conviction along Lockean lines. It should immediately be added, however, that in his day Locke was by no means alone in thinking about these matters as he did; genius though he was, Locke was not a *solitary* genius. The truth is that Locke articulated better than anyone else a philosophical way of thinking about religion that was gaining currency around the end of the seventeenth and the beginning of the eighteenth century in northwest Europe.

Locke's philosophy of religion was almost entirely an *epistemology* of religious knowledge and belief; and in this epistemology of religion he regularly distinguished between *natural* religion and *revealed* religion – Christianity being of course the "revealed religion" on which he mainly reflected. The distinction between natural and revealed religion was current in Locke's day among those who wrote and spoke about religion; no doubt the distinction should be seen as a descendant of the distinction between the *preambles* of faith and the *articles* of faith found in medieval philosophers such as Aquinas. But why the concentration on epistemology? Because, apart from his political philosophy, Locke's general philosophical reflections were oriented almost entirely around two questions: (1) what is the scope of human knowledge? and (2) how ought we to govern our assent when we lack knowledge? In turn, the fact that Locke's philosophical thoughts were focused almost entirely on politics and on epistemology reflects the social and cultural situation of his day.

Locke was an engaged philosopher. Let me speak about the conditions leading to the epistemological side of his reflections.

For hundreds of years Western intellectuals had thought of the body of texts bequeathed to them by "pagans," Jews, Christians, and Muslims, as presenting, for the most part, a highly articulated, unified, body of wisdom. Exceptions had to be made; there were heresies and other sorts of mistakes. But it was widely believed that once these not-very-substantial points of error had been excised, then whatever disagreements there appeared to be would fade away and a richly articulated body of truth would be revealed if one used the appropriate strategies of interpretation and made the right distinctions. Saint Paul and Virgil, Aristotle and Augustine, would all be seen to fit together. And if at some point in one's life one found oneself in a quandary as to what to believe on some matter of ethics or religion, or even cosmology, the best recourse was to consult this venerable tradition and let oneself be guided by its articulate wisdom. Many medieval philosophers also held that a dialectical appropriation of this tradition was the best preparation for engaging in that highest of intellectual activities, the practice of *scientia*.

By Locke's time and in Locke's situation, in the latter half of the seventeenth century in England and Holland, this view of the textual tradition had become thoroughly implausible and was generally rejected. Hardly anyone supposed that what Protestants in their various sects were saying all fitted together into some larger unity, let alone that what Protestants were saying fitted together with what Catholics were saying. And even the view that the pre-Reformation Christian tradition was a unified body of truth had become increasingly hard to defend in the face of humanist ways of reading texts and the Lutheran-Calvinist assault on the papacy.

But if in situations of quandary one can no longer consult the wisdom of a unified tradition, then obviously on the cultural agenda there is the question, how do we go about deciding what to believe; how do we conduct our understanding? And if one's culture presents one repeatedly with questions that are debated intensely without any agreed resolution turning up, then the suggestion is likely to arise that there is something misconceived about these questions. One possibility is that these questions are dealing with matters beyond the limits of human knowledge and adjudication. These were exactly Locke's questions: are there limits to human knowledge; if so, what are those limits; and how is one to conduct one's understanding when one deals with matters beyond the limits? In his "Epistle to the Reader" at the beginning of the *Essay concerning Human Understanding* Locke says that

Were it fit to trouble thee with the history of this essay, I should tell thee that five or six friends meeting at my chamber, and discoursing on a subject very remote from this, found themselves quickly at a stand, by the difficulties that rose on every side. After we had a while puzzled our selves, without coming any nearer a resolution of those doubts which perplexed us, it came into my thoughts, that we took a wrong course; and that, before we set our selves upon enquiries of that nature, it was necessary to examine our own abilities, and see, what objects our understandings were, or were not fitted to deal with. This, I proposed to the company, who all readily assented; and thereupon it was agreed, that this should be our first enquiry. (E Epis: 7)

We know, from a notation in the hand of Tyrrell, that it was on matters of morality and revealed religion that the friends were discoursing (Cranston 1957: 140–41). Locke's incessant insistence on the inadequacies of tradition leave one with little doubt that he perceived himself as philosophizing in a situation of cultural and social crisis; he set out to address himself to that crisis.

It would be appropriate to ask which part of Locke's thought, in the preceding comments, I am denominating his "philosophy of religion"? For a striking feature of Locke's thought is that religious considerations enter into all parts of his thought; Locke's philosophy as a whole bids fair to be called a Christian philosophy (Ashcraft 1969). It is artificial to isolate part of his thought as his philosophy of religion. Worse, it is misleading to do so. Our common practice of treating the seventeenth- and eighteenth-century European philosophers as if they were secular philosophers does most of them a very ill turn.

But we must set limits here; our project is not to discuss the whole of Locke's philosophy. Thus I shall concentrate on that part of Locke's thought that we would nowadays tend to call his "philosophy of religion" – without on this occasion probing into the propriety of this tendency of ours. I shall not talk about what we would nowadays call his theology. Neither will I talk about what he has to say on the topic of religious toleration. I will not even talk about what he says on the topic of moral theory, though here what he says is so tightly interwoven with religious considerations as to make any attempt at separation futile (see Colman 1983). I will focus just on what he says when he is talking *about* natural and revealed religion – and within this, on those passages in which he is, *by our lights,* talking about religion *qua* philosopher rather than *qua* theologian.

The notion that science, art, religion, politics, personal relations, and the like have each their own peculiar modes of knowing and each their own peculiar grounds for entitled belief, so that each requires its own particular and peculiar epistemology, was not part of Locke's way of thinking. Knowledge for him was one thing, no matter what it was knowledge of; and the grounds of entitlement were everywhere of the same sort. Locke's epistemology of religious knowledge and belief was thus, self-consciously, an application to the particular area of religion of his general epistemology. To understand his philosophy of religion we must, then, begin with that general epistemology. I shall have to be brief and brisk, lest we have no time left for the application.

Fundamental in Locke's epistemology was his distinction between *knowledge* and *assent (belief)*. We are confronted, however, with a difference between the official and visionary way in which Locke makes the distinction and his unofficial qualified way. In the course of his discussion Locke found himself forced to concede that his official way of making the distinction was not satisfactory. Yet the official way remains in the text; Locke did not blot it out and confine it to preliminary notebooks. I think we must conclude that a certain elegant and powerful picture of knowledge and entitled belief never ceased to work its spell on Locke's mind – this in spite of the fact that, when immersed in the attempt to work out the details, he conceded that it would not do. Here, as in many places in Locke, to understand the pattern of his philosophy one must discern both the vision and the qualifications; to lose sight of either is to miss a fundamental dimension of his thinking. Of course we could join forces with that large body of Locke commentators who dwell on Locke's inconsistencies. But to do that and stop there, not to see the pattern of vision presented and vision undercut, is to be oblivious to both sides of Locke's genius. Locke was both philosophical visionary and philosophical craftsman. What he never managed to do was bring these two sides of his genius together.

On the official doctrine, knowledge and assent are fundamentally different phenomena. Locke held, indeed, that assent always accompanies knowledge; but he denied what has become a fundamental tenet of epistemology in our own day, namely, that knowledge is a *species* of assent. Assent or belief, says Locke, is *taking* some proposition to be true, whereas knowledge is *seeing* it to be true. To know is to be directly acquainted with some fact, to be immediately aware of it, to perceive it; or, to put the point from the other side, knowledge occurs when some fact is presented directly to the mind.

The question arises, of what sorts of facts can we human beings be directly aware; what is the potential scope of knowledge? Here too we have to distinguish between Locke's official and his unofficial answer. His official answer was that we can have knowledge only of what nowadays (after Kant) we would call *conceptual truths.* Hence the famous opening of Book IV of the *Essay:* Knowledge is *"nothing but the perception of the connexion and agreement, or disagreement and repugnancy of any of our Ideas.* In this alone it consists. Where this Perception is, there is Knowledge, and where it is not, there, though we may fancy, guess, or believe, yet we always come short of Knowledge" (E IV.i.2: 525).

This, I say, is Locke's official doctrine as to the scope of insight. In the course of his discussion we find him conceding that insight goes beyond these narrow boundaries. We find him conceding that often we "see" that we are engaging in such-and-such a mental act and having such-and-such an idea – where "idea" now denotes not just what we would nowadays call concepts but mental objects in general. We also find him conceding that often we "see" various nonnecessary relationships among our ideas and mental acts. And we find him conceding that we each "see" that we ourselves exist. Beyond this, though, there is no insight. One has insight only into the existence of one's mind, into one's having of ideas and one's performing of mental acts, and into the interrelationships of these. The representatives of that long tradition, articulated powerfully already by Plato, which held that we have insight into a whole realm of necessity existing independently of us, would feel themselves profoundly claustrophobic if they thought and imagined their way into Locke's picture.

Knowledge is awareness of some fact; belief or assent, by contrast, is taking something to be a fact. That is Locke's official doctrine. Now for the unofficial. Locke held that knowledge is *certain*; and he held that certainty is a gamut on a continuum whose other gamut, on the positive end of the continuum, is probability. What is this continuum a continuum *of*? That is to say, what entities bear the property of having a particular degree of certainty or probability? For probability the answer is clear: it is believings and assentings that are more or less probable. And what about certainty? Well, Locke speaks about certainty as adjoining probability on the continuum; and he not infrequently speaks of assent as accompanying insight. The obvious suggestion is that the continuum is of *assentings* and *believings*. But if this suggestion is correct, then, since Locke identifies one's knowing P with P's being certain for one, it follows that knowledge is a species of assent.

So far this is a significant, though not destructive, revision of Locke's official doctrine of knowledge. Given that Locke regards insight as always accompanied by assent that is certain, then, though his officially stated preference is to speak only of insight as knowledge, an implication of his ascription of certitude to knowledge is that it is the accompanying *assent* that is knowledge. But this is not the end of the matter. Certitude acquires a life of its own. In the details of this discussion Locke cites cases of assent that, though certain, are not the accompaniment of insight. This undercuts the suggestion he makes here and there that insight is what accounts for certainty. But worse: such cases confront him with an unwelcome choice. Will he maintain his identification of knowledge with insight, and concede that assent may be certain without being the accompaniment of knowledge; or will he maintain his claim that a hallmark of knowledge is certitude, and grant that some cases of assent are cases of knowledge even though they are not the accompaniment of insight? Will he conclude that certainty outstrips knowledge, or that knowledge outstrips insight?

It's clear how he chooses: knowledge outstrips insight. That this is how he chooses is clearest in his discussion of memory. Locke holds that some of our rememberings constitute knowledge. For

example, some, though not all, ways of remembering a fact one once
perceived are such that examples count as one's knowledge of that
fact, even though one is not then perceiving that fact. Indeed, Locke
himself calls such knowledge "habitual" knowledge in the course
of distinguishing it from the "actual" knowledge that fits his official
formula. Once Locke has made this concession, then it is open to
him to say, as he does, that we not only have immediate knowledge
of facts but also *demonstrative* knowledge – this latter (typically)
involving a blend of present and remembered insight (cf. E IV.ii.7:
533–34). And this in turn makes it possible for him to hold that
examples of certain ways of remembering what one once demonstrated, not only of what one once perceived immediately, are examples of knowledge.

Locke never explores the implications of this concession; that reflects, so it seems to me, the reluctance with which he makes it.
What never ceased to shape Locke's thought were the visionary convictions that at certain points we human beings have direct insight
into the facts of reality and that all belief and assent which is not
the direct accompaniment of such insight ought to be *based on* such
points of insight. The qualifications he introduced not only refine
but undercut this vision; yet he never surrenders it.

But whether knowledge be identified with insight, or with assent
that is certain, it was clear to Locke that for life it is indispensable
that we *take* certain things to be true without seeing, or even being
certain, that they *are* true. The workings of our assent- and belief-
forming faculties must, however, be governed. We are not to let
them do their work without supervision and direction. We are to in-
tervene.

Why is that? Because there is a certain goal with respect to our
assentings and believings that we ought each to try our best to
achieve; and if we allow our assent- and belief-forming faculties to
work ungoverned, we will not be trying our best. What is that goal?
Unfortunately Locke never presents a clear and decisive formulation. It has to do with that merit in believing which consists of the
believed proposition being true, and that demerit which consists of
the believed proposition being false. But many alternative views are
possible as to what might be our obligation with respect to this
merit and this demerit; and such phrases as Locke is fond of, as for
example that we are to search for truth for truth's sake, or that we

are to keep away from mistake and error, scarcely sort out the alternatives. One thinks here of the contemporary epistemologist Roderick Chisholm, who also holds that each of us, just by virtue of being an intellectual being capable of believing and withholding belief from propositions, has a certain obligation. In his *Foundations of Knowing* Chisholm formulates this obligation as "the general requirement to try to have the largest possible set of logically independent beliefs that is such that the true beliefs outnumber the false beliefs" (Chisholm 1982: 7). In his earlier *Theory of Knowledge* he suggested that the requirement is that of each person "trying his best to bring it about that for any proposition *h* he considers, he accepts *h* if and only if *h* is true" (Chisholm 1977: 14).

It is my guess – I call it a "guess" because I cannot cite decisive textual evidence – that Locke, if confronted with this option and others similar, would choose the latter of Chisholm's two proposals. With one very significant exception, however: Locke did not think that one has this obligation with respect to *all* propositions that one considers. So let us adapt Chisholm's suggestion and say that someone has *the alethic obligation* with respect to a certain proposition P at a certain time just in case that person is obligated at that time to try his or her best to bring it about that he or she accepts P if and only if P is true.

The question we face then is this: what will one try to do if one tries one's best; how ought one to conduct one's understanding? It was to this question of *regulative epistemology* that Locke addressed himself in the second main part of book IV of the *Essay* – from Chapter xiv to the end. The best summary of what he wishes to say occurs when he begins to discuss the relation of faith and reason – faith being for him a species of assent:

Faith is nothing but a firm Assent of the Mind: which if it be regulated, as is our Duty, cannot be afforded to any thing, but upon good Reason; and so cannot be opposite to it. He that believes, without having any Reason for believing, may be in love with his own Fancies; but neither seeks Truth as he ought, nor pays the Obedience due to his Maker, who would have him use those discerning Faculties he has given him, to keep him out of Mistake and Errour. He that does not this to the best of his Power, however he sometimes lights on Truth, is in the right but by chance; and I know not whether the luckiness of the Accident will excuse the irregularity of his proceeding. This at least is certain, that he must be accountable for whatever Mistakes he runs into: whereas he that makes use of the Light and Faculties God has given him, and seeks sincerely to discover Truth, by those Helps and Abilities he has, may have this satisfaction in doing his Duty as a rational Creature, that though he should miss Truth, he will not miss the Reward of it. For he governs his Assent right, and places it as he should, who in any Case or Matter whatsoever, believes or disbelieves, according as Reason directs him. He that does otherwise, transgresses against his own Light, and misuses those Faculties, which were given him to no other end, but to search and follow the clearer Evidence, and greater Probability. (E IV.xvii.24: 687–88)

Before I attempt to unpack what Locke is saying here, a word should be said about his interpretation of *obligation*, since his doctrine on this point may with reason be regarded as part of his philosophy of religion. "Amongst the simple *Ideas*, which we receive both from *Sensation* and *Reflection*, *Pain* and *Pleasure* are two very considerable ones," says Locke (E II.xx.1: 229). And he goes on to say that things "are Good or Evil, only in reference to Pleasure or Pain. That we call *Good*, which *is apt to cause or increase Pleasure, or diminish Pain in us; or else to procure, or preserve us the possession of any other Good, or absence of any Evil.* And on the contrary we name that *Evil*, which *is apt to produce or increase any Pain or diminish any Pleasure in us; or else to procure us any Evil, or deprive us of any Good*" (E II.xx.2: 229). Locke's subsequent discussion makes clear that the words "pain" and "pleasure" are misleading as names for the phenomena he has in mind. Locke, I suggest, is taking note of the fundamental fact that much of our experience is phenomenally "charged": some of what we experience we like, some we dislike. That this is different from the pleasure-pain contrast is easily seen by observing, for example, that persons sometimes like pain. Locke himself says that "By *Pleasure* and *Pain* . . . I must all along be understood . . . to mean, not only bodily Pain and Pleasure, but whatsoever *Delight* or *Uneasiness* is felt by us, whether arising from any grateful, or unacceptable Sensation or Reflection" (E II.xx.15: 232).

Good and evil, thus understood, enter crucially into Locke's explication of the nature of morality. The morality of a voluntary action, such actions constituting the scope of morality, is determined by its conformity or lack of conformity to a certain kind of rule – namely, to a rule that is a law (E II.xxviii.4–5: 350–51). A rule for voluntary action is a law if someone who wills that that rule be followed has the power to attach, and does attach, rewards and punishments – that is, good and evil – to the observance or breach of the rule. *"Morally Good and Evil* then, is only the Conformity or Disagreement of our voluntary Actions to some Law, whereby Good or Evil is drawn on us, from the Will and Power of the Law-maker; which Good and Evil, Pleasure or Pain, attending our observance, or breach of the Law, by the Decree of the Law-maker, is that we call *Reward* and *Punishment"* (E II.xxviii.5: 351). "What Duty is, cannot be understood without a Law; nor a Law be known, or supposed without a Law-maker, or without Reward and Punishment" (E I.iii.12: 74).

Locke went on to distinguish three sorts of moral rules, or laws: "1. The *Divine* Law. 2. The *Civil* Law. 3. The Law of *Opinion* or *Reputation,* if I may so call it. By the Relation they bear to the first of these, Men judge whether their Actions are Sins, or Duties; by the second, whether they be Criminal, or Innocent; and by the third, whether they be Vertues or Vices" (E II.xxviii.7: 352). It is when we are confronted with the divine law that we are in the domain, not just of morality, but of moral *obligation.*

And what is divine law? Divine law is "that Law which God has set to the actions of Men, whether promulgated to them by the light of Nature, or the voice of Revelation" (E II.xxviii.8: 352). Locke had no doubt whatsoever that there is a law that is divine. "That God has given a Rule whereby Men should govern themselves, I think there is no body so brutish as to deny," he says. God "has a right to do it, we are his Creatures: He has Goodness and Wisdom to direct our Actions to that which is best: and he has Power to enforce it by Rewards and Punishments, of infinite weight and duration, in another Life: for no body can take us out of his hands." Locke then once again emphasizes his main point: "This is the only true touchstone of *moral Rectitude;* and by comparing them to this Law, it is, that Men judge of the most considerable *Moral Good* or *Evil* of their Actions; that is, whether as *Duties, or Sins,* they are like to procure them happiness, or misery, from the hands of the ALMIGHTY" (ibid.).

Locke never defends his view that we each have what I have called "the alethic obligation" with respect to various propositions. That is to say, he never defends his view that for each of us there are certain propositions such that God will reward us if we try our best to bring it about that we believe them if and only if they are true, and will punish us if we do not. It is, though, to this view that he is alluding when, in the passage quoted from E IV.xvii.24, he says that the person who seeks sincerely to discover truth, though he may miss it, "will not miss the Reward of it."

Once again, then: what does one do so as to carry out one's alethic obligations? I shall present Locke's answer in the form of four principles. The first is this:

Principle of Immediate Belief: One is to believe something immediately only if it is certain for one – that is, only if one knows it.

Often Locke will say that we are to believe something immediately only if we *perceive* it. But as we have seen, he finds himself forced to move away from that preferred position.

The remaining principles for *trying one's best* pertain to *mediate* assent to propositions. Locke himself singled out for special attention those cases of mediate assent to some proposition which are such that one knows the proposition demonstratively. The principle is that if one knows that some proposition is entailed by something that one knows immediately, then one is entitled to believe that proposition with near maximal firmness. In fact, however, this principle is entailed by Locke's principles for mediate belief generally; accordingly I shall not single it out for special attention.

As Locke never tired of emphasizing, for most of the propositions that come our way it is impossible to *know* whether or not they are true. So what does trying one's best require, with respect to mediate belief, when so far as one can see the proposition in question is not entailed by what one knows? The passage in which Locke gives the best brief statement of most elements of his view is this:

the Mind if it will proceed rationally, ought to examine all the grounds of Probability, and see how they make more or less, for or against any probable Proposition, before it assents to or dissents from it, and upon a due balancing the whole, reject, or receive it, with a more or less firm assent, proportionably to the preponderancy of the greater grounds of Probability on one side or the other. (E IV.xv.5: 656)

Doing one's best with respect to some proposition that one does not know immediately requires proportioning the firmness of one's assent to the proposition to the probability of that proposition on evidence. So it is with evidence that one must begin. Clearly Locke does not think that we may proceed with whatever evidence we just happen to have. The evidence must be of a quality that makes it satisfactory. And the evidence must consist of things one knows. Belief is to be based on knowledge, on certitude: ideally, on insight. Otherwise it dangles loose and we drift about; or to change the metaphor, otherwise we wander in darkness. Locke's "principle of evidence," as we may call it, can then be formulated as follows:

Principle of Evidence: One is not to believe something mediately until one has acquired evidence for it such that each item of evidence is something that one knows and such that the totality of one's evidence is satisfactory.

Locke thinks of collecting satisfactory evidence as often an imposing and daunting task, requiring considerable expenditure of time and energy. It is for this reason that we each have the alethic responsibility with respect to only a relatively small proportion of the propositions that come our way. For most of the propositions that come our way, we neither can nor should try our best to bring it about that we believe them if and only if they are true. Indeed, we are often *obligated not to try our best.* To try our best would require flouting other more weighty obligations. Nonetheless it was Locke's view that "no Man is so wholly taken up with the Attendance on the Means of Living, as to have no spare Time at all to think of his Soul, and inform himself in Matters of Religion" (E IV.xx.3: 708). Every person has the alethic obligation concerning moral and religious matters, and those immediately practical matters which most concern him or her. For these are of most importance to the person; and everyone, no matter how much a "beast of burden" he or she may be, has time to "try one's best" for these. Locke makes it clear that the alethic obligation is much more expansive in its scope if one is a member of the leisured class than of the working class.

What does trying one's best require once satisfactory evidence is in hand? It requires determining the probability of the proposition in question on that evidence. Let us call this requirement, the "principle of appraisal." It may be formulated as follows:

Principle of Appraisal: One is not to believe some proposition mediately until, having satisfactory evidence, one has examined that evidence to determine its logical force and one has "seen" what, on that evidence, is the probability of the proposition.

Locke thinks of probability in frequency terms; or, more cautiously, in some passages he is clearly thinking of probability in frequency terms and in no passage is it clear that he is thinking of it in another way. He regarded the evidence for determinations of probability as in general of two sorts: observations we ourselves have made concerning the frequency of some property or event in some "population"; and testimony concerning such frequency. Before an item of testimony is accepted it must itself be appraised for the probability of its being true. In such appraisal one must consider "1. The Number. 2. The Integrity. 3. The Skill of the Witnesses. 4. The Design of the Author, where it is a Testimony out of a Book cited. 5. The Consistency of the Parts, and Circumstances of the Relation. 6. Contrary Testimonies" (E IV.xv.4: 656).

Once one has determined the probability, on satisfactory evidence, of the proposition in question, then one is ready to apply the last principle – call it the "principle of proportionality":

Principle of Proportionality: Having determined the probability, on one's satisfactory evidence, of the proposition in question, one ought to adopt a level of confidence in it which is proportioned to its probability, on that evidence.

Where is reason in all this? Over and over Locke says that in the governance of our beliefs we are to let reason be our guide – or in another metaphor, to listen to the voice of reason. In fact reason is right before us, though without having been mentioned. Locke takes reason to be a faculty, a faculty yielding insight; more specifically, the faculty yielding insight into the logical relations among propositions – understanding a proposition's having such-and-such a probability on a certain body of evidence as a logical relation between the proposition and that evidence. For Locke to say that we are to let reason be our guide in the governance of our assent is thus to say that in such governance we are to make use of the deliverances of our faculty for insight into the entailment and probability relations among propositions. Of course he presupposes that we are to do so in the way specified in the principles of evidence, appraisal, and proportionality.

We are ready now to consider how Locke applied this general epistemology – a descriptive epistemology concerning the nature of knowledge and a regulative epistemology concerning the governance of belief – to religious knowledge and religious belief. It is perhaps important to say here at the outset that in his beliefs Locke was a thoroughly religious person of latitudinarian Anglican conviction. That God calls us to obedience remained central in Locke's framework of conviction. It is indeed fairly clear that in his theological views Locke was a Socinian (unitarian) for the last decade and a half of his life. In his late book, *The Reasonableness of Christianity*, he was entirely silent about Christological and Trinitarian matters, arguing merely that the teaching of the Gospels is that Jesus was the Messiah; when this pattern of argument led to suspicion, he confined himself to insisting that he had nowhere affirmed Socinianism. But this unorthodoxy concerning the Trinity by no means led to indifference concerning Christianity and its Scriptures. The *Reasonableness* is informed by a close and perceptive reading of the Gospels, just as his later paraphrases of some of the letters of Saint Paul are informed by a close and perceptive reading of those parts of the New Testament; and though the moral content of the New Testament loomed very large for him, Locke never ceased to regard Christianity as a message of salvation. It may be added that his turn to close scriptural exegesis and exposition in his last decade was a consequence of his growing conviction that a true *scientia* of morality, though in principle possible, was in fact nowhere in view. To know God's full will for us we must, de facto, turn to the New Testament. (For easily the finest discussion of Locke's personal religion and theology, see Marshall 1990.)

Locke held that certain conceptual truths involving the concept of God can be known *immediately* – for example, that God would offer to us for our believing on God's say-so only what is true. But concerning any proposition that entails the existence of God, Locke was what has been called an *evidentialist*. Let me explain.

Evidentialism comes in many forms, at the heart of all forms being the notion of *satisfactory evidence being required* – with evidence understood as consisting of *propositions* which are *known*, or at least *believed*. (There are phenomena with good title to being called "evidence" other than believed propositions; for example, one's evidence for one's belief that one feels dizzy is one's feeling dizzy.) For one thing, there is a diversity of states or conditions for which, it may be claimed, satisfactory evidence is required: the state of being *entitled* to believe something, the state of being *warranted* in believing something, the state of *knowing* something, and so forth. Second, it will be for propositions *of certain sorts* that satisfactory evidence, so it is claimed, is required: for propositions concerning physical objects, for propositions entailing the existence of God, or whatever. Third, the claim will be that the evidence must be related to the state or condition in a certain way: to be entitled to believe P one must *have* satisfactory evidence for P, or one must believe P *on the basis of* satisfactory evidence, and so forth. Obviously there will also be a diversity of views as to what makes evidence *satisfactory*.

Locke was an evidentialist concerning all propositions that entail the existence of God – call these "theistic propositions." His claim was that satisfactory evidence is required both for knowing any such proposition and for being entitled to assent to any such proposition. And pretty clearly he assumed that either to know or be entitled to believe any such proposition, one must not merely *have* satisfactory evidence but must know or believe the proposition *on the basis of* satisfactory evidence.

Locke's particular form of evidentialism concerning theistic propositions followed straightforwardly from his general foundationalist epistemology, plus his contention that everybody has the alethic obligation with respect to such propositions. Everybody has the time, on Sundays if on no other day, to collect satisfactory evidence for such propositions and to appraise the logical force of that evidence; and the great importance of such propositions for one's temporal and eternal welfare has the consequence that one's obligation to apply the principles of evidence, appraisal, and proportionality is not defeasible.

It was Locke's doctrine, let us recall, that the only facts we can directly "perceive" are facts concerning the mind's existence and its modifications. Likewise it was his doctrine that beyond the assent or belief accompanying such "perception," the only immediate beliefs that are certain are memory beliefs concerning what one did perceive. God is never directly present to the mind; that assumption is fundamental to Locke's epistemology of religion. One's *idea*, one's concept, of God is directly present to the mind; but not God. The sacramental view, that at least some of us human beings at some points in our lives experience God, was not an assumption Locke made. If asked about it, he would firmly have rejected it. And not only are we not directly presented with any fact of which God is a constituent; no immediate assent to any such fact is certain. Of course Locke also assumed that none of us is directly acquainted with another human being, or with a physical object; and that no assent to a fact of which such an entity is a constituent is certain. Only the mind and its acts and objects are directly present to the mind; and the only cases of immediate assent that are certain are those which accompany one's perception of facts consisting of the existence and interrelationship of such entities, plus one's memory of having perceived such facts. Insofar as we know or are entitled to believe anything else, that knowledge or entitlement comes by way of inference from such facts, and requires that the absent thing be "represented" by some "idea." To believe a theistic proposition immediately, or to believe it on the basis of less than satisfactory evidence, is to act irresponsibly, to flout one's God-given obligations.

Though immediate knowledge of theistic propositions is unavailable to us human beings, Locke did not think that religion is all belief, no knowledge. Quite to the contrary: he held that a good deal of natural theology can be known by demonstration. What can be demonstrated is that there is an eternal, most powerful, and most knowing being – which, "whether any one will please to call *God*, it matters not" (E IV.x.6: 621); and "from this *Idea* duly considered, will easily be deduced all those other Attributes, which we ought to ascribe to this eternal Being" (ibid.).

Though the demonstration of God's existence "requires Thought and Attention," and though "the Mind must apply it self to a regular deduction of it from some part of our intuitive Knowledge, or else we shall be as uncertain, and ignorant of this, as of other Propositions, which are in themselves capable of clear Demonstration" (E IV.x.1: 619), nonetheless the demonstration is pretty obvious, Locke thinks. It is in fact "the most obvious Truth that Reason discovers" (ibid.), so that we cannot "justly complain of our Ignorance in this great Point, since [God] has so plentifully provided us with the means to discover, and know him, so far as is necessary to the end of our Being, and the great concernment of our Happiness" (ibid.). "The Thing is evident," Locke says (E IV.x.6: 621). Elsewhere he says that "'tis as certain, that there is a God, as that the opposite Angles, made by the intersection of two straight Lines, are equal" (E I.iv.16: 94–95), adding that "there was never any rational

Creature, that set himself sincerely to examine the truth of these Propositions, that could fail to assent to them."

Locke acknowledges that not all persons have in fact set themselves sincerely to examine the argument in question. Yet the thought that a whole *people* would lack knowledge of God's existence is to him incredible: "the visible marks of extraordinary Wisdom and Power, appear so plainly in all the Works of the Creation, that a rational Creature, who will but seriously reflect on them, cannot miss the discovery of a *Deity* . . . it seems stranger to me, that a whole Nation of Men should be any where found so brutish, as to want the Notion of a God; than that they should be without any Notion of Numbers, or Fire" (E I.iv.9: 89).

The demonstration Locke has in mind opens, for each person, with one's "*clear Perception of [one's] own Being*" (E IV.x.2: 619). Next,

Man knows by an intuitive Certainty, that bare *nothing can no more produce any real Being, than it can be equal to two right Angles*. . . . If therefore we know there is some real Being, and that Non-entity cannot produce any real Being, it is an evident demonstration, that from Eternity there has been something; since what was not from Eternity, had a Beginning; and what had a Beginning, must be produced by something else. (E IV.x.3: 620)

What remains to be established is that this eternal being is most powerful and most knowing. "It is evident," says Locke, "that what had its Being and Beginning from another, must also have all that which is in, and belongs to its Being from another too. All the Powers it has, must be owing to, and received from the same Source. This eternal Source then of all being must also be the Source and Original of all Power; and so *this eternal Being must be also the most powerful*" (ibid.). Let it be noted that what Locke purports to have proved is just that there is an eternal being more powerful than any other being – not an eternal being such that no more powerful being can be conceived, nor such that no being more powerful is possible.

Similarly, this being is most knowledgeable – not the most knowledgeable possible, nor the most knowledgeable conceivable, just more knowledgeable than any other. "A man finds in himself perception, and knowledge," says Locke. So there was a time then, when there was no knowing Being, and when Knowledge began to be; or else, there has been also *a knowing Being from Eternity.* If it be said, there was a time when no Being had any Knowledge, when that eternal Being was void of all Understanding. I reply, that then it was impossible there should ever have been any Knowledge. It being as impossible, that Things wholly void of Knowledge, and operating blindly, and without any Perception, should produce a knowing Being, as it is impossible, that a Triangle should make it self three Angles bigger than two right ones. For it is as repugnant to the *Idea* of senseless Matter, that it should put into it self Sense, Perception, and Knowledge, as it is repugnant to the *Idea* of a Triangle, that it should put into it self greater Angles than two right ones. (E IV.x.5: 620–21)

And so, says Locke, "from the Consideration of our selves, and what we infallibly find in our own Constitutions, our Reason leads us to the Knowledge of this certain and evident Truth, that *there is an eternal, most powerful, and most knowing Being*" (E IV.x.6: 621). The existence of God is a condition of one's own existence.

When compared to other variants, and formulations of variants, of the cosmological argument for God's existence, this is surely among the weakest, making use at several points of premises whose questionableness Locke's subsequent discussion does nothing to eliminate, and making moves that are either fallacious or dependent upon unstated and dubious premises. However, I do not think it worthwhile to lay out the argument in detail and to appraise its various elements. Better to move on to Locke's epistemology of revealed religion. To do so is to enter Locke's discussion of faith and reason.

Locke stands in that long line of Christian reflection according to which *faith* is understood as the correlate of *revelation.* "Faith . . . is the assent to any Proposition . . . upon the Credit of the Proposer, as coming from GOD in some extraordinary way of Communication. This way of discovering Truths to Men we call *Revelation*" (E IV.xviii.2: 689). For Locke, the decisive consideration establishing that faith, thus understood, is not knowledge is that faith lacks the certitude requisite to knowledge. In his letter to Stillingfleet, the bishop of Worcester, he says that "the certainty of faith, if your lordship thinks fit to call it so, has nothing to do with the certainty of knowledge. And to talk of the certainty of faith, seems all one to me, as to talk of the knowledge of believing; a way of speaking not easy to me to understand" (W IV: 146). Locke does speak in the same passage of "the assurance of faith," and he says, of his assent to an article of the faith, that "I steadfastly venture my all upon it" (ibid.). But whatever he may have meant by that, he insists that "Faith stands . . . upon grounds of its own," different from those of knowledge. "Their grounds are so far from being the same, or having anything common, that when it is brought to certainty, faith is destroyed; it is knowledge then, and faith no longer" (ibid.).

We must thus make a threefold distinction in how human beings hold theistic beliefs. Sometimes they are held just as matters of *opinion* on the basis of tradition or whatever. Sometimes they are held in such a way as to constitute that special form of opinion which is *faith*. And then, third, as we have seen, quite a bit about God can be *known* – though only demonstratively, not immediately.

Faith is not a mode of knowledge. It consists in believing things on the basis of one's belief that they have been revealed by God rather than on the basis of the premises of some demonstration – it being assumed that there is no proposition such that it can be *demonstrated* that God has revealed that proposition. Let us be clear that it is not the proposition *that God has revealed P* which is the object of faith (unless one believes it to have been revealed that P has been revealed – see E IV.xviii.6: 693). Rather it is P itself, the proposition one believes to have been revealed by God, that is the object of faith. It is important to realize that even though faith is not and cannot be a species of knowledge, nonetheless Locke assumed that the same proposition may be held by faith and by reason – and also by a form of opinion which is not faith. I surmise, however – I do not find him explicit on the point – that Locke would agree with Aquinas that a given person cannot at a given time both believe something on the basis of a demonstration and believe it on the basis of revelation. Reason overcomes faith.

We must distinguish two types of revelation. In *original revelation* an impression "is made immediately by GOD, on the Mind of" the person (E IV.xviii.3: 690). *Traditional revelation*, by contrast, occurs when someone communicates to another what has been originally revealed to himself or someone else. Faith in response to this latter type of revelation consists of accepting as revealed by God what that person communicates as having been (originally) revealed to someone.

We can be certain that whatever God reveals is true. This we know immediately. "Whatever GOD hath revealed, is certainly true," says Locke, "no Doubt can be made of it" (E IV.xviii.10: 695). Locke never considers the possibility that God might offer to us for our belief things that are not strictly speaking true but will serve to direct our feet on the paths of life. He just takes it as necessarily true that if God reveals P, then P is true. But that God did in fact reveal something on some occasion cannot be known, nor can it be known what he revealed. About such matters only belief, not knowledge, is possible. At three points in E IV.xviii.4–5 Locke does speak of us as *knowing* that God revealed something. But I think we must regard these as slips of the pen on his part. They conflict with his repeated and emphatic insistence that the certainty required for knowledge is lacking in these cases. Further, if we *were* sometimes certain that God had revealed P, then, given that we are also certain that if God revealed P, P is true, it also seems to be the case that we would be, or could be, certain *that P*. But then that would no longer be a case of faith – for definitive of faith, as we have seen, is that it *lacks* certitude. We can be certain neither that an occurrence of revelation has occurred nor that we have correctly interpreted the content of some purported occurrence of revelation. The belief that God revealed P always lacks for us the certitude requisite for knowledge.

And just as we can never be certain *that God revealed P,* so assenting to P itself can never be certain for us when we accept P on the ground of its having been revealed by God. "For whatsoever Truth we come to the clear discovery of, from the Knowledge and Contemplation of our own *Ideas,* will always be certainer to us, than those which are conveyed to us by *Traditional Revelation.* For the Knowledge, we have, that this *Revelation* came at first from GOD, can never be so sure, as the Knowledge we have from the clear and distinct Perception of the Agreement, or Disagreement of our own *Ideas*" (E IV.xviii.4: 690–91). What Locke says here concerning traditional revelation, he meant for revelation in general.

In deciding whether to accept P, on the ground of its having been revealed by God, we must appraise the probability on satisfactory evidence of the proposition *that God has revealed P.* Only if, on such evidence, this is more probable than not, are we entitled to believe P itself – unless, of course, we have independent reason for accepting P. Locke makes clear that he is not insisting that we need evidence in favor of P itself – in favor of the content of the purported revelation – to be entitled to accept it. Quite to the contrary; the very genius of revelation is that, by this means, God can present to us for our belief things that we would not be entitled to believe by the unaided use of our own faculties. What is required is not satisfactory evidence directly in favor of P but satisfactory evidence in favor of the proposition *that God has revealed P*. It may be added that, nevertheless, Locke's project in his own book, *The Reasonableness of Christianity*, was not to show that it is probable on satisfactory evidence that the New Testament records revelation from God, but to show that a great deal of the *content* of the revelation there recorded can be arrived at by reason – that is, can either be demonstrated or shown to be probably true.

Beliefs about the occurrence and interpretation of revelation are not, though, to be treated as totally independent of beliefs about content. If the purportedly revealed proposition P is one that (self-evidently) contradicts something of which one is intuitively certain, then one must reject the proposition *that God has revealed P*.

Since no evidence of our Faculties, by which we receive such *Revelations* can exceed, if equal, the certainty of our intuitive Knowledge, we can never receive for a Truth any thing, that is directly contrary to our clear and distinct Knowledge . . . *no Proposition can be received for Divine Revelation, or obtain the Assent due to all such, if it be contradictory to our clear intuitive Knowledge.* Because this would be to subvert the Principles, and Foundations of all Knowledge, Evidence, and Assent whatsoever. (E IV.xviii.5: 691–92)

What then about the case in which, though P is not self-evidently false, nonetheless on satisfactory evidence it is *impossible*, whereas the proposition *that God has revealed P* is probable on satisfactory evidence? Am I somehow to weigh up the strength of the evidence for the proposition *that God has revealed P* against the strength of the evidence against P itself and go with the stronger (remembering that to determine the former I must consider both the strength of the evidence for the proposition that I am confronted with an occurrence of revelation and the strength of the evidence for the proposition that I am correctly interpreting the content of that purported occurrence)? Though Locke is far from lucid on this matter, I think his answer is yes – as indeed in his system it should be. He says that "since GOD in giving us the light of *Reason* has not thereby tied up his own Hands from affording us, when he thinks fit, the light of *Revelation* in any of those Matters, wherein our natural Faculties are able to give a probable Determination, *Revelation*, where God has been pleased to give it, *must carry it, against the probable Conjectures of Reason*" (E IV.xviii.8: 694).

There is yet one more connection between content and presentation. Though Locke regularly speaks of the assurance of faith, this is to be a tempered assurance. The firmness with which we believe P is not to be in excess of that with which we are entitled to believe *that God has revealed P*. In the case of faith, "our Assent can be rationally no higher than the Evidence of its being a Revelation, and that this is the meaning of the Expressions it is delivered in. If the Evidence of its being a Revelation, or that this its true Sense be only on probable Proofs, our Assent can reach no higher than an Assurance or Diffidence, arising from the more, or less apparent Probability of the Proofs" (E IV.xvi.14: 667–68).

And what, finally, is Locke willing to accept as evidence for the occurrence of revelation? It was in dealing with this point that Locke inserted into the fourth edition of the *Essay* a vigorous, even biting, attack on the enthusiasts who "flatter'd themselves with a perswasion of an immediate intercourse with the Deity, and frequent communications from the divine Spirit" (E IV.xix.5: 699). Before we look at Locke's own positive view as to what would constitute satisfactory evidence for revelation, let us glance at how he conducts this attack on the enthusiasts.

He does not deny, indeed he affirms, that God can, and perhaps sometimes still does, "enlighten Mens Minds in the apprehending of certain Truths, or excite them to Good Actions by the immediate influence and assistance of the Holy Spirit" (E IV.xix.16: 705). "GOD . . . cannot be denied to be able to enlighten the Understanding by a Ray darted into the Mind immediately from the Fountain of Light" (E IV.xix.5: 699). But Locke was confident that in the case of the enthusiasts it was not God's enlightenment that accounted for their convictions but a disordered psyche, a "warmed or overweening Brain" (E IV.xix.7: 699). The people who succumb to enthusiasm are those "in whom Melancholy has mixed with Devotion," along with those "whose conceit of themselves has raised them into an Opinion of a greater familiarity with GOD, and a nearer admittance to his Favour than is afforded to others" (E IV.xix.5: 699). "Their Minds being thus prepared, whatever groundless Opinion comes to settle it self strongly upon their Fancies, is an Illumination from the Spirit of GOD, and presently of divine Authority: And whatsoever odd Action they find in themselves a strong Inclination to do, that impulse is concluded to be a call or direction from Heaven, and must be obeyed" (E IV.xix.6: 699).

Thus Locke charged the enthusiasts with irresponsibility. He repeats in vivid language his general point that if one is to believe responsibly that God revealed so-and-so on such-and-such occasion, one must believe in accord with the "dictates of Reason." And he assumes that the only alternative to his own view as to what we must do with the dictates of reason is a policy of "anything goes" – antinomianism in religious belief.

God when he makes the Prophet does not unmake the Man. He leaves all his Faculties in their natural State, to enable him to judge of his Inspirations, whether they be of divine Original or no. When he illuminates the Mind with supernatural Light, he does not extinguish that which is natural. If he would have us assent to the Truth of any Proposition, he either evidences that Truth by the usual Methods of natural Reason, or else makes it known to be a Truth, which he would have us assent to, by his Authority, and convinces us that it is from him, by some Marks which Reason cannot be mistaken in. *Reason* must be our last Judge and Guide in every Thing. I do not mean, that we must consult Reason, and examine whether a Proposition revealed from God can be made out by natural Principles, and if it cannot, that then we may reject it: But consult it we must, and by it examine, whether it be a *Revelation* from God or no: And if *Reason* finds it to be revealed from GOD, *Reason* then declares for it, as much as for any other Truth, and makes it one of her Dictates. Every Conceit that throughly warms our Fancies must pass for an Inspiration, if there be nothing but the Strength of our Perswasions, whereby to judge of our Perswasions: If *Reason* must not examine their Truth by something extrinsical to the Perswasions them selves; Inspirations and Delusions, Truth and Falshood will have the same Measure, and will not be possible to be distinguished. (E IV.xix.14: 704)

But is it clear that the enthusiasts are violating Locke's principles for responsible belief? Does not their religious experience supply them with the evidence required? Locke thinks not. For when we interpret their metaphors, we see that to the question why they believe that God has spoken to them, their answer is just that they believe it strongly.

> If they say they know it to be true, because it is a *Revelation* from GOD, the reason is good: but then it will be demanded, how they know it to be a Revelation from GOD. If they say by the Light it brings with it, which shines bright in their Minds, and they cannot resist; I beseech them to consider, whether this be any more, than what we have taken notice of already, *viz.* that it is a Revelation because they strongly believe it to be true. For all the Light they speak of is but a strong, though ungrounded perswasion of their own Minds that it is a Truth. (E IV.xix.11: 702)

In short, "their Confidence is mere Presumption: and this Light, they are so dazzled with, is nothing, but an *ignis fatuus* that leads them continually round in this Circle. *It is a Revelation, because they firmly believe it*, and *they believe it, because it is a Revelation*" (E IV.xix.10: 702). It is regrettable that, beyond this highly tendentious attack on the enthusiasts, Locke never explores the possibility that religious experience, of one sort or another, can provide evidence for theistic belief.

If not inner experience, what then is Locke willing to accept as evidence for the occurrence of revelation? Miracles. But he gives the matter lamentably short shrift:

> We see the holy Men of old, who had *Revelations* from GOD, had something else besides that internal Light of assurance in their own Minds, to testify to them, that it was from GOD. They were not left to their own Perswasions alone, that those perswasions were from GOD; But had outward Signs to convince them of the Author of those Revelations. And when they were to convince others, they had a Power given them to justify the Truth of their Commission from Heaven; and by visible Signs to assert the divine Authority of the Message they were sent with. (E IV.xix.15: 705)

Locke then proceeds to offer several examples of biblically reported miracles. He assumes that if we do as we ought and subject the testimony of the gospel writers to the same evidential tests to which we subject any other testimony (E IV.xviii.4: 690–91), we will arrive at the conclusion that their testimony is reliable. In particular, Locke never doubted that the deeds of Jesus to which the gospel writers testify and which they interpreted as miracles, were in fact miracles; and further, that these miracles authenticated Jesus' prophetic status: "The evidence of our Saviour's mission from heaven is so great, in the multitude of miracles he did before all sorts of people, that what he delivered cannot but be received as the oracles of God, and unquestionable verity. For the miracles he did were so ordered by the divine providence and wisdom, that they never were, nor could be denied by any of the enemies or opposers of Christianity" (W VII: 135).

This view, traditional though it is, that miracles are evidence for divine revelation, bristles with problems. To mention just one: how much of what a person claims to be divinely revealed is confirmed as divinely revealed by his performance of a miracle? To these problems Locke never addressed himself, nor did he address himself to the question Hume raised: under what circumstances, if any, are we permitted to accept testimony to the effect that a miracle has occurred?

Our survey of Locke's epistemology of religious knowledge and belief is complete. Locke regarded the "natural philosophy" coming to birth in his day, in the work of people like Boyle and Newton, as a paradigmatic application of his regulative epistemology. The way we ought to conduct our understanding was the way they did conduct it; and that way is specified in his principle of immediate belief, plus his principles of evidence, appraisal, and proportionality. But Locke's view of the religious belief of his day was profoundly different from his view of the new natural philosophy. With the exception perhaps of the beliefs of a small group of Latitudinarians, Locke regarded his regulative epistemology as unillustrated and unexampled in religion. He presented his epistemology as an attack on current religious belief, as a critique. The attack was at its sharpest when Locke attacked the role of experience in the beliefs of the enthusiasts; his rhetoric would have been no less sharp, though, if he had devoted a chapter to those who accept their religious beliefs on the say-so of others, or devoted a chapter to those who accept their religious beliefs on the unexamined authority of the Bible or tradition or church councils.

This assumed contrast between the epistemic status of natural science and that of religion has not ceased to cast its spell over Western intellectuals in the time between us and Locke. Natural science as we know it illustrates responsibly governed belief; religion as we know it represents a failure of responsibly governed belief. The scientist has responsibly listened to the voice of reason; the religious person has not responsibly listened. Many if not most reflective intellectuals of the modern Western world have shared with Locke the conviction that the only alternative to foundationalism of a Lockean sort is antinomianism. They have agreed with Locke that the twin of antinomianism is arbitrary dogmatism. And they have agreed that religious belief for the most part fails the demands of Lockean foundationalism.

But things are changing. Philosophers and historians of science over the past twenty-five years have looked with care at how our natural science does in fact go rather than making presumptions about how it goes; on the basis of this scrutiny they have concluded that, in important ways, it does not follow the Lockean model. That has presented them and us with a choice: shall we say so much the worse for our natural science, or so much the worse for the Lockean model? I know of no one who has chosen the former – whereas, by contrast, when discrepancy was discerned between *religion* and the Lockean model, many if not most Western intellectuals concluded, so much the worse for religion. During roughly these same twenty-five years developments in systematic philosophy have led to powerful attacks on, and widespread rejection of, foundationalism of the Lockean sort.

These two developments have joined hands to make Locke's evidentialist epistemology of religious belief seem questionable to many. Locke was right on this: religious belief does not, with rare exceptions, satisfy his evidentialist demands. But whereas previously the dominant response was either to give up on religious belief as incurable, in violation of intellectual responsibility, or to try to revise or ground it so that it becomes acceptable, now a significant number of philosophers have begun to suggest that it is rather Locke's evidentialist demands that ought to be given up for religion as well as for science and other matters. "Reformed epistemologists" (the present writer included) have suggested that in certain situations, not at all uncommon, it is entirely proper to believe certain theistic propositions immediately. And "Wittgensteinians" have argued that the practice of religion neither needs grounding, nor is open to objections, in the way Locke suggested; it's in order as it is.

Thus with respect to epistemology in general and the epistemology of religious belief in particular, we are living in a new intellectual situation; none of us has any idea whatsoever as to what form this new situation will eventually take. The worry to which Locke addressed himself remains with us, however: when the tradition handed down to one is fractured and pluralized, so that one can no longer order one's life and belief by the wisdom of unified tradition, to what then does one turn? The answer that Locke articulated and defended with visionary power and philosophical subtlety was that one is to appeal to the deliverances of reason – or more broadly and fundamentally, to those points of direct insight into the facts of reality. That answer, in my view and the view of many others, is unacceptable. But once we have rejected Locke's answer we are back to his question: when tradition is fractured, to what does one turn for the ordering of life and belief?

8   Locke's moral philosophy

Locke's failures are sometimes as significant as his successes. His views on morality are a case in point. He published little on the subject, and what little he did publish raised more problems for his readers than it solved. Some of the difficulties contemporaries perceived in Locke's ethics are indicated in a retort by a critic, who was piqued by Locke's suggestion that the critic was part of a plot against him:

As to the *Storm* you speak of, preparing against you, I know nothing of it . . . ; yet I can blame none that desire such Principles of *Humane Understanding* as may give them Proofs and Security against such a System as this, Cogitant Matter, a Mortal Soul, a Manichean God (or a God without Moral Attributes,) and an Arbitrary Law of Good and Evil. . . . The ready way to prevent any such *Storm*, is to give such a plain Explication of your Principles, without Art or Chicane, as may cure and remove any Fears of this Nature. (Burnet 1697: 11)

Friends as well as critics asked Locke several times to give a "plain explication" of his moral theory, but in his published writings he did not do so, and his rejections of his friends' requests could be testy.[1] Though one or two of Locke's acquaintances knew that he had written extensively on natural law when he was a young Oxford don, suggestions that he revise or release the early work went unheeded. There is no doubt that Locke took compliance with the requirements of morality to be important for such happiness as we can attain in this life and indispensable for reward in the next. Some of his remarks indicate, moreover, that he thought he had a comprehensive ethical theory explaining how reason could show what moral requirements we must satisfy; yet he left his readers to infer what this theory might be from a number of brief, scattered and sometimes puzzling passages.

Locke's statements on ethics in the first published work that he openly claimed as his, the *Essay concerning Human Understanding*, generated in more than one critic the kinds of concern expressed in the preceding quotation. In this essay I begin with a review of what Locke tells us about morality in the *Essay* and then go on to explain just why his remarks seem to raise these problems. In the third section I sketch the developments in philosophical thought about morality that generated the issues that Locke thought he had to resolve. Next I consider briefly some of the points Locke made about morality in his other writings. And in conclusion I indicate the historical significance of the difficulties Locke's readers found in his theory of morality.

I

As part of his general attack on innate ideas in Book I of the *Essay*, Locke specifically denied that morality has any innate aspect. Moral principles or maxims command less agreement than speculative ones, so that if disagreement shows that the latter are not innate, there is even less reason to hold the former to be so (E I.iii.1–2: 65–66). Some speculative principles, though not innate, are at least self-evident, needing no proof. For any practical principle, however, we can rightly ask the reason; and this could not be if such principles were innate (E I.iii.4: 68). The general agreement that virtue is praiseworthy can be explained as a result of the general awareness that virtue is useful to society (E I.iii.6: 69). Since there are many ways other than reading what is "written on their hearts" by which men can learn the principles of morals, there is no need to claim that the principles are innate in the conscience. Conscience is simply one's opinion of the rightness or wrongness of one's own action, and one's opinions can come from education, or custom, or the company one keeps (E I.iii.8: 70). People frequently break basic moral rules with no inner sense of shame or guilt, thereby showing that the rules are not innate (E I.iii.9–13: 70–75). Finally, no one has been able to state these allegedly innate rules. Attempts to do so either fail to elicit agreement or else contain utterly vacuous propositions that cannot guide action. It is no help to be told, for instance, that the principle "men must repent of their sins" is innate, unless that knowledge gives the details of what counts as sin – and no one has shown that it does (E I.iii.14–19: 76–80).

In these few pages Locke attacked a widely held view about the source of moral knowledge and set up some tests that any satisfactory replacement of that view must pass. The attack was deeply offensive to received opinion not only because it ran counter to entrenched philosophical commonplaces but also because it was meant as a polemical interpretation of the biblical support for those commonplaces, Saint Paul's central dictum in Romans 2.14–15:

For when the Gentiles, which have not the law, do by nature the things contained in the law, these, having not the law, are a law unto themselves: Which shew the work of the law written in their hearts, their consciences also bearing witness . . .

Every theorist of natural law from Aquinas onward had cited this passage as an authoritative warrant for the claim that there is a moral law discoverable by reason. But Locke seemed to be dismissing Saint Paul. Moreover by stressing the enormous role played by custom, education, common opinion, and superstition in creating the varied moral beliefs people actually have, he seemed to be casting doubt on the existence of any justifiable universal morality. Locke emphatically asserted that he was not denying the truth of basic moral principles (E I.iii.13: 75; Letter 1309: C IV: 112–23). But to give the strongest possible rebuttal to his critics, he needed to offer an actual demonstration of rules; and on the standards for a satisfactory demonstration implicit in his objections to innatist views, this would plainly be difficult.

By giving a further reason for his denial of innate moral principles, Locke indicated some central features of his own understanding of morality. The ideas required to frame and understand moral principles are not themselves innate. For morality concerns laws and obligation, and these require concepts that can only be understood in terms of a lawmaker. The first lawmaker involved in morality is God. His ability to obligate us requires a life after this observable one, since it is plain that he does not make us obey him by rewarding and punishing in our present life (E I.iv.8: 87–88; E I.iii.12: 74). Moral principles could only be innate, then, if the ideas of God, law, obligation, punishment, and immortality were so, and this, Locke argued, is plainly not the case.

Underlying the technical objections to innate ideas is Locke's belief that God gave us a faculty of reason sufficient to enable us to discover all the knowledge needed by beings such as we are. It would have been useless therefore for him to have given us innate ideas or innate knowledge. He meant us to think for ourselves (E I.iv.12: 91). To claim that certain principles are innate is to claim that there is no need for further thought about the matters they cover; and this in turn is an excellent tactic for anyone who wants certain principles taken on authority, without inquiry. But God could not have meant our rational faculties to be blocked in this way (E I.iv.24: 101–2). The theme of the importance of thinking for oneself was as central to Locke's vision of moral personality as was his belief that we are under God's laws and owe him obedience.

We know that the *Essay* grew out of discussions concerning morality (see Aaron 1936: xii), but the topic has no privileged place within it. Locke explains moral ideas and beliefs in the terms that suffice for all our other ideas and beliefs, and the latter are his main concern. He does not claim that any separate faculty or mental operation is involved in getting moral ideas or deriving moral knowledge. Our ideas of good and evil are constructed from our ideas of pleasure and pain: good is what causes pleasure, evil what causes pain (E II.xx.2: 229). The ideas of distinctively moral good and evil, though more complex, still involve no new faculty. To call a voluntary action morally good is to mark its conformity to a law which the lawmaker backs by attaching natural good to compliance and evil to disobedience, that is, by offers of rewards or threats of punishment (E II.xxviii.5: 351).

Locke goes on to note the sorts of rules or laws by which men in fact usually judge actions: the divine law, the civil law, and the law of "opinion or reputation" (E II.xxviii.7: 352). We must refer to these kinds of law, he thinks, to explain how we come to have various moral ideas. If we judge by the divine law – the law God makes known either by revelation or by the light of reason – we get ideas of acts as either sins or duties. The application of the laws of our government gives us the ideas of acts as either criminal or innocent. And when we consider acts as they stand in the general estimation of others in our society, we have the ideas of them as virtuous or vicious (E II.xxviii.8–10: 352–54). Locke insists that he is only explaining how we come by certain ideas and what rules we actually use. Yet he does pause to suggest the warrant for one set of rules, the divine laws. No one can deny that God has given us a law, which is the "only true touchstone of *moral Rectitude.*"

He has a Right to do it, we are his Creatures: He has Goodness and Wisdom to direct our Actions to that which is best: and he has Power to enforce it by Rewards and Punishments, of infinite weight and duration, in another Life: for no body can take us out of his hands. (E II.xxviii.8: 352)

The science of ethics, Locke held, teaches us the rules that lead us to happiness (E IV.xxi.3: 720). Since the point is to improve practice, the rules must be effective guides to action. What, then, moves us to action? Locke was a hedonist about motivation, holding that only prospects of pleasure and pain can motivate us. From the second edition of the *Essay* onward, he provided a sophisticated version of that view. Desire is awakened only by the prospect of the agent's own happiness or pleasure (E II.xxi.41–42: 258–59). But we are not mechanically moved by desires. We are free agents, and our freedom consists in our ability to suspend action while we consider the different desires and aversions we feel, to decide which of them to satisfy, and then to act on our decision. Only the person, not the will, is properly said to be free. The will is the power of considering ideas and of suspending and deciding on action, and it makes no sense to speak of a power as free (E II.xxi.5: 236; E II.xxi.8–14: 237–40; E II.xxi.21–28: 244–48).[2]

Thus what moves us to voluntary action is ultimately our own choice; and the choice is determined, Locke held, by a present felt uneasiness. We may or may not be made uneasy by the thought of some possible future good. We do not all care for the same things. One person may like hunting, another chess, another wine. Each of them is pleasant yet not all are equally to everyone's taste. From these remarks about the diversity of likings and desires, Locke drew two significant conclusions.

First, there is no point in discussing the highest good or summum bonum, as the ancient philosophers did. They asked what kind of life would give us the greatest happiness. Locke knew of Gassendi's attempt to revive the Epicurean answer, that the good life consists in pleasure and the absence of pain. He agreed with Gassendi on the importance of pleasure and pain, but differed from Epicurus in not offering any advice about a specific way of living that will bring the one and avoid the other. For Locke "pleasure" is simply a stand-in for "whatever you incline toward or prefer." The greatest happiness consists, then, in having what pleases and avoiding what pains; but since "these, to different Men, are very different things" (E II.xxi.55: 269), the ancient question cannot be answered in a way that is both generally valid and useful in guiding action.

Second, the will is not determined by our beliefs about what course of action would bring us the greatest amount of good. If it were, Locke argues, no one would sin, since the prospect of eternal bliss or torment would outweigh every other. We can feel more uneasiness from a present lack of food than from a desire for heaven, and the will prompts us to act to relieve the greater uneasiness (E II.xxi.31–38: 250–56). Nonetheless only thoughts of pleasures and pains can arouse uneasiness, so that laws not backed by sanctions would be quite pointless. They could not move us to act.

Locke takes these considerations to show that the elements he thinks he needs to explain our moral ideas – ideas of God, law, good, will, reward, and happiness – can all be obtained from data given by experience. We need no other ideas to build up our complex repertoire of moral concepts. One example will illustrate the point. The idea of murder involves ideas of the act of terminating human life, of doing so purposefully and voluntarily, and of the act being disapproved by most people in my society or forbidden by civil or divine law. Thus like all other complex ideas this one is made up of simple ideas "originally received from Sense or Reflection" (E II.xxviii.14: 358).[3]

It is a matter of considerable importance to Locke that moral ideas are complex ideas of the kind he calls "mixed modes." They are constructed by us, not copied from observation of given complexes. They are not intended to mirror or be adequate to some external reality, as ideas of substances are. They are rather "Archetypes made by the Mind, to rank and denominate Things by," and can only err if there is some incompatibility among the elements we bring together in them (E II.xxx.4: 373–74; E II.xxxi.3–4: 376–77). Consequently, if we are perfectly clear about the moral ideas our moral words stand for, we know the real and not only the nominal essences of moral entities (E III.iii.18: 418; E III.xi.15: 516). This feature of moral ideas and terms is what enables Locke to make his strongest claims about the demonstrability of morality (E III.xi.17–18: 516–17; E IV.xii.8: 643).

Although men commonly look to the law of opinion and the civil law in framing their moral views, the true law of morality is the law God has laid down for us. That law concerns us more nearly than any other, since our eternal happiness or misery is determined by the extent of our compliance with it. How then are we to know what God's law tells us to do? In a famous passage Locke tells us what kind of answer we may expect to this question:

> The *Idea* of a supreme Being, infinite in Power, Goodness, and Wisdom, whose Workmanship we are, and on whom we depend; and the *Idea* of our selves, as understanding, rational Beings, being such as are clear in us, would, I suppose, if duly considered, and pursued, afford such Foundations of our Duty and Rules of Action, as might place *Morality among the Sciences capable of Demonstration:* wherein I doubt not, but from self-evident Propositions, by necessary Consequences, as incontestable as those in Mathematicks, the measures of right and wrong might be made out, to any one that will apply himself. (E IV.iii.18: 549)

The existence of God, considered as an eternal, most powerful and most knowledgeable being, can be demonstrated, Locke tells us in *Essay* IV.x, and it is obvious that as his creatures we are dependent upon him. If we then simply consider the ideas of two such beings, we will "as certainly find that the Inferior, Finite, and Dependent, is under an Obligation to obey the Supreme and Infinite" as we will see that two and two are more than three if we will consider those ideas (E IV.xiii.3: 651).

Locke gives an example to show how demonstrations of more specifically moral truths are to be constructed. Consider some moral concept, such as injustice. It contains as a part the concept of property, which in turn is the idea of something to which someone has a right. "Injustice" is the name given to the mixed-mode idea of violating someone's right to something. It follows demonstrably that where there is no property, there is no injustice. Here is a model for other demonstrations of morality. We are left to get to work producing others (E IV.iii.18: 549).

Locke allows that there are special difficulties in doing so. Moral ideas are harder to clarify, and "commonly more complex," than those involved in mathematics.[4] Private interests and party allegiances lead men to quarrel about moral demonstrations, but not about mathematics (E IV.iii.20–21: 552–53).[5] Nonetheless Locke thinks he has shown how moral demonstrations can produce certainty, which is just "the Perception of the Agreement, or Disagreement of our *Ideas*." Even if no virtuous person ever existed, it is still demonstrably certain that a just man never violates another's rights. Of course we must agree about the ideas to which we attach names. If God has defined certain moral names, Locke says, "it is not safe to apply or use them otherwise"; but where we are dealing only with human definitions, the worst that can happen is verbal impropriety. And if we work with the complex ideas themselves instead of using only names, we can always obtain demonstrations (E IV.iv.7–10: 565–68).

In several places Locke tells us that our main business is to live well and prepare ourselves for the afterlife. Moral law provides the indispensable guidance for this task. Locke makes much of the limitations on our ability to attain speculative knowledge. What matters more is our ability to know the practical laws of morals (E I.i.5–6: 45–46; E II.xxiii.12: 302).

II

It is not hard to see how Thomas Burnet could have been led to say that Locke was presenting "a God without moral attributes." Moral goodness, on Locke's account, is what we predicate of action that complies with a law backed by sanctions. No one could impose such a law on God, so his actions could not be morally good or evil. Similarly, his acts can be neither sins nor duties, since both presuppose laws backed by divine sanctions. Locke insists in several places, moreover, that there is nothing in nature that corresponds to our mixed-mode moral ideas (E III.ix.5: 477; E III.ix.11: 481; E III.xi.9: 513). There can be nothing in nature, then, to set a moral limit to God's will. If neither law nor nature can constrain Locke's God, then Locke is taking the voluntarist position, that God's will alone makes right acts right. God's power makes him, of course, a cause of pleasure and pain, and so he can be thought to be good or evil in a nonmoral way. But this hardly helps matters. The possession of

unlimited power merely enables God to be at best a benevolent despot, at worst a tyrant. There seems to be a good case for Burnet's
claim that on Locke's view the laws God has laid down for us are
"entirely arbitrary."

Locke might rebut the charge if he could show that God possesses
not only unlimited power and knowledge but unlimited goodness as
well – that his aim is to cause as much good or pleasure for his
creatures as possible. And as the quotation from *Essay* II.xxviii.8
indicates, this is Locke's belief.[6] But the proof he offers of God's existence does not show that God is naturally good. Put briefly, the argument is this. We know that we ourselves exist, and that we can perceive and know. The only possible explanation of this fact is that we
were made by an eternal most powerful and most intelligent being
(E IV.x.3–5: 620–21). Locke claims that "from this *Idea* duly considered, will easily be deduced all those other Attributes, which we
ought to ascribe to this eternal Being" (E IV.x.6: 621). Neither in the
expansion of this proof that occupies the rest of this chapter nor
anywhere else in the *Essay* does Locke show how to deduce God's
essential benevolence. If the deduction seemed easy to him, it has
not seemed so to his readers.[7]

Locke's view of how to demonstrate moral truths makes matters
worse, because it suggests that there cannot be a demonstration of
a moral principle that satisfies Locke's own standards. Locke insisted, as I have noted, that a principle must offer genuine guidance.
It must not be trivial or vacuous, a mere verbal statement that does
not enable us to pick out right acts. Although Locke said we must
start our moral demonstrations from self-evident principles, he also
said that there are no self-evident moral principles with substantial
content. Demonstration consists, Locke held, in making explicit the
ideas assembled in one complex mode and showing, perhaps by using an intermediate complex idea, their literal overlap with the ideas
in another. As a contemporary critic pointed out, it is hard to see
how this could yield much more than the kind of "trifling" or vacuous proposition Locke criticized the innatists for offering.[8] And the
problem is increased by Locke's claim that we ourselves assemble
the elements of moral ideas. What guarantee have we that the moral
ideas we construct will inform us of God's will for us? To say, as
Locke did, that God may have constructed some complex moral
ideas that we ignore at our peril is of no use unless we can determine

which moral ideas those are; and, in the *Essay* at least, Locke did not tell us or show us how to decide.

Locke's moral psychology compounded all these difficulties. He made it clear that only what affects our own personal happiness provides motivating reasons. We may indeed place our interests in the well-being of others, just as we may find our happiness in a variety of pursuits and achievements having nothing to do with others. But while Locke allowed that we can have an immediate concern for the well-being of others, he did not stress it. His account of the role of the will mitigates his apparent egoism only slightly. It allows that a present uneasiness felt after mature consideration is what determines us when we act, and not a calculated maximum of benefit to self. Yet his constant insistence that only sanctions will bring about compliance with the laws of morality makes him sound as if he thinks that a narrowly egoistic view of motivation is accurate for most, if perhaps not all, people. An untrammeled ruler giving arbitrary direction to a selfish population seems indeed to emerge as his model of the moral relations between God and human beings. And if one allowed, as Locke notoriously did (E IV.iii.6: 539–43), that matter might think, how could one hope to obtain the certainty of the immortality of the soul that on Locke's view is so necessary to induce us to obey God's laws?

III

The difficulties Locke faced in constructing an understanding of morality adequate for his purposes arose from his analysis of the problems of morality and politics in his own time. He lived in circumstances that forced on him an awareness of the genuine possibility of political chaos and social disintegration. Controversies and conflicts, about property and about religion, seemed ineliminable, but they would have to be contained if there were to be any hope of sustaining decent societies. Moral skepticism of the kind to which Montaigne had given wide currency, and the dogmatic certainties of religious enthusiasts, seemed equally unlikely to foster the peaceful settlement of disputes. A morality to which God's existence and providence was immaterial would have been socially ineffectual and was personally unacceptable to Locke. His thought about morality reflected all these constraints.

He was not alone in seeing the problems of morality in these terms. His reiterated praise of Pufendorf's work on natural law points to his allegiances.[9] Although he used and valued Richard Hooker's great treatise *Of the Laws of Ecclesiastical Polity* (1593–1661),[10] and although Hooker opens with a magisterial exposition of a theory of natural law, Locke did not accept his version of that theory. Hooker believed that the laws of nature can be known through reason because they are written in everyone's conscience, and that the general agreement of mankind about what those laws require provides evidence of the divine origin of our basic moral convictions. Locke rejected the first of these views and doubted the very existence of the *consensus gentium* presupposed by the second. Hooker's theory was Thomistic, as was that published in England in 1652 by Nathanael Culverwell, who followed closely the exposition of Thomistic natural law doctrine by the Spanish Jesuit Francisco Suárez (1612). Protestants in general felt no need to disavow this part of Catholic teaching. Such distinguished seventeenth-century divines of the Church of England as Robert Sanderson and Jeremy Taylor made Thomistic natural law theory the basis for their work on conscience and casuistry. Locke knew the work of Sanderson and Culverwell but the view of natural law he used in his political writings and briefly explained elsewhere was not Thomistic. In recommending Pufendorf he was linking himself to a type of natural law thought that had only begun to develop in his own century in the work of the Dutch lawyer Hugo Grotius.[11]

Grotius used a vocabulary of natural law while dropping much of the Thomistic theory previously carried by it. He portrayed humans as sociable not only because we need one another's help but also because we simply enjoy one another's company.[12] At the same time, he held, we are self-interested and competitive. Natural law on his view has nothing to do with cosmic harmonies or with showing individuals how they are to attain their own perfection or highest good. (Grotius in fact said nothing about the highest good, dismissing the whole question of the best way of living in part of a sentence.)[13] Rather natural law provides the solution to the problem of how rational beings, constituted as we are, can live together. Each of us, Grotius held, is naturally the possessor of certain rights. We may give up any or all of our rights, which thus provide the bargaining chips we hold when we consider entering or staying within a community. The basic law of nature is that no one's rights may be violated. Violation of rights constitutes injustice, and only positive laws that avoid injustice are valid. God makes and enforces laws to protect our rights but the rights are prior both to those laws and to the human societies we construct by giving some of them to those who rule and who are therefore to protect our enjoyment of those we have not ceded. Protection is necessary because, given the unsocial sociability of our nature, competition and conflict will inevitably continue, even in the best-ordered society.[14] Morality is what sets the ground rules for that competition and for the actions of the ruler in keeping society going.

Grotius was first of all an international lawyer, concerned with disputes between Protestant and Catholic nations. To provide a basis for settling such disputes, he tried to invent a way of reasoning about moral and political issues that avoided skepticism, that in matters of religion appealed only to beliefs shared by all reasonable people, and that enabled observable facts to determine the laws of nature. He elaborated the first successful code of international law, without however working out in detail the foundations he thought it needed. Thus he never explained what sort of attribute a right is; he distinguished between advising or counseling someone that it would be good for him to do something, and obligating him to do the act, but he offered no theory of obligation; and his claim that God merely sanctioned laws backing up independent rights seemed to relegate the divinity to a secondary place in morality. His considerable influence in moral philosophy was in large part a result of the fact that many later thinkers accepted his assumptions about the constraints a satisfactory theory of morality would have to observe. Their own efforts to work out the Grotian problematic yielded varied results.

Hobbes was in many respects a Grotian theorist. He saw competitive drives as a standing threat to society; and he was more interested in politics than in the details of individual morality. While he elaborated more fully than Grotius a philosophical ethics, he did so in a way that shocked generations of Europeans and forced them into attempts to find less drastic terms, with less appalling political consequences, for dealing with the human tendency to conflict. Hobbes provided something Grotius had not, a theory of obligation; but at the same time he was taken to have carried the Grotian sidelining of religion to an extreme, making God nearly irrelevant to the moral life. And if it was clear that the Grotians needed a theory of obligation, it was also clear from the response to Hobbes that no view that left God out of morality would win general agreement.

We can see some of the difficulties the post-Hobbesian Grotians faced in working out a comprehensive theory by looking briefly at Pufendorf's views.[15] Pufendorf – by far the most widely read of all the Grotian natural lawyers – built God securely into morality at the start, by adopting the medieval voluntarist view of the status of natural law and of evaluation generally.[16] God's creation of the physical universe, Pufendorf held, is conceptually different from his creation of morality. The latter was imposed by God's will after the former was complete. Humans can create moral entities – institutions and persons as represented in normative concepts – just as God can, but our creation of such entities is limited by God's prior legislation, while God is totally untrammeled in laying down laws for us.[17] Morality thus exists solely because God has willed us to act in certain ways. To hold anything else – to believe that God's sovereignty could be limited by something outside himself – would be impious.

There is a second way in which God is indispensable for morality. The laws of nature were intended by God to indicate the kinds of actions that would enable us to live peacefully and profitably with one another. We can find out what those laws are by means of empirical examination of human nature. We have only to note the main special features of our nature, such as our ability to use language, and take them as pointing to God's will for us. If we turn our special attributes to good purposes, we will be acting as God wants us to. Yet unless there is more to be said than this, morality would be merely a matter of God's advice about how we can prosper. If obligation and law are to enter the scene, the indications of God's will provided by our nature must be backed by the threat of sanctions for noncompliance. Since God provides that threat, Pufendorf explains obligation as the necessity of doing an action commanded by a rightful superior who has sufficient power to compel inferiors to obey.

Pufendorf was aware of the traditional difficulties with a voluntarist position. If God's will is entirely untrammeled in creating moral entities, is he anything more than a powerful tyrant? And if obligation is simply the necessity of doing an act commanded by that tyrant and backed by sanctions, are we not caught in the worst aspects of Hobbes's view of morals as self-interested precepts that become obligatory, and can be carried out, only when they are turned into the enforceable commands of a political sovereign? Pufendorf suggested that we could see from empirical evidence that God is benevolent, so that we should be grateful for his bounty to us. Gratitude, therefore, gives us a reason to do as God commands, a reason not the same as the selfish fear of punishment. Still, he admitted that most people would not be moved by gratitude and that sanctions are needed to obtain enough obedience to make society possible. And this left Pufendorf with yet another problem. He did not think that reason unaided by revelation could assure us that there is a future life in which punishments and rewards are distributed on the basis of behavior in this life. Without that assurance, however, no one, on his view, could know that there are any other obligations than those of positive law. Such an admission threatened the whole Grotian project of deriving a natural law morality from propositions capable of being defended on empirical grounds.

Another line of thought was followed by Richard Cumberland, whose treatise on natural law was published in the same year as Pufendorf's. Cumberland, avowing himself an admirer of Grotius, argued that the sanctions for God's laws are built into the ordinary course of nature: transgress, and you will suffer, just as you suffer the pains of headache if you drink too much wine. So obligation can be explained without appeal to unknowable sanctions in another life. The natural law itself is easily discovered from ordinary facts and we can then see that compliance pays and disobedience does not. The problem of course is that while such an arrangement of the natural world and our relation to it may show the benevolence of God, it does not really give him any active role in sustaining morality. Once the world is created morality would be as much a self-sustaining mechanism as the movements of the heavenly bodies. A deist or even an atheist could accept a Cumberlandian view of ethics. Locke, deeply committed to an understanding of God as calling for obedience to him as our personal creator, could not.

IV

We can see that Locke was aware of the problems Pufendorf and Cumberland had encountered by looking at some of his other writings that concern morality.[18] I can touch here on only three of them: the early unpublished work that its first editor entitled *Essays on the Law of Nature*,[19] the second of the *Two Treatises of Government*, and the late work, *The Reasonableness of Christianity*.

The *Essays* do not provide a completely coherent ethical theory.[20] In two or three places, for instance, Locke speaks of the moral law as innate (EL I: 117; QL I: 113), yet he devotes much space to arguing that moral knowledge cannot be innate. One of his aims, indeed, is to explain how we can derive knowledge of natural law from ordinary experience. In this, as in much else, the arguments of these *Essays* display in rudimentary form what Locke came to say more fully in his main work on knowledge; and on one topic – the nature of obligation – Locke goes into more detail than he later did. Since Locke refused to publish the *Essays* it is not clear how much of what they say we can suppose to represent his own considered opinion. Still, they certainly show us some issues in ethical theory to which he devoted considerable attention, and allow us to see some problems he ran into at this early stage of his development.

In the *Essay concerning Human Understanding* Locke does not say which simple ideas are combined to make up the mixed-mode idea of obligation (E II.xxii.1: 288). One of the *Essays* helps us, however, as Locke argues for an affirmative answer to the question whether the law of nature is binding on all men (EL VI; QL VIII). The account of obligation he gives in the course of his discussion is the standard view of the time. Obligation is "the bond of the law of nature by which everyone is constrained to discharge a debt of nature," that is, a debt that arises from human nature rather than from civil law.[21] The term "obligation" does not refer to the act a subject is constrained to do, but to the constraint itself. Hence Locke can speak of the obligation of our duty, since our duty is the specific act we are to do, while obligation is the bond that ties us to do it or to suffer the penalty for noncompliance.[22]

Locke promptly adds that "no one can oblige or constrain us to do anything unless he has right and power over us" (EL VI: 181–83; QL VIII: 205), and the explanation of this right is given forthwith:

this [kind of] obligation seems to derive at times from the divine wisdom of the legislator, and at times from that right which the creator has over his creation. For every [kind of] obligation can ultimately be referred back to god, to the command of whose will we must show ourselves obedient. We are obligated because we have received both our being and proper function from him, on whose will both depend, and we ought to observe the limit he has prescribed. Nor is it any less proper that we should do what has been decided by him who is all-knowing and supremely wise. (EL VI: 183; QL VIII: 205–7)

At the start of the discussion, Locke (following Suárez as well as Grotius and Pufendorf) distinguishes what is advisable in the light of our own desires or purposes from what is obligatory because commanded by another. Against Hobbes (as he thinks), he holds that obligation could not arise from a desire for self-preservation alone. Only the will of another creates obligation. But that other, he insists in the passage just quoted, must have authority or right as well as power sufficient to compel compliance. Obligation does not arise from coercive power alone: "it is not fear of punishment that binds us but our determination of what is right" (EL VI: 185; QL VIII: 207).[23] Our conscience judges us and tells us that we deserve – and do not merely fear – punishment if we have transgressed.

Two grounds for God's authority are thus indicated. One is his wisdom. God has aims and, being all-knowing, surely chooses the best means to them. We are in no position to dispute him. This alone, of course, might be true of a merely tyrannical god, but Locke makes it clear that he does not view God as a tyrant. He notes that to obey a king merely out of fear of his power to compel us "would be to establish the power of tyrants, thieves, and pirates" (EL VI: 189; QL VIII: 213). To avoid charging God with tyranny Locke appeals to the principle that a creator has the right to control his creations.

Locke held to the principle of creator's right throughout his life (E II.xxviii.8: 352).[24] But neither in the *Essays* nor anywhere else does he attempt to justify it.[25] It seemed, perhaps, so obvious to him as to need no justification, but in his own mature philosophy, as was noted earlier, he allows no self-evident moral principles. And if his later thought is to be consistent, there are two further problems about the concept of obligation.

There is first the question of whether Locke can give an account of what he can take terms such as "right" and "authority" to mean. All ideas come either from the senses or from inner perception of feelings and mental operations. From these Locke thinks we can get ideas of pleasure and pain, which enable him to define the ideas of good and evil in their "natural" sense. But the moral sense of the terms, as we have seen, depends on law, and law requires authority and right. From introspection we get the idea of power (E II.xxi.4: 235), but that idea by itself does not suffice to account for the idea of authority. Locke admits no other senses to give us simple ideas. He offers no explicit account of authority as an idea, nor of the idea of right, and it is hard to see how he could do so without showing quite clearly that his epistemology does not contain the resources to enable him to draw the distinction he needs between them and mere power.

The second problem concerns motivation. In the *Essays* it seems clear that Locke does not think that the fear of punishment alone serves to move us to obey God's natural laws. Somehow the simple recognition of God's rightful laws suffices to move us. Now on Locke's mature view, what moves us is always connected (however indirectly) with our anticipation of pleasure or pain. A late manuscript note indicates his awareness of the problem this set for any position like his own early one on natural law:

That which has very much confounded men about the will and its determination has been the confounding of the notion of moral rectitude and giving it the name of moral good. The pleasure that a man takes in any action or expects as a consequence of it is indeed a good in the self able and proper to move the will. But the moral rectitude of it considered barely in itself is not good or evil nor any way moves the will, but as pleasure and pain either accompanies the action itself or is looked on to be a consequence of it. Which is evident from the punishments and rewards which God has annexed to moral rectitude or pravity as proper motives to the will, which would be needless if moral rectitude were in itself good and moral pravity evil.[26]

A ruler's subjects can know what the laws are without knowing what good their obedience will bring, because the laws themselves do not specify that good. What motive have they then to obey? Locke's later hedonism made the answer inevitable: fear of punishment, hope of reward. The early sketch of natural law offered no escape from the unpalatable view of human moral motivation suggested in the *Essay concerning Human Understanding*.

The early work is also not much help in explaining how we come to know what it is that God commands us to do. Locke argues that we learn this from experience, not from direct revelation, tradition, innate ideas, or general consent. Experience shows us that there is a "powerful and wise creator" of all things whom we are naturally disposed to worship (EL IV: 153; QL V: 161); it shows that we tend to preserve ourselves; and it shows that we are disposed to live sociably and are equipped, by our possession of language, to do so. But how exactly we are to go from there to knowledge of the laws governing our duties to God, self, and others is not made clear.[27]

The *Two Treatises of Government* give us no help in working out the details of a Lockean theory of the nature of obligation or of motivation, but they point toward an elaboration of Locke's view of how we could come to know which mixed-mode moral ideas God intended us to make central to our lives and societies. This is not the main focus of the *Treatises,* but in the second of them there are indications of a line of argument that Locke's contemporaries would have found familiar. Locke there says that God made man in such a way that "it was not good for him to be alone." He therefore "put him under strong Obligations of Necessity, Convenience, and Inclination to drive him into *Society,*" and equipped him with reason and speech, which would make it possible (T II.vii.77: 336). If these strongly marked special features of human beings indicate God's will for us, then it must also be his will that we do what is needful to carry it out. Locke suggests that in the earliest stages of human history not much in the way of morality was required. Members of families naturally accommodate to one another, and in the "Golden Age" personal and social life would have been so simple and so lacking in material goods that conflict would not have been a major problem (T II.viii.110–11: 359–61). But our natural propensity to increase our level of well-being leads inevitably to greater wealth and to competition. To manage it, Locke argues, we are led to form political organizations.[28]

Locke's political philosophy is not our subject here. The point of recalling it is to indicate how it might have helped solve the problem of determining which complex moral ideas God intends us to use. He intends us to use those, Locke might have said, that we need in order to live as the special features of our nature show us he meant us to live: sociably and with an increasing degree of prosperity brought about in part by precisely the self-interested competitiveness that makes it difficult for us to live together. The related concepts of justice and of property in a broad sense thus have an obvious place in God's plans for us. If this makes it at least probable that we ought to use those ideas as basic, the question that remains is whether this kind of argument can ground the "Obligation to mutual Love amongst Men," which along with the maxim of justice Locke takes to be fundamental (T II.ii.5: 288). Locke says little about it in his published work, and although, as I noted earlier, he allows that we can take a disinterested and direct concern in the well-being of others, he is more emphatic about the sources of discord in our nature than about our love of one another. Actual love of others, to the point of self-sacrifice, is not such a salient feature of our constitution as Locke sees it that our nature as plainly points to charity as it does to justice.

It must be noted that Locke himself did not claim that the argument of the *Second Treatise* was intended to fill out his moral theory. We may read it as doing so, but as Locke did not acknowledge the work it is doubtful that he meant us to do so. Moreover it may well be, as Colman claims, that it was the impossibility of giving this kind of grounding for the great maxim of charity that prevented Locke from completing and publishing a demonstrative morality (Colman 1983: 204). But once again we do not have any published statement by Locke to this effect and no evidence that his readers took the lack of such an argument to be what worried them about the little he did say about moral philosophy. I will return to this issue, after remarking on a feature of Locke's ethics that emerges only in *The Reasonableness of Christianity*. In the course of arguing that Christianity demands of its adherents only the minimal doctrinal belief that Jesus is the Messiah or Savior, Locke raises the question, "What need was there of a Saviour? What advantage have we by Jesus Christ?" (W VII: 134). The question arises because Locke has argued that reason could have taught even those to whom the Jewish and Christian revelations were not delivered the crucial rudiments of religious truth. Reason could have shown, for instance, that the natural law requires that we forgive our enemies. So reason could teach that the author of that law – whose existence, we recall, can be learned by reason – will forgive us if we repent our transgressions and resolve to improve. But the belief that we can be forgiven is a prerevelation counterpart to the belief that Jesus is the Messiah, and belief in it would make the heathen eligible for salvation (W VII: 133). Why, then, was Christ's actual coming necessary?

Part of the answer is that reason alone could not have prevailed on most people sufficiently to teach them God's existence, while Christ's personal presence enabled the belief to spread. Another part is that the human race needed a clearer knowledge of morals than reason alone had been able to give it. The heathen philosophers did not discover all or even the most important of the laws of nature, and it seems in general, Locke says, "that it is too hard a task for unassisted reason to establish morality in all its parts, upon its true foundation, with a clear and convincing light" (W VII: 139). But suppose that a compendium of non-Christian moral teaching had been made, including even the wisdom of Confucius, and suppose that it had included what is commanded by the laws of nature: what then? "The law of nature is the law of convenience too"; no wonder therefore if "men of parts" should find out what is right simply by its beauty and convenience.[29] But as thus discovered and taught, the precepts would still have amounted only to counsel or advice from wise men about how to live a happy life. The precepts could not have been taught as laws that obligate. Only the knowledge that the precepts are the command of a supreme lawgiver who rewards and punishes could transform them into moral laws; and the heathen did not adequately possess that knowledge, which had then to be taught by Christ (W VII: 140–43).

Now that Christ has made it clear that God lays down laws, and told us what God's laws are, we can show them to be reasonable, and so we come to think we might have discovered them ourselves. But even if reason could have uncovered and proved the whole of the law of nature, rational demonstrations would not be sufficient to move ordinary people to act morally. "The greatest part of mankind want leisure or capacity for demonstration; . . . you may as soon hope to have all the day-labourers and tradesmen, the spinsters and dairy maids, perfect mathematicians, as to have them perfect in ethics" by proving moral laws to them. "Hearing plain commands," Locke continues, "is the sure and only course to bring them to obedience and practice. The greatest part cannot know, and therefore they must believe." Christ coming in glory from heaven is needed to convince most people to comply with the laws of nature (W VII: 146).

Locke's doubts about the ability of reason to discover and to teach effectively the laws of nature do not contradict his belief that those laws, once revealed, can be rationally demonstrated. But they do require us to interpret with caution those passages in which Locke says that the law of nature is "plain and intelligible to all rational Creatures" (T II.ix.124: 369). This is no slip into a rationalist claim that the laws are self-evident. But neither is it the claim that knowledge of the laws of nature is equally available to everyone alike. The laws are plain enough so that the day-laborer and the spinster can obey, once they have been instructed. But they will not necessarily be able to see for themselves why the laws are binding on them. They will be obeying God by obeying other men.

V

Locke, I have suggested, was concerned to combat both skeptical doubts about morality and enthusiastic claims to insight into it. Skepticism and enthusiasm both work against the possibility of constructing a decent and stable society. An empiricist naturalism seemed to him the only response that could take care of both these dangers. And only an understanding of morality to which God was essential could win the assent of the vast majority of Europeans. For these reasons Locke aimed to show morality to require God's active participation while invoking only natural human knowledge. He shared these aims with the natural law thinkers who saw Grotius as the originator of the problems on which they worked. If Locke did less than others to present a detailed system of natural law, he devoted more attention than they to working out the epistemology of moral knowledge.

His view, as I have indicated, was that the best way to naturalize moral knowledge would be to show that it is explicable in the way that ordinary empirical knowledge is. This would link it firmly with scientific and mathematical knowledge and with the knowledge Locke thought we could have – revelation apart – of God. We could explain moral concepts by appeal to information gained by the senses, and reach moral conclusions by showing how the ideas involved in moral beliefs are necessarily connected with one another. On the assumption that people perceive, enjoy, and reason about the world in basically the same ways, these moves, if successful, would effectively exclude the claims to special insight of the enthusiast and the nihilism of the relativist or skeptic.

What we now think of as reductionism in ethics has seemed to many philosophers to be a hopeless enterprise, and a nonreductionistic naturalism does not seem to have been an option Locke considered. (He might, indeed, have rejected it if he had, as merely a subtle opening for enthusiasm.) The problem Locke's readers had with his reductive view was not the objection raised by twentieth-century critics of ethical naturalism, that that kind of theory gets the meanings of words wrong. Their problem was that naturalism would force on us a misconstrual of our relations with God. Locke could not portray God's dominion over us as resting on anything but his power and skill as creator. He could admit no difference between God's rule and that of a benevolent despot except at the cost of allowing into his scheme concepts that could not be explained in terms drawn from the experience of our senses.

We have seen how Thomas Burnet put the point.[30] And we know from the early *Essays on the Law of Nature* that Locke too wanted to hold that God has moral attributes and is not merely a powerful tyrant who is, though this could not be proved, also beneficent. There are no doubt difficulties for Locke in giving a Pufendorfian argument from special features of human nature to a divine intention that we obey the great maxim of Charity; but they are not much greater than the difficulties with Pufendorfian arguments from special features to other laws, and Locke seems to have accepted some form of this argumentation. It was not the problem about charity, I suggest, that made Locke refuse to publish a deductive ethic. It was his embarrassment at his inability to give Burnet a satisfactory explanation of how we could even say and mean that God is a just ruler (let alone prove it) that prevented him from doing so. He could not allow for the kind of relation between God and his creatures that many Christians – he himself among them – believed to exist.

The significance of Locke's failure was considerable. It drew attention to the moral consequences of empiricism in a way that previous empiricist ethics had not done. We can see why if we contrast the relative importance in Locke's work of epistemology and ethics with their balance in other writers in the Grotian tradition.

Hobbes offered at least the elements of a reductionist empiricism, but his epistemology was massively overshadowed by his extremely contentious political views, and he seemed to his readers to be deeply irreligious.[31] His work therefore raised problems more urgent than any that might arise from a connection between empiricism and religious voluntarism. Pufendorf was a voluntarist who, like Locke after him, rejected innate ideas and held that all knowledge is based in experience.[32] His empiricism allowed him to claim that the reasoning he used to derive particular laws of nature was religiously neutral and that anyone could check his data and his arguments. Yet he did not develop a general theory of the derivation of concepts from experience or try to show that the knowledge we need concerning moral laws can be stated and proved in experiential terms. His interest was in the detailed development of a code of natural law, usable as a guide to positive legislation. Readers could reject Pufendorf's voluntarism and his theory of moral entities – both of which he in fact omitted from his popular brief textbook – and still accept his code.

With Locke it was different. Locke was more interested in the epistemology of natural law than in working out a code. As a result the connection between voluntarism and empiricism stood out more starkly in his view of ethics, fragmentary though it was, than in Pufendorf's. The connection seems clear. Locke aimed to account for all ideas by showing how they can be built up from atomic simples derived from experience. Experience shows us how things are and teaches us what we enjoy. It yields no inherently normative ideas. Norms come only from will, but the only ideas we have available for understanding the law-making operation of will are those of power and sanction. The empiricist epistemology cuts off any other source of normative force. God's will then can only be understood as arbitrary.

Since epistemology was so obviously the center of Locke's theory, his readers could hardly avoid seeing that if, like him, they embraced reductionist empiricism about moral concepts as a way of excluding religious authoritarianism and enthusiasm, then they would be forced into voluntarism – unless they left God entirely out of morality. Locke's voluntarism, like Pufendorf's, undoubtedly had a deeply religious motivation. But one unintended consequence of his work was to make it even plainer than Hobbes had done that if strong voluntarism is unacceptable because of its moral consequences, then so too is empiricism.[33]

It is a striking fact that after Locke no major thinker tried to work out a Grotian theory of natural law in voluntarist terms. Grotian natural law continued – largely through the enormous popularity of Pufendorf's writings – to be a major force in European culture, from Russia to the American colonies. But the post-Lockean philosophers all turned to new ways of attempting to understand morality. Even those who were as concerned as Locke to show that the true morality was what Christianity had always taught did not try Locke's way of showing this. They interpreted Christianity differently and found new ways of accommodating it to the natural powers of human reason. Locke's *Essay* was one of the most widely read philosophical works of the period. I believe that the main innovative directions taken by moral philosophy after Locke can profitably be seen as efforts to respond to the failure of the Grotian project, which Locke's work made evident.

NOTES

1 See the letter to Tyrrell of August 4, 1690 (Letter 1309: C IV: 110–13). His responses to Burnet were also tart and unhelpful.

2 Some commentators claim that there is an inconsistency between Locke's hedonistic theory of motivation and the ethical "rationalism" according to which "reason alone can determine what is truly good" (Aaron 1971: 257), or between his hedonism and his voluntaristic view that laws arise from God's commands (Laslett 1967: 82n). But even if the good consists in pleasure, there is no inconsistency in claiming that reason must be used to tell us where the good is to be found, since it is easy to have mistaken views about what will bring the greatest pleasure to us in the long run. I find no clear and unequivocal suggestion in Locke's published work of any intuitionist rationalism about the laws of morality. And if obedience to God's commands ultimately leads to our own greatest happiness, then on an egoistic hedonistic view of motivation we can be moved to obey them, although the commands depend only on his will.

3 In *An Introduction to the History of Particular Qualities* (1671), Robert Boyle said:

there are some things that have been looked upon as qualities which ought rather to be looked upon as states of matter, or complexions of particular qualities, as *animal, inanimal,* &c, *health,* and *beauty,* which last attribute seems to be made up of *shape, symmetry* or comely proportion, and the *pleasantness of the colours* of the particular parts of the face. (Boyle 1979: 97)

Boyle here suggests a naturalistic and reductionistic account of beauty, of the kind Locke gives of moral ideas. In explaining what he means by "mode" Locke gives as one example the idea of beauty, "consisting of a certain composition of Colour and Figure, causing delight in the Beholder" (E II.xii.5: 165).

4 The "Discourses of Religion, Law, and Morality," are of the "highest concernment" to us and also "the greatest difficulty" (E III.ix.22: 489).

5 Among such interests and allegiances are those involved in disputes about correct religious doctrine and practice, of the kind that engaged Locke in his writings on toleration.

6 See also E IV.xiii.3: 651, where Locke says that we can see that we are dependent on a being "who is eternal, omnipotent, perfectly wise and good."

7 Lord King's biography prints a manuscript dated August 7, 1681, in which Locke argues that since God is totally perfect and needs nothing he cannot use his power for his own good, and therefore must use it for the good of his creatures (L I: 228–30). Whatever the merits of this argument, which if taken seriously would raise all the difficulties of the problem of evil, Locke did not publish it. In *The Reasonableness of Christianity*, Locke says that "the works of nature show [God's] wisdom and power: but it is his peculiar care of mankind most eminently discovered in his promises to them, that shows his bounty and goodness" (W VII: 129). How then are God's promises to be known? If by reason, as Locke suggests in saying that "God had, by the Light of Reason, revealed to all Mankind . . . that he was good and merciful" (ibid.), the original problem is unresolved.

8 Henry Lee (Lee 1702: 252) objects to the triviality of the conclusions Locke's method would enable us to deduce and notes that such propositions "can be of no use according to his own Principles, because they are in sense *Identical*." The matter is arguable.

9 See TE 186: 239; also "Some Thoughts concerning Reading and Study for a Gentleman," where Pufendorf's large treatise on natural law is described as "the best book of that kind" (W III: 296).

10 See Laslett 1967: 56–57 and the references there given.

11 Thus I disagree with von Leyden, who treats as not significant Locke's affiliation with Grotius as well as with Selden, and who thinks Locke had little in common with Pufendorf (von Leyden 1954: 37–39).

12 Contrast this with the way Aquinas shows that we are social animals. Man cannot secure the necessities of life by himself and "therefore it is natural for man to live in association with his fellows." Moreover he

knows only in a general way what he needs in order to thrive; only collaboration with others can increase and specify man's knowledge; and "thus it is necessary for him to live in society." Our ability to talk is adduced simply as an aspect of our ability to aid one another (Aquinas 1988: 14–15).

13 "Just as, in fact, there are many ways of living, one being better than another, and out of so many ways of living each is free to select that which he prefers" (Grotius 1925: 104).

14 The phrase "unsocial sociability" is used by Kant in his "Idea for a Universal History" (Kant 1963: 15).

15 For a fuller discussion, and for further bibliography, see Schneewind 1987. Dr. Fiametta Palladini has pointed out some errors in this article; they do not, however, affect the present discussion.

16 A view also held by Descartes, who asserted that God created the eternal truths of mathematics as well as those of morals. Descartes, however, did not develop a comprehensive philosophical ethics or theory of law.

17 This may be one of the sources of Locke's view of moral ideas as mixed-mode ideas constructed by us.

18 See Colman 1983 for extended discussion, and the forthcoming book by John Marshall, to be drawn from his Johns Hopkins Ph.D. dissertation (Marshall 1990), to which I am indebted.

19 This is W. von Leyden, whose edition appeared in 1954. I follow von Leyden in referring to this work as "Essays." A new edition and translation, by Robert Horwitz, Jenny Strauss Clay, and Diskin Clay (1990), calls the work "Questions concerning the Law of Nature." In his introduction to this edition, Horwitz argues that Locke here wrote "disputed questions" in a medieval style of debate still current in the Oxford in which he was teaching at the time. This may well be true, but I am not convinced by Horwitz's claim (Horwitz 1990: 55) that it would be of major significance for our interpretation of the work. (I shall, however, cite both the von Leyden and the Horwitz editions in my references to this work, using the abbreviations "EL" and "QL," respectively. And I shall quote from the latter's translation, done by Diskin Clay.)

20 The best discussion of the *Essays* is that in Colman 1983: 29–50.

21 The Latin word translated as "bond" in this quotation is *vinculum*, which means "cord" and "fetter" and "chain," as well as "bond."

22 In the *Essay* itself there are only some fourteen sections in which the term "obligation" occurs. Locke speaks of the obligation of rules or the obligation to obey laws or the obligation to obey God (E I.iii.6–8, 11: 69–70, 72–73; E I.iv.8: 87; E II.xxviii.3: 350; E IV.xiii.3: 651; and E IV.xx.11: 714). As in the *Essays*, "obligation" here means something like "what binds one to obey or perform" (and not the act or class of acts to whose performance one is obligated). At E II.xxviii.2: 349 Locke

thus speaks of "the Obligations of several Duties amongst Men." (My thanks to the Intelex computerized Locke text for the count and the references.)

23 The Latin phrase here is *recti ratio nos obligat:* "right reason binds us." See also T II.xvi.186–87: 410–11, where Locke says that force alone does not create obligation to an earthly ruler.

24 See Colman 1983: 46, and the valuable discussions in Tully 1980.

25 We find in the *Essays* exactly the same transition that (as was earlier noted) there is in the *Essay,* from the empirical conclusion that a powerful and wise agent created the world to the further conclusion "that there is some superior authority to which we are rightly subject" – and in just the same way the transition is not spelled out (EL IV: 153–54; QL V: 163).

26 Voluntas: B MS Locke c.28: 114 (quoted by von Leyden 1954: 72–73; also quoted by Colman 1983: 48–49).

27 That the salient features of human nature are indicators of God's intentions for us and that these three characteristics are our important salient features is a doctrine that goes back, as von Leyden notes (von Leyden 1954: 159n1), to Aquinas. Locke's *Essays* antedate Pufendorf but, as suggested earlier, would have been reinforced by his work: see Schneewind 1987: 134–38.

28 There are suggestions in Pufendorf of a historical evolution toward government and private property, and Locke may here be picking up some of them. See Hont 1987.

29 And see E I.III.6: 69 for an earlier statement of the point.

30 Leibniz, criticizing Pufendorf some years later, put the objection by saying that the failure of an account like Pufendorf's (here very close to Locke's) will be obvious once we "pay attention to this fact: that God is praised because he is just." Unable to account for this fact, such theories have no way to explain proper authority as distinct from power, and leave us therefore subjected to a tyrant, not carrying out the part a just and merciful God has assigned us in bringing about aims we can all understand and share (Leibniz 1988: 71–73).

31 His nominalism and the deductivism associated with it may also have obscured the strong empiricist element in his theory.

32 See Pufendorf's account of Romans 2.14–15 in *On the Law of Nature and of Nations* II.iii.13 (Pufendorf 1934: 201–2).

33 Descartes's voluntarism was not, of course, a consequence of any empiricist view. But neither – as Leibniz made plain – is voluntarism entailed by rationalism.

9   Locke's political philosophy

Locke's political philosophy has generally been presented and assessed in terms of certain conclusions drawn from a few basic premises. Since Locke's political theory was not constructed according to the presuppositions of analytical philosophy, such an interpretive approach to his political thought seems better designed to portray Locke as an inconsistent or unclear thinker than to provide the reader of the *Two Treatises of Government* with an understanding of what Locke was attempting to do in writing that work.

I propose in this essay to follow another interpretive path by beginning with Locke's conclusion, namely, that "it is lawful for the people . . . to *resist* their King" (T II.xix.232: 437), and ask how and why did he come to that conclusion? If, as I shall argue, it was part of Locke's intentional objective in writing the *Two Treatises* to persuade his readers that they should resist the king, then putting the question in this form will assign considerable importance to determining the relationship between political theorizing and engagement in political actions.

To state summarily a point that I hope will be demonstrated throughout this essay, Locke believed that political theorizing was an exercise in practical reasoning. He took political actions to be guided by beliefs grounded upon probable evidence constrained by a few fundamental tenets of a theologically structured morality. Since I view the writing of the *Two Treatises of Government* as a political action, I shall assess the arguments within that text in terms of the probable evidence they supplied for Locke's beliefs and the extent to which they expressed his basic religious convictions.

Before considering those arguments, it should be noted that reformulating the interpretive problem as I have suggested effectively alters the nature and status of the evidence presented as an interpretation of Locke's political thought. In asking what Locke's purpose was in writing the *Two Treatises*, what the point of that action was, I am assuming that information regarding the author's (or actor's) intentions will supply some guidelines for determining the meaning of the action and, in this case, of various arguments advanced in the text. Yet few actions executed by individuals can be characterized with such simplicity as to suggest a single intentional objective. If, as seems evident, writing a work of political theory is a complex action, then in writing the *Two Treatises*, Locke was attempting to realize several objectives. These might include, for example, supplying a solution to the intellectual problem, drawn from the writings of Hugo Grotius or Samuel Pufendorf, of how to conceptualize property, or offering a justification for the act of tyrannicide in the specific context of the resistance by Locke's countrymen to the actions of Charles II or James II. In other words, since the meaning of a particular argument in the *Two Treatises* is referable, in part, to the multiple intentional objectives of the author, what the interpreter of that text offers the reader is a plausible reconstruction of its meaning that is always underdetermined in relation to the available evidence. I say "in part" because the author's beliefs and intentions are referable to social practices, conventions, and institutions that also provide a range of possible meanings in terms of which a particular concept, argument, or action may be understood.[1]

What I have attempted to do in this essay, therefore, is to provide a plausible reading of the *Two Treatises of Government* from the perspective of Locke's effort to supply a justification for active resistance to the illegitimate authority of the king. While I believe that this is the most important political objective that Locke wished to realize through the writing of that work, it is simply one of several interpretive frameworks according to which the meaning of the arguments in that text may be assessed.

If the actions of the king may be resisted, the first question is, under what conditions should individuals engage in such resistance? Since Locke's most general answer is that resistance is called for when the king becomes a tyrant, the problem becomes one of showing how such a specific transformation comes about and of supplying a general justification for resistance to tyranny.

Locke provides two convergent answers as to what constitutes "tyranny." One derives from classical political theory, and the other, though rooted in medieval political thought, must ultimately be seen in terms of the originality of Locke's formulation of the question. Tyranny occurs, Locke argues, "when the Governour, however intituled, makes not the Law, but his Will, the Rule; and his Commands and Actions are not directed to the preservation of the Properties of his People, but the satisfaction of his own Ambition, Revenge, Covetousness, or any other irregular Passion." In other words, tyranny is the ruler's use of his political power "not for the good of those, who are under it, but for his own private separate Advantage" (T II.xviii.199: 416–17). Thus, Locke maintains, "the difference betwixt a *King* and a *Tyrant* [consists] only in this, That one makes the Laws the Bounds of his Power, and the Good of the Publick, the end of his Government; the other makes all give way to his own Will and Appetite" (T II.xviii.200: 418). In Locke's restatement of the classical position, all political power must be exercised for the good of the community, and no ruler can be supposed to have "a distinct and separate Interest" from that of his people (T II.xiv.163: 394; cf. T II.xi.138: 378–79; T II.xii.143: 382; T II.xiv.164: 395). It is a subversion of "the end of government" – tyranny – for political power to be used to advance the self-interest of the ruler.

Although a number of specific queries must be answered in order to apply Locke's definition of tyranny to a particular situation – I will return to this problem later – the definition itself is clear. What I wish to note here is the structural constraint Locke places upon the concept of "self-interest" by formulating his political argument in this way. With respect to the exercise of political power, not only will the common good always take precedence over self-interest but, also, government will have to be constituted in such a manner as to rule out a Hobbesian Sovereign or a divinely instituted monarch who retains an interest that is distinct and separate from that of his subjects. On the other hand, if the latter are presumed – as they are by Locke – to have legitimate self-interests (e.g., religious beliefs and practices), their priority can be defended only by excluding them absolutely from the "ends of government" (as Locke maintains they are in the *Letter concerning Toleration*).

Locke's second definition of tyranny is "*the exercise of Power beyond Right*" (T II.xviii.199: 416), or as he more commonly phrases it, "the use of *force* without Authority" (T II.xiii.155: 389;

T II.xviii.202: 418–19; T II.xix.227: 434; T II.xix.232: 437). Thus, "whosoever in Authority exceeds the Power given him by the Law, and makes use of the Force he has under his Command, to compass that upon the Subject, which the Law allows not, ceases in that to be a Magistrate, and acting without Authority, may be opposed, as any other Man, who by force invades the Right of another" (T II.xviii.202: 418–19). This limitation upon the ruler's power is more formally stated than the first definition of tyranny, since it does not presuppose that the ruler's exercise of power necessarily contravenes the substantive common good of society, but only that the action "exceeds" the limitations imposed upon the ruler's power "by the Law."[2] To be sure, this argument depends upon a distinction between the ruler's will and the law, analogous to the self-interest/ common good distinction of the first definition of tyranny, but the thrust of the argument is directed toward providing an account of the nature and limits of authority. If the first definition proscribed tyranny in relation to the ends of government, the second, by focusing on "authority," raises the issue of the origins of political power.

For Locke, as for medieval Christian thinkers, political authority derived either from God or from the people. Having rejected Robert Filmer's particular defense of the first view in the *First Treatise*, Locke takes it as axiomatic that *"Politick Societies* all *began* from a voluntary Union, and the mutual agreement of Men" (T II.viii.102: 353; cf. T II.viii.106: 355–56; T II.viii.112: 361–62; T II.xvi.175: 402–3). Against Filmer's theory of divine right, Locke has good reasons for claiming that consent of the people as the source of political authority is the traditional view (T I.ii.6: 162), though, as we shall see, his interpretation of this proposition represents a departure from medieval political thought in several important respects. That political authority derives from the consent of the people collectively constituted means that the ruler must "be considered as the . . . Representative of the Commonwealth." That is, he is "the publick Person vested with the Power of the Law" as enacted "by the will of the Society, declared in its Laws; and thus he has no Will, no Power, but that of the Law." If he acts contrary to "the publick Will of the Society" expressed as law, he loses his authority "and is but a single private Person without Power," to whom the members of society no longer owe their obedience (T II.xiii.151: 386).

Putting aside for the moment the precise manner in which society enacts its will into laws, Locke's argument is premised upon the assumption that popularly enacted laws establish limits to a ruler's exercise of power, and when these limits are exceeded, the ruler loses his authority, which then returns to the people as the original source of all political authority. Since this transformation from ruler to tyrant changes his status from a "public" to a "private" person, as the latter, he has no "right" to use force against the people. Indeed, the people have a right to defend themselves, and thus to resist with force the actions of a tyrant.

In support of this argument, Locke cites the authority of William Barclay, an early seventeenth-century defender of absolutism who, notwithstanding his attack upon the *Vindiciae contra tyrannos*, the writings of George Buchanan, and other advocates of the right to resistance, conceded that *"the Body of the People"* could *"resist intolerable Tyranny"* (T II.xix.233: 439). Locke, however, pushes the argument further, rejecting Barclay's distinction between a "moderate" and an "intolerable" tyranny, maintaining that both, and not merely the latter, may be resisted. Locke also rejects Barclay's attempt to preserve the "superior" status of the king (tyrant) vis-à-vis an "inferior" subject, arguing that in exceeding the bounds of the law, the ruler forfeits all his privileges and power and puts himself into a state of war with any or all of his subjects; and in a state of war, "all former Ties are cancelled, all other Rights cease, and every one has a *Right* to defend himself, and *to resist the Aggressor"* (T II.xix.232: 437). And as this statement indicates, Locke does not accept Barclay's limitation of the right of resistance to the "Body of the People," but rather extends that right to "every one" or any individual, thus sanctioning tyrannicide as one possible form of resistance to tyranny (T II.xiv.168: 397–98; T II.xviii.208: 422; T II.xix.241: 445).

Thus far, it can be argued that in distinguishing between a lawful ruler and a tyrant, in identifying the ends of government with the use of political power for the common good of the people, and in tracing the origins of political authority to the consent of the people viewed as a corporative entity, Locke's theory of resistance preserves and is structured around a core of traditional political ideas. At the same time, Locke's references to the "right" of every individual and his underlying assumption of equality regarding the exercise of those rights not only point away from classical or medieval sources, but they also require a set of arguments – not yet introduced – to make them defensible aspects of Locke's political thought. Moreover, although the "misuse" of power is a defining characteristic of tyranny, "it is hard to consider it aright . . . without knowing the Form of Government in which it happens" (T II.xix.213: 426). Hence, Locke's theory of resistance requires both an elaboration of his fundamental presuppositions concerning political society and a more detailed and concrete characterization of how tyranny has occurred within the political society in which the readers of the *Two Treatises of Government* live so that they will be persuaded to resist it.

It might be supposed that the reconstruction of Locke's conception of political society requires that we turn immediately to a consideration of his basic assumptions about human nature and social relationships. But, in keeping with the interpretive approach of this essay, reasoning from the desired action – resistance – to the beliefs and evidence that justify and encourage it, Locke must show that tyranny exists (or existed) in late seventeenth-century England, for otherwise, regardless of the general principles concerning human behavior or the definitions of authority or tyranny his readers shared with him, they would not be persuaded to take political action against their government or to accept the justification offered on behalf of those who did. Of course, Locke's readers also hold certain religious and philosophical beliefs, but he does not have to show that his recommendation of resistance is logically deducible from these or some other set of beliefs, only that such action is compatible with and does not contravene the holding of those beliefs.

In his analysis of tyranny, Locke "supposes" a form of government such as England has, namely, a hereditary monarch, "an Assembly of Hereditary Nobility," and "an Assembly of Representatives chosen *pro tempore*, by the People" (T II.xix.213: 426). This analysis of tyranny is offered by Locke within the framework of the general question he is considering: under what conditions can the existing form of government be said to have "dissolved" and what happens to political power when this occurs?

Apart from foreign conquest, governments are generally dissolved, Locke argues, when the law-making authority established by the people – "the Legislative," as Locke refers to it – is altered or destroyed. Since "the *Constitution of the Legislative* is the first and fundamental Act of Society," establishing how the laws will be "made by persons authorized thereunto, by the Consent and Appointment of the People, . . . [w]hen any one, or more, shall take upon them to make Laws, whom the People have not appointed so to do, they make Laws without Authority, which the People are not therefore bound to obey." In these circumstances, the originally constituted government has dissolved, and the people, as a collective entity, "may constitute to themselves a *new Legislative,* as they think best, being in full liberty to resist the force of those, who without Authority would impose any thing upon them" (T II.xix.212: 425–26). Clearly, Locke has restated the general elements of his definition of tyranny – exceeding the law, violating the public will, using force without authority, and so forth – in such a way as to give these terms a specific meaning within the context of an institutional structure, namely, the English government.

In Locke's interpretation of the English government, Parliament is "the Legislative," and therefore "*the supream power* of the Common-wealth." No edict or command "of any Body else, . . . by what Power soever backed, [can] have the force and obligation of a *Law*" without the sanction of the legislative power (Parliament) (T II.xi.134: 374). "In well order'd Commonwealths," which Locke believes England to be, "the *Legislative* Power is put into the hands of divers Persons who duly Assembled, have by themselves, or jointly with others, a Power to make Laws, which when they have done, being separated again, they are themselves subject to the Laws, they have made" (T II.xii.143: 382; cf. T II.xiii.153: 387; T II.xiv.159: 392–93). Not only does this passage reaffirm one of the defining features of Locke's conception of political society – that everyone is subject to and no one is above the law (T II.vii.94: 347–48; T II.viii.97: 350; T II.xi.138: 378–79; T II.xi.142: 381) – but it also establishes a link between the people and their legislative assembly. Thus the latter is "made up of Representatives chosen . . . by the People" and "this power of chusing must also be exercised by the People, either at certain appointed Seasons, or else when they are summon'd to it" (T II.xiii.154: 388). In a well-ordered or "Constituted Commonwealth" (T II.xiii.153: 387), Locke insists that there is a continuous connection between the people and their government maintained through the medium of elections, whereby the people give their consent to the laws enacted by their deputies or representatives.

It is neither necessary nor convenient, Locke argues, for the legislature to be always in session, but it is essential that the laws be continuously enforced by the executive (T II.xii.144: 382–83; T II.xiii.153: 387–88; T II.xiv.159–60: 392–93). Between meetings of the legislature, therefore, the executive (king) may appear to hold "supreme power," but, Locke insists, he is always subordinate to the legislative power, even if, as in the case of England, he retains a share of legislative power through the use of a veto (T II.xiii.151–53: 386–88). However, since Locke also assumes that the calling of Parliament into session is left to the judgment of the executive (T II.xiii.154: 388; T II.xiii.156: 389–90; T II.xiii.158: 391–92; T II.xiv.167: 396), he is forced to consider the general problem of a conflict between the executive and the legislative powers of government if (as happened in England between 1681 and 1685) the king decides not to call Parliament into session.

"What if," he asks, "the Executive Power being possessed of the Force of the Commonwealth, shall make use of that force to hinder the *meeting* and *acting* of the Legislative, when the Original Constitution, or the publick Exigencies require it?" Locke answers that

using Force upon the People without Authority, and contrary to the Trust put in him, that does so, is a state of War with the People, who have a right to *reinstate* their *Legislative in the Exercise* of their Power. For having erected a Legislative, with an intent they should exercise the Power of making Laws, either at certain set times, or when there is need of it; when they are hindr'd by any force from, what is so necessary to the Society, . . . the People have a right to remove it by force. (T II.xiii.155: 388)

Locke has thus offered his reader a specific example of tyranny and a particular reason for engaging in resistance, namely, the restoration of an elected legislative assembly. When he restates the problem a few paragraphs later, the executive's refusal to convene the legislature is portrayed as a deprivation of the "right" of the people to have an elected legislature through the executive's "Exercise of a power without right" in denying this claim, leaving the people with "a liberty to appeal to Heaven" to justify their resistance in accordance with that "Law antecedent and paramount to all positive Laws," that is, the Law of Nature (T II.xiv.168: 397–98).

Locke relies primarily upon the definition of tyranny as an action contravening the common good, supposing that if it was the original intention of the people to place the law-making power in the hands of an elected assembly, it can never be in their common good for anyone to hinder or prevent that legislature from meeting whenever there is a "need" for it to do so (T II.xiii.155: 388; T II.xiv.163: 394–95; T II.xiv.166: 396). Although the question of who determines when there is a need for the legislature to meet is open-ended in the sense that the decision depends upon the prudential judgment of the executive, Locke makes it clear that this power is "a fiduciary trust" granted the executive by the people, who retain the right to judge whether it is being properly used (T II.xii.147: 383–84; T II.xiii.149: 385; T II.xiii.151: 386; T II.xiii.156: 389–90; T II. xiv.161: 393; T II.xiv.167–68: 396–98).

Having laid the foundations of his argument for resistance in the right of the people to have an elected legislature, Locke considers a number of specific actions the king might take – in addition to not calling Parliament into session (T II.xix.215: 427) – that effectively alter the legislative power as originally constituted and therefore dissolve the government, returning political power into the hands of the people. In the absence of a sitting legislature, the king may attempt to introduce "new Laws" or to substitute "his own Arbitrary Will in place of the Laws" (T II.xix.214: 426–27). He may alter the "ways of Election" according to which the legislature is chosen by the people (T II.xix.216: 427). He may attempt "to corrupt the *Representatives*" through bribery or intimidation, coercing them into voting according to "his designs" prior to or regardless of the outcome of elections, so that it cannot be said that the representatives were "freely chosen" by the people. All such actions by the king constitute a *"breach of trust"* and "a design to subvert the Government" (T II.xix.222: 431). Since Locke is showing how a constitutional government degenerates into tyranny, he argues that anyone who destroys the authority the people originally established "actually *introduce*[s] *a state of War*, which is that of Force without Authority," and such rulers – not the people – are therefore *"guilty of Rebellion"* (T II.xix.227: 434; T II.xix.230: 435–36; T II.xix.232: 437). Since all of these examples, as well as other actions cited by Locke that dissolve the government, such as the delivery of the commonwealth into the hands of a foreign power (T II.xix.217: 427–28) or the executive's abandonment of his duty so that the laws are not executed (T II.xix.219: 429), refer to the specific actions of Charles II or

James II, Locke has supplied his reader with what are in his estimation examples of tyranny and the grounds for resisting their king.[3]

Given that, as we have seen, the assumption underlying Locke's discussion of the right to resistance is the legitimacy and decline into tyranny of the English form of government, he arguably could have formulated his position in terms of the balancing – or imbalance – of political power distributed among king, lords, and commons, according to the "ancient constitution" of England.[4] Restoring the House of Commons to its rightful place in that constitution could certainly serve as a justificatory premise for resistance to the arbitrary and/or absolute power of the king. Yet Locke, rather notoriously, avoided using the historical and legalistic language of the ancient constitution approach, relying instead upon an appeal to natural law and an argument based upon natural rights.

One reason Locke did not structure his political theory around historical or legal precedents is his belief that "at best an Argument from what has been, to what should of right be, has no great force" (T II.viii.103: 354). Or, as he put it in one of his journal notes, the study of history is useful only "to one who hath well settled in his mind the principles of morality, and knows how to make a judgment on the actions of men" (Journal 1677: L I: 202). Mention of the principles of morality is significant because, according to Locke, "true politicks ... [is] a Part of Moral Philosophie." Not only does the latter include an inquiry "into the Ground and Nature of Civil Society; and how it is form'd into different Models of Government"; but it also presupposes, for Locke, some consideration of "the natural Rights of Men, and the Original and Foundations of Society, and the Duties resulting from thence" (Letter 2320: C VI: 215; Letter 3328: C VIII: 58; TE 186: 239). Thus, any decision to engage in resistance against the established government requires (1) a contextual knowledge of its particular form, the specific actions that comprise a "misuse of power" by the ruler, and the exercise of prudential judgment by the body of the people in concluding that *"great mistakes"* or "many wrong" actions constitute "a long train of Abuses ... all tending the same way" (T II.xix.225: 433; T II.xix.230: 435–36), that is, a pattern of tyranny; and (2) a defense of the natural rights of individuals and an understanding of the origins of political society grounded upon universal principles of morality.

Interestingly, "property" is a concept that is crucial to both aspects of Locke's argument in the *Two Treatises*. On the one hand, Locke maintains that an elected legislative assembly is essential to the protection and security of the property rights of individuals in Restoration England, and, on the other, he argues that property ownership precedes the establishment of political society and therefore must be understood in terms of the moral principles pertaining to the rights and duties of individuals and the origins of political society.

"The *Supream Power*," Locke declares, "*cannot take* from any Man any part of his *Property* without his own consent." For if someone could take "any part" of my property without my consent, he could take it all, and then it could not be said that I have any property at all.

Hence it is a mistake to think, that the Supream or *Legislative Power* of any Commonwealth, can do what it will, and dispose of the Estates of the Subject *arbitrarily*, or take any part of them at pleasure. This is not much to be fear'd in Governments where the *Legislative* consists, wholly or in part, in Assemblies which are variable, whose Members upon the Dissolution of the Assembly, are Subjects under the common Laws of their Country, equally with the rest. (T II.xi.138: 378–79)

The two alternatives to this form of government, "where the *Legislative* is in one lasting Assembly always in being, or in one Man, as in Absolute Monarchies," do present a problem, however, since it is difficult to imagine what obtaining my consent might mean, or how my giving that consent could function as an institutional barrier to the exercise of absolute or arbitrary power (T II.xi.138–39: 378–80).

That Locke is concerned to establish such a barrier is evident from his discussion of taxes. "For if any one shall claim a *Power to lay* and levy *Taxes* on the People, by his own Authority, and without such consent of the People, he thereby invades the *Fundamental Law of Property*, and subverts the end of Government." Since "Governments cannot be supported without great Charge," and this revenue must be raised through taxation, the latter can only be legitimized through "the Consent of the Majority, giving it either by themselves, or their Representatives chosen by them" (T II.xi.140: 380). It is one of the boundaries that "the Law of God and Nature, have *set to the Legislative* Power of every Commonwealth, in all Forms of Government," that the latter "must not raise Taxes on the

Property of the People, *without the Consent of the People*, given by themselves, or their Deputies." How this condition could be met in those societies where deputies are not "from time to time chosen" by the people, Locke does not make clear (T II.xi.142: 381).

Nor is it clear what limits Locke wishes to place upon a government that does have the consent of the people, expressed through their elected representatives, with respect to individuals' property. On the one hand, "every Man" upon joining political society "submits to the Community those Possessions, which he has, or shall acquire," and both his person and "his Land" are thereafter "regulated by the Laws of the Society" (T II.viii.120: 366). This reaffirms Locke's earlier statement that "in Governments the Laws regulate the right of property, and the possession of land is determined by positive constitutions" (T II.v.50: 320). Now it is possible to interpret such passages as simply the formalization of individuals' property rights through the laws or constitution of society. But it should be remembered that the purpose of all laws, including taxation, is to provide for the common good, and the only formal restraint upon legal taxation – the confiscation of private property to be used for the public good – is that it be done with "the consent of the people" or their representatives. In this regard, consider Locke's declaration in his 1667 *Essay concerning Toleration* that "the magistrate having a power to appoint ways of transferring proprieties from one man to another, may establish any, so they be universal, equal and without violence and suited to the welfare of that society" (B MS Locke c.28: Laslett 1967: 366n). On the other hand, while observing that "the utmost Bounds" of the Legislative power "is *limited to the publick good* of the Society," Locke insists that this power "can never have a right . . . designedly to impoverish the Subjects" (T II.xi.135: 375–76). Thus, political power is to be used "to secure [individuals] in the Possession and Use of their Properties" – which for Locke means "that Property which Men have in their Persons as well as Goods" – and to provide for the good of society as a whole (T II.xv.173: 401; cf. T II.xv.171: 399–400).

There is simply no recognition by Locke in the *Two Treatises* of a general problem arising out of a conflict between the government's obligation to secure the individual's "use" of property and its obligation to appropriate that property (through taxation) for the public good. What he is concerned to show, however, is that a government in which the law-making power is placed in the hands of an elected legislative assembly is less likely to act in an arbitrary or despotic manner, whatever laws it enacts with respect to property, than a form of government where this institutional feature is not present. It is not difficult to see why Locke structured his argument in this way, given the political context of the 1680s, when the Whigs were seeking to persuade the gentry that their property was more secure when Parliament was sitting than it was when, in the absence of Parliament, the king effectively exercised political power as an absolute monarch (Ashcraft 1986: 228–85).

Thus far, we have considered the implications for the use and distribution of political power of Locke's proposition that "the preservation of Property [is] the end of Government," but, as he points out, this "necessarily supposes and requires, that the People should *have Property*" at the time when they constitute political society (T II.xi.138: 378; italics in original). Since "the great end of Mens entering into Society," according to Locke, is "the enjoyment of their Properties in Peace and Safety," he must provide an account of how individuals come to have property prior to the formation of political society (T II.xi.134: 373–74; cf. T II.ix.124: 368–69).

It could be said that Locke, in positing a state of nature as the prepolitical condition of mankind, is engaging in counterfactual reasoning by removing the characteristic features of government from the social life of individuals. This view of Locke's approach to the problem, however, is too narrow and fails to capture the full significance of Locke's reliance upon the concept of the state of nature in the formulation of his political theory. What Locke emphasizes in the *Second Treatise* are the positive moral features of the natural state of man. He does so not because he is ignorant of the empirical data relating to the diverse and disruptive behavior of individuals – Locke was an avid reader of the anthropological reports contained in the voyage and travel literature of the seventeenth century – but because his notion of the state of nature is structured in terms of certain fundamental religious beliefs he held regarding the relationship between God and man. In other words, whereas men are wholly responsible for whatever they make of themselves in political society, what individuals are in their natural state primarily depends upon what one assumes God made them to be.

A "right" understanding of the nature and origins of political power, Locke argues, can only be built upon the assumption that all men have a *"perfect Freedom* to order their Actions, and dispose of their Possessions, and Persons as they think fit, within the bounds of the Law of Nature, without . . . depending upon the Will of any other Man." Since no one has more "Power" or "Jurisdiction" than another, this is "a *State* also *of Equality."* In justifying "this *equality* of Men by Nature" with respect to the use of power, Locke offers the ontological proposition "that Creatures of the same species" who have "the use of the same faculties" are equal, in the absence of a "manifest Declaration" or a "clear appointment" of divine will to the contrary, such as Filmer's political theory had supposed to exist (T II.ii.4–5: 287–88; T I.vi.67: 208). He then relates this "self evident" proposition of natural reason to the intentions of the Deity as man's creator. "For Men being all the Workmanship of one Omnipotent, and infinitely wise Maker . . . [are] sent into the World by his order and about his business." Thus, "the *State of Nature* has a Law of Nature to govern it, which obliges every one" and "that Law teaches all Mankind . . . that being all equal and independent, no one ought to harm another in his Life, Health, Liberty, or Possessions" (T II.ii.6: 289). The Law of Nature "is that measure God has set to the actions of Men, for their mutual security" (T II.ii.8: 290–91; T II.ii.11: 291–92; cf. T II.xi.135: 375–76).

Having supposed that God created all men free and equal and that they are under an obligation to obey His will, as expressed in natural law, Locke argues that the latter not only requires that we refrain "from doing hurt to one another," but it also places us under a positive obligation to promote the *"Preservation of all Mankind"* (T II.ii.6–8: 288–90; T II.ii.11: 291–92). That is, as members of "one Community of Nature," everyone's actions must "be conformable to the Law of Nature, *i.e.* to the Will of God, of which that is a Declaration, and the *fundamental Law of Nature* [is] *the preservation of Mankind"* (T II.xi.135: 375–76). This law presupposes, of course, that everyone *"is bound to preserve himself"* as part of an inclusive duty to preserve *"the rest of Mankind,"* but although Locke concedes human fallibility with respect to the application of this principle of action to particular cases, what he is concerned to demonstrate is that the "right" use of power by any individual in relation to another is directed toward preserving everyone (T II.ii.6: 288–89; T II.xi.135: 375–76; T II.xiv.159: 392–93; T II.xv.171: 399–400; T II.xvi.183: 408–9).

Thus, in the state of nature, Locke argues, "every one has a right to punish the transgressors of" the Law of Nature. Locke derives this proposition not only from the moral obligation that every individual *qua* individual has to act to preserve mankind, but he also assumes that every person in the state of nature will see a violation of natural law as "a trespass against the whole Species" and a threat to everyone in the "community" of nature, rather than as an act committed by one individual against another individual (T II.ii.7–8: 289–90; T II.ii.10–11: 291–92). This point has been insufficiently emphasized in the secondary literature on Locke, but it is crucial to his concept of power that it be inextricably linked to acting for the common good in the state of nature. For, as he observes, if the ruler's power cannot be understood in terms of "the common right" of every individual to act for the common good in the state of nature, then the exercise of that power within political society can claim no moral status whatsoever. "The *Municipal Laws* of Countries," Locke argues, "are only so far right, as they are founded on the Law of Nature, by which they are to be regulated and interpreted" (T II.ii.9: 290–91; T II.ii.11–12: 291–93; cf. T II.xi.135: 375–76; T I.ix.92: 227–28; T I.xi.126: 251). In providing an account of the origins and right use of political power, what Locke believes he has demonstrated with respect to the latter is "that the *end and measure of this Power*, when in every Man's hands in the state of Nature, being the preservation of all of his Society, that is, all Mankind in general, it can have no other *end or measure*, when in the hands of the Magistrate, but to preserve the Members of that Society in their Lives, Liberties, and Possessions" (T II.xv.171: 399–400; cf. T II.xi.134–35: 373–76).

Before turning to Locke's discussion of the origins of property, it will prove helpful to relate several arguments advanced in the *First Treatise* to Locke's usage of the concept of the state of nature in the *Second Treatise*. First, Filmer tried to establish in *Patriarcha* a necessary connection between property ownership and political power, arguing that God had made Adam both the proprietor and the ruler of the earth. He was then forced to maintain that Adam's political power and his title to property were inherited by Adam's

heirs. Locke offers a devastating critique of Filmer's position, showing that these "two Titles of Dominion ... cannot descend together"; that is, "the Sovereignty founded upon *Property*" ownership cannot sustain this inseparable linkage with the transmission
of political power over time (T I.vii.74–77: 214–17). Locke's detailed
examination of Filmer's statements, which are no longer of much
interest to present-day readers of the *Two Treatises*, has unfortunately obscured an important general point that emerges from this
attack; namely, that there is no necessary connection between property ownership and the exercise of political power.

As previously noted, Locke argues that the origin of political society is founded in the consent of individuals, a proposition with
which he concludes his chapter in the *Second Treatise* on the state
of nature (T II.ii.15: 295–96). In other words, political power is derived from personal consent, and what Locke tries to demonstrate
in the *First Treatise* is that property ownership cannot, in itself, convey any power over other persons. He observes that even if one assumed that "*Adam* was made sole Proprietor of the whole Earth,
what will this be to his Soveraignty?" It is simply not the case,
Locke insists, "that *Property* in Land gives a Man Power over the
Life of another" or that "the Possession even of the whole Earth"
can "give any one a Sovereign Arbitrary Authority over the Persons
of Men" (T I.iv.41–42: 187–88; cf. T I.ix.97–98: 230–31). Neither
Filmer nor anyone else can "prove that Propriety in Land ... gave
any Authority over the Persons of Men"; rather, "only [a] Compact"
between individuals can convey such authority (T I.iv.43: 188–89).
This argument and the distinction upon which it is based is reas-
serted in the *Second Treatise*. "Every Man," Locke declares, "is born
with a double Right: *First, A Right of Freedom to his Person,* which
no other Man has a Power over, but the free Disposal of it lies in
himself. *Secondly, A Right,* before any other Man, to *inherit,* with
his Brethren, his Fathers Goods" (T II.xvi.190: 411–12). There, as
elsewhere throughout the *Two Treatises,* Locke asserts the necessary connection between the freedom of one's person, consent, and
political power (T II.xvi.192: 412).

Locke's argument, in other words, not only rejects Filmer's historical and logical connection between property ownership and political power, but it also rejects any assumption that attempts to explain the nature or legitimacy of political power in terms of the

distribution of property ownership. To put it another way, if we could just assume that those who own property exercise political power in society, we could understand this relationship in terms of a straightforward empirical characterization of social relations, formulated in a manner similar to that adopted by Aristotle in the *Politics*. One of the purposes of Locke's employment of the concept of the state of nature, however, is to undermine the force of the presupposition that political authority is simply derived from and reflective of the social relations of property ownership by showing that political authority must be linked with the consent given by persons who are equal and independent. Hence, there is a moral autonomy to the realm of politics. The latter, for Locke, could never be understood merely as the protective outgrowth of the interests of property owners.

A second issue concerning property arising out of Locke's critique of Filmer in the *First Treatise* involves explaining the relationship between a definition of property in terms of "common use" by everyone in the original state of nature and a definition of property as exclusive use by individuals that comes into being at some later stage of human development, but prior to the institution of political society. Against Filmer's assertion that Adam was the sole proprietor of the earth, Locke interprets the Scriptures as providing "a Confirmation of the Original Community of all things among the Sons of Men" (T I.iv.40: 186–87). Locke's interpretation of this traditionally held view lays the foundation for any concept of property in a connection between "use," "subsistence," and God's purposes. Since God did not intend "that so curious and wonderful a piece of Workmanship" as man should perish, Locke argues that he specifically conveyed to every individual a right "to the use of those things, which were serviceable for his Subsistence." "Man had a right to a use of the Creatures, by the Will and Grant of God. . . . And thus Man's *Property* in the Creatures, was founded upon the right he had, to make use of those things, that were necessary or useful to his Being" (T I.ix.86: 222–23). Moreover, this is "an equal Right" and "a right in common" that everyone has to "provide for their Subsistence." Any successive development or notion of property, Locke argues, presupposes this fundamental right to subsistence, which all individuals can claim as a natural right (T I.ix.87–92: 224–28). It is worth noting in passing that Locke employs this general principle as the basis for a critique of the practice of primogeniture, which is not reconcilable with the equal right all children have to their parents' property according to the Law of Nature (T I.ix.88–91: 224–27; T I.ix.93: 228; T I.ix.97: 230–31).

Not only has the importance of this argument received insufficient attention from commentators on the *Two Treatises*, but many of them have denied that Locke defended everyone's natural right to subsistence. Such a view fails to appreciate the role this proposition plays as the core element of Locke's descriptive characterization of property, its role as a natural law claim in the context of Locke's theory of social relations, and the fact that such a claim can be incorporated into an enforceable economic policy within political society.

Locke begins the chapter on property in the *Second Treatise* with a restatement of the argument we have just considered, maintaining that both natural reason and Scripture support the view that individuals "have a right . . . to Meat and Drink, and such other things, as Nature affords for their Subsistence" (T II.v.25: 303–4). How this assertion fits into Locke's discussion of property in that chapter, we shall see in a moment. My point here is to show that it constitutes, as Locke maintained that it did in the *First Treatise*, the starting point for any theory of property.

Speaking of the relationship between God and mankind, Locke observes that he gave "them all a Right, to make use of the Food and Rayment, and other Conveniencies of Life . . . for their Subsistence" (T I.iv.41: 187–88). It is on the basis of this intentional design and authority of the Deity that a "needy Brother" may claim "a Right to the Surplusage" of his brother's goods, which "cannot justly be denied him, when his pressing Wants call for it." The same natural law principle of charity "gives every Man a Title to so much out of another's Plenty, as will keep him from extream want, where he has no means to subsist otherwise" (T I.iv.42: 188). Later, Locke invokes "the Fundamental Law of Nature . . . that all, as much as may be, should be preserved" in order to show that in a conflict of rights between the property a just conqueror might claim and the subsistence claims of the wives and children of the conquered soldiers, the latter claim takes precedence, since "he that hath, and to spare, must . . . give way to the pressing and preferable Title of those, who are in danger to perish without it" (T II.xvi.183: 408–9).

Following the Glorious Revolution, Locke was appointed a member of the Board of Trade, whose duties included the formulation and administration of the government's economic policy. In connection with a request from the king for the board to suggest revisions in the Poor Laws, Locke drafted a memorandum reflecting his views on the subject, in which he declares that "every one must have meat, drink, clothing, and firing. So much goes out of the stock of the kingdom, whether they work or no" (Fox Bourne 1876: 2:382). Not only does Locke assume this natural right of subsistence to be included within his concept of the common good, to which the legal and economic resources of the government may be directed in the form of poor relief, but he also proposes that it be made a crime chargeable against the administrative officer of such relief in each parish if any person dies of starvation for want of that relief (Fox Bourne 1876: 2:390). In short, Locke clearly believed that the natural right to subsistence was an enforceable right, that is, one of those instances in which "the Obligations of the Law of Nature, cease not in Society, but . . . have by Humane Laws known Penalties annexed to them, to inforce their observation" (T II.xi.135: 375–76).

Turning to a consideration of the chapter on property in the *Second Treatise,* I will limit my discussion to those points that illustrate the connections Locke is attempting to forge in the *Two Treatises* as a whole between a few fundamental philosophical and religious beliefs and the political objectives to be realized through collective action. First, Locke must explain how the transition from a stage of subsistence property and common right to one of individual and unequal property ownership occurs prior to the institution of political society, and why this transition is consonant with the precepts of natural law. Second, given this transition, he wants to show that the stability and prosperity of property ownership depends upon a constitutional form of government and that neither can be sustained under an absolute monarchy.

"Every Man," Locke declares, "has a *Property* in his own *Person*" which "no Body has any Right to but himself." Expressed through the action of labor, the latter is "the unquestionable Property of the Labourer" and "no Man but he can have a right to what that is once joyned to." This definition of property rooted in the freedom of the person "excludes the common right of other Men" to what the individual's labor has produced, at least, Locke adds, "where there is

enough, and as good left in common for others" (T II.v.27: 305–6).
As the elaborative discussion that follows makes clear, "the common right of every one" and the Law of Nature precepts applicable
to "the *beginning of Property*" describe a condition prior to "private
Possession" as understood by "the Civiliz'd part of Mankind" where
compacts and "positive Laws . . . determine Property," so that having
"enough and as good left in common for others" is a restrictive condition upon an individual's productive labor within the context of a
claim to subsistence others might make with respect to the products of that labor (T II.v.28–30: 306–8). Thus, Locke argues, the Law
of Nature establishes limits to what an individual "may by his labour fix a Property in," namely, to what he "can make use of to any
advantage of life before it spoils" (T II.v.31: 308). Locke extends the
argument beyond acorns and deer to land, so that "*as much Land
as a Man Tills, Plants, Improves, Cultivates, and can use the Product
of, so much is his Property*" (T II.v.32–33: 308–9).

Locke is still describing, as he had in the *First Treatise*, the condition of mankind at the beginning of the world, when "God gave the
World to Men in Common." In that condition, "the measure of Property . . . [is] set, by the Extent of Mens *Labour*," and the meaning of
"use" is limited by the consumption needs of the individual and his
family. "This *measure* did confine every Man's *Possession*, to a very
moderate Proportion," and constituted no "Injury to any Body in the
first Ages of the World" when there was plenty of land and relatively
few people (T II.v.34–36: 309–11). Thus, "Men had a Right to appropriate, by their Labour, each one to himself, as much of the things
of Nature, as he could use," and "he had *no Right, farther than his
Use* called for" any goods of nature, to appropriate more than he
could consume. If he did so, "he offended against the common Law
of Nature" for having "invaded his Neighbour's share," and he "was
liable to be punished" for violating natural law (T II.v.37: 312–23;
T II.v.46: 317–18; T II.v.51: 320). "For the most part," however, individuals in this first stage of the state of nature, "contented themselves with what un-assisted Nature offered to their Necessities"
(T II.v.45: 317). In other words, Locke assumes that it is obvious that
"the necessity of subsisting made the first Commoners of the World
look after" those commodities which, "if they are not consumed by
use, will decay and perish of themselves." And "of those good things
which Nature hath provided in common, every one had a Right . . .

to as much as he could use, and had a Property in all that he could affect with his Labour." If he attempted "to hoard up more than he could make use of," "he took more than his share, and robb'd others" (T II.v.46: 317–18). This moral terminology derives from the structure of Locke's argument, for not only had a man no "right" to take "more than his share" of what God had given to mankind in common for their subsistence, he also has, according to the Law of Nature, a positive duty to act in a manner that seeks to preserve mankind, which principle, in Locke's view, the actions of hoarding and waste violate.

In the last paragraph of the chapter on property, Locke summarizes the moral and social parameters of life in the first stage of the state of nature:

it is very easie to conceive . . . *how Labour could at first begin a title of Property* in the common things of Nature, and how the spending it upon our uses bounded it. So that there could then be no reason of quarrelling about Title, nor any doubt about the largeness of Possession it gave. Right and conveniency went together; for as a Man had a Right to all he could employ his labour upon, so he had no temptation to labour for more than he could make use of. This left no room for Controversie about the Title, nor for Encroachment on the Right of others; what Portion a Man carved to himself, was easily seen; and it was useless as well as dishonest to carve himself too much, or take more than he needed. (T II.v.51: 320; cf. T II.v.39: 314)

What I have been arguing is that to understand Locke's argument in the chapter on property it is essential to see it in terms of the structure of his political theory in the *Two Treatises*, in which moral foundations are linked to practical objectives. Hence the first stage of the state of nature – the original condition in which God placed mankind – is one in which property is defined in naturalistic and moral terms, where the key concepts are freedom of one's person, labor, use, the right to subsistence, and the Law of Nature or God's will. This stage, or way of life, for which the Indians in America provide a useful illustration (T II.v.26: 304–5; T II.v.30: 307–8; T II.v.41: 314–15; T II.v.43: 316–17; T II.v.46: 317–18; T II.v.48–49: 319; T II.viii.105: 354–55; T II.viii.108: 357–58), must be grasped holistically; Locke is, after all, offering a developmental picture of the state of nature, its transition from one stage to another, where both stages precede the institution of political society. It is a mistake to believe that the moral features characteristic of the first stage simply disappear with the invention of money and the other historical developments that characterize the second stage of the state of nature (see Macpherson 1962 and Strauss 1953). For, as we have seen, Locke certainly believes that the natural right to subsistence is carried forward in time as an enforceable moral claim in the most advanced or civilized state of society.

Locke's description of the second stage of the state of nature represents an empirical (historical) extension of the first stage. The key concepts of this stage are consent, exchange, commerce, cities, and money. As Locke makes clear in Paragraph 36, the *"Rule of Propriety"* governing the subsistence stage of the state of nature is transformed through the consent of individuals to accept money in exchange for the goods produced through their labor, thus allowing individuals a "Right" to "larger Possessions" (T II.v.36: 310–11). This "mutual consent" to exchange perishable goods for money "did no injury" to anyone else nor did it waste "the common Stock" of mankind. In fact, Locke maintains that by encouraging the productive use of labor and the cultivation of the land, this process of exchange results in an "increase [in] the common stock of mankind," and it therefore represents a positive contribution to the preservation of mankind (T II.v.37: 312–23; T II.v.46–47: 317–19).

Apart from demonstrating that the use of money is consonant with the purposes of natural law, Locke supplies a historical account of how "Families increased" and people "settled themselves together, and built Cities, and then, by consent, . . . and by Laws within themselves, settled the *Properties* of those of the same Society" (T II.v.38: 313–14; T II.v.45: 317). In addition to these demographic changes, Locke identifies the invention of money with commerce and trade, and a productive use of labor beyond that necessary to supply the consumption needs of the individual's family (T II.v.46–48: 317–19; T II.v.50: 319–20). Thus, in Locke's terms, one moves from a labor-use-familial-consumption stage of existence to a production-for-exchange society, where men require laws to regulate their property rights. "And so, *by Compact* and Agreement," individuals "settled the Property which Labour and Industry began." Once men settled in cities, "common Consent" and *"positive agreement"* rather than "natural common Right" determined the boundaries of property (T II.v.45: 317). This progressive development in the social relations of property assumes that everyone benefits in a society devoted to trade. Hence, Locke argues that the day-laborer in England is better off than "a King of a large and fruitful Territory" in America (T II.v.41: 314–15). In other words, Locke assumes, as an empirical proposition, that a money-exchange economy benefits every member of society because the wealth of society as a whole filters down to the individuals of the lowest socioeconomic status in that society, giving them a comparative advantage over individuals (e.g., Indians) who remain at a subsistence stage of economic development. Given the structure of Locke's moral argument, this means that the well-being of individuals must be viewed not merely in material terms but also as a progressive fulfillment of the obligation to preserve mankind by improving the conditions that make the execution of this obligation possible.

Economic development, however, carries with it certain problems, chief among which are disputes over property rights, where the latter are established by "mutual consent" or contracts. In a subsistence society, Locke observes, "there could be then little room for Quarrels or Contentions about Property" (T II.v.31: 308; T II.v.39: 314). Since Locke believes that "quarrelling about Title" or "about the largeness of Possession" of property is the major source of those controversies among individuals that make it necessary to institute government as an umpire to resolve them (T II.v.51: 320; T II.vi.75: 335–36; T II.viii.107–8: 356–58), there is a rather direct connection in Locke's argument between economic development from the first to the second stage of the state of nature and the necessity of some form of government.

Summarizing the characteristics of individuals in the early stage of the state of nature, Locke writes that "the equality of a simple poor way of liveing confineing their desires within the narrow bounds of each man's smal propertie made few controversies, and so no need of many laws to decide them." Because "their Possessions, or way of living . . . afforded little matter for Covetousness or Ambition . . . there were but few Trespasses, and few Offenders" against the Law of Nature (T II.viii.107: 356–57). Thus, "want of People and Money gave Men no Temptation to enlarge their Possessions of land, or contest for wider extent of Ground" (T II.viii.108: 357). In the absence of such controversies over property rights, there was "no contest betwixt Rulers and People about Governours or Government" (T II.viii.111: 361). Nor did they require many laws (T II.viii.107: 356–57; T II.xiv.162: 394), from which it follows for Locke – he is here providing a historical account of the origins of government – that people did not have to concern themselves with how to institute a law-making power as the first prerequisite of political society. Rather, "*Monarchy* being simple, and most obvious to Men" as a form of government as an extension of a patriarchal family, it was "also best suited to their present State and Condition" because they "stood more in need of defence against foreign Invasions and Injuries, than of multiplicity of Laws" (T II.viii.107: 356–57).

The presuppositions underlying this argument, that simple forms of government (monarchy) are "best suited" to simple socioeconomic conditions, also support, of course, an argument that a form of government more complicated than placing all political power in the hands of one man is "best suited" to more complex socioeconomic conditions, where controversies over property rights are more frequent and "a multiplicity of Laws" may be necessary to resolve them. Thus Locke observes that as the wealth of society increased, "Ambition and Luxury . . . taught Princes to have distinct and separate Interests from their People," a condition that makes "the oppression of tyrannical dominion" a much more likely occurrence. In these circumstances, "Men found it necessary to examine more carefully *the Original* and Rights of *Government;* and to find out ways to *restrain the Exorbitances,* and *prevent the Abuses* of that Power which they [had] intrusted in another's hands only for their own good." This reconsideration of the nature and purposes of political power led the people "to think of Methods of . . . ballancing the Power of Government, by placing several parts of it in different hands" (T II.viii.107: 356–57; T II.viii.111: 360–61). Or, as Locke states the point unequivocally in another passage, it might be true historically that during "the negligent, and unforeseeing Innocence of the first Ages" of mankind, political power was placed in the hands of one man, but, he argues, "the People finding their Properties not secure under the Government, as it then was, . . . could never be safe nor at rest, *nor think themselves in Civil Society,* till the Legislature was placed in collective Bodies of Men, call them Senate, Parliament, or what you please" (T II.vii.94: 347–48).

Constitutional government, as a balancing of powers that includes an elected legislative body, thus provides that security for the properties of individuals living in a money-exchange economy which monarchy as a form of government is unlikely and/or unable to provide. Locke's discussion of property in the *Two Treatises*, therefore, does much more than provide a description of and a moral justification for the origin of private property; he also offers a defense of constitutional government based upon his developmental account of property.

What I have tried to offer in this essay is an interpretive reading of the *Two Treatises of Government* that illustrates the extent to which the practical objectives to be achieved through collective action – resistance to tyranny – structure the theoretical framework of Locke's political thought as expressed in that text. Locke's defense of constitutional government, on the one hand, is grounded upon the theological and moral principles he identifies with the Law of Nature; and, at the same time, is a recognizable facsimile of the specific political institutions of seventeenth-century England. Yet Locke's natural law argument is not simply a compilation of moral precepts, abstractly stated (see Dunn 1969a and Grant 1987). When viewed in relation to Locke's developmental account of the stages of the state of nature and the origins of property, Locke's natural law argument is capable of defending both the moral economy of a natural right to subsistence and the beneficial features of a market society. This defense of commerce is also employed by Locke as a political weapon against absolute monarchy, or, to put it in more positive terms, as part of his normative and historical justification for the emergence of constitutional government, which, at a minimum, includes within the notion of "consent" the right of individuals to elect a representative legislative assembly.

This right of the people to have an elected legislature redress grievances was, as I suggested at the outset, the starting point for any understanding of the political arguments advanced by the radical Whigs led by the earl of Shaftesbury in the 1680s, and for an interpretive understanding of why Locke wrote the *Two Treatises of Government*. That work thus supplies a historical and theoretical basis for linking the discourses of revolution and democracy through an activist interpretation of the concept of popular sovereignty. These arguments, in turn, are premised upon assumptions concerning the moral equality, rationality, and independence of individuals and their capacity to direct their actions to achieve the common good. How far the implications of the arguments presented in the *Two Treatises* were meant by Locke to extend is a vexing question, about which interpreters of the text may reasonably disagree. But it is hardly claiming too much to see in Locke's political thought the intellectual foundations for the struggles in the eighteenth and nineteenth centuries to achieve political independence and to extend the practices and institutions of democracy.

NOTES

1 Quentin Skinner has provided arguments for and illustrative examples of this interpretive approach to political theory. A bibliography as well as a critical assessment of Skinner's writings can be found in Tully 1988b.
2 An example relevant to Locke's argument and to English politics would be the attempt by the king to impose a tax that, regardless of its consequential benefits to society, would be deemed to be an exercise of power beyond his authority.
3 I have elaborated upon Locke's analysis of tyranny in the context of the political events of the 1680s in Ashcraft 1986: esp. 286–337 and 521–89.
4 In fact, while Locke could certainly have defended a policy of resistance framed in the language of the ancient constitution, I do not think he could have developed the arguments for moral egalitarianism (of individuals in the state of nature) within the framework of that language. For an analysis of the structure of political debate at the time of the Glorious Revolution that is sensitive to the political implications of the language and arguments employed by political writers, see Goldie 1980.

10   Locke's influence

I

John Locke is the most influential philosopher of modern times. His *Essay* initiated the vigorous and lasting philosophical tradition that is known as British empiricism, but Locke's importance reaches far beyond the limits of what has since his time become recognized as the professional discipline of philosophy. His influence in the history of thought, on the way we think about ourselves and our relations to the world we live in, to God, nature and society, has been immense. His great message was to set us free from the burden of tradition and authority, both in theology and knowledge, by showing that the entire grounds of our right conduct in the world can be secured by the experience we may gain by the innate faculties and powers we are born with. God "commands what reason does" (W VII: 11) are the words that best reveal the tenor and unity of Locke's thought.[1]

Leslie Stephen wrote that Locke was "the intellectual ruler of the eighteenth century" (Stephen 1876: 1:86). Voltaire, who throughout his career was Locke's devoted champion, called him the "Hercules of metaphysics" because he had fixed the bounds of the human mind (Voltaire, Letter of 1768 to Horace Walpole; cited by Stewart 1816–21: 1:220n). Within less than ten years of Locke's death, Addison and Steele regularly referred to and cited Locke in their periodical the *Spectator*, which aimed to meet the interests of the growing middle-class reading audience. In 1717, at the age of fourteen, Jonathan Edwards read the *Essay* in New Haven with excitement that had lasting consequences for his thought (Miller 1956: 175–83). Samuel Johnson took his basic view of language from Locke and included some thirty-two hundred quotations from him in his famous dictionary, more than from any other source (McLaverty 1986: 384). Laurence Sterne said his genius had been nourished by lifelong dedication to the reading of Locke, whose psychology shaped both Sterne's characters and the innovative technique of his fiction (Howes 1974: 414). When the enterprising publisher Charles Joseph Panckoucke began, late in the century, to issue his *Encyclopédie méthodique*, he devoted four volumes to "logique et métaphysique." Taking the first of these volumes as a sample, we find Locke represented by the entire chapter "Of the Association of Ideas" (E II.xxxiii) and, in the article "Idea," by Chapters i–xii and xxix–xxxi of the *Essay*'s Book II. The introduction to the four volumes explains that since it was the aim to make them "a compilation of the best treatises, dissertations, and articles on metaphysics and logic . . . the reader will understand that it is chiefly Locke and Condillac who have provided most of the entries" (*Encyclopédie méthodique* 1786–91: 1:xv–xvi). A little index-hopping would quickly produce a wealth of other nontrivial mentions of Locke in the print world of eighteenth-century Europe.

It would obviously be useless to pursue Locke into every nook and cranny of eighteenth-century life and thought, but it is useful to ask the general and fundamental question: what were the features of his thought that gave Locke the acceptance and appeal he enjoyed both in England and on the Continent (where most of his works became known in French translations even before his death in 1704)? It will be the first aim of this essay to give a compact answer to that question. I shall next, chiefly drawing on the *Essay*, by a few examples or soundings seek to illustrate some of the variety of ways in which particular aspects of Locke's philosophy gained attention and even popularity in eighteenth-century thought. I shall, thirdly, treat Locke's role in the new philosophy of language, chiefly associated with Condillac, that is one of the great and enduring achievements of the eighteenth century. Finally, I shall briefly deal with Locke's fall from favor – or rather grace – in the century of Coleridge, Victor Cousin, Carlyle, and Emerson, before I conclude with the revival of Locke studies, which during the last generation has greatly increased the understanding of his thought and our respect for his achievement.

Let us first, however, call to mind a few facts about the world in which Locke lived. The seventeenth century has often been called the century of reason and genius. This distinction is readily granted when we recall such names as Descartes, Poussin, Hobbes, Corneille, Milton, Molière, Pascal, Spinoza, Leibniz, and Locke, and when we contemplate the astonishing emergence of the new way of understanding nature and creation that we associate with the science of Kepler, Galileo, Boyle, and Newton. This science was soon felt to be so important and productive of welfare that its promotion became institutionalized in scientific societies both in Paris and London already during the 1660s. But this spirited picture is only one face of that remarkable century.

For the vast majority of the men and women who lived in Europe during Locke's century, the immediate reality was very different. It was a time of violence, death, rape, war, and devastation on a vast scale. It was years of religious strife caused by sectarian disputes over the right reading of Scriptures and the flaunting of royal despotism justified by the doctrine of the divine right of kings. It was a world of constant religious and political intolerance and repression, and of ensuing dislocation that made fugitives wander across the lands of Europe in search of peace and security. England had its share of this reality in the religious enthusiasm and apocalyptic promises of life in an egalitarian society that largely caused the disorders and violence of the 1640s and 1650s.

In England the Restoration of 1660 promised a return to order, but on what principles was that order to be based, since the mere claim of royal prerogative would not alone prevail? We get a sense of one weighty answer in the programmatic pronouncement by Thomas Sprat, speaking for the Royal Society and its new science, that "the intellectual Disposition of this Age is bent upon a rational Religion" (Sprat 1667: 374). The sense is clear: since science is the study of God's revelation in creation, it will encourage all humanity to join together in peaceful living by inculcating the ecumenical lesson of rationality and order, which our senses and reason, acting in consort, teach us in the study of nature. Sprat emphasized that it was not the society's aim to give its work any particular national or religious cast, but to found "a Philosophy of Mankind" (Sprat 63). Both the *Essay* and Locke's other works were written in the spirit of this universalist union of faith and knowledge.[2]

II

The vast appeal and influence of Locke's thought flow chiefly from what was judged to be his successful application of the method of natural philosophy to the study of what pertains to the mind. Max Weber talked about "the disenchantment of the world" as the mark of modernity and secularization, by which he meant the effect of the increasing mastery of the physical world that makes us confident we can understand things rationally, that is, without belief in magic or thoughts of mysterious little creatures that rush in and get busy when we start the car. With the *Essay* Locke performed a corresponding disenchantment of the human world, and it was this disenchantment that more than any other factor provided the thrust for Locke's influence. The *Essay*, Sterne said, is "a history-book . . . of what passes in a man's own mind" (Howes 1974: 44). In his famous thirteenth letter in *Letters concerning the English Nation*, Voltaire noted that after so many had written "the Romance of the Soul, a Sage at last arose, who gave, with an Air of the greatest Modesty, the History of it. Mr. *Locke* . . . every where takes the Light of Physicks for his Guide" (Voltaire 1733: 248; see Voltaire 1734: 222–27 for other texts on Locke; see also Bonno 1947, who shows that Voltaire was not the first Frenchman to cast Locke in that role).

A much weightier tribute to Locke appeared in 1751 in d'Alembert's important *Preliminary Discourse* to that great monument of eighteenth-century thought and culture, the *Encyclopédie*, which d'Alembert was then editing with Denis Diderot. Locke, he wrote, had "created metaphysics [i.e., philosophy], almost as Newton had created physics. . . . In a word, he reduced metaphysics to what it really ought to be: the experimental physics of the soul" (d'Alembert 1751: 83–84). In the work cited earlier Voltaire had already joined Newton with Locke, and this pairing became a commonplace – which shows how well the eighteenth century understood Locke's deed of disenchantment. We can best understand how Locke performed this radical turn by looking at a familiar detail of his thought.

The best-known and most dramatic feature of Locke's thought is the dismissal of innate ideas and principles from epistemology and the philosophy of mind, on the grounds that no matter how he looked at the issue he found it impossible to distinguish what was claimed to be innate ideas and principles from what we can acquire by our natural faculties, which of course are innate. For Locke even the idea of God was not innate, but will invariably be discovered, that is acquired, by a rational mind that seriously reflects on the works of creation (E I.iv.9: 89) – so why would God have wasted his efforts by furnishing us with innate knowledge when we are capable of gaining the same knowledge by the faculties He has put into our nature (E I.iv.21: 98–99)? The innateness doctrine is esoteric and thus open to repressive exploitation by people in positions of authority who claim to be the guardians of these hidden truths, a point Locke made more than once with great emphasis in the opening book of the *Essay*. The rejection of innate ideas immediately involved Locke in controversy with theologians who found his argument a threat to religious belief and the maintenance of church discipline. The innateness doctrine was in fact theological rather than philosophical, and its rejection played over a large register, from Descartes to the apocalyptic enthusiasts of the 1640s and 1650s. Natural philosophy can only admit knowledge that is open to all, that is, drawn from the shareable experience of reflection and sensation, of reason and the senses. Locke often insisted that the enthusiasts' claims to truth by private revelation were empty and socially disruptive.

It was common in the seventeenth century to cite the angels and Adam before the Fall as creatures whose knowledge was perfect because it was innate. Descartes even aspired to recapture "the primordial knowledge" of the angels (Aarsleff 1993). In this view the model of truth was in the past, at the beginning, and the improvement of knowledge would become possible only by reversing the moral and spiritual causes of our loss – truth itself was a religious issue. It was for this reason that Descartes had to put himself in the angelic or Adamic position of having assurance of the existence of God before he could trust what his senses told him about the world. For the same reason he also held that unbelievers could not be trusted as philosophers, even in mathematics. Similarly, for Descartes there was no possibility of natural theology, no basis for Deism, because God is too inscrutable for us to understand His plan of creation.

Since they were part and parcel of the innateness doctrine, Locke rejected these claims about the relation between prelapsarian begin-

nings and our present state. In place of the recovery of timeless sta-
sis he offered process and progress. Well aware, of course, of the
theological bases of these claims, Locke directed his attack at the
heart of the matter by asserting what has felicitously been called
Adam's ordinary humanity. In the first of the *Two Treatises of Government* Locke demolished Robert Filmer's Adamic patriarchalism,
which asserted that the right of royal power had descended by primogeniture in Adam's line, a doctrine that by its very strangeness
to us reveals the century's trust in the Adamic archetype. It is well
known that Locke in the *Second Treatise* places the origin of political obligation in the free and contractual passage from the state of
nature into civil society. Kings do not rule by divine right. Societies,
states, and sovereignty are human institutions. Locke brought equal
force to bear against two other substantial claims in the Adamic
theology.

In the *Essay* Locke repeatedly, especially in Book III, asserted that
words become signs of ideas "not by any natural connexion, that
there is between particular articulate Sounds and certain *Ideas*, for
then there would be but one Language amongst all Men" (E III.ii.1:
405) – as was claimed for the postulated Adamic language – but only
"*by a perfectly arbitrary Imposition*" (E III.ii.8: 408). A language
works only by the tacit consent among its speakers to respect the
familiar use of words, that is, by contract. Locke several times talks
about "the beginners of languages," and though he never expressly
says so, these beginnings must have been contractual, like the con-
tinuance by tacit consent in the case of civil society. Locke's rejection of the Adamic language doctrine was at the same time a repeti-
tion of what he had done for innateness in Book I, for current
interpretation of Genesis had based Adam's epistemological privilege of innate knowledge on his naming of the animals according to
their true natures and essences – the very essences that Locke argued we could never know (on Adam's ordinary humanity, see also
E III.vi.44–51: 466–71).

Finally, in the opening pages of *The Reasonableness of Christianity* Locke dismissed the doctrine of original sin both because he
found no support for it in the Bible and because he found it contrary
to reason and unworthy of our idea of God and His benevolence.
Christ did not redeem mankind from original sin, but from the loss
of immortality that, Locke argued, was the consequence of the Fall.

Christ came as the restorer of all men to "that life, which they receive again at the resurrection" (W VII: 9). It is no wonder that Locke was charged with being anti-Trinitarian and Socinian, that is, roughly what we today would call unitarian. Locke was ever acutely aware of our passionate and sinful impulses, of how hard it is to perform God's will by being rational in thought and deed, but he wished to make sure that each individual was held responsible only for his own actions, and for that reason he was committed to the position that a philosophy for all mankind – we recall Sprat's phrase – could not fairly be based on what had not by the word been revealed to all. There is no doubt at all that Locke himself was a pious believer in scriptural revelation, but his public philosophy was directed toward God's manifest revelation in creation because it, by being open to the reason and senses of all, allows for equality of knowledge for all.

It requires effort to grasp the radical nature of Locke's moves against contemporary arguments for political, epistemological, and religious authority. Even such a rational man as Locke's near-contemporary Henry More defended innate ideas because he feared that belief in the reality of witchcraft would be lost without them. By banishing all thought of innate culpability and natural inferiority that had to be relieved by the intercession of traditionally sanctioned authorities, Locke gave mankind total autonomy in the conduct of its affairs in this world, even for the rightness of conduct that might merit a life among the blessed hereafter.

This autonomy became possible because the abandonment of the innate doctrine opened the way for three features that must be counted among the most widely influential in Locke's thought: the notion that knowledge is cumulative and progressive, the necessity of communication, and curiosity about cultural variety or what we today with a technical term would call comparative anthropology. None of these would have any legitimacy for those who believed that our epistemological task is the recovery of lost and perfect knowledge and that cultural differences were the result of degrees of moral degeneration from the archetype. In Book I of the *Essay* Locke supported his argument against innateness with copious examples from travel accounts that showed the total absence in many populations of the very conceptions that were claimed to be innate. Such accounts gave information about human nature much like the knowledge the scientist could gain by experiment. Locke's library

was especially rich in travel literature, and he may even have had
a hand in preparing the large four-volume collection that his own
publishers brought out in the year of his death. Books of travel were
widely – even wildly – popular in the eighteenth century, and a good
number of them gained a place in philosophy proper.

Locke believed that cultural differences had their source not in
uneven natural endowments, but in unequal opportunities for time
and leisure to develop our faculties. "We are born to be, if we please,
rational creatures," he wrote, "but it is use and exercise only that
makes us so" (Conduct 6: W III: 220). When he compared people of
different stations in life, from the ordinary workman to the "country gentleman," he charged the wide variations of intellectual at-
tainments that he noted, not to inequality of "natural parts," but to
the "different scope that has been given to their understandings to
range in, for the gathering up of information, and furnishing their
heads with ideas" (Conduct 3: W III: 212). In this respect he found
that "porters and coblers of great cities" surpass the modest craftsman of a country town, who in turn does somewhat better than "the
day-labourer of a country-village." The level of intellectual culture
is largely determined by the opportunity for communication; the
progress of mind and knowledge (phrases that Locke used with some
frequency) is more likely to occur in cities than in the isolation of
the countryside. The same principle applied to populations in distant parts of the world. Thus Locke believed that the "ancient savage
Americans . . . come no way short of those of the most flourishing
and polite Nations" in regard to "natural Endowments and Provis-
ions" (E IV.xii.11: 646).

Locke often spoke harshly of the dull minds of the common
people, but he was just as severe in his opinion of scholars who, he
found, were much given to narrow views and sectarian reading that
induced dangerous error and illusion. Children, by contrast, he
found more rational than they were generally given credit for being.
Education for wise, rational, and happy living was one of Locke's
deepest concerns, evident not only in the educational writings but
also in the *Essay*. Habit and exercise of our natural talents make the
great difference. Self-improvement and progress are possible both for
the individual and for the group. Rationality is a personal achievement, which in turn entails a heavy responsibility for individual
conduct.

Locke's inquiry "into the Original, Certainty, and Extent of humane Knowledge; together, with the Grounds and Degrees of Belief, Opinion, and Assent" (E I.i.2: 43) – properly called an "essay" – was both in its private nature and its public effect not unlike Freud's self-analysis two hundred years later. For Locke himself the writing of the *Essay* was the sort of education to humanity that he hoped others would seek to attain. When an early critic pointed out that much in the *Essay* could have been cited from books, Locke agreed while at the same time giving the confident answer that since his aim was "to copy nature, and to give an account of the operations of the mind in thinking," he could "look into nobody's understanding" but his own "to see how it wrought." The *Essay*, he said, was "a copy of my own mind," and he had no hesitation publishing it because he believed "that the intellectual faculties are made, and operate alike in most men" (W IV: 138–39). Others would be qualified to judge what he wrote, for he did not claim infallibility and even granted that the tastes of our understandings can differ (E Epis: 8). Readers were not to take him on trust and treat him as a superior authority, for "it is thinking makes what we read ours," as he laconically said in *The Conduct of the Understanding* (Conduct 20: W III: 241; see also Conduct 24: W III: 250). If the *Essay* gained a wider readership than such works commonly enjoy, which seems certain, it may in part have been because it engaged in a measure of intimacy with the reader, apparent, for instance, in the "Epistle to the Reader," which addresses its audience in the intimate second-person "thou" rather than the usual "you." In the passage already cited from his *Preliminary Discourse*, d'Alembert wrote that for Locke "the principles of metaphysics . . . are the same for the philosophers as for the general run of the people" (d'Alembert 1751: 84). Like Freud, Locke offered more than an analysis of the mind. He was rightly understood to offer a program of reform that would make us happy in this world and in the world hereafter.

III

It is familiar history that the *Essay* is the beginning of the philosophical tradition that late in the nineteenth century became known as British empiricism. It is marked by a tendency to stay close to the common sense shared by ordinary people, to avoid raising paradox into profound truth, to accept without much fuss the fact of an external world that our senses tell us something about, and to grant reason the role of supreme arbiter. Its chief interest is epistemology, and for that reason it has generally been responsive to new events in science. Empiricism is also a mode of philosophy that thrives on communication and discussion, does not expect that truth will come in a flash (if it ever comes), and has a low estimate of the claims of isolated genius and of speculative brooding on deep matters. It treasures good style, a certain vivacity of mind, humor, and the gratifications of social life, combined with a sense of responsibility for the welfare of all. It was by its nature well placed to thrive when philosophy gained an assured place in the universities. Though Locke's outlook contained a good portion of Cartesian thought, the *Essay* moved philosophy to the point of being counted the refutation of Descartes. The idealism of the German tradition beginning with Kant was too foreign to invite accommodation or even interest. British empiricism has for long been the preferred mode of anglophone philosophical discourse, from Berkeley and Hume, the Scottish philosophers, and John Stuart Mill to Bertrand Russell and A. J. Ayer. Its history has received ample treatment, and I shall not attempt to deal with it within the limited scope of this essay.

Given the barely concealed controversial cast of the *Essay* and Locke's other writings, including *The Reasonableness of Christianity*, it is not surprising that the first reactions came from theology. It was after all Locke's position that the authority, tradition, and dogmas of the church, not to mention its ceremonies (which he bracketed under the phrase "all the little things"), were surpassed by scriptural and manifest revelation and that the discourse of scriptural revelation was subject to the correction of reason – "God commands what reason does," we recall. Locke was early on accused of being a Socinian and a Deist. His most persistent opponent was Edward Stillingfleet, the bishop of Worcester, whose three published criticisms Locke met with as many answers at such length that they occupy a separate 500-page volume in standard editions of the works. The fact that they were all written within an eighteen-month period, beginning in the fall of 1696, when Locke was also very busy with other things, is a measure of the urgency of the issues under debate.

One general issue was that Locke's "new way of ideas" – which is the useful phrase first launched by Stillingfleet – posed a danger to the mysteries of the faith, which, one must grant, might have difficulty being sustained by our contemplation of objects of thought, namely ideas, that our own experience has formed by reflection and sensation. But Locke was not a friend of mysteries; he looked for public understanding. Another issue was Locke's elimination of the prevailing doctrine of substance, in the sense that though Locke granted there were real substances, he also urged that we have no epistemological access to them. We know only the sensible properties of substances, that is, what Locke rather provocatively called their "nominal essence." This the bishop found a serious threat to the doctrine of the Trinity. A third awesome issue was raised in the famous chapter "Of Identity and Diversity," which is Chapter xxvii of Book II. Here Locke argued that personal identity depends on the same continued consciousness inhering in "a thinking thing," much as we consider the identity of an animal to consist not in some particular substance, for the matter that makes up the animal will change over time, but in "the unity of one continued Life" (E II.xx–vii.10: 336). The bishop and others were quick to point out that Locke's conception of the self caused difficulty for the doctrine of the resurrection of the dead.

The formulation and discussion of the problem of personal identity would seem to be Locke's distinct contribution to philosophy, and it has right up to the present time been discussed largely in the terms that Locke first outlined. But what can perhaps with some justice be called its revolutionary – and disturbing – implications soon had an effect also in literature, for if there is no abiding substantial self, what is the self? What happens to our conception of a person if we have to grasp a friend or a fictional character in terms of a succession of memories with many gaps or, even more unsettling, as a tangle of chance associations of the sort Locke took to be the mark of a mind that, at least for a while, has lost its rationality and lapsed into "a sort of madness"? On August 9, 1714, a piece in Addison's and Steele's *Spectator* opened with a passage from Locke's chapter as a preamble to the retelling of a Persian tale, which the author was "mightily pleased [to find] in some Measure applicable to this Piece of Philosophy" (Addison and Steele 1714: 4:575–76). Soon the group of English literati called the Scriblerians also had fun with Locke's problem of identity. With its emphasis on consciousness and the awareness of self, Locke's analysis encouraged a new intimacy and even inwardness in the conception and portrayal of character that we recognize as an innovative feature of the English novel in the eighteenth century (Fox 1988: 7–78; see also MacLean 1936: 98–102). It is a notable detail of Locke's analysis that he raised the issue whether a man can fairly be punished for actions committed while unconscious, for instance, while being too drunk to have any self-awareness.

The Stillingfleet controversy raised still one more problem of great import, but before turning to it, let me first cite the full subtitle to Locke's last answer (which ran to three hundred pages) in order to give an air of authenticity to these arcane matters. It was, the title page said, an answer "wherein, besides other incident Matters, what his Lordship has said concerning Certainty by Reason, Certainty by Ideas, and Certainty by Faith; the Resurrection of the Body; the Immateriality of the Soul; the Inconsistency of Mr. Locke's Notions with the Articles of the Christian Faith, and their Tendency to Scepticism; is examined" (W IV: [191]). This catalogue shows how many sensitive topics the *Essay* discussed, topics that are largely lost to us unless we dig for them. It will also remind us that the *Essay* was not merely about knowledge. It was about faith and knowledge (see Ashcraft 1969).

The fourth issue was one that Locke briefly raised by way of suggestion in an unusually long section (E IV.iii.6: 539–43). Here the point he wished to make was the limitations of our knowledge even where we could imagine having it. Thus we have the ideas of a square, a circle, and equality, but may never be able to prove a square and a circle equal in regard to surface size. We also have the ideas of matter and of thinking, but cannot know "whether any mere material Being thinks, or no" (E IV.iii.6: 540). This immediately led Locke to the observation that he saw "no contradiction in it, that the first eternal thinking Being should, if he pleased, give to certain Systems of created sensless matter, put together as he thinks fit, some degrees of sense, perception, and thought" (E IV.iii.6: 541). This may seem quite an innocent remark about divine omnipotence and our ignorance, but the bishop did not allow ignorance in such matters, for he did not admit probability in regard to knowledge that pertained to faith – hence one reason for the mention of certainty in the title cited earlier. As the bishop saw it, if "matter may have a power of thinking . . . it is impossible to prove a spiritual substance in us" (W IV: 32). Locke's impertinent suggestion was held to support both materialism and atheism. Locke replied that if by "spiritual" the bishop meant "immaterial," then he had not proved what the bishop was after, nor did Locke think it could be demonstrated, but merely made highly "probable, that the thinking substance in us is immaterial. But your lordship thinks not probability enough" (W IV: 33).

Here we encounter a basic feature of Locke's epistemology, namely the notion that since we cannot know the real essences of substances, it is not possible for natural science to become demonstrative in the sense geometry is. In fact, for Locke, if we insist on certainty, we will quite lose our bearings in the world, for we are not equipped for it – we are not angels. Within a page of the passage about thinking matter just quoted, Locke wrote "that it becomes the Modesty of Philosophy" for us not to speak too confidently where we lack grounds of knowledge, and "that it is of use to us, to discern how far our Knowledge does reach; for the state we are at present in, not being that of Vision, we must, in many Things, content our selves with Faith and Probability" (E IV.iii.6: 541–42). By "state of vision" he meant the instant and nondiscursive intuition of the angels, which for Descartes was the only legitimate model of knowing. Here we clearly see the rift that separates the silently contemplating Descartes along with the infallibly (because divinely, as they claimed) inspired enthusiasts on the one hand from the discoursing and communicating Locke on the other, rigid certainty from livable probability. Elsewhere in the *Essay* we read that "our Business here is not to know all things, but those which concern our Conduct" (E I.i.6: 46; cf. E I.i.5: 45–46 and E II.xxiii.12: 302–3). It was this modesty that Voltaire remarked on when he called Locke the Hercules of metaphysics. (On the doctrine of substance and on thinking matter in the early English reception of the *Essay*, see Yolton 1956: 126–66.)[3]

Locke's suggestion about thinking matter became the single most disputed issue raised by the *Essay*, both in England and especially on the Continent. It became widely known in France, first, because the second edition (1729) of the French translation to the relevant passage (E IV.iii.6: 539–43) added a long note that summarized the Locke-Stillingfleet controversy (with reliance on the much longer note in the fifth English edition) and, second, because Voltaire gave it half the space of his influential account of Locke in the *Letters concerning the English Nation* (Voltaire 1733: 246–53). Here Voltaire did not at all celebrate the potential materialism, but kept true to Locke by urging that the lesson of the problem is our ignorance of what many people vainly claim to know with certainty. But he did something just as dangerous by treating the problem as a pivotal issue in Locke's philosophy, on a par with the rejection of innate ideas. He cited the words that we "possibly shall never be able to know, whether any material Being thinks, or no," and applauded Locke's belief that "all the great Ends of Morality and Religion, are well enough secured, without philosophical Proofs of the Soul's Immateriality." He also related Locke's suggestion to the long-debated question of animal souls and Cartesian beast machines, thus raising the thought that Locke believed that humans barely differed from brutes. In the final paragraph Voltaire placed Locke in the suspect company of Spinoza and Hobbes as well as the deistical writers John Toland and Anthony Collins. It is not at all surprising, therefore, that what for Locke was an innocent remark became the subject of sharp debates between believers and nonbelievers, between those for whom Locke was a wicked skeptic and those for whom he was the voice of freedom and secular autonomy. One result was that the publication of Locke became prohibited in some countries.

The controversy was given ample prominence in the periodicals of the time – if we had something like the *Arts and Humanities Citation Index* for the century of Voltaire and Diderot, Locke would probably have as many columns as Nietzsche and Derrida have today. John Yolton has devoted two books (Yolton 1983 and Yolton 1991) to the impact of Locke's problem in England and in France. The second book is useful also for giving a sense of Locke's standing with the French philosophes, including Diderot who wrote the entry on Locke in the *Encyclopédie* (Diderot 1765a), as well as other entries that pay much attention to Locke, for example, the article "Logique" (Diderot 1765b). Yolton's recent book (Yolton 1991) pays some attention to Locke's presence in the periodical literature, a subject that receives illuminating treatment in Schøsler's monograph on *La Bibliothèque Raisonnée* (Schøsler 1986). It would of course be senseless to ask who won the debate, but there is no doubt that the thinking-matter question contributed much to Locke's reputation for radical skepticism, which came to be so severely held against him in the nineteenth century.

The second edition of the *Essay* (1694), in which the twenty-page chapter on personal identity first appeared, also contained a short addition of less than one page that made just as great a stir in the world. This addition introduced what has ever since been known as Molyneux's problem, named after Locke's most congenial philosophical correspondent William Molyneux of Dublin, a philosopher and scientist who had translated Descartes's *Meditations* into English and written an admired treatise on optics that was used by George Berkeley. Citing a letter from his friend, Locke placed the problem in the chapter "Of Perception" in Book II in which he had argued that our ideas of sensation sometimes, without our awareness, are altered by judgment from a partial to a correct idea of what we are experiencing. Thus, looking at a sphere, the eyes will merely see a "flat Circle variously shadow'd," but owing to past experience we will in fact see a sphere because "the Judgment presently, by an habitual custom, alters the Appearances into their Causes" (E II.ix.8: 145). Thus the cooperation of the senses performs a correction of the initial idea created by a single sense, a typically Lockean argument that was at variance with the traditional doctrine that the mind by reason alone (or a postulated *sensus communis*) would produce the right perception of the object without support from another sense.

It was at this point that Locke introduced Molyneux's problem as an especially pointed test of his own argument. The problem is this: if we imagine that sight is suddenly restored to a person blind from birth who has learned to distinguish by touch a sphere from a cube, will that person be able to distinguish the two shapes by sight alone, all along assuming that they are roughly equal in size and made of the same material? Molyneux's answer was no and Locke agreed, at the same time inviting the reader to consider "how much he may be beholding to experience, improvement, and acquired notions, where he thinks, he has not the least use of, or help from them" (E II.ix.8: 146). The question was destined to attract attention because it raised issues that involved optics, geometry, the theory of knowledge, the psychology of perception, and even the physiology of the eye (see Morgan 1977, Simms 1982, and Evans 1985).

The post-Lockean tradition of British empiricism was inaugurated by the young Berkeley's *Essay towards a New Theory of Vision* (1709), which was also a prelude to the philosophy he first expounded the following year in his *Treatise on the Principles of Human Knowledge:* his claim that we perceive only ideas and his rejection of Locke's distinction between primary and secondary qualities. Berkeley's entire essay can be seen as an extended analysis of the problem Molyneux had raised, though the essay actually cites Locke's passage only near the end. Berkeley agreed with Molyneux's and Locke's negative answer though on quite different grounds – one aspect of the problem that caused continued discussion was that it had been so loosely formulated to begin with. At first only a thought experiment, the problem gained sensational prominence when the English surgeon William Cheselden in 1728 performed a cataract operation on a youth who had been blind nearly from birth; the operation was successful, the youth could see and was duly observed by the surgeon, who published a brief and murky report that was taken to confirm what Berkeley had earlier concluded on the basis of reasoning alone.

On the Continent the popularity of the question became assured when Voltaire, in his widely read and influential *Eléments de la philosophie de Newton,* devoted a couple of pages to it, with mention of Locke and Berkeley as well as a reference to Cheselden's report (Voltaire 1738: 318–20). From this source the question was taken up by La Mettrie, Buffon (see Roger 1989: 214–18), and Condillac, who in two separate works submitted it to detailed analyses that arrived at different conclusions. Voltaire also became the source of citation and discussion in several entries in the *Encyclopédie.* But by far the most important treatment occurred in Diderot's *Letter on the Blind for the Use of Those who See* (Diderot 1749), a work whose title conveyed the startling suggestion that those who have sight have something to learn from the blind. Diderot shifted the interest in blindness away from the mere distinction of shapes to the larger question of how a blind person thinks and feels. His philosophy and morality, Diderot suggested, will be different from ours. His sense of vice and virtue is not the same. He will not, for instance, understand our concern with clothes for the sake of sexual modesty, and he will not share our compassion with suffering because he will not see the expression of pain but only hear the victim's cries, which, Diderot implies, are less conducive to compassion than the sight of pain and suffering – a suggestion that anticipates a similar observation in Diderot's *Letter on Deaf-mutes for the Use of Those who Hear and Speak* (Diderot 1751), which in turn anticipates the argument of *Laokoon* (1766) by Diderot's great admirer Lessing.

Diderot's reflections on the world of the blind culminate in the fictive deathbed confession of the real-life mathematics professor at Cambridge, Nicholas Saunderson, who cannot at all share the prevailing optimism about the beauty and wisdom of creation, which, it is suggested, is a conception that results from excessive attachment to the appearances of sight. Diderot knew as well as Locke that we do not now live in "a state of vision." He was alert to what Wordsworth called the tyranny of the eye. Diderot is one among many mid-eighteenth-century figures who illustrated the seismic shift Locke was causing away from the dominance of vision, intuition, and reason to sound, speech, and expression. This was one of the effects of Locke's commitment to the necessity of communication. This shift was a move onto romanticism. In his fictive confession, the blind Saunderson revealed his estrangement from the transparent stillness of Newton's clockwork universe. He had a dark sentiment – which was also a presentiment – of a world that presented only the illusion of order and had come into being by a continual tendency toward destruction of successive waves of beings struggling for life and existence. Here we may seem far removed from the initial question, yet Diderot's pointed challenge to conventional thought began with blindness and the modes of sensation. His aim was to tell us that we have been mistaken about our pride in reason, for we learn, unawares, much more from the senses than we have allowed ourselves to believe. And our immediate concern is to understand that without Locke we would not have the Diderot we know.[4]

The association of ideas made its first appearance in the fourth edition (1700) of the *Essay* as the last chapter of Book II. The same edition also had the new chapter "Of Enthusiasm" (E IV.xix), which is about the ways in which the association of ideas nourishes religious fanaticism and subverts what Sprat called "rational religion." "Of the Association of Ideas" has undoubtedly been the single most productive chapter in the *Essay*, right from the eighteenth century to the present; its importance in the history of philosophy and psychology as well as in psychoanalysis is too obvious to require elaboration. The decision to add the chapter on association points to a remarkable feature of the *Essay*, namely that Locke, though his purpose certainly was to show us how to be reasonable, devoted so much space to telling us how we could go wrong, fall into error, put trust in illusions, and become unreasonable. The entire Book III, about "words and language in general," may be taken as a single long therapeutic effort to remedy what Locke called "the cheat of words."

Association is "a weakness," "a disease," even a "sort of madness," but we are all liable to fall into it. Self-interest, obstinacy, and especially careless education may favor it, but in general it is an everyday phenomenon that puts obstacles in the way of our best rational endeavors. It consists in cementing a "strong Combination of *Ideas*, not ally'd by Nature" (E II.xxxiii.6: 396), as contrasted with the "natural Correspondence and Connexion [of our ideas] one with another" (E II.xxxiii.5: 395). Locke consistently contrasts the term "association" with "connection," as when he elsewhere says that "when we find out an *Idea*, by whose Intervention we discover the Connexion of two others, this is a Revelation from God to us, by the Voice of Reason" (E IV.vii.11: 598; cf. E IV.i.2: 525: "*Knowledge* then seems to me to be nothing but *the perception of the connexion and agreement, or disagreement and repugnancy of any of our Ideas*"). Association is the enemy of reasonableness, and children's education in particular should be designed to guard against it.

Nothing shows more clearly than his conception of the association of ideas that Locke's human norm was rationality. For him association was harmful, but in the eighteenth century it quickly took on quite another role. Whether he meant to subvert Locke's terminology or not, it is a fact that Hume early in the *Treatise of Human Nature* had a section he entitled "Of the connexion or association of ideas." This association, he explained, has three modes: "RESEMBLANCE, CONTIGUITY in time or place, and CAUSE and EFFECT"; and he called association "a kind of ATTRACTION, which in the mental world will be found to have as extraordinary effects as in the natural," thus invoking the example of Newton as the model for his own new science of human nature (Hume 1739–40: 10–13). It is Hume's conception of it that has given association a constructive role in knowledge, though this role has often falsely been taken to be in accord with Locke's intentions. This mistake is an expression of the nineteenth century's slight knowledge of Locke and the hostility to his thought that made it convenient to lump him with the more openly suspect Hume.

There were, however, some who understood Locke correctly and found a positive application of his association, namely in art. Thus Condillac observed that poetry is governed by association in the expression of emotion and passion, whereas prose, being the rational discourse of the philosopher, relies on the "connection of ideas." Condillac was one of the few who observed Locke's distinction between association and connection (Aarsleff 1975: 221–22). It has also been argued that Francis Hutcheson's notion of an aesthetic sense that immediately recognizes beauty was ultimately laid to rest when it was replaced by arguments from association (Kivy 1976: 174–218). There is a curious detail that seems to suggest that Locke would have allowed an aesthetic role for association. The final sections of *The Conduct of the Understanding* are devoted to a treatment of association that is more wide-ranging than the chapter in the *Essay*, though of course less known. Here he referred to what he had said in the *Essay* in connection with the Molyneux problem about one sense correcting the other, then continued: "Let any one not skilled in painting be told, when he sees bottles, and tobacco-pipes, and other things so painted as they are in some places shown, that he does not see protuberances, and you will not convince him but by the touch: he will not believe that, by an instantaneous leger-demain of his own thoughts, one idea is substituted for another" (Conduct 41: W III: 278). In this passage Locke is saying that the habitual cooperation of the senses is a mode of association and that this mode causes the illusion of depth to arise from the flat surface of the canvas. Elsewhere Locke told of a blind man who associated the color scarlet with the sound of a trumpet (E III.iv.11: 425), a remark that was often quoted. This observation can of course be taken as a small example of synesthesia, which was a phenomenon that became popular during the eighteenth century as fascination with the ways of sensation began to invade the old domain of the rational mind. Henry James spoke of novels that were loose and baggy monsters; in its own genre of philosophical writing the *Essay* was also quite a capacious monster, but it was not least this roominess that made it so human, suggestive, and influential. Its effect and relevance were spread far and wide over the fertile ground of eighteenth-century thought.

IV

The most spectacular and pervasive influence of the *Essay* occurred in the new philosophy of language that was developed during the eighteenth century. By contrast to Adamicism, which it replaced, this philosophy would deserve the name of humanism if that word had not already been put to other uses. Locke shared Descartes's fear of language; both were committed to the principle that knowledge is served well only by the wordless discourse of the mind, by concentration on "*Ideas* by themselves, their Names being quite laid aside" (E IV.vi.1: 579). Locke devoted an entire book of the *Essay* to the discussion of "words and language in general" because he wished, by a sort of intensive therapy, to make people "reflect on their own Use of Language" in order to provide lasting protection against the bewitchment and cheat of words. He admitted, it seems with surprise, that what he had to say on the subject "appears to me new, and a little out of the way" (E III.v.16: 437), but he could hardly have had a premonition that it was so far out of the way that the effect became the very opposite of what he had intended. Instead of securing that language kept its place as the docile servant of thought, his discussion gave so much power to words that they were poised to become the very agency of mental life. If we are so readily caught in the web that language casts over thought, it no longer seemed plausible to believe that words could be "quite laid aside." Locke had gotten caught in a dilemma from which there was no escape without a new view of language. It became the central doctrine of this new conception that language (as speech) has a human origin and that both its creation and its continued use are primal expressions of our humanity.

Locke said nothing about the origin of language, except to leave no doubt that it was human, not divine and Adamic, but in the *Essay* he more than once suggested that attention to the beginning of language throws light on the relations between thought and speech. His fundamental principle that, since only individuals exist in nature, "*General and Universal . . . are the Inventions and Creatures of the Understanding . . . and concern only Signs,* whether Words, or *Ideas"* (E III.iii.11: 414), raised the question of how words are made, and to this Locke gave a firm answer: general names were not made by philosophers and logicians, but "received their Birth and Signification, from ignorant and illiterate People, who sorted and denominated Things" into kinds or species according to convenience and need "by those sensible Qualities they found in them" (E III.vi.25: 453). Our classifications are not made with regard for truth to nature, but are, so to speak, people-oriented. In his vastly popular, multivolume *Histoire naturelle,* Buffon adopted this principle in the division of animals, while at the same time (in the opening discourse) ridiculing the overly intricate and abstract classifications of such "methodists" as Linnaeus – again a clash with Adamicism, for Linnaeus saw himself as a second Adam. In the same discourse Buffon also, like Maupertuis and Diderot in those years, criticized the overestimation of the place of mathematics in science. Good science is the work of genius rather than method (Buffon 1749).

Locke was entirely committed to this popular language, and it was this language alone that he discussed in Book III. He did not at all think that the learned could do any better, and he rejected with scorn the thought of replacing it with a universal and philosophical language (E III.xi.2: 509), a position that was of course entirely in accord with his epistemology. In this rejection he was followed by the philosophes, for example by Condillac, who insisted that what he called "a well-made language" can only be an improvement of an ordinary national language, never a perfect, universal, philosophical, and ahistorical replacement for it (Condillac 1798: 2:463b). For Locke languages have a history that reflects the experience and thought of their speakers. And if they have a human history, they also have a human origin which it may prove as illuminating to explore as the state of nature had proved to be in political philosophy.

Toward the pursuit of this line of thought another section of the *Essay* gave a still stronger impulse. Early in Book III Locke cited such words as *"Imagine," "Apprehend," "Comprehend," "Adhere," "Conceive," "Spirit"* (which "in its primary signification, is Breath"), and *"Angel,* a Messenger" to illustrate the principle that words for actions and things that "fall not under our Senses" have had "their first rise from sensible *Ideas"* (E III.i.5: 403). From this, he concluded, "we may give some kind of guess, what kind of Notions they were, and whence derived, which filled their Minds, who were the first Beginners of Languages" (ibid.). This conclusion had vast consequences, for it made the urgent suggestion that the beginning of language confirms the core of Locke's philosophy: the rejection of innate ideas and the rehabilitation of sensation. The conclusion was also just one step from saying that the genetic epistemology or progress of the mind is recorded in words. With this step taken, Locke's section became the rationale for using etymology to reveal the trains of thought that had been in the minds of speakers in the course of the progress of the mind. From having been the history of things, etymology became the history of thought. The section that Locke had subtitled "words ultimately derived from such as signify sensible ideas" became the most quoted and pervasively influential passage in the *Essay*.

One proof of this influence is the famous and often-cited article on "Etymology" that appeared in the sixth volume of the *Encyclopédie* in 1756. The author was the young philosophe Turgot, who later became known as a great economist and administrator. Here, saying that he was "speaking according to Locke," Turgot called etymology "an interesting branch of experimental metaphysics," thus echoing d'Alembert's words about Locke having made philosophy the "experimental physics of the soul." Words being like grains of sand that humanity has left in its course, they alone can show us the path the mind has followed in its progress toward the present. Using a stronger metaphor, Turgot proclaimed that "those who study the march of the human mind in the history of past modes of thought must march with the torch of etymology in hand to avoid falling into a thousand errors" (Turgot 1756: 108a-b). The metaphor of the torch became a commonplace for celebrating the power and lessons of etymology, almost as if we were entering Plato's cave with our own light.

A year earlier the previous volume of the *Encyclopédie* had contained Diderot's magnificent article "Encyclopédie," in which he wrote that "the language of a nation gives its vocabulary, and the vocabulary is quite a faithful record of the entire range of knowledge of that nation; by the mere comparison of the vocabulary of a nation at different times, we can form an idea of its progress" (Diderot 1755: 637va). Similar lessons could be gained by the comparison of the languages of different nations. Early in the nineteenth century, in one of the founding texts of the new historical and comparative study of languages, Rasmus Rask called Turgot's article on etymology "perhaps the best that has been written on this subject in modern times" (Rask 1818: 1:25). A forward-looking French anthropological text from the year 1800 proclaimed that the proper study of native languages "would be one of the master-works of philosophy," for in studying them we travel in time and are "taken back to the first period of our own history" by learning about "the origin and generation of ideas," the "formation and development of language," and "the relations between these two processes" (Degérando 1800: 63, 70). With his own philosophical interest in comparative anthropology, Locke would have been happy to see this vigorous effect of his "Historical, plain Method." The central conception of these views of the nature of language is the familiar romantic notion that the genius of a nation is expressed and revealed in the genius of its language. Etymology changed our sense of the past not least by making historicism possible because it gave us the means to understand history by entering the minds of those who had lived and acted in it.

Locke's remarks about the language making of the common folk would have been impertinent if he had not rejected the doctrine of a rational and ordered beginning. This rejection called forth some other fundamental conceptions that also gained prominence in the new philosophy of language. One of these appears in his reason for admiring Richelet's acclaimed monolingual French dictionary (1680), which Locke (writing in French to Toinard) thought had "found the true secret of good dictionary-making, for the usual manner of rendering the words of one language by those of another is no more reasonable than sending to France for a case for an English instrument that is unknown in France both in regard to form and use, for the words of different languages do not agree any better than that" (Letter 596: C II: 310; see Aarsleff 1964: 76). French and English are incongruent, and this is a fact that creates the problem of translation, on which Locke often was quite explicit in the *Essay* (see, e.g., E II.xxii.6: 290–91 and E III.v.8: 432–33). Being rather like the collective minds of their nations, the two languages each have their own genius.

This individuality also operates on the level of speakers of the same language; a certain privacy will always cling to the meanings of words because they depend "very much on the Thoughts, Notions, and *Ideas* of him that uses them," a problem Locke found so pronounced in ancient Greek that each author in it had "a distinct Language, though the same Words" (E III.ix.22: 489; cf. on classical philology E III.ix.10: 481). Locke quite often remarked on this private aspect to the meaning of words (e.g., E III.ii.8: 408; E III.vi.30: 457–58; and E III.ix.7: 478–79). This is not, however, the Wittgensteinian conception of a private language (as these passages make clear). It is rather the privacy that Wilhelm von Humboldt had in mind when he said that "all understanding is also a not-understanding": in saying this he was repeating what Diderot, following Condillac, had written in the 1750s when he noted that speaking and hearing are reciprocal activities that both demand creative effort in order to reduce the element of privacy.

The work that initiated the new philosophy of language – and with it a new epistemology – by turning Locke's argument upside-down was Condillac's *Essay on the Origin of Human Knowledge*, first published in French in 1746 and ten years later in English translation. It quickly became one of the most influential texts of the century in France as well as in Scotland and especially in Germany (Aarsleff 1974: 146–209). Condillac admired Locke as the greatest of modern philosophers, but he also believed that Locke, for all his good insight into the workings of language, had failed to realize that his ideal of wordless discourse was a chimera. Condillac was committed to the position that the "use of signs is the principle which unfolds all our ideas as they lye in the bud," and, further, that "men are incapable of making [i.e., creating] any signs, but by living in society" (Condillac 1746: 11, 134). The origin of language as speech becomes the condition for the beginning of knowledge. Language is constitutive of thought, and our very sociability as human beings makes us creatures of language. Starting from Locke, Condillac offered a global theory of human expression that embraced both aesthetics and epistemology, both art and science, poetry and prose. The origin of our shared public language is the archetype of human creativity.

It was this creativity that prompted the making of the signs that are the words of our discourse. The crucial condition for this innovation was what Condillac called the language of action, by which he meant the expression of states of mind by spontaneous gestures, including vocal sounds, that are natural and thus the same for all. The first step toward human speech and language would occur, so Condillac argued, when our capacity for reflection induced the deliberate – that is, nonnatural – use of one of these vocal gestures as a sign, for this reflective use would in turn suggest the further expansion of the range of communicative possibility by the creation of our own artificial signs with sounds that are arbitrary in relation to their meanings. This human language will release us from the instinctive boundedness of the animals, and it will meet the shared needs of its speakers in a process of continuing analytical refinement, thus evolving toward the discursive prose that serves the ends of philosophy and knowledge. But this prose still remains a secondary development of poetry, which is the primal form of language, just as the primal form of art is the expression of emotion and passion in the language of action, in which all the arts have their common source (Condillac 1746: 7–8, 299). For Condillac, therefore, "the style of all languages was originally poetical," and at this stage language was shaped by imagination, which inspires "the mode of speaking by action and gesture" (Condillac 1746: 228, 214). By contrast, prose is the work of analysis that obstructs the imagination just as philosophy dampens art (Condillac 1746: 90, 293–94). Imagination has taken the place of intuition and reason as the foremost agent of mental life: "The man of imagination is a creative spirit," who "creates things that exist only in his own mind" (Condillac 1775: 1:413b). In the article "Encyclopédie" Diderot wrote that "a man of genius can put a nation in a state of fermentation, shorten centuries of ignorance, and carry knowledge to a point of astonishing perfection." Geniuses are rare, but among them we will hardly ever "find any who have not improved language. Creative people have that special quality . . . It is the heat of imagination that enriches language with new expressions" (Diderot 1755: 638va).

In these conceptions of poetry, prose, art, philosophy, language, genius, and imagination it is, for good reason, easy to discern the familiar features of the aesthetics of romanticism. The crucial formative role assigned to the language of action caused a shift in the conception of the nature of art from imitation to expression, a shift that is brilliantly explored in the aesthetic writings of Diderot. All this may seem a good distance from Locke, yet it all happened because he let the language genie out of the bottle.

The priority given to the language of action in the formation and expression of thought also had an important effect in philosophy: it undermined the authority of traditional logic and caused a shift to a holistic conception of meaning, that is, to the notion that not words but entire sentences are the natural semantic units. Professor Quine has compared this shift in semantics to the Copernican turn in astronomy (Quine 1981: 69). Traditional logic assumed that the linear subject-predicate sequence typical of French and English expresses the prior and natural ordering of ideas in the mind. Thus, since the word order was unproblematic, it was enough to concentrate on words and the ideas behind them – this is what Locke did, which explains why the *Essay*'s Book III was called Locke's logic. This view corresponds, I believe, to what Quine has called "the impossible term-by-term empiricism of Locke and Hume" (Quine 1951: 42; it might perhaps better be called term-by-term rationalism: see Passmore 1953). By contrast, the language of action expresses not propositional sequences of terms but states of mind, each of which is an undifferentiated whole without dimension in time, or in Condillac's words, "to those who are used to it, a single gesture is oftentimes equivalent to a whole sentence" (Condillac 1746: 214). Thus words are artificial and secondary units that came into being owing to the inescapable successivity of speech, which forced the decomposition of the simultaneity of states of mind (Diderot 1751: 64) – it is not least for this reason that our thought itself is changed by language, which so to speak forces its constitutiveness on thought. It follows that the basic units of meaning are not words but entire sentences and even passages of discourse. Condillac once devoted a chapter to showing how a long prose passage presented successively what was in the author's mind all at once, and on another occasion he devoted ten pages to what he called the fabric or web of discourse, "du tissu du discours" (Condillac 1775: 1:447b–50a, 1:580–90; the web metaphor was also used by Diderot: see Diderot 1751: 70).

It was left for the maverick but brilliant political radical John Horne Tooke to write the largest work on language in response to Locke, no less than a thousand pages in two large volumes entitled *The Diversions of Purley* (1786–1805). This was a work of great originality, based on the belief that the title of Locke's *Essay* was "a lucky mistake (for it was a mistake) ... For some part of the inestimable benefit of that book has, merely on account of its title, reached to many thousands more than, I fear, it would have done, had he called it (what it is merely) A *Grammatical* Essay, or a Treatise on *Words*, or on *Language*" (Tooke 1786–1805: 1:31n). For Tooke the mind had no other business in regard to language than to have sensations; his philosophy was a sort of linguistic materialism. All that Locke had said about "the composition, abstraction, complexity, generalization, relation, &c., of Ideas, does indeed merely concern *Language*" (Tooke 1786–1805: 1:39; see Aarsleff 1967: 54 and Quine 1981: 67–68). Tooke's answer was fantastic and endless etymologizing in order to reduce all particles, and especially prepositions, to the names of sensations. Thus he sought to confirm the very term-by-term empiricism (or rationalism) that the conception of the language of action had shown to be untenable. Tooke's book greatly impressed James Mill, who relied on it heavily in his *Analysis of the Phenomena of the Human Mind* (1829), which in turn had considerable authority with John Stuart Mill and other Utilitarians. (See Aarsleff 1967: 44–114 for more on Tooke's doctrines and influence.)

V

The nineteenth century was not a good time for Locke. In that century Locke meant the *Essay*, and the contents and tenor of the *Essay* were largely equated with the thought of the encyclopedists and philosophes, who already by 1800 were being held collectively responsible for the French Revolution. Throughout the century informed critics remarked that the denigrators of Locke could hardly, if they were honest, have read him, but the denigration continued all the same. In the opening years of the century, Coleridge concluded after close study that Locke's style was deplorable, that his philosophy was unoriginal and a mere unacknowledged plagiarism of Gassendi and Hobbes, that he owed his reputation to the advocacy of popular arguments for political freedom, and that he had so thoroughly misunderstood Descartes that he had repeated him with new errors (Coleridge 1955: 67–109). These themes were, independently of Coleridge, common throughout the century. Coleridge was reported to speak "as usual . . . with contempt of *Locke's* Essay," because "it led to the destruction of Metaphysical Science by encouraging the unlearned to think that with good sense they might dispense with study" (Coleridge 1955: 97). Carlyle said that Locke "had paved the way for banishing religion from the world" (Carlyle 1828: 1:215), a statement that reveals the kind of thought-warp world in which the dominant part of nineteenth-century opinion felt at home. The ultraconservative Joseph de Maistre, who had a following among influential people in England, made Locke the evil genius of the "theophobia" of the eighteenth century (for which in his view the Revolution was the well-deserved divine retribution) and proclaimed that in philosophy contempt of Locke was the beginning of wisdom (de Maistre 1821: 4:379). It became the commonly accepted opinion that Locke had made the mind a puny, passive, mechanical thing because he was a sensualist, a materialist, a skeptic, an atheist, and a Utilitarian.

That was the real problem; in the rhetoric of the time Locke was one of "the false apostles" owing to the role he, like the Utilitarians, gave to pleasure and pain in morality, with grand disregard of the fact that pain and pleasure for Locke were providential and not physiological phenomena – again the thought warp. Locke was treated with particular severity at Cambridge in the 1830s and 1840s because Utilitarian thought was gaining support among the students at that time. William Whewell, the powerful master of Trinity College, wrote in 1841, soon after he had assumed the chair of moral philosophy, that he had "already used [his] influence to introduce an Anti-Lockian philosophy, and intend[ed] to use it for other good purposes" (Douglas 1881: 248). Whewell believed that the importance accorded to Locke's philosophy was an eighteenth-century error, and whether owing to him or not, it was certainly in his spirit that the regulations for the moral sciences tripos at Cambridge, for the subject of "mental philosophy," required the reading of Locke's *Essay* along with Victor Cousin's *Philosophie de Locke* (Cousin 1829; see Aarsleff 1971: 130). Cousin's extensive writings on Locke were widely trusted in spite of the fact that prominent and well-informed reviews as well as an entire book demonstrated that Cousin's "criticism is not only an insult to the memory of Locke – it is an insult to Philosophy and to common sense" (Webb 1857: 13; cited by Yolton 1991: 210). In France Cousin was chiefly responsible for the revival of Descartes, whose thought with its advocacy of innate ideas was judged congenial with religion and traditional values. In a similar move, Coleridge had urged that Locke did not deserve the company of Newton, for whom he judged Bacon a worthier mate (Coleridge 1955: 75). One could say that Bacon was reinvented in the 1830s to take the place of the unwanted Locke. When G. H. Lewes was writing his history of philosophy in the mid-1840s, he found "the sneers and off-hand charges" against Locke so frequent that, in his words, "we, who had read him in our youth with delight, began to suspect that the admiration had been rash" (Lewes 1845–46: 3:187). Fortunately, Lewes stayed with his first assessment and devoted fifty strong pages to Locke in his book. But throughout the century the good writing on Locke was chiefly devoted to defending him against his detractors, with the result that little original work was done on his philosophy.[5]

Separate mention should be made of two works that have retained their importance, both of which, oddly, were published in 1876. Fox Bourne's two-volume biography is still valuable. In the preface the author explained that "more than half of the contents of this work are derived from hitherto unused manuscripts; and by them, in addition to their independent worth, altogether new light is thrown on most of the information that is not actually new" (Fox Bourne 1876: 1:vii). But in spite of its fresh approach and the new material, this biography does not seem to have inspired renewed interest in Locke at the time. The other work is Leslie Stephen's wonderful *English Thought in the Eighteenth Century*. Here Locke has a prominent position throughout, but especially in the treatment of Deism in the first volume (Stephen 1876). Deism is a subject that would not today be so closely bound to Locke because we have a stronger awareness of Locke's piety; but it is perhaps characteristic that a work written in the nineteenth-century climate of opinion should have placed the weight differently.

The long years of controversy and denigration were over, but Locke was still sinking into virtual oblivion, at least in Britain. Late in the century, the situation was rather different in America. C. S. Peirce found that "Locke's grand work was substantially this: Men must think for themselves, and genuine thought is an act of perception. . . . We cannot fail to acknowledge a superior element of truth in the practicality of Locke's thought, which on the whole should place him nearly upon a level with Descartes" (Peirce 1890: 254–55). William James spoke fondly of "the good Locke," of his "dear old book," and rejoiced in Locke's "devotion to experimentalism, his common sense, and his hatred of obscure, misty ideas" (Perry 1935: 1:545).

The final event of the nineteenth century was almost bizarre. It was the publication in 1894, under the distinguished imprint of the Clarendon Press, of the first critical edition of the *Essay*, "collated and annotated, with biographical, critical, and historical prolegomena," by Alexander Campbell Fraser (Locke 1894). This all sounds very impressive, even Teutonic, but the edition quite failed to live up to its claims, the reviews were poor, and the publisher never reissued it when it went out of print. This caused the quite remarkable situation that for many years the *Essay* was not available in the regular book trade, but could only be bought at second hand, until an American paperback publisher put out the two Fraser volumes in 1959, thus giving new life and even authority to this edition, whose notes are surely the greatest display of *Besserwisserei* in history, treating Locke rather like a schoolboy who should have known better than not to grasp, for instance, the moral seriousness of innate ideas.

But by the 1950s things were changing. After having been brought to Oxford for safekeeping during the war, the large collection of Locke papers known as the Lovelace Collection was acquired by the Bodleian Library and soon made available to scholars. During the same period and for related reasons Peter Laslett published in 1960 his edition of the *Two Treatises of Government*, with an extensive introduction that convincingly argued that the *Treatises* were not written after 1688 as a retrospective rationale for the Revolution of 1688, but before 1688 as a political brief for it (Laslett 1967). Laslett's edition also gained attention – at the time almost to the point of sensationalism – because it raised the question of Locke's influence in America. In 1922 Carl Becker had argued at some length that Locke was the source of the ideas that Jefferson put into the Declaration of Independence (Becker 1922: 62), and his argument came to be widely accepted and amplified (see, e.g., Hartz 1955). But by the 1960s the Becker thesis had lost its appeal, and the issue seemed settled by John Dunn's argument that Locke's political philosophy in fact had received much less attention in England and America than had commonly been assumed. But Dunn's argument has recently elicited much work that tends to reaffirm, though in somewhat different terms from those earlier claimed, Locke's presence in eighteenth-century political thought.[6]

One other productive trend became evident around 1960: students of Locke saw that he could not be properly understood without close attention to the intellectual, religious, and political context in which he lived and wrote. This has, rather cumbersomely, been called the historicization of Locke, something that had begun to happen to Descartes a couple of generations earlier. We see the beginnings of this trend in 1956 with John Yolton's book *John Locke and the Way of Ideas*, which for the first time treated the intellectual context and Locke's reception in the manner that had long been applied to literary figures, theologians, and even some philosophers. Several essays in a volume edited by Yolton (Yolton 1969a) are also historical; and in the same year appeared John Dunn's book with its "historical account of the argument of the *Two Treatises*" (Dunn 1969a). The culmination of this recent activity has been the new Clarendon Edition of the Works of John Locke, which is already far advanced, most notably with the first true critical edition of the *Essay* by Peter H. Nidditch, and E. S. de Beer's magisterial edition of Locke's correspondence (see the Bibliography at the end of this volume). (It is a sign of the intervening eclipse of Locke that the last previous printing of the old edition of his works had occurred in 1854.) In 1991 came Michael Ayers's two-volume work, which is historical as well as philosophical in its treatment of Locke's philosophy (Ayers 1991). It is hard to say whether Locke's philosophical stature has increased as a result of this recent work, but there is no doubt that his achievement and importance are now much better understood and respected than they have been for some one hundred fifty years.

VI

At the beginning I cited Locke's word that "God commands what reason does" as an expression of his fundamental outlook. In closing it is useful to remember another statement that has equal force. It occurs in Section 38 of *The Conduct of the Understanding:* "God has made the intellectual world harmonious and beautiful without us; but it will never come into our heads all at once; we must bring it home piecemeal, and there set it up by our own industry, or else we shall have nothing but darkness and a chaos within, whatever order and light there be in things without us" (W III: 272). To understand fully what Locke means with those words is also to understand his thought and the grounds of his philosophy.

NOTES

1 Information about the secondary works cited in this chapter is given in the list of References at the end of the chapter. Citations of Locke's *Conduct of the Understanding* include the word "Conduct," followed by a section number, as well as a reference to Volume III of Locke's *Works*.

2 Readers who wish to follow the printings and translations of Locke's writings will find Attig 1985 a rich source. Yolton and Yolton 1985 is a useful annotated guide to writings about Locke 1689–1982. Hall and Woolhouse 1983 covers Locke scholarship in the last eighty years. These items all have very full indices.

3 The controversy with Stillingfleet received a great deal of attention in the fifth edition of the *Essay* (published in 1706 after Locke's death) in the form of nine notes. It is uncertain whether Locke authorized these notes or what share he had in them (see Nidditch 1975: xxxii), though they are in part styled in the first person. The notes teem with references to Locke's own as well as Stillingfleet's writings and to the Scriptures. Though omitted from current editions (but noted in their proper places in the Nidditch edition), these notes were in the past retained in the standard editions of the works, the issues thus being available to readers who might otherwise not have heard of Stillingfleet and his arguments. The longest of these notes is the one to *Essay* IV.iii.6 on thinking matter, no less than fourteen pages in small print. These notes are clear evidence of the *Essay*'s close engagement with theology and religion.

4 Saunderson's confession is one of the texts published around 1750 that signaled disaffection with mathematics and Newtonian mechanics in favor of a movement toward biological thinking and the life sciences. Other texts are Buffon's Premier discours to his *Histoire Naturelle* (Buffon 1749) and Diderot's *Pensées sur l'interprétation de la nature* (Diderot 1753). Condillac's preference for organic metaphors is another sign of this change of orientation. Yet, the anglophone world is wedded to the absurd idée fixe of "the 'hard' mechanistic and mathematical culture of the Enlightenment" as opposed to "the 'soft,' fluid, speculative culture of the Romantic life sciences," to quote a recent review in the *New York Review of Books* (June 27, 1991: 51). Since the very word "Enlightenment" gets such reactions, I have entirely avoided it. On this matter see the excellent

book by Kondylis, especially the sections on "Der polemische Charakter des Denkens in der Aufklärung und in ihren Interpretationen" and "Die Herabsetzung der Mathematik" (Kondylis 1981: 19–35 and 291–98).

5 Further information and references on Locke's reputation in the nineteenth century are provided by Aarsleff 1971: 120–45 and Aarsleff 1986. Coleridge 1955 is a rich source. Everett 1829 is excellent: it is a critical review of four books by Victor Cousin, who is cited at length along with Joseph de Maistre. Everett finds it surprising that on the Continent some see Locke "as the great apostle of irreligion, immorality, impurity, and sedition" (Everett 1829: 81). Curti 1937 is valuable for its discussion of Locke's standing in America during the important period it covers, with a wealth of references.

6 See Dunn 1969b, Wills 1979, Moore 1991, Pocock 1991, and Wootton 1993. Pocock 1987 is a useful introduction to the issues and literature concerning this topic; Wootton, among other things, stresses Locke's Socinianism. (I am grateful to David Wootton and Knud Haakonssen for some of these references.)

REFERENCES

Aarsleff, Hans. 1964. Leibniz on Locke on Language. *American Philosophical Quarterly* 1: 165–88; repr. in Aarsleff 1982: 42–83.
Aarsleff, Hans. 1967. *The Study of Language in England 1780–1860* (Princeton: Princeton University Press).
Aarsleff, Hans. 1971. Locke's Reputation in Nineteenth-century England. *Monist* 55: 392–422; repr. in Aarsleff 1982: 120–45.
Aarsleff, Hans. 1974. The Tradition of Condillac. In *Studies in the History of Linguistics*, ed. Dell Hymes (Bloomington: Indiana University Press) 93–156; repr. in Aarsleff 1982: 146–209.
Aarsleff, Hans. 1975. Condillac's Speechless Statue. *Studia Leibnitiana* Supp. 15: 287–302; repr. in Aarsleff 1982: 210–24.
Aarsleff, Hans. 1982. *From Locke to Saussure: Essays on the Study of Language and Intellectual History* (Minneapolis: University of Minnesota Press).
Aarsleff, Hans. 1986. Joseph de Maistre and Victorian Thought on the Origin of Language and Civilization. In *Studies in the History of Western Linguistics*, ed. F. R. Palmer and Theodore Bynon (Cambridge: Cambridge University Press) 96–108.
Aarsleff, Hans. 1993. Descartes and Augustine on Genesis, Language, and the Angels. In *Leibniz and Adam*, ed. Marcelo Dascal and Elhanan Yakira (Tel Aviv: University Publishing Projects).

Addison, Joseph, and Steele, Joseph, eds. 1714. *The Spectator* No. 578 (Monday, August 9); in *The Spectator*, ed. Donald F. Bond. 5 vols. (Oxford: Oxford University Press, 1965) 4:575–79.

Ashcraft, Richard. 1969. Faith and Knowledge in Locke's Philosophy. In Yolton 1969: 194–223.

Attig, John C. 1985. *The Works of John Locke: A Comprehensive Bibliography from the Seventeenth Century to the Present* (Westport CT: Greenwood Press).

Ayers, Michael R. 1991. *Locke*. 2 vols. (London: Routledge).

Becker, Carl. 1922. *The Declaration of Independence: A Study in the History of Political Ideas* (New York: Harcourt, Brace).

Bonno, Gabriel. 1947. The Diffusion and Influence of Locke's *Essay concerning Human Understanding* in France before Voltaire's *Lettres philosophiques*. *Proceedings of the American Philosophical Society* 91: 421–25; repr. in Yolton 1990: 75–85.

Buffon, Georges-Louis Leclerc. 1749. Premier discours. In *Histoire naturelle*. 15 vols. (Paris, 1749–67) 1:3–62.

Carlyle, Thomas. 1828. Goethe. *Foreign Review* 2: 80–127; in *Critical and Miscellaneous Essays*, by Thomas Carlyle. 5 vols. (New York: Scribner, 1900–1) 1:198–257.

Coleridge, Samuel Taylor. 1955. *Coleridge on the Seventeenth Century*, ed. Roberta Florence Brinkley (Durham NC: Duke University Press).

Condillac, Etienne Bonnot de. 1746. *Essai sur l'origine des connaissances humaines* (Amsterdam); tr. as *An Essay on the Origin of Human Knowledge*, by Thomas Nugent (London, 1756); repr. (Gainesville FL: Scholars' Facsimiles & Reprints, 1971).

Condillac, Etienne Bonnot de. 1775. *Cours d'études* (Paris); in *Oeuvres philosophiques de Condillac*, ed. Georges le Roy. 3 vols. (Paris: Presses Universitaires de France, 1947–51) 1:395–776; 2:1–237.

Condillac, Etienne Bonnot de. 1798. *La langue des calculs* (Paris); in *Oeuvres philosophiques de Condillac*, ed. Georges le Roy. 3 vols. (Paris: Presses Universitaires de France, 1947–51) 2:417–529.

Cousin, Victor. 1829. Leçons 15–25. In *Cours de l'histoire de la philosophie: Histoire de la philosophie du XVIIIe siècle*. 2 vols. (Paris) 2:65–560; 4th ed. as *La philosophie de Locke* (Paris 1861).

Curti, Merle. 1937. The Great Mr. Locke: America's Philosopher, 1783–1861. *Huntington Library Bulletin* No. 11: 107–51.

D'Alembert, Jean le Rond. 1751. Discours préliminaire des éditeurs. In *Encyclopédie . . . 1751–65*: 1:i-xlv; tr. as *Preliminary Discourse to the Encyclopedia of Diderot*, by Richard N. Schwab (Indianapolis: Bobbs-Merrill, 1963).

de Maistre, Joseph Marie. 1821. *Soirées de Saint Petersbourg* (Paris); in

Oeuvres complètes de Joseph de Maistre. 14 vols. (Lyon, 1884–86) Vol. 4.

Degérando, Joseph-Marie. 1800. *Considérations sur les méthodes à suivre dans l'observation des peuples sauvages* (Paris); tr. as *The Observation of Savage Peoples*, by F. C. T. Moore (Berkeley and Los Angeles: University of California Press, 1969).

Diderot, Denis. 1749. *Lettre sur les aveugles à l'usage de ceux qui voient* (Paris).

Diderot, Denis. 1751. *Lettre sur les sourds et muets à l'usage de ceux qui entendent et qui parlent* (Paris); ed. Paul Hugo Meyer in *Diderot Studies* 7 (1965) 1–232.

Diderot, Denis. 1753. *Pensées sur l'interprétation de la nature* (Paris).

Diderot, Denis. 1755. Encyclopédie. In *Encyclopédie . . .* 1751–65: 5:635ra-648vb.

Diderot, Denis. 1765a. Locke, Philosophie de. In *Encyclopédie . . .* 1751–65: 9:625b-627a; tr. as Locke, Philosophy of, by Jean S. Yolton, in Yolton 1990: 254–60.

Diderot, Denis. 1765b. Logique. In *Encyclopédie . . .* 1751–65: 9:637b-641b.

Douglas, Janet Mary [Douglas, Mrs. Stair]. 1881. *The Life and Selections from the Correspondence of William Whewell* (London).

Dunn, John. 1969a. *The Political Thought of John Locke: An Historical Account of the Argument of the* Two Treatises of Government (Cambridge: Cambridge University Press).

Dunn, John. 1969b. The Politics of Locke in England and America in the Eighteenth Century. In Yolton 1969: 45–80.

Encyclopédie, ou Dictionnaire raisonnée des sciences, des arts et des métiers, ed. Denis Diderot et al. 1751–65. 17 vols. (Paris, 1751–57; Neufchâtel, 1765); repr. 3 vols. (New York: Readex, 1969).

Encyclopédie méthodique: Logique et métaphysique, ed. M. Lacretelle. 1786–91. 4 vols. (Paris: Panckoucke).

Evans, Gareth. 1985. Molyneux's Question. In *Collected Papers*, by Gareth Evans (Oxford: Oxford University Press) 364–99.

Everett, Alexander H. 1829. History of Intellectual Philosophy. *North American Review* 29: 67–123.

Fox, Christopher. 1988. *Locke and the Scriblerians: Identity and Consciousness in Early Eighteenth-century Britain* (Berkeley and Los Angeles: University of California Press).

Fox Bourne, H. R. 1876. *The Life of John Locke*. 2 vols. (London).

Hall, Roland, and Woolhouse, Roger. *80 Years of Locke Scholarship: A Bibliographical Guide* (Edinburgh: Edinburgh University Press, 1983).

Hartz, Louis B. 1955. *The Liberal Tradition in America: An Interpretation of American Political Thought since the Revolution* (New York: Harcourt, Brace).

Howes, Alan B., ed. 1974. *Sterne: The Critical Heritage* (London: Routledge & Kegan Paul).

Hume, David. 1739–40. *A Treatise of Human Nature.* 3 vols. (London); ed. L. A. Selby-Bigge (Oxford: Oxford University Press, 1888); 2nd ed., ed. P. H. Nidditch (1978).

Kivy, Peter. 1976. *The Seventh Sense: A Study of Francis Hutcheson's Aesthetics and its Influence in Eighteenth-century Britain* (New York: Burt Franklin).

Kondylis, Panajotis. 1981. *Die Aufklärung im Rahmen des neuzeitlichen Rationalismus* (Stuttgart: Klett-Cotta).

Laslett, Peter. 1960. Introduction and Notes. In *Two Treatises of Government,* by John Locke, ed. Peter Laslett (Cambridge: Cambridge University Press); 2nd. ed. (1967) 1–152 et passim.

Lewes, George Henry. 1845–46. *A Biographical History of Philosophy.* 4 vols. in 2 (London).

Locke, John. 1894. *An Essay concerning Human Understanding,* ed. Alexander Campbell Fraser. 2 vols. (Oxford: Oxford University Press); repr. (New York: Dover, 1959).

MacLean, Kenneth. 1936. *John Locke and English Literature of the Eighteenth Century* (New Haven: Yale University Press).

McLaverty, James. 1986. From Definition to Explanation: Locke's Influence on Johnson's *Dictionary. Journal of the History of Ideas* 47: 377–94.

Mill, James. 1829. *Analysis of the Phenomena of the Human Mind.* 2 vols. (London).

Miller, Perry. 1956. *Errand into the Wilderness* (Cambridge MA: Harvard University Press).

Moore, James. 1991. Theological Politics: A Study of the Reception of Locke's *Two Treatises of Government* in England and Scotland in the Early Eighteenth Century. In Thompson 1991: 62–82.

Morgan, Michael J. 1977. *Molyneux's Question: Vision, Touch and the Philosophy of Perception* (Cambridge: Cambridge University Press).

Nidditch, Peter H. 1975. Introduction. In *Essay concerning Human Understanding,* by John Locke, ed. Peter H. Nidditch (Oxford: Oxford University Press) ix-liv.

Passmore, John. 1953. Descartes, the British Empiricists, and Formal Logic. *Philosophical Review* 62: 545–53.

Peirce, Charles Sanders. 1890. Review of *Locke* by A. C. Fraser. *Nation* 51 (September 25) 254–55.

Perry, Ralph Barton. 1935. *The Thought and Character of William James.* 2 vols. (Boston: Little, Brown).

Pocock, J. G. A. 1987. Between God and Magog: The Republication Thesis and the Ideologia Americana. *Journal of the History of Ideas* 48: 325–46.

Pocock, J. G. A. 1991. Negative and Positive Aspects of Locke's Place in Eighteenth-Century Discourse. In Thompson 1991: 45–51.

Rask, Rasmus. 1818. Undersøgelse om Det gamle Nordiske eller Islandske Sprogs Oprindelse. In Rasmus Rask Ausgewählte Abhandlungen, ed. Louis Hjelmslev. 3 vols. (Copenhagen: Levin & Munksgaard, 1932–37) Vol. 1.

Quine, W. V. 1951. Two Dogmas of Empiricism. Philosophical Review 60: 20–43; repr. in From a Logical Point of View, by W. V. Quine (Cambridge MA: Harvard University Press, 1953) 20–46.

Quine, W. V. 1981. Five Milestones of Empiricism. In Theories and Things, by W. V. Quine (Cambridge MA: Harvard University Press) 67–72.

Roger, Jacques. 1989. Buffon, un philosophe au jardin du roi (Paris: Fayard).

Schøsler, Jorn. 1986. La Bibliothèque Raisonnée (1728–1753): Les réactions d'un périodique français à la philosophie de Locke au XVIIIe siècle (Odense: Odense University Press).

Simms, J. G. 1982. William Molyneux of Dublin, ed. P. H. Kelly (Blackrock: Irish Academic Press).

Sprat, Thomas. 1667. History of the Royal Society (London); ed. Jackson I. Cope and Harold Whitmore Jones (St. Louis MO: Washington University Studies, 1958).

Stephen, Leslie. 1876. History of English Thought in the Eighteenth Century. 2 vols. (London).

Stewart, Dugald. 1816–21. Dissertation First: Exhibiting a General View of the Progress of Metaphysical, Ethical, and Political Philosophy, Since the Revival of Letters in Europe. In Supplement to the 4th and 5th Editions of the Encyclopedia Britannica (Edinburgh); repr. in The Collected Works of Dugald Stewart, ed. Sir William Hamilton. 11 vols. (Edinburgh, 1854–60) Vol. 1.

Thompson, Martyn P., ed. 1991. John Locke und/and Immanuel Kant: Historical Reception and Contemporary Relevance (Berlin: Duncker und Humblot).

Tooke, John Horne. 1786–1805. EPEA PTEROENTA, or the Diversions of Purley. 2 vols. (London).

Turgot, Anne-Robert-Jacques. 1756. Etymologie. In Encyclopédie ... 1751–65: 6:98a–111b.

Voltaire [Arouet, François-Marie]. 1733. Letter XIII. on Mr. Locke. In Letters concerning the English Nation (London) 94–108; repr. in Yolton 1990: 246–53.

Voltaire [Arouet, François-Marie]. 1734. Lettres philosophiques (Paris); ed. Raymond Naves (Paris: Garnier, 1956); tr. as Letters concerning the English Nation, by John Lockman (London, 1733).

Voltaire [Arouet, François-Marie]. 1738. Eléments de la philosophie de

Newton (Amsterdam); ed. Robert L. Walters and W. H. Barber (Oxford: Voltaire Foundation, 1992).

Webb, Thomas. 1857. *The Intellectualism of Locke: An Essay* (Dublin).

Wills, Garry. 1979. *Inventing America: Jefferson's Declaration of Independence* (New York: Vintage).

Wootton, David. 1993. Introduction. In *John Locke: Political Writings*, ed. David Wootton (Harmondsworth: Penguin) 5–122.

Yolton, Jean S., ed. 1990. *A Locke Miscellany: Locke Biography and Criticism for All* (Bristol: Thoemmes).

Yolton, Jean S., and Yolton, John W. 1985. *John Locke: A Reference Guide* (Boston: G. K. Hall).

Yolton, John W. 1956. *John Locke and the Way of Ideas* (Oxford: Oxford University Press).

Yolton, John W., ed. 1969. *John Locke: Problems and Perspectives* (Cambridge: Cambridge University Press).

Yolton, John W. 1983. *Thinking Matter: Materialism in Eighteenth-Century Britain* (Minneapolis: University of Minnesota Press).

Yolton, John W. 1991. *Locke and French Materialism* (Oxford: Oxford University Press).

BIBLIOGRAPHY

This bibliography is divided into two parts. The first lists Locke's own works, both as published during his lifetime and in later collections and editions. The second contains works relating to Locke and his thought, some by his contemporaries and near successors but most of more recent vintage. Both lists are highly selective. Fuller bibliographies, some covering primary as well as secondary sources, are provided by Christophersen 1930, Hall and Woolhouse 1983, Attig 1985, and Yolton and Yolton 1985, and by the "Recent Publications" section in Roland Hall's annual *Locke Newsletter*. Details about these bibliographical resources are given herein.

LOCKE'S OWN WORKS

Individual works published during or just after Locke's lifetime

Abrégé d'un ouvrage intitulé Essai philosophique touchant l'entendement (Amsterdam, 1688); tr. as *An Extract of a Book, Entituled,* A Philosophical Essay upon Human Understanding (London, 1692).
Epistola de tolerantia (Gouda, 1689); tr. as *Letter on Toleration,* by William Popple (London, 1689); 2nd ed. (1690).
Two Treatises of Government (London, 1690); 2nd ed. (1694); 3rd ed. (1698).
An Essay concerning Human Understanding (London, 1690); 2nd ed. (1694); 3rd ed. (1695); 4th ed. (1700); 5th ed. (1706).
An Essay concerning Human Understanding, 4th ed. (London, 1700); tr. as *Essai philosophique concernant l'entendement humain,* by Pierre Coste (Amsterdam, 1700).
An Essay concerning Human Understanding, 4th ed. (London, 1700); tr. as *De intellectu humano,* by Ezekiel Burridge (London, 1701).
A Second Letter concerning Toleration (London, 1690).

A Third Letter for Toleration, to the Author of The Third Letter concerning Toleration (London, 1692).

Some Considerations of the Consequences of the Lowering of Interest, and Raising the Value of Money (London, 1692); 2nd ed. (1696).

Some Thoughts concerning Education (London, 1693); 2nd ed. (1693); 3rd ed. (1695); 4th ed. (1699); 5th ed. (1705).

Short Observations on a Printed Paper, Intituled, For Encouraging the Coining Silver Money in England, and After for Keeping it Here (London, 1695).

Further Considerations concerning Raising the Value of Money (London, 1695); 2nd ed. (1695).

The Reasonableness of Christianity, As Delivered in the Scriptures (London, 1695); 2nd ed. (1696).

A Vindication of the Reasonableness of Christianity, &c. from Mr. Edwards's Reflections (London, 1695).

A Second Vindication of the Reasonableness of Christianity, &c. (London, 1697).

A Letter to the Right Reverend Edward, Lord Bishop of Worcester, Concerning some Passages relating to Mr. Locke's Essay of humane Understanding: In a late Discourse of his Lordship's, in Vindication of the Trinity (London, 1697).

Mr. Locke's Reply to the Right Reverend the Lord Bishop of Worcester's Answer to his Letter, concerning Some Passages Relating to Mr. Locke's Essay of Humane Understanding: in a Late Discourse of his Lordships, in Vindication of the Trinity (London, 1697).

Mr. Locke's Reply to the Right Reverend the Lord Bishop of Worcester's Answer to his Second Letter: Wherein, besides other incident Matters, what his Lordship has said concerning Certainty by Reason, Certainty by Ideas, and Certainty by Faith. The Resurrection of the Same Body. The Immateriality of the Soul. The Inconsistency of Mr. Locke's Notions with the Articles of the Christian Faith, and their Tendancy to Scepticism, is Examined (London, 1699).

A Paraphrase and Notes on the Epistles of St. Paul. 6 vols. (London, 1705–7).

Collections and later editions (Abbreviations for editions and sources cited are given in brackets.)

Posthumous Works of Mr. John Locke [including *An Examination of P. Malebranche's Opinion of Seeing All Things in God* (1693), *Of the Conduct of the Understanding* (1697), *A Discourse of Miracles* (1702), et al.] (London, 1706).

Some Familiar Letters between Mr. Locke, and Several of his Friends (London, 1708).

The Works of John Locke Esq. 3 vols. (London, 1714).

A Collection of Several Pieces of Mr. John Locke, Never Before Printed, or not Extant in his Works, ed. Pierre Desmaizeaux [including *Remarks upon some of Mr. Norris's Books* (1693), *The Elements of Natural Philosophy* (1698ff.), *Some Thoughts concerning Reading and Study for a Gentleman* (1703), et al.] (London, 1720).

The Works of John Locke, new ed., corrected. 10 vols. (London, 1823); repr. (Aalen: Scientia, 1963). [W]

Manuscripts in the Bodleian Library. [B]

The Clarendon Edition of the Works of John Locke, ed. Peter H. Nidditch, John W. Yolton, et al. 30 vols. (Oxford: Oxford University Press, 1975–).

Essays on the Law of Nature.

The writings on toleration.

Two Treatises of Government.

An Essay concerning Human Understanding, ed. Peter H. Nidditch (1975); repr. (1979). [E]

Drafts for the Essay concerning Human Understanding, *and Other Philosophical Writings*, ed. Peter H. Nidditch and G. A. J. Rogers. 3 vols. (1990–). [D]

Locke on Money, ed. Patrick Hyde Kelly. 2 vols. (1991).

Some Thoughts concerning Education, ed. John W. Yolton and Jean S. Yolton (1989). [TE]

The Reasonableness of Christianity.

The Stillingfleet correspondence.

A Paraphrase and Notes on the Epistles of St. Paul, ed. Arthur W. Wainwright. 2 vols. (1987).

Two or three volumes of writings on medicine and religion and of "bits and pieces."

Journals 1675–1704, ed. H. A. S. Shankula. 4 vols. (forthcoming).

The Correspondence of John Locke, ed. E. S. de Beer. 9 vols. (1976–). [C]

The Life of John Locke, by Peter, Lord King (London, 1829); new ed. 2 vols. (London, 1830). [L]

An Essay concerning the Understanding, Knowledge, Opinion, and Assent, ed. Benjamin Rand (Cambridge MA: Harvard University Press, 1931).

An Early Draft of Locke's Essay, ed. R. I. Aaron and Jocelyn Gibb (Oxford: Oxford University Press, 1936).

Essays on the Law of Nature, ed. W. von Leyden (Oxford: Oxford University Press, 1954). [EL]

Locke's Essay on Respiration, ed. Kenneth Dewhurst. *Bulletin for the History of Medicine* 24 (1960) 257–73.

Two Tracts on Government, ed. Philip Abrams (Cambridge: Cambridge University Press, 1967).

Two Treatises of Government, ed. Peter Laslett (Cambridge: Cambridge University Press, 1960); 2nd ed. (1967). [T]

Locke's First Reply to John Norris, by Richard Acworth. *Locke Newsletter* 2 (1971) 7–11.

Locke and Ethical Theory: Two Ms. Pieces, by Thomas Sargentich. *Locke Newsletter* 5 (1974) 24–31.

John Locke's Essay on Infallibility: Introduction, Text, and Translation, by John C. Biddle. *Journal of Church and State* 19 (1977) 301–27.

Locke on Power and Causation: Excerpts from the 1685 Draft of the *Essay,* by Ruth Mattern. *Philosophy Research Archives* 7 (1981) 835–995.

Questions concerning the Law of Nature, ed. and tr. Robert Horwitz, Jenny Strauss Clay, and Diskin Clay (Ithaca: Cornell University Press, 1990). [QL]

WORKS RELATING TO LOCKE

Aaron, Richard I. Introduction. In *An Early Draft of Locke's Essay,* ed. R. I. Aaron and Jocelyn Gibb (Oxford: Oxford University Press, 1936) xi–xxviii.

Aaron, Richard I. *John Locke* (Oxford: Oxford University Press, 1937); 3rd ed. (1971).

Aarsleff, Hans. Leibniz on Locke on Language. *American Philosophical Quarterly* 1 (1964) 165–88; repr. in *From Locke to Saussure,* by Hans Aarsleff (Minneapolis: University of Minnesota Press, 1982) 42–83.

Aarsleff, Hans. The State of Nature and the Nature of Man in Locke. In *John Locke: Problems and Perspectives,* ed. John W. Yolton (Cambridge: Cambridge University Press, 1969) 99–136.

Aarsleff, Hans. Locke's Reputation in Nineteenth-century England. *Monist* 55 (1971) 392–422; repr. in *From Locke to Saussure,* by Hans Aarsleff (Minneapolis: University of Minnesota Press, 1982) 120–45.

Aarsleff, Hans. *From Locke to Saussure: Essays on the Study of Language and Intellectual History* (Minneapolis: University of Minnesota Press, 1982).

Abrams, Philip. Introduction. In *Two Tracts on Government,* by John Locke, ed. Philip Abrams (Cambridge: Cambridge University Press, 1967) 1–114.

Adams, Robert M. The Locke-Leibniz Debate. In *Innate Ideas,* ed. Stephen P. Stich (Berkeley and Los Angeles: University of California Press, 1975) 37–67.

Adams, Robert M. Where Do Our Ideas Come From?–Descartes vs. Locke.

In *Innate Ideas,* ed. Stephen P. Stich (Berkeley and Los Angeles: University of California Press, 1975) 71–87.

Alexander, Peter. Boyle and Locke on Primary and Secondary Qualities. *Ratio* 16 (1974) 51–67; repr. in *Locke on Human Understanding,* ed. I. C. Tipton (Oxford: Oxford University Press, 1977) 62–76.

Alexander, Peter. Curley on Locke and Boyle. *Philosophical Review* 83 (1974) 229–37. Discussion of Curley 1972.

Alexander, Peter. Locke on Substance-in-General. *Ratio* 22 (1980) 91–105; 23 (1981) 1–19.

Alexander, Peter. *Ideas, Qualities and Corpuscles: Locke and Boyle on the External World* (Cambridge: Cambridge University Press, 1985).

Allison, Henry E. Locke's Theory of Personal Identity: A Re-examination. *Journal of the History of Ideas* 27 (1966) 41–58; repr. in *Locke on Human Understanding,* ed. I. C. Tipton (Oxford: Oxford University Press, 1977) 105–22.

Alston, William P., and Bennett, Jonathan. Locke on People and Substances. *Philosophical Review* 97 (1988) 25–46.

Anscombe, G. E. M. The Intentionality of Sensation: A Grammatical Feature. In *Analytical Philosophy: Second Series,* ed. R. J. Butler (Oxford: Blackwell, 1965) 158–80.

Aquinas, Thomas. *St. Thomas Aquinas on Politics and Ethics,* ed. and tr. Paul E. Sigmund (New York: Norton, 1988).

Aristotle. *The Complete Works of Aristotle,* ed. Jonathan Barnes. 2 vols. (Princeton: Princeton University Press, 1984).

Armstrong, D. M. *Belief, Truth and Knowledge* (Cambridge: Cambridge University Press, 1973).

Armstrong, R. L. Cambridge Platonists and Locke on Innate Ideas. *Journal of the History of Ideas* 30 (1969) 187–202.

Aronson, C., and Lewis, Douglas. Locke on Mixed Modes, Knowledge and Substances. *Journal of the History of Philosophy* 8 (1970) 193–99. Discussion of Perry 1967. Discussed by Woolhouse 1972.

Ashcraft, Richard. Locke's State of Nature: Historical Fact or Moral Fiction? *American Political Science Review* 62 (1968) 898–915.

Ashcraft, Richard. Faith and Knowledge in Locke's Philosophy. In *John Locke: Problems and Perspectives,* ed. John W. Yolton (Cambridge: Cambridge University Press, 1969) 194–223.

Ashcraft, Richard. Revolutionary Politics and Locke's *Two Treatises of Government:* Radicalism and Lockean Political Theory. *Political Theory* 8 (1980) 429–86.

Ashcraft, Richard. *Revolutionary Politics and Locke's* Two Treatises of Government (Princeton: Princeton University Press, 1986).

Ashcraft, Richard. *Locke's Two Treatises of Government* (London: Unwin Hyman, 1987).

Ashcraft, Richard, ed. *John Locke: Critical Assessments*. 4 vols. (London: Routledge, 1991).

Ashworth, E. J. Descartes' Theory of Clear and Distinct Ideas. In *Cartesian Studies*, ed. R. J. Butler (Oxford: Blackwell, 1972) 89–105.

Ashworth, E. J. The Scholastic Background to Locke's Theory of Language. In *Progress in Linguistic Historiography*, ed. K. Koerner (Amsterdam: Benjamins, 1980) 59–68.

Ashworth, E. J. 'Do Words Signify Ideas or Things?' The Scholastic Sources of Locke's Theory of Language. *Journal of the History of Philosophy* 19 (1981) 299–326.

Ashworth, E. J. Locke on Language. *Canadian Journal of Philosophy* 14 (1984) 45–73.

Ashworth, E. J. Traditional Logic. In *The Cambridge History of Renaissance Philosophy*, ed. Charles B. Schmitt and Quentin Skinner (Cambridge: Cambridge University Press, 1988) 143–72.

Atherton, Margaret. Locke and the Issue over Innateness. In *How Many Questions? Essays in Honor of Sidney Morgenbesser*, ed. Leigh S. Cauman et al. (Indianapolis: Hackett, 1983) 223–42.

Atherton, Margaret. Locke's Theory of Personal Identity. *Midwest Studies in Philosophy* 8 (1983) 273–93.

Atherton, Margaret. The Inessentiality of Lockean Essences. *Canadian Journal of Philosophy* 14 (1984) 277–93.

Atherton, Margaret. Knowledge of Substance and Knowledge of Essence in Locke's *Essay*. *History of Philosophy Quarterly* 1 (1984) 413–28.

Atherton, Margaret. Corpuscles, Mechanism, and Essentialism in Berkeley and Locke. *Journal of the History of Philosophy* 29 (1991) 47–67.

Attig, John C. *The Works of John Locke: A Comprehensive Bibliography from the Seventeenth Century to the Present* (Westport CT: Greenwood Press, 1985).

Ayers, Michael R. Substance, Reality, and the Great, Dead Philosophers. *American Philosophical Quarterly* 7 (1970) 38–49. Discussion of Bennett 1965.

Ayers, Michael R. The Ideas of Power and Substance in Locke's Philosophy. *Philosophical Quarterly* 25 (1975) 1–27; repr. in *Locke on Human Understanding*, ed. I. C. Tipton (Oxford: Oxford University Press, 1977) 77–104.

Ayers, Michael R. Locke versus Aristotle on Natural Kinds. *Journal of Philosophy* 78 (1981) 247–71; repr. in *Philosopher's Annual* 5 (1982) 41–66.

Ayers, Michael R. Locke's Doctrine of Abstraction: Some Aspects of its

Historical and Philosophical Significance. In *John Locke: Symposium Wolfenbüttel 1979*, ed. Reinhard Brandt (Berlin: de Gruyter, 1981) 5–24.

Ayers, Michael R. Locke's Logical Atomism. *British Academy Proceedings* 67 (1981) 209–25.

Ayers, Michael R. Mechanism, Superaddition and the Proof of God's Existence in Locke's Essay. *Philosophical Review* 40 (1981) 210–51. Discussed by Wilson 1982.

Ayers, Michael R. Are Locke's 'Ideas' Images, Intentional Objects or Natural Signs? *Locke Newsletter* 17 (1986) 3–36.

Ayers, Michael R. *Locke*. 2 vols. (London: Routledge, 1991).

Barnes, Jonathan. Mr. Locke's Darling Notion. *Philosophical Quarterly* 22 (1972) 193–214.

Barnes, Jonathan. Enseigner la vertu? *Revue Philosophique* (1991) 571–89.

Behan, D. P. Locke on Persons and Personal Identity. *Canadian Journal of Philosophy* 9 (1979) 53–75.

Bennett, Jonathan. Substance, Reality, and Primary Qualities. *American Philosophical Quarterly* 2 (1965) 1–17; repr. in *Locke and Berkeley: A Collection of Critical Essays*, ed. C. B. Martin and D. M. Armstrong (Garden City NY: Doubleday, 1968) 86–124. Discussed by Ayers 1970.

Bennett, Jonathan. *Locke, Berkeley, Hume: Central Themes* (Oxford: Oxford University Press, 1971).

Bennett, Jonathan. *Linguistic Behaviour* (Cambridge: Cambridge University Press, 1976).

Bennett, Jonathan. Substratum. *History of Philosophy Quarterly* 4 (1987) 197–215.

Bennett, Jonathan, and Remnant, Peter. How Matter Might at First be Made. *Canadian Journal of Philosophy* Supp. 4 (1978) 1–11.

Berkeley, George. *The Works of George Berkeley Bishop of Cloyne*, ed. A. A. Luce and T. E. Jessop. 9 vols. (London: Nelson, 1948–57).

Berlin, Isaiah. Hobbes, Locke and Professor Macpherson. *Political Quarterly* 35 (1963) 444–68. Discussion of Macpherson 1962.

Bill, E. W. G. *Education at Christ Church Oxford 1660–1800* (Oxford: Oxford University Press, 1988).

Bolton, Martha Brandt. The Origins of Locke's Doctrine of Primary and Secondary Qualities. *Philosophical Quarterly* 26 (1976) 305–16.

Bolton, Martha Brandt. Substances, Substrata, and Names of Substances in Locke's Essay. *Philosophical Review* 85 (1976) 488–513.

Bolton, Martha Brandt. A Defense of Locke and the Representative Theory of Perception. *Canadian Journal of Philosophy* Supp. 4 (1978) 101–20.

Bolton, Martha Brandt. Locke and Pyrrhonism: The Doctrine of Primary and Secondary Qualities. In *The Skeptical Tradition*, ed. Myles Burnyeat (Berkeley and Los Angeles: University of California Press, 1983) 353–75.

Bolton, Martha Brandt. Locke on Substance Ideas and the Determination of Kinds: A Reply to Mattern. *Locke Newsletter* 19 (1988) 17–45. Discussion of Mattern 1986.

Bolton, Martha Brandt. The Epistemological Status of Ideas: Locke compared to Arnauld. *History of Philosophy Quarterly* 9 (1992) 409–24.

Boyle, Robert. *Selected Philosophical Papers of Robert Boyle,* ed. M. A. Stewart (Manchester: Manchester University Press, 1979).

Brandt, Reinhard, ed. *John Locke: Symposium Wolfenbüttel 1979* (Berlin: de Gruyter, 1981).

Brandt, Reinhard. Locke und die Auseinandersetzungen über sein Denken. In *Die Philosophie des 17. Jahrhunderts,* ed. Jean-Pierre Schobinger, Vol. 3: *England* (Basel: Schwabe, 1988) 607–802.

Bricke, John. Locke, Hume and the Nature of Volitions. *Hume Studies* 10th Anniversary Issue (1985) 15–51.

Burnet, Thomas. *Second Remarks upon an Essay concerning Humane Understanding, In a Letter address'd to the Author* (London, 1697); repr. (New York: Garland, 1984).

Butler, R. J. Substance Un-Locked. *Aristotelian Society Proceedings* 74 (1973–74) 131–60.

Campbell, John. Locke on Qualities. *Canadian Journal of Philosophy* 10 (1980) 567–85.

Carter, W. B. The Classification of Ideas in Locke's *Essay. Dialogue* 2 (1963–64) 25–41.

Chappell, Vere. Locke and Relative Identity. *History of Philosophy Quarterly* 6 (1989) 69–83.

Chappell, Vere. Locke on the Ontology of Matter, Living Things, and Persons. *Philosophical Studies* 60 (1990) 19–32.

Chappell, Vere. Locke on the Freedom of the Will. In *Locke's Philosophy: Content and Context,* ed. G. A. J. Rogers (Oxford: Oxford University Press, 1994).

Chisholm, Roderick M. *Theory of Knowledge* (Englewood Cliffs NJ: Prentice-Hall, 1966); 2nd ed. (1977).

Chisholm, Roderick M. *The Foundations of Knowing* (Minneapolis: University of Minnesota Press, 1982).

Christophersen, H. O. *A Bibliographical Introduction to the Study of John Locke* (Oslo: I Kommisjon hos Jacob Dybwad, 1930); repr. (New York: Burt Franklin, 1968).

Cicovacki, P. Locke on Mathematical Knowledge. *Journal of the History of Philosophy* 28 (1990) 511–24.

Clark, Lorenne M. G. Women and John Locke; or, Who Owns the Apples in the Garden of Eden? *Canadian Journal of Philosophy* 7 (1977) 699–724; repr. in *The Sexism of Social and Political Theory,* ed. Lorenne M. G.

Clark and Lynda Lange (Toronto: University of Toronto Press, 1979) 16–40.

Cohen, Joshua. Structure, Choice, and Legitimacy: Locke's Theory of the State. *Philosophy and Public Affairs* 15 (1986) 301–24.

Colie, Rosalie. The Essayist in his *Essay*. In *John Locke: Problems and Perspectives*, ed. John W. Yolton (Cambridge: Cambridge University Press, 1969) 234–61.

Colman, John. *John Locke's Moral Philosophy* (Edinburgh: Edinburgh University Press, 1983).

Cooney, B. John Sergeant's Criticism of Locke's Theory of Ideas. *Modern Schoolman* 50 (1973) 143–58.

Cox, Richard H. *Locke on War and Peace* (Oxford: Oxford University Press, 1960).

Crane, R. S. Notes on the Organization of Locke's *Essay*. In *All These to Teach: Essays in Honor of C. A. Robertson*, ed. R. A. Bryan et al. (Gainesville: University of Florida Press, 1965) 144–58.

Cranston, Maurice. *John Locke: A Biography* (London: Longman, 1957); repr. (Oxford: Oxford University Press, 1985).

Culverwell, Nathanael. *An Elegant and Learned Discourse of the Light of Nature* (London, 1652); repr. (New York: Garland, 1978).

Cumberland, Richard. *De legibus naturae* (London, 1672); tr. as *A Treatise of the Laws of Nature*, by John Maxwell (London, 1727); repr. (New York: Garland, 1976).

Cummins, Robert. Two Troublesome Claims about Qualities in Locke's *Essay*. *Philosophical Review* 84 (1975) 401–18.

Curley, Edwin M. Locke, Boyle, and the Distinction between Primary and Secondary Qualities. *Philosophical Review* 81 (1972) 438–64. Discussed by Alexander 1974.

Curley, Edwin M. Leibniz on Locke on Personal Identity. In *Leibniz: Critical and Interpretive Essays*, ed. Michael Hooker (Minneapolis: University of Minnesota Press, 1982) 302–26.

Day, J. P. Locke on Property. *Philosophical Quarterly* 16 (1966) 207–20.

De Almeida, C. Locke on Knowledge and Trifling Propositions. *Locke Newsletter* 22 (1991) 31–55.

Dennett, Daniel C. *Brainstorms* (Cambridge MA: MIT Press, 1978).

Dewhurst, Kenneth. *John Locke (1632–1704) Physician and Philosopher* (London: Wellcome Historical Medical Library, 1963).

Dijksterhuis, E. J. *The Mechanization of the World Picture* (Oxford: Oxford University Press, 1961).

Downing, Lisa. Are Corpuscles Unobservable in Principle for Locke? *Journal of the History of Philosophy* 30 (1992) 33–52.

Drury, S. B. John Locke: Natural Law and Innate Ideas. *Dialogue* 19 (1980) 531–45.

Duchesneau, François. Locke et le savoir de probabilité. *Dialogue* 11 (1972) 185–203.

Duchesneau, François. *L'empirisme de Locke* (The Hague: Martinus Nijhoff, 1973).

Duchesneau, François. L'analyse d'idées selon Locke. *Etudes philosophiques* (1977) 67–94.

Dunn, John. Consent in the Political Theory of John Locke. *Historical Journal* 10 (1967) 153–82.

Dunn, John. Justice and the Interpretation of Locke's Political Theory. *Political Studies* 16 (1968) 68–87.

Dunn, John. *The Political Thought of John Locke: An Historical Account of the Argument of the* Two Treatises of Government (Cambridge: Cambridge University Press, 1969).

Dunn, John. The Politics of Locke in England and America in the Eighteenth Century. In *John Locke: Problems and Perspectives*, ed. John W. Yolton (Cambridge: Cambridge University Press, 1969) 45–80.

Dunn, John. The Concept of 'Trust' in the Politics of John Locke. In *Philosophy in History*, ed. Richard Rorty et al. (Cambridge: Cambridge University Press, 1984) 279–301.

Dunn, John. *Locke* (Oxford: Oxford University Press, 1984).

Dunn, John. What is Living and What is Dead in the Political Theory of John Locke? In *Interpreting Political Responsibility: Essays 1981–1989*, by John Dunn (Princeton: Princeton University Press, 1990).

Edwards, John. *Some Thoughts Concerning the Several Causes and Occasions of Atheism, Especially in the Present Age* (London, 1695); repr. (New York: Garland, 1984).

Edwards, John. *Socinianism Unmask'd* (London, 1696); repr. (New York: Garland, 1984).

Farr, James. "So Vile and Miserable an Estate": The Problem of Slavery in Locke's Political Thought. *Political Theory* 14 (1986) 263–89.

Farr, James. The Way of Hypotheses: Locke on Method. *Journal of the History of Ideas* 48 (1987) 51–72.

Farrell, D. M. Coercion, Consent, and the Justification of Political Power: A New Look at Locke's Consent Claim. *Archiv für Rechts- und Sozialphilosophie* 65 (1979) 521–43.

Ferreira, M. Jamie. Locke's 'Constructive Skepticism'–A Reappraisal. *Journal of the History of Philosophy* 24 (1986) 211–22.

Filmer, Sir Robert. *Patriarchia: Of the Natural Power of Kings* (London, 1680).

Firpo, M. John Locke e il socinianesimo. *Rivista Storica Italiana* 92 (1980) 35–124.

Flage, D. E. Locke's Relative Ideas. *Theoria* 47 (1981) 142–59.

Flew, Antony. Locke and the Problem of Personal Identity. *Philosophy* 26 (1951) 53–68; repr. in *Locke and Berkeley: A Collection of Critical Essays*, ed. C. B. Martin and D. M. Armstrong (Garden City NY: Doubleday, 1968) 155–78.

Fox Bourne, H. R. *The Life of John Locke*. 2 vols. (London, 1876).

Frank, Robert G., Jr. *Harvey and the Oxford Physiologists* (Berkeley and Los Angeles: University of California Press, 1980).

Franklin, Julian H. *John Locke and the Theory of Sovereignty* (Cambridge: Cambridge University Press, 1978).

Garber, Daniel. Locke, Berkeley, and Corpuscular Skepticism. In *Berkeley: Critical and Interpretive Essays*, ed. Colin M. Turbayne (Minneapolis: University of Minnesota Press, 1982) 174–93.

Gauthier, David. Why Ought One Obey God? Reflections on Hobbes and Locke. *Canadian Journal of Philosophy* 7 (1977) 425–46.

Gibson, James. *Locke's Theory of Knowledge and its Historical Relations* (Cambridge: Cambridge University Press, 1917).

Goldie, Mark. The Revolution of 1689 and the Structure of Political Argument. *Bulletin of Research in the Humanities* 83 (1980) 473–564.

Goldie, Mark. John Locke and Anglican Royalism. *Political Studies* 31 (1983) 61–85.

Gough, J. W. *John Locke's Political Philosophy: Eight Studies* (Oxford: Oxford University Press, 1950).

Goyard-Fabre, S. *John Locke et la raison raisonnable* (Paris: Vrin, 1986).

Grant, Ruth W. *John Locke's Liberalism* (Chicago: University of Chicago Press, 1987).

Grave, S. A. *Locke and Burnet* (Perth: University of Western Australia, 1981).

Greenlee, Douglas. Locke and the Controversy over Innate Ideas. *Journal of the History of Ideas* 33 (1972) 251–64.

Grice, H. P. Personal Identity. *Mind* 50 (1941) 330–50.

Grotius, Hugo. *De jure belli ac pacis* (Paris, 1625); tr. as *The Law of War and Peace*, by Francis W. Kelsey et al. (Oxford: Oxford University Press, 1925).

Haley, K. H. D. *The First Earl of Shaftesbury* (Oxford: Oxford University Press, 1968).

Hall, Roland, ed. *Locke Newsletter* 1– (1970–).

Hall, Roland. Recent Publications. *Locke Newsletter* 1– (1970–).

Hall, Roland. Locke and Sensory Experience. *Locke Newsletter* 18 (1987) 11–31.

Hall, Roland. 'Idea' in Locke's Works. *Locke Newsletter* 21 (1990) 9–26.

Hall, Roland, and Woolhouse, Roger. *80 Years of Locke Scholarship: A Bibliographical Guide* (Edinburgh: Edinburgh University Press, 1983).

Hargreaves-Mawdsley, W. N. *Oxford in the Age of John Locke* (Norman: Oklahoma University Press, 1973).

Harris, John. Leibniz and Locke on Innate Ideas. *Ratio* 16 (1974) 226–42; repr. in *Locke on Human Understanding*, ed. I. C. Tipton (Oxford: Oxford University Press, 1977) 25–40.

Harris, N. G. E. Locke's Triangles. *Canadian Journal of Philosophy* 18 (1988) 31–41.

Harrison, John, and Laslett, Peter. *The Library of John Locke* (Oxford: Oxford University Press, 1965); 2nd ed. (1971).

Heil, John. The Molyneux Question. *Journal for the Theory of Social Behavior* 17 (1987) 227–41.

Helm, Paul. Locke on Faith and Knowledge. *Philosophical Quarterly* 23 (1973) 52–66.

Helm, Paul. John Locke's Puzzle Cases about Personal Identity. *Locke Newsletter* 8 (1977) 53–68.

Helm, Paul. Locke's Theory of Personal Identity. *Philosophy* 54 (1979) 173–85.

Hobbes, Thomas. *De cive* (Amsterdam, 1646); tr. as *Philosophicall Rudiments Concerning Government and Society* (London, 1651); ed. Howard Warrender (Oxford: Oxford University Press, 1984).

Hobbes, Thomas. *De corpore, Part I: Computatio sive Logica* (London, 1655); tr. as *Logic*, by Aloysius Martinich (New York: Abaris, 1981).

Hoffheimer, Michael H. Locke, Spinoza and the Idea of Political Equality. *History of Political Thought* 7 (1986) 341–60.

Hont, Istvan. The Language of Sociability and Commerce: Samuel Pufendorf and the Theoretical Foundations of the 'Four-Stages Theory'. In *The Languages of Political Theory in Early-Modern Europe*, ed. Anthony Pagden (Cambridge: Cambridge University Press, 1987) 253–76.

Hooke, Robert. *Micrographia* (London, 1665); repr. (Weinheim: Cramer, 1961).

Hooker, Richard. *Of the Laws of Ecclesiastical Polity: Eight Books* (London, 1593–1661); ed. Georges Edelen et al., 4 vols. (Cambridge MA: Harvard University Press, 1977–82).

Horton, John, and Mendus, Susan, eds. *John Locke: A Letter Concerning Toleration in Focus* (London: Routledge, 1991).

Horwitz, Robert. Introduction. In *Questions concerning the Law of Nature*, by John Locke, ed. and tr. Robert Horwitz, Jenny Strauss Clay, and Diskin Clay (Ithaca: Cornell University Press, 1990) 1–62.

Horwitz, Robert. John Locke's *Questions concerning the Law of Nature:* A Commentary, ed. M. Zuckert. *Interpretation* 19 (1992) 251–306.

Hughes, M. W. Personal Identity: A Defence of Locke. *Philosophy* 50 (1975) 169–87.

Jackson, Reginald. Locke's Distinction between Primary and Secondary Qualities. *Mind* 38 (1929) 56–76; repr. in *Locke and Berkeley: A Collection of Critical Essays,* ed. C. B. Martin and D. M. Armstrong (Garden City NY: Doubleday, 1968) 53–77.

Jackson, Reginald. Locke's Version of the Doctrine of Representative Perception. *Mind* 39 (1930) 1–25; repr. in *Locke and Berkeley: A Collection of Critical Essays,* ed. C. B. Martin and D. M. Armstrong (Garden City NY: Doubleday, 1968) 125–54.

Jacob, James R. Locke's *Two Treatises* and the Revolution of 1688–1689: The State of the Argument. *Annals of Scholarship* 5 (1987–88) 311–33.

Jenkins, John J. *Understanding Locke* (Edinburgh, 1983).

Johnson, C. L. Samuel Johnson's Moral Psychology and Locke's 'Of Power'. *Studies in English Literature 1500–1900* 24 (1984) 563–82.

Jolley, Nicholas. *Leibniz and Locke: A Study of the* New Essays on Human Understanding (Oxford: Oxford University Press, 1984).

Kain, P. J. Locke and the Development of Political Theory. *Annals of Scholarship* 5 (1987–88) 334–61.

Kant, Immanuel. *On History,* ed. and tr. Lewis White Beck et al. (Indianapolis: Bobbs-Merrill, 1963).

Kelly, Patrick Hyde. 'All Things Richly to Enjoy': Economics and Politics in Locke's *Two Treatises of Government. Political Studies* 36 (1988) 273–93.

Kelly, Patrick Hyde. General Introduction. In *Locke on Money,* ed. Patrick Hyde Kelly. 2 vols. (Oxford: Oxford University Press, 1991) 1–109.

Kelly, P. J. John Locke: Authority, Conscience and Religious Toleration. In *John Locke:* A Letter Concerning Toleration *in Focus,* ed. John Horton and Susan Mendus (London: Routledge, 1991) 125–46.

Kilcullen, John. Locke on Political Obligation. *Review of Politics* 45 (1983) 323–44.

King, Peter, Lord. *The Life of John Locke* (London, 1829); new ed. 2 vols. (1830).

Kretzmann, Norman. The Main Thesis of Locke's Semantic Theory. *Philosophical Review* 77 (1968) 175–96; repr. in *Locke on Human Understanding,* ed. I. C. Tipton (Oxford: Oxford University Press, 1977) 123–40.

Kroll, Richard W. F. The Question of Locke's Relation to Gassendi. *Journal of the History of Ideas* 45 (1984) 339–60.

Krüger, Lorenz. *Der Begriff des Empirismus: Erkenntnistheoretische Studien am Beispiel John Lockes* (Berlin: de Gruyter, 1973).

Krüger, Lorenz. The Concept of Experience in John Locke. In *John Locke: Symposium Wolfenbüttel 1979*, ed. Reinhard Brandt (Berlin: de Gruyter, 1981) 74–89.

Kulstad, Mark A. Locke on Consciousness and Reflection. *Studia Leibnitiana* 16 (1984) 143–67.

Landesman, Charles. Locke's Theory of Meaning. *Journal of the History of Philosophy* 14 (1976) 23–35.

Laslett, Peter. The English Revolution and Locke's *Two Treatises of Government. Cambridge Historical Journal* 12 (1956) 40–55.

Laslett, Peter. John Locke, the Great Recoinage, and the Origins of the Board of Trade, 1695–1698. *William and Mary Quarterly* 14 (1957) 370–402; repr. in *John Locke: Problems and Perspectives*, ed. John W. Yolton (Cambridge: Cambridge University Press, 1969) 137–64.

Laslett, Peter. Introduction and Notes. In *Two Treatises of Government*, by John Locke, ed. Peter Laslett (Cambridge: Cambridge University Press, 1960); 2nd. ed. (1967) 1–152 et passim.

Laudan, Laurens. The Nature and Sources of Locke's Views on Hypotheses. *Journal of the History of Ideas* 28 (1967) 211–23; repr. in *Locke on Human Understanding*, ed. I. C. Tipton (Oxford: Oxford University Press, 1977) 149–62.

Le Clerc, Jean. Review of *An Essay concerning Human Understanding . . .*, the fifth Edition. *Bibliothèque Choisie* 12 (1707) 80–123.

Le Clerc, Jean. Review of *Some Familiar Letters between Mr. Locke and Several of his Friends. Bibliothèque Choisie* 17 (1709) 234–41.

Lee, Henry. *Anti-Scepticism: or, Notes Upon each Chapter of Mr. Lock's Essay concerning Humane Understanding* (London, 1702); repr. (New York: Garland, 1984).

Leibniz, G. W. *Nouveaux essais* (Amsterdam, 1765); ed. Andre Robinet and Heinrich Schepers (Berlin, 1962); tr. as *New Essays on Human Understanding*, by Peter Remnant and Jonathan Bennett (Cambridge: Cambridge University Press, 1981).

Leibniz, G. W. *Die philosophischen Schriften von Gottfried Wilhelm Leibniz*, ed. C. J. Gerhardt. 7 vols. (Berlin, 1875–90).

Leibniz, G. W. *Leibniz: Political Writings*, ed. and tr. Patrick Riley (Cambridge: Cambridge University Press, 1988).

Leites, Edmund. Conscience, Leisure, and Learning: Locke and the Levellers. *Sociological Analysis* 39 (1978) 36–61.

Leites, Edmund. Locke's Liberal Theory of Parenthood. In *Having Children*, ed. Onora O'Neill and William Ruddick (New York: Oxford University

Press, 1979) 306–18; repr. in *John Locke: Symposium Wolfenbüttel 1979*, ed. Reinhard Brandt (Berlin: de Gruyter, 1981) 90–112.

Lennon, Thomas M. Locke's Atomism. *Philosophy Research Archives* 9 (1983) 1–28.

Lewis, Douglas. The Existence of Substances and Locke's Way of Ideas. *Theoria* 35 (1969) 124–46.

Lievers, Menno. The Molyneux Problem. *Journal of the History of Philosophy* 30 (1992) 399–416.

Limborch, Philippus van. *Theologia Christiana* (Amsterdam, 1686); tr. as *A Compleat System, or Body of Divinity*, by William Jones. 2 vols. (London, 1702); 2nd ed. (1713).

Lough, John. *Locke's Travels in France 1675–1679* (Cambridge: Cambridge University Press, 1953).

Lowde, James. *A Discourse concerning the Nature of Man* (London, 1694).

Lowe, E. J. Necessity and Will in Locke's Theory of Action. *History of Philosophy Quarterly* 3 (1986) 149–63.

Mabbott, J. D. *John Locke* (London: Macmillan, 1973).

Mackie, J. L. *Problems from Locke* (Oxford: Oxford University Press, 1976).

Mackie, J. L. Locke and Representative Perception. In *Logic and Knowledge: Selected Papers*, by J. L. Mackie, Vol. 1 (Oxford: Oxford University Press, 1985) 214–24.

MacLean, Kenneth. *John Locke and English Literature of the Eighteenth Century* (New Haven: Yale University Press, 1936).

Macpherson, C. B. *The Political Theory of Possessive Individualism: Hobbes to Locke* (Oxford: Oxford University Press, 1962). Discussed by Berlin 1963.

Mandelbaum, Maurice. Locke's Realism. In *Philosophy, Science, and Sense Perception*, by Maurice Mandelbaum (Baltimore: Johns Hopkins University Press, 1964) 1–60.

Marshall, John. *John Locke in Context: Religion, Ethics, and Politics*. Unpublished Ph.D. Dissertation (Baltimore: Johns Hopkins University, 1990); published version (Cambridge: Cambridge University Press, forthcoming).

Martin, C. B., and Armstrong, D. M., eds. *Locke and Berkeley: A Collection of Critical Essays* (Garden City NY: Doubleday, 1968).

Martin, C. B., and Deutscher, Max. Remembering. *Philosophical Review* 75 (1966) 161–96.

Mattern, Ruth. Locke: "Our Knowledge, Which All Consists in Propositions". *Canadian Journal of Philosophy* 8 (1978) 677–95.

Mattern, Ruth. Locke on Active Power and the Obscure Idea of Active

Power from Bodies. *Studies in History and Philsophy of Science* 11 (1980) 39–77.

Mattern, Ruth. Moral Science and the Concept of Persons in Locke. *Philosophical Review* 89 (1980) 24–45.

Mattern, Ruth. Locke on Clear Ideas, Demonstrative Knowledge, and the Existence of Substances. *Midwest Studies in Philosophy* 8 (1983) 259–71.

Mattern, Ruth. Locke on Natural Kinds as the "Workmanship of the Understanding." *Locke Newsletter* 17 (1986) 45–92. Discussed by Wolfram 1987. Discussed by Bolton 1988.

Matthews, Gareth B. Senses and Kinds. *Journal of Philosophy* 69 (1972) 149–57.

Matthews, H. E. Locke, Malebranche and the Representative Theory. *Locke Newsletter* 2 (1971) 12–21; repr. in *Locke on Human Understanding*, ed. I. C. Tipton (Oxford: Oxford University Press, 1977) 55–61.

Matthews, H. E. Descartes and Locke on the Concept of a Person. *Locke Newsletter* 8 (1977) 9–34.

McCann, Edwin. Lockean Mechanism. In *Philosophy, Its History and Historiography*, ed. A. J. Holland (Dordrecht: Reidel, 1985) 209–31. Discussed by Milton 1985.

McCann, Edwin. Cartesian Selves and Lockean Substances. *Monist* 69 (1986) 458–82.

McCann, Edwin. Locke on Identity: Matter, Life, and Consciousness. *Archiv für Geschichte der Philosophie* 69 (1987) 54–77.

McRae, Robert. "Idea" as a Philosophical Term in the Seventeenth Century. *Journal of the History of Ideas* 26 (1965) 175–90.

Mendus, Susan. Personal Identity and Moral Responsibility. *Locke Newsletter* 9 (1978) 75–86.

Mendus, Susan. Locke: Toleration, Morality and Rationality. In *John Locke: A Letter Concerning Toleration in Focus*, ed. John Horton and Susan Mendus (London: Routledge, 1991) 147–62.

Mendus, Susan, and Horton, John. Locke and Toleration. In *John Locke: A Letter Concerning Toleration in Focus*, ed. John Horton and Susan Mendus (London: Routledge, 1991) 1–11.

Meyers, Robert G. Locke, Analyticity and Trifling Propositions. *Locke Newsletter* 10 (1979) 83–96. Discussion of Wolfram 1978. Discussed by Wolfram 1980.

Michael, F. S., and Michael, Emily. The Theory of Ideas in Gassendi and Locke. *Journal of the History of Ideas* 51 (1990) 379–99.

Mill, John Stuart. *A System of Logic, Ratiocinative and Inductive.* 2 vols. (London, 1843); ed. J. M. Robson, 2 vols. (Toronto: University of Toronto Press, 1973–74).

Milton, J. R. John Locke and the Nominalist Tradition. In *John Locke: Symposium Wolfenbüttel 1979*, ed. Reinhard Brandt (Berlin: de Gruyter, 1981) 128–45.

Milton, J. R. The Scholastic Background to Locke's Thought. *Locke Newsletter* 15 (1984) 25–34.

Milton, J. R. Lockean Mechanism: A Comment. In *Philosophy, Its History and Historiography*, ed. A. J. Holland (Dordrecht: Reidel, 1985) 233–39. Discussion of McCann 1985.

Milton, J. R. John Locke and the Fundamental Constitutions of Carolina. *Locke Newsletter* 21 (1990) 111–33.

Milton, J. R. Locke and Gassendi: A Reappraisal. In *Studies in Seventeenth-Century Philosophy*, ed. M. A. Stewart (Oxford: Oxford University Press, forthcoming).

Mitchell, Neil J. John Locke and the Rise of Capitalism. *History of Political Economy* 18 (1986) 291–305.

Molyneux, William. *Dioptrica Nova* (London, 1692).

Moyal, Georges J. D. Locke, Innate Ideas and the Ethics of Belief. *Locke Newsletter* 10 (1979) 97–127.

Murphy, Jeffrie G. A Paradox in Locke's Theory of Natural Rights. *Dialogue* 8 (1969) 256–71.

Nathanson, Stephen L. Locke's Theory of Ideas. *Journal of the History of Philosophy* 11 (1973) 29–42.

Neill, Alex. Locke on Habituation, Autonomy, and Education. *Journal of the History of Philosophy* 27 (1989) 225–45.

Nicholson, Peter. John Locke's Later Letters on Toleration. In *John Locke: A Letter Concerning Toleration in Focus*, ed. John Horton and Susan Mendus (London: Routledge, 1991) 163–87.

Nidditch, Peter H. Introduction. In *Essay concerning Human Understanding*, by John Locke, ed. Peter H. Nidditch (Oxford: Oxford University Press, 1975) ix–liv.

Noonan, H. Locke on Personal Identity. *Philosophy* 53 (1978) 343–52.

Norris, John. *Cursory Reflections upon a Book Call'd, An Essay concerning Human Understanding* (London, 1690).

Nuchelmans, Gabriel. *Judgment and Proposition: From Descartes to Kant* (Amsterdam: North-Holland, 1983).

O'Connor, D. J. *John Locke* (Harmondsworth: Penguin, 1952).

O'Donnell, Sheryl Rae. Mr. Locke and the Ladies: The Indelible Words on the *Tabula Rasa*. *Studies in Eighteenth Century Culture* 8 (1979) 151–64.

O'Donnell, Sheryl. "My Idea in your Mind": John Locke and Damaris Cudworth Masham. In *Mothering the Mind: Twelve Studies of Writers and their Silent Partners*, ed. Ruth Perry and Martine Watson Brownley (New York: Holmes and Meier, 1984) 26–46.

Odegard, Douglas. Locke as an Empiricist. *Philosophy* 40 (1965) 185–96.

Odegard, Douglas. Locke and the Unreality of Relations. *Theoria* 35 (1969) 147–52.

Odegard, Douglas. Locke and Substance. *Dialogue* 8 (1969–70) 243–55.

Odegard, Douglas. Locke and Mind-Body Dualism. *Philosophy* 45 (1970) 87–105.

Olivecrona, Karl. Locke's Theory of Appropriation. *Philosophical Quarterly* 24 (1974) 220–34.

Ollion, Henri. *La philosophie générale de John Locke* (Paris: Alcan, 1908).

Osler, M. J. John Locke and the Changing Ideal of Scientific Knowledge. *Journal of the History of Ideas* 31 (1970) 3–16.

Owen, David. Locke on Real Essence. *History of Philosophy Quarterly* 8 (1991) 105–18.

Oxford English Dictionary, Compact Edition. 2 vols. (Oxford: Oxford University Press, 1971).

Parker, Samuel. *A Free and Impartial Censure of the Platonick Philosophie* (Oxford, 1666).

Parry, Geraint. *John Locke* (London: Allen & Unwin, 1978).

Passmore, John. Locke and the Ethics of Belief. *British Academy Proceedings* 64 (1980) 185–208.

Pelletier, F. J. Locke's Doctrine of Substance. *Canadian Journal of Philosophy* Supp. 4 (1978) 121–40.

Perry, D. L. Simple Ideas. *Philosophy and Phenomenological Research* 27 (1966–67) 278–80.

Perry, D. L. Locke on Mixed Modes, Relations, and Knowledge. *Journal of the History of Philosophy* 5 (1967) 219–35. Discussed by Aronson and Lewis 1970.

Perry, John. Personal Identity, Memory, and the Problem of Circularity. In *Personal Identity*, ed. John Perry (Berkeley and Los Angeles: University of California Press, 1975) 135–55.

Perry, John. The Importance of Being Identical. In *The Identities of Persons*, ed. Amélie Oksenberg Rorty (Berkeley and Los Angeles: University of California Press, 1976) 67–90.

Phemister, Pauline. Real Essences in Particular. *Locke Newsletter* 21 (1990) 27–55.

Polin, Raymond. *La politique morale de John Locke* (Paris: Presses Universitaires de France, 1960).

Polin, Raymond. John Locke's Conception of Freedom. In *John Locke: Problems and Perspectives*, ed. John W. Yolton (Cambridge: Cambridge University Press, 1969) 1–18.

Proast, Jonas. *The Argument of the Letter concerning Toleration, Briefly Consider'd and Answer'd* (Oxford, 1690); repr. (New York: Garland, 1984).

Proast, Jonas. *A Third Letter concerning Toleration: In Defense of The Argument of the Letter concerning Toleration, briefly Consider'd and Answer'd* (Oxford, 1691); repr. (New York: Garland, 1984).

Pufendorf, Samuel. *De jure naturae et gentium* (Lund, 1672); tr. as *On the Law of Nature and of Nations,* by C. H. Oldfather and W. A. Oldfather (Oxford: Oxford University Press, 1934).

Pufendorf, Samuel. *De officio hominis et civis* (Lund, 1673); tr. as *The Duty of Man and Citizen,* by Frank Gardner Moore (Oxford: Oxford University Press, 1927).

Puster, Rolf W. *Britische Gassendi-Rezeption am Beispiel John Lockes* (Stuttgart: Frommann-Holzboog, 1991).

Rabb, J. D. Are Locke's Ideas of Relation Complex? *Locke Newsletter* 5 (1974) 41–55.

Rabb, J. D. Reflection, Reflexion, and Introspection. *Locke Newsletter* 8 (1977) 35–52.

Reid, Thomas. *An Inquiry into the Human Mind* (Edinburgh, 1764); ed. Timothy Duggan (Chicago: University of Chicago Press, 1970).

Reid, Thomas. *Essays on the Intellectual Powers of Man* (Edinburgh, 1785); ed. Sir William Hamilton (Edinburgh, 1846).

Riley, Patrick. On Finding an Equlibrium between Consent and Natural Law in Locke's Political Philosophy. *Political Studies* 22 (1974) 432–52.

Riley, Patrick. Locke on "Voluntary Agreement" and Political Power. *Western Political Quarterly* 29 (1976) 136–45.

Rogers, G. A. J. Boyle, Locke and Reason. *Journal of the History of Ideas* 27 (1966) 205–16.

Rogers, G. A. J. Locke's *Essay* and Newton's *Principia. Journal of the History of Ideas* 39 (1978) 217–32.

Rogers, G. A. J. The Empiricism of Locke and Newton. In *Philosophers of the Enlightenment,* ed. S. C. Brown (Brighton: Harvester, 1979) 1–30.

Rogers, G. A. J. Locke, Newton, and the Cambridge Platonists on Innate Ideas. *Journal of the History of Ideas* 40 (1979) 191–205.

Rogers, G. A. J. Locke, Law and the Laws of Nature. In *John Locke: Symposium Wolfenbüttel 1979,* ed. Reinhard Brandt (Berlin: de Gruyter, 1981) 146–62.

Russell, Paul. Locke on Express and Tacit Consent: Misinterpretations and Inconsistencies. *Political Theory* 14 (1986) 291–306.

Ryan, Alan. Locke and the Dictatorship of the Bourgeoisie. *Political Studies* 134 (1965) 219–30; repr. in *Locke and Berkeley: A Collection of Critical Essays,* ed. C. B. Martin and D. M. Armstrong (Garden City NY: Doubleday, 1968) 231–54.

Ryle, Gilbert. John Locke on the Human Understanding. In *John Locke: Tercentenary Addresses,* ed. J. L. Stocks (Oxford: Oxford University

Press, 1933) 15–38; repr. in *Locke and Berkeley: A Collection of Critical Essays,* ed. C. B. Martin and D. M. Armstrong (Garden City NY: Doubleday, 1968) 14–39; repr. in *Collected Papers,* by Gilbert Ryle, Vol. 1 (London: Hutchinson, 1971) 126–46.

Ryle, Glibert. John Locke. *Critica* 1 (1967) 3–16; repr. in *Collected Papers,* by Gilbert Ryle, Vol. 1 (London: Hutchinson, 1971) 147–57.

Sanford, D. H. Does Locke Think Hardness is a Primary Quality? *Locke Newsletter* 1 (1970) 17–29.

Sanford, D. H. Locke, Leibniz, and Wiggins on Being in the Same Place at the Same Time. *Philosophical Review* 79 (1970) 75–82.

Schankula, H. A. S. Locke, Descartes, and the Science of Nature. *Journal of the History of Ideas* 41 (1980) 459–77; repr. in *John Locke: Symposium Wolfenbüttel 1979,* ed. Reinhard Brandt (Berlin: de Gruyter, 1981) 163–80.

Schneewind, J. B. Pufendorf's Place in the History of Ethics. *Synthese* 72 (1987) 123–55.

Schobinger, Jean-Pierre, ed. *Die Philosophie des 17. Jahrhunderts,* Vol. 3: *England* (Basel: Schwabe, 1988).

Schochet, Gordon J. The Family and the Origins of the State in Locke's Political Philosophy. In *John Locke: Problems and Perspectives,* ed. John W. Yolton (Cambridge: Cambridge University Press, 1969) 81–98.

Schouls, Peter A. The Cartesian Method of Locke's *Essay concerning Human Understanding. Canadian Journal of Philosophy* 4 (1974–75) 579–601.

Schouls, Peter A. *The Imposition of Method: A Study of Descartes and Locke* (Oxford: Oxford University Press, 1980).

Schouls, Peter A. Locke and the Dogma of Infallible Reason. *Revue Internationale de Philosophie* 42 (1988) 115–32.

Schouls, Peter A. *Reasoned Freedom: John Locke and the Enlightenment* (Ithaca: Cornell University Press, 1992).

Seliger, Martin. *The Liberal Politics of John Locke* (London: Allen & Unwin, 1968).

Sergeant, John. *Solid Philosophy Asserted, Against the Fancies of the Ideists: or, the Method to Science Farther Illustrated* (London, 1697); repr. (New York: Garland, 1984).

Shapiro, B. J. *Probability and Certainty in Seventeenth-Century England* (Princeton: Princeton University Press, 1983).

Simmons, A. J. Tacit Consent and Political Obligation. *Philosophy and Public Affairs* 5 (1976) 274–91.

Simmons, A. J. Inalienable Rights and Locke's *Treatises. Philosophy and Public Affairs* 12 (1983) 175–204.

Simmons, A. J. Locke's State of Nature. *Political Theory* 17 (1989) 449–70.

Simmons, A. J. *The Lockean Theory of Rights* (Princeton: Princeton University Press, 1992).

Snyder, David C. Faith and Reason in Locke's *Essay*. *Journal of the History of Ideas* 47 (1986) 197–213.

Snyder, David C. Locke on Natural Law and Property Rights. *Canadian Journal of Philosophy* 16 (1986) 723–50.

Soles, David E. Locke on Knowledge and Propositions. *Philosophical Topics* 13 (1985) 19–30.

Soles, David E. Locke's Empiricism and the Postulation of Unobservables. *Journal of the History of Philosophy* 23 (1985) 339–69.

Soles, David E. Intellectualism and Natural Law in Locke's *Second Treatise*. *History of Political Thought* 8 (1987) 63–81.

Soles, David E. Locke on Ideas, Words, and Knowledge. *Revue Internationale de Philosophie* 42 (1988) 150–72.

Specht, Rainer. *John Locke* (München: C. H. Beck, 1989).

Spellman, W. M. The Christian Estimate of Man in Locke's *Essay*. *Journal of Religion* 67 (1987) 474–92.

Spellman, W. M. *John Locke and the Problem of Depravity* (Oxford: Oxford University Press, 1988).

Spellman, W. M. Locke and the Latitudinarian Perspective on Original Sin. *Revue Internationale de Philosophie* 42 (1988) 215–28.

Sprute, Jürgen. John Lockes Konzeption der Ethik. *Studia Leibnitiana* 17 (1985) 127–42.

Stewart, M. A. Locke's Mental Atomism and the Classification of Ideas: I. *Locke Newsletter* 10 (1979) 53–82.

Stewart, M. A. Locke's Mental Atomism and the Classification of Ideas: II. *Locke Newsletter* 11 (1980) 25–62.

Stillingfleet, Edward. *A Discourse in Vindication of the Doctrine of the Trinity: with an Answer to the Late Socinian Objections against it from Scripture, Antiquity and Reason* (London, 1697).

Stillingfleet, Edward. *The Bishop of Worcester's Answer to Mr. Locke's Letter, concerning Some Passages Relating to his Essay of Humane Understanding, mention'd in the Late Discourse in Vindication of the Trinity* (London, 1697).

Stillingfleet, Edward. *The Bishop of Worcester's Answer to Mr. Locke's Second Letter; Wherein his Notion of Ideas is Prov'd to be Inconsistent with it self, and with the Articles of the Christian Faith* (London, 1698).

Strauss, Leo. *Natural Right and History* (Chicago: University of Chicago Press, 1953). Discussed by Yolton 1958.

Strauss, Leo. Locke's Doctrine of Natural Law. *American Political Science Review* 52 (1958) 490–501.

Stroud, Barry. Berkeley v. Locke on Primary Qualities. *Philosophy* 55 (1980) 149–66.

Suárez, Francisco. *De legibus ac Deo legislatore* (Coimbra, 1612); tr. as *On Law and God the Lawgiver*, by Gladys Williams et al., in *Selections from Three Works of Francisco Suárez*, Vol. 2 (Oxford: Oxford University Press, 1944).

Tarcov, Nathan. *Locke's Education for Liberty* (Chicago: University of Chicago Press, 1984).

Tarlton, Charles D. A Rope of Sand: Interpreting Locke's *First Treatise of Government. Historical Journal* 21 (1978) 43–73.

Tarlton, Charles D. "The Rulers now on Earth": Locke's *Two Treatises* and the Revolution of 1688. *Historical Journal* 28 (1985) 279–98.

Thiel, Udo. Locke's Concept of a Person. In *John Locke: Symposium Wolfenbüttel 1979*, ed. Reinhard Brandt (Berlin: de Gruyter, 1981) 181–92.

Thiel, Udo. *Locke's Theorie der personalen Identität* (Bonn: Bouvier, 1983).

Thomas, Janice. On a Supposed Inconsistency in Locke's Account of Personal Identity. *Locke Newsletter* 10 (1979) 13–32.

Thompson, Martyn P., ed. *John Locke und/and Immanuel Kant: Historical Reception and Contemporary Relevance* (Berlin: Duncker und Humblot, 1991).

Thomson, Judith Jarvis. Molyneux's Problem. *Journal of Philosophy* 71 (1974) 637–50.

Tipton, Ian C., ed. *Locke on Human Understanding* (Oxford: Oxford University Press, 1977).

Tipton, Ian C. *Locke–Reason and Experience* (Milton Keynes: Open University Press, 1983).

Toland, John. *Christianity not Mysterious* (London, 1696); repr. (New York: Garland, 1984).

Troyer, John. Locke on the Names of Substances. *Locke Newsletter* 6 (1975) 27–39.

Tully, James. The Framework of Natural Rights in Locke's Analysis of Property. In *Theories of Property*, ed. Anthony Parel and Thomas Flanagan (Waterloo: Wilfrid Laurier University Press, 1979) 115–38.

Tully, James. *A Discourse of Property: John Locke and his Adversaries* (Cambridge: Cambridge University Press, 1980).

Tully, James. Governing Conduct. In *Conscience and Casuistry in Early Modern Thought*, ed. Edmund Leites (Cambridge: Cambridge University Press, 1988) 12–71.

Tully, James, ed. *Meaning and Context: Quentin Skinner and his Critics* (Princeton: Princeton University Press, 1988).

Uzgalis, William L. The Anti-Essential Locke and Natural Kinds. *Philosophical Quarterly* 38 (1988) 330–39.

Van Leeuwen, H. G. *The Problem of Certainty in English Thought 1630–1690* (The Hague: Martinus Nijhoff, 1963); 2nd ed. (1970).

Vaughn, Karen Iversen. *John Locke: Economist and Social Scientist* (Chicago: University of Chicago Press, 1980).

Vienne, Jean-Michel. *Expérience et raison: Les fondements de la morale selon Locke* (Paris: Vrin, 1991).

Vienne, Jean-Michel. Malebranche and Locke: The Theory of Moral Choice, a Neglected Theme. In *Nicolas Malebranche: His Philosophical Critics and Successors*, ed. Stuart Brown (Assen: Van Gorcum, 1991) 94–108.

Vinci, Thomas. A Functionalist Interpretation of Locke's Theory of Simple Ideas. *History of Philosophy Quarterly* 2 (1985) 179–94.

von Leyden, W. Introduction and Notes. In *Essays on the Law of Nature*, by John Locke, ed. W. von Leyden (Oxford: Oxford University Press, 1954) 1–106 et passim.

von Leyden, W. John Locke and Natural Law. *Philosophy* 31 (1956) 23–35.

von Leyden, W. What is a Nominal Essence the Essence Of? In *John Locke: Problems and Perspectives*, ed. John W. Yolton (Cambridge: Cambridge University Press, 1969) 224–33.

von Leyden, W. La loi, la liberté et la prérogative dans la pensée de John Locke. *Revue Philosophique* 163 (1973) 187–203.

Wainwright, Arthur W. Introduction and Notes. In *A Paraphrase and Notes on the Epistles of St. Paul*, by John Locke, ed. Arthur W. Wainwright. 2 vols. (Oxford: Oxford University Press, 1987).

Waldron, Jeremy. Locke: Toleration and the Rationality of Persecution. In *Justifying Toleration*, ed. Susan Mendus (Cambridge: Cambridge University Press, 1988) 61–86; repr. in *John Locke: A Letter Concerning Toleration in Focus*, ed. John Horton and Susan Mendus (London: Routledge, 1991) 98–124.

Waldron, Jeremy. John Locke: Social Contract versus Political Anthropology. *Review of Politics* 51 (1989) 3–28.

Wall, G. Locke's Attack on Innate Knowledge. *Philosophy* 49 (1974) 414–19; repr. in *Locke on Human Understanding*, ed. I. C. Tipton (Oxford: Oxford University Press, 1977) 1–18.

Wallace, Dewey D., Jr. Socinianism, Justification by Faith, and the Sources of John Locke's *The Reasonableness of Christianity*. *Journal of the History of Ideas* 45 (1984) 49–66.

Webb, Thomas. *The Intellectualism of Locke: An Essay* (Dublin, 1857).

Wedeking, Gary. Locke's Metaphysics of Personal Identity. *History of Philosophy Quarterly* 4 (1987) 17–31.

White, P. J. Materialism and the Concept of Motion in Locke's Theory of Sense-Idea Causation. *Studies in History and Philosophy of Science* 2 (1971–72) 97–134.

Wieand, Jeffrey. Locke on Memory. *Locke Newsletter* 11 (1980) 63–75.

Wiggins, David. Locke, Butler and the Stream of Consciousness: and Men as a Natural Kind. *Philosophy* 51 (1976) 131–58.

Williams, Stephen N. John Locke on the Status of Faith. *Scottish Journal of Theology* 40 (1987) 591–606.

Williams, Stephen N. Restoring 'Faith' in Locke. *Enlightenment and Dissent* 6 (1987) 95–113.

Willis, Thomas. *Thomas Willis's Oxford Lectures,* ed. Kenneth Dewhurst (Oxford: Sandhurst Publications, 1980).

Wilson, Margaret D. Leibniz and Locke on "First Truths." *Journal of the History of Ideas* 28 (1967) 347–66.

Wilson, Margaret D. Superadded Properties: The Limits of Mechanism in Locke. *American Philosophical Quarterly* 16 (1979) 143–50.

Wilson, Margaret D. Superadded Properties: A Reply to M. R. Ayers. *Philosophical Review* 91 (1982) 247–52. Discussion of Ayers 1981.

Winchester, S. J. Locke and the Innatists. *History of Philosophy Quarterly* 2 (1985) 411–20.

Winkler, Kenneth P. Locke on Personal Identity. *Journal of the History of Philosophy* 29 (1991) 201–26.

Wolfram, Sybil. On the Mistake of Identifying Locke's Trifling-Instructive Distinction with the Analytic-Synthetic Distinction. *Locke Newsletter* 9 (1978) 27–53. Discussed by Meyers 1979.

Wolfram, Sybil. Locke's Trifling-Instructive Distinction–A Reply. *Locke Newsletter* 11 (1980) 89–99. Discussion of Meyers 1979.

Wolfram, Sybil. Locke and "Natural Kinds." *Locke Newsletter* 18 (1987) 75–103. Discussion of Mattern 1986.

Wolterstorff, Nicholas. The Assurance of Faith. *Faith and Philosophy* 7 (1990) 396–417.

Wood, Neal. The Baconian Character of Locke's *Essay. Studies in History and Philosophy of Science* 6 (1975) 43–84.

Wood, Neal. *The Politics of Locke's Philosophy: A Social Study of "An Essay Concerning Human Understanding"* (Berkeley and Los Angeles: University of California Press, 1983).

Woodbridge, F. J. E. Locke's *Essay. Studies in the History of Ideas* 3 (1935) 243–54.

Woolhouse, R. S. Substance and Substances in Locke's *Essay. Theoria* 35 (1969) 153–67.

Woolhouse, R. S. Locke's Idea of Spatial Extension. *Journal of the History of Philosophy* 8 (1970) 313–18.

Woolhouse, R. S. *Locke's Philosophy of Science and Knowledge* (Oxford: Blackwell, 1971).

Woolhouse, R. S. Locke on Modes, Substances, and Knowledge. *Journal of* the History of Philosophy 10 (1972) 417–24. Discussion of Aronson and Lewis 1970.

Woolhouse, R. S. Locke, Leibniz, and the Reality of Ideas. In John Locke: Symposium Wolfenbüttel 1979, ed. Reinhard Brandt (Berlin: de Gruyter, 1981) 193–206.

Woolhouse, R. S. Locke (Brighton: Harvester, 1983).

Wootton, David. Introduction. In John Locke: Political Writings, ed. David Wootton (Harmondsworth: Penguin, 1993) 5–122.

Woozley, A. D. Introduction. In An Essay concerning Human Understanding, by John Locke, ed. A. D. Woozley (London: Collins, 1964) 9–51.

Woozley, A. D. Some Remarks on Locke's Account of Knowledge. Locke Newsletter 3 (1972) 7–17; repr. in Locke on Human Understanding, ed. I. C. Tipton (Oxford: Oxford University Press, 1977) 141–48.

Yolton, Jean S., ed. A Locke Miscellany: Locke Biography and Criticism for All (Bristol: Thoemmes, 1990).

Yolton, Jean S., and Yolton, John W. John Locke: A Reference Guide (Boston: G. K. Hall, 1985).

Yolton, John W. Locke and the Seventeenth-Century Logic of Ideas. Journal of the History of Ideas 16 (1955) 431–52.

Yolton, John W. John Locke and the Way of Ideas (Oxford: Oxford University Press, 1956).

Yolton, John W. Locke on the Law of Nature. Philosophical Review 67 (1958) 477–98. Discussion of Strauss 1953.

Yolton, John W. The Concept of Experience in Locke and Hume. Journal of the History of Philosophy 1 (1963) 53–71; repr. in Locke and Berkeley: A Collection of Critical Essays, ed. C. B. Martin and D. M. Armstrong (Garden City NY: Doubleday, 1968) 40–52.

Yolton, John W., ed. John Locke: Problems and Perspectives (Cambridge: Cambridge University Press, 1969).

Yolton, John W. The Science of Nature. In John Locke: Problems and Perspectives, ed. John W. Yolton (Cambridge: Cambridge University Press, 1969) 183–93.

Yolton, John W. Locke and the Compass of Human Understanding: A Selective Commentary on the Essay (Cambridge: Cambridge University Press, 1970).

Yolton, John W. Locke on Knowledge of Body. In Jowett Papers 1968–1969 (Oxford: Blackwell, 1970) 69–94.

Yolton, John W. Ideas and Knowledge in Seventeenth-Century Philosophy. Journal of the History of Philosophy 13 (1975) 145–65.

Yolton, John W. On Being Present to the Mind: A Sketch for the History of an Idea. Dialogue 14 (1975) 373–88.

Yolton, John W. *Thinking Matter: Materialism in Eighteenth-Century Britain* (Minneapolis: University of Minnesota Press, 1983).

Yolton, John W. *Perceptual Acquaintance from Descartes to Reid* (Minneapolis: University of Minnesota Press, 1984).

Yolton, John W. *Locke: An Introduction* (Oxford: Blackwell, 1985).

Yolton, John W. Mirrors and Veils, Thoughts and Things: The Epistemological Problematic. In *Reading Rorty: Critical Responses to Philosophy and the Mirror of Nature (and Beyond)*, ed. Alan R. Malachowski (Oxford: Blackwell, 1990) 58–73.

Yolton, John W. *Locke and French Materialism* (Oxford: Oxford University Press, 1991).

Yolton, John W. *A Locke Dictionary* (Oxford: Blackwell, 1993).

Yolton, John W., and Yolton, Jean S. Introduction. In *Some Thoughts concerning Education*, by John Locke, ed. John W. Yolton and Jean S. Yolton (Oxford: Oxford University Press, 1989) 1–75.

Yost, R. M., Jr. Locke's Rejection of Hypotheses about Sub-Microscopic Events. *Journal of the History of Ideas* 12 (1951) 111–30.

Zuckert, M. P. An Introduction to Locke's *First Treatise*. *Interpretation* 8 (1980) 58–74.

INDEX OF NAMES AND SUBJECTS

Aaron, Richard I., 202, 222

Aarsleff, Hans, 144, 256, 270, 275, 278, 279, 284

Abrams, Philip, 25

abstraction, 38–44, 127–30; see also idea, abstract

action, 94, 95, 97, 200, 202, 203, 204, 206, 211, 275, 276, 277; voluntary, 94, 95, 180, 202, 203

Adam, 240, 242, 256, 257, 272

Addison, Joseph, and Richard Steele, 252, 262

aesthetics, 270

agreement, 229

Alexander, Peter, 80, 81, 87, 88

Alston, William, and Jonathan Bennett, 114

America, 222, 248, 280, 281, 284

Anglican Church, see Church of England

Anscombe, G. E. M., 32

appraisal, 183, 184, 186, 191

Aquinas, Thomas, 172, 190, 201, 223, 224, 225

Aristotelianism, 64, 66, 67, 116, 117, 159, 162, 164

Aristotle, 84, 119, 144, 171, 173, 242

Armstrong, D. M., 98

Arnauld, Antoine, 33

Aronson, C., and Douglas Lewis, 170

art, 270, 276

Ashcraft, Richard, 14, 25, 174, 238, 251, 263

Ashworth, E. J., 122, 144, 152

assent, 172–98

association of ideas, see ideas, association of

atheism, 75, 264

atom, 56, 57, 62, 67, 106, 107, 114, 158, 221

atomism, 56, 57, 75, 158, 159; see also corpuscularianism

Attig, John C., 4, 283

authority, 202, 214, 225, 227, 228, 229, 230, 232, 234, 241, 242, 252, 258

awareness, direct, 176, 186

Ayer, A. J., 261

Ayers, Michael R., 33, 45, 46, 82, 88, 145, 282

Bacon, Francis, 23, 115, 280

bad, see good

Barnes, Jonathan, 151

beauty, 223, 270

Becker, Carl, 281

behavior, 89, 93, 97, 103, 238

belief, 91, 92, 93, 97, 103, 146, 147, 154, 155, 156, 161, 164, 166, 172–98, 202, 204; immediate, 182, 186; mediate, 182, 183; religious, 166, 167, 172, 185, 190, 194, 195, 196, 197

Bennett, Jonathan, 77, 87, 103

Berkeley, George, 43, 63, 76, 87, 89, 127, 261, 266, 267

Bible, 7, 17, 23, 167, 195, 196, 201, 257

Bill, E. W. G., 25

Bodleian Library, 25, 281

body, 56–88, 90, 169; see also matter; substance, material

body, science of, see science, natural

Bolton, Martha Brandt, 88, 145
Bonno, Gabriel, 255
Boyle, Robert, 6, 7, 8, 9, 56, 57, 58, 59,
    60, 63, 65, 67, 68, 75, 86, 162, 196,
    222, 223
Brandt, Reinhard, 144
British empiricism, see empiricism,
    British
Buffon, Georges-Louis Leclerc, 267, 272,
    283
Burnet, Thomas, 199, 206, 220, 222
Butler, Joseph, 109

Carlyle, Thomas, 279
Cartesianism, 57, 58, 59, 85, 100,
    265
Catholicism, 7, 13, 166, 173, 209, 210
causation, 50, 51, 53, 57–88, 90, 99,
    100–4, 111, 112, 116, 124
certainty, 163, 164, 168, 177, 182, 183,
    186, 189, 191, 206, 264
Chappell, Vere, 114
charity, 243; see also love
Charles II, 13, 227, 234
Charleton, Walter, 86
Chisholm, Roderick M., 179
Christ, 185, 195, 217, 218, 257
Christianity, 20, 24, 172, 173, 174, 185,
    189, 217, 220, 222
Church of England, 7, 15, 21, 22, 87,
    185, 209
Clarendon Edition, 4, 282
classification, 116–45, 272
Coleridge, Samuel Taylor, 278, 279, 280,
    284
Colman, John, 175, 217, 224, 225
common good, 228, 229, 230, 233, 237,
    240, 244, 251
concept, 44–49
Condillac, Etienne Bonnot de, 253, 267,
    270, 272, 275, 276, 277, 283
Conduct of the Understanding, The,
    23, 25
conscience, 200, 209, 214
consciousness, 105, 108, 109, 110, 111,
    262
consent, 229, 230, 232, 236, 237, 241,
    242, 247, 250, 257
constitution, 235, 237, 251
constitution of a body, 65, 66, 68, 69,

70, 72, 74, 82, 83, 118, 131, 133, 134,
    137, 139, 140, 158, 159, 163
corpuscle, see atom
corpuscularianism, 56–88, 116, 132,
    135, 145, 159; see also atomism
Cousin, Victor, 279, 284
Cranston, Maurice, 25, 174
Culverwell, Nathanael, 209
Cumberland, Richard, 212
Curley, Edwin M., 104
Curti, Merle, 284

d'Alembert, Jean le Rond, 255, 260, 273
de Beer, E. S., 4, 282
Declaration of Independence, 281
Degérando, Joseph-Marie, 274
Deism, 22, 168, 256, 261, 265, 280
de Maistre, Joseph Marie, 279, 284
democracy, 250
demonstration, 72, 75, 161, 162, 165,
    168, 187, 190, 201, 205, 207, 219
demonstration of morality, see morality,
    science of
Dennett, Daniel C., 103
Descartes, René, 7, 12, 28, 33, 63, 85,
    86, 89, 90, 98, 112, 114, 152, 224, 225,
    256, 261, 264, 266, 271, 278, 279, 282
desire, 91, 93, 94, 96, 97, 103, 203, 214
determinism, 94
Dewhurst, Kenneth, 3, 25
Diderot, Denis, 255, 265, 267, 268, 272,
    273, 275, 276, 277, 283
Dijksterhuis, E. J., 57
divine right, see right, divine
Douglas, Janet Mary [Mrs. Stair Doug-
    las], 279
dualism, 89–90, 98, 99, 114; see also
    mind and body
Dunn, John, 250, 282, 284
duty, 202, 206, 213

economics, 3, 10, 18, 244, 248
education, 3, 259, 260, 269
Edwards, John, 20, 23
egoism, 208, 222
empiricism, 36, 37, 48, 61, 149, 219,
    220, 221, 225; British, 252, 260, 266
Encyclopédie, 255, 265, 267, 273
Encyclopédie méthodique, 253

England, 13, 173, 231, 232, 236, 248, 250, 254, 264, 265, 279, 281
entailment, 182, 184
enthusiasm, 168, 193, 194, 196, 208, 219, 220, 221, 254, 256, 264, 268
Epicurus, 158, 204
epistemology, 1, 172, 175, 176, 184, 197, 219, 220, 221, 261; regulative, 179, 184, 196
epistemology of religion, 172, 175, 186, 197
equality, 230, 239, 242, 251, 259
Essay concerning Human Understanding, An, 1, 2, 11, 13, 15, 16, 17, 19, 20, 22, 23, 146, 202, 283
essence, 112, 130–40, 159, 257; nominal, 131, 132, 133, 156, 157, 158, 159, 160, 161, 204, 262; real, 51, 71, 81, 82, 130, 131, 133, 134, 135, 136, 139, 145, 156, 157, 158, 159, 160, 161, 162, 163, 165, 204
ethics, 199, 200, 210, 213, 220, 221, 224
Evans, Gareth, 266
Everett, Alexander H., 284
evidence, 183, 184, 185, 186, 191, 192, 193, 194, 195, 196
evidentialism, 185, 186, 197
evil, 223; *see also* good
exchange, 247, 250
executive, 233
experience, 36, 37, 77, 84, 111, 116, 148, 149, 150, 152, 155, 156, 161, 165, 180, 204, 211, 212, 213, 214, 216, 219, 221, 252, 256, 262; religious, 186, 194, 195, 196
explanation, 60, 65, 67, 68, 70, 71, 84, 93, 97, 100, 101, 103, 116, 118, 131, 133, 134, 150, 157, 158, 159, 207
extension, 56, 57, 60, 61, 73, 74, 87, 88, 99, 112, 169

faith, 167, 179, 189, 190, 193, 262, 263
Ferreira, M. Jamie, 170
Filmer, Sir Robert, 14, 229, 240, 241, 242, 257
Flew, Antony, 114
foundationalism, 186, 197
Fox, Christopher, 263
Fox Bourne, H. R., 25, 244, 280
France, 12, 25, 253, 264, 265, 275, 279

Frank, Robert G., Jr., 3, 25
free will, *see* freedom
freedom, 94, 96, 203, 232, 239, 241, 244, 246
Frege, Gottlob, 93
functionalism, 93, 97

Galilei, Galileo, 63, 86, 158
Gassendi, Pierre, 7, 12, 56, 75, 86, 158, 203, 278
generality, 38–44, 118, 126–30, 134, 153, 271; *see also* idea, general; term, general
Genesis, 257
geometry, *see* mathematics
Gibson, James, 170
God, 45, 50, 51, 53, 54, 70, 72, 73, 74, 75, 80, 88, 102, 147, 148, 150, 158, 165, 167, 168, 169, 170, 181, 185, 186, 189, 190, 191, 193, 194, 195, 199–225, 229, 238, 239, 240, 242, 243, 245, 246, 252, 256, 257, 282; argument for the existence of, 71, 74, 75, 101, 104, 165, 187–89, 205, 207, 225; as lawgiver, 165, 201, 218
Goldie, Mark, 251
good, 95, 96, 180, 202, 203, 204, 206, 207, 209, 215, 222, 223
Gospels, 166, 167, 185, 195
government, 225, 228, 231, 232, 235, 238, 248, 249; constitutional, 234, 250; end of, 228, 229, 230, 238; English, 231, 232, 233, 235, 251
Grant, Ruth W., 250
Grice, H. P., 106, 109
Grotianism, 211, 222
Grotius, Hugo, 209, 210, 212, 214, 219, 223, 224, 227

Haley, K. H. D., 25
Hall, Roland, 4
Hall, Roland, and Roger Woolhouse, 4, 283
happiness, 199, 203, 204, 205, 208, 222, 260
Harrison, John, and Peter Laslett, 25
Hartz, Louis B., 281
hedonism, 215, 222
Hobbes, Thomas, 6, 86, 98, 119, 144,

145, 158, 210, 212, 214, 220, 221, 228,
  265, 278
Holland, 14, 15, 16, 173
Hont, Istvan, 225
Hooke, Robert, 162
Hooker, Richard, 209
Horton, John, and Susan Mendus, 3
Horwitz, Robert, 224
Howes, Alan B., 253, 255
human nature, see man
Hume, David, 105, 155, 196, 261, 269
Hutcheson, Francis, 270
Huygens, Christiaan, 162

idea, 26–55, 62, 63, 64, 81, 84, 91, 92,
  116, 120, 121, 122, 123, 124, 125, 127,
  141, 143, 148, 149, 152, 161, 165, 168,
  176, 186, 202, 204, 205, 206, 214, 216,
  219, 221, 257, 262, 266, 267, 277; abstract, 38–44, 45, 127, 128, 129, 130,
  132, 133, 136, 145, 156; adequate,
  49–52; complex, 37–38, 39, 42, 50–52,
  77, 87, 127, 132, 141, 152, 156, 204,
  207; general, 38–44, 45, 48; innate,
  46, 90, 111, 151, 165, 202, 221, 255–
  59, 273; particular, 38–44, 45, 48; real,
  49–52; simple, 35, 36–37, 39, 41, 50–
  52, 99, 128, 132, 141, 156, 180, 204,
  213, 215; true, 49
idea of God, see God
idea of substance, see substance
ideas, association of, 268–71
identity, 104–8, 109, 110, 113–14
identity, personal, 104–5, 108–12, 112–
  24, 262–63
image, 44–45; see also idea
immortality, 201, 208, 212, 257, 258
impact, see impulse
impulse, 56, 62, 68, 90, 100, 101
Indian, American, 170, 246, 248
injustice, see justice
innate idea, see idea, innate
innate knowledge, see knowledge,
  innate
insight, see intuition
intentionality, 29
interest, 147, 228
intuition, 161, 168, 176, 177, 178, 183,
  184; see also knowledge, intuitive

James II, 13, 227, 235
James, William, 280
Jefferson, Thomas, 281
Johnson, Samuel, 252
judgment, 154, 266
justice, 205, 210, 217

Kant, Immanuel, 93, 176, 224, 261
Kelly, Patrick Hyde, 3, 25
kind, see sort
king, 226, 227, 228, 233, 234, 235, 238,
  251
Kivy, Peter, 270
knowledge, 48, 92, 146–71, 175, 176,
  177, 182, 183, 185, 186, 188, 189, 190,
  202, 219, 258, 263; a posteriori, 155,
  163, 219; a priori, 155, 163, 176; degrees of, 153; demonstrative, 153, 154,
  168, 178, 182, 187, 190, 264; extent
  of, 67–76, 147, 148, 168, 172, 173,
  176, 206, 263; immediate, 178, 182,
  185, 187, 191; inferential, 187; innate,
  76, 111, 148, 149–51, 153, 166, 171,
  200, 201, 202, 213, 255–59; intuitive,
  153, 154, 166, 168, 187, 192, 264; sensitive, 153, 168, 170
knowledge of essence, 68, 82, 133, 134,
  135, 136, 140, 157, 158, 159, 160, 161,
  164, 257, 264
knowledge of existence, 153, 166, 168,
  176, 185, 207
Kondylis, Panajotis, 284
Kretzmann, Norman, 144

labor, 244, 245, 246, 247
La Mettrie, Julien Offray de, 267
language, 48, 115–45, 152, 163, 206,
  216, 224, 257, 271–78; abuse of, 116,
  140, 145; imperfection of, 115, 116,
  124, 125, 126, 140–44; origin of, 257,
  271, 273
Laslett, Peter, 14, 222, 223, 237, 281
Latitudinarianism, 185, 196
law, 180, 202, 203, 204, 206, 215, 218,
  224, 228, 229, 230, 232, 233, 237, 247,
  249; civil, 202, 210, 213, 221; divine,
  181, 202, 205; moral, 165, 181, 200,
  201, 202, 205, 206, 208, 213; natural,
  201, 209, 210, 211, 212, 213, 215, 217,

law (*cont.*)
219, 221, 222, 233, 235, 239, 240, 243, 245, 246, 247, 250
law of nature, *see* law, natural
le Clerc, Jean, 16
Lee, Henry, 223
legislature, 231, 232, 233, 234, 236, 238, 249, 250
Leibniz, Gottfried Wilhelm, 76, 92, 95, 101, 102, 136, 138, 225
Lessing, Gotthold Ephraim, 268
Lewes, George Henry, 280
liberty, *see* freedom
Limborch, Philippus van, 16
Locke, John: influence, 252–89; journals, 12; letters to Stillingfleet, 22, 78, 87, 99, 261, 263, 264, 283; life, 5–25; religion, 7, 24, 185, 221, 226; writings on education, 19; writings on the law of nature, 2, 8, 25, 213, 224; writings on money, 10, 18, 20; writings on toleration, 7, 10, 15, 16, 17, 25
Locke Newsletter, 4
logic, 277
logical positivism, 163
Lough, John, 25
love, 217; *see also* charity
Lovelace Collection, 4, 281
Lowde, James, 150, 170
Luther, Martin, 166

Mackie, J. L., 33, 139, 140
MacLean, Kenneth, 263
Macpherson, C. B., 247
Malebranche, Nicolas, 19, 33
man, 104, 209, 211, 213, 216, 218, 220, 223, 225, 231, 238, 242, 243, 257, 260, 265
Mandelbaum, Maurice, 82, 88
Marshall, John, 3, 185, 224
Martin, C. B., and Max Deutscher, 114
Masham, Damaris, 18, 19, 24, 25
materialism, 98, 114, 264, 265
mathematics, 43, 132, 154, 155, 156, 159, 160, 161, 162, 165, 169, 206, 219, 224, 264
matter, 56, 57, 69, 73, 74, 76, 80, 87, 101, 112, 158; thinking, *see* thinking matter
Matthews, Gareth B., 35

maxim, 43, 162, 164, 171
McLaverty, James, 253
McRae, Robert, 152
meaning, 116, 118–26, 139, 140, 143, 144, 156, 274, 277
mechanical philosophy, 6, 9, 57
mechanism, 56, 67–76, 85, 86, 102
medicine, 3, 6, 8, 9, 15, 25
memory, 45, 46, 47, 48, 53, 109, 110, 111, 112, 168, 177, 186
Mill, James, 278
Mill, John Stuart, 120, 155, 261, 278
Miller, Perry, 252
mind, 26–55, 63, 69, 85, 89–114, 152, 169, 176, 186, 255, 260
mind and body, 69, 73, 85, 100–4, 169; *see also* dualism
miracle, 195, 196
misery, *see* happiness
mode, 38, 50, 99, 156, 159, 160, 161, 165, 207, 223; mixed, 131, 132, 138, 141, 204, 206, 213, 216, 224
Molyneux, William, 20, 166, 266
Molyneux problem, 20, 266–68, 270
monarch, *see* king
monarchy, 231, 249, 250
money, 247, 250
Montaigne, Michel de, 208
Moore, James, 284
morality, 94, 147, 151, 166, 167, 168, 170, 174, 175, 180, 181, 183, 185, 199–225, 226, 235, 236, 238, 240, 242, 246, 248, 250, 279; science of, 156, 161, 165, 166, 185, 203, 205, 207, 217, 220
More, Henry, 258
Morgan, Michael J., 266
motivation, 94, 95, 97, 203, 204, 208, 215, 216, 222

name, *see* language
natural law, *see* law, natural
natural philosophy, *see* science, natural
natural right, *see* right, natural
natural science, *see* science, natural
naturalism, 219, 220
nature, 53, 54, 117, 126, 127, 129, 135, 136, 138, 139, 145, 206, 212; human, *see* man; law of, *see* law, natural; state of, *see* state of nature

necessity, 71, 75, 76, 153, 156, 162, 163, 164, 176, 211, 219
New Testament, 17, 185, 192
Newton, Isaac, 17, 19, 86, 162, 196, 255, 268, 280, 283
Nidditch, Peter H., 4, 282, 283
Norris, John, 19, 31

object, 27, 29–35; external, 29, 30, 52, 54; intentional, 33–35; material, see body; substance, material
obligation, 147, 180, 181, 201, 210, 211, 213, 214, 216, 224, 237, 239, 240, 244, 248; epistemic, 178, 179, 181, 182, 183, 186
observation, 154, 155, 162, 163, 184, 204
Ockham, William of, 30
opinion, see belief
original sin, see sin, original
Oxford, 5, 8, 15, 18, 25, 224
Oxford English Dictionary, 32

pain, see pleasure
Palladini, Fiametta, 224
Paraphrase and Notes on the Epistles of St. Paul, A, 3, 23, 25, 185
Parker, Samuel, 150, 170
parliament, see legislature
Parliament, English, 13, 232, 233, 235, 238
particular, 39–43, 62, 126, 127, 129, 131, 168, 170; bare, 76, 77, 80, 81, 83
passion, 91
Passmore, John, 277
patriarchy, 257
Paul, Saint, 23, 173, 185, 201
Peirce, Charles Sanders, 280
people, 229, 230, 231, 232, 234, 235, 250
perception, 26–55, 80, 91, 93, 152, 153, 154, 168, 176, 186, 267
Perry, John, 114
Perry, Ralph Barton, 281
person, 104–12, 113, 203, 244
personal identity, see identity, personal
philosophy, 1, 2; mechanical, see mechanical philosophy; natural, see science, natural; political, 1, 226–27, 251
philosophy of religion, 2, 172
Plato, 119, 176, 273

Platonism, 116
pleasure, 180, 202, 203, 204, 206, 215, 222, 279
Pocock, J. G. A., 284
poetry, 270, 276
politics, 7, 10, 13, 25, 208, 210, 216, 226–51, 257
power, 47, 50, 51, 60, 63, 64, 71, 76, 81, 181, 188, 203, 206, 211, 213, 214, 215, 225, 228–51
Proast, Jonas, 18
probability, 154, 177, 182, 183, 184, 191, 192, 193
proof, 153
property, 205, 208, 217, 225, 227, 235, 236, 237, 238, 240, 241, 242, 243, 250; origin of, 238, 244–50; use of, 242, 245, 246
proportionality, 184, 186
proposition, 91, 97, 150, 153, 154, 176, 178, 179, 181, 182, 183, 184, 185, 186; general, 168; trifling, 163, 207, 223
Protestantism, 7, 15, 173, 209, 210
Pufendorf, Samuel, 209, 211, 212, 214, 220, 221, 222, 223, 225, 227
punishment, see reward

quality, 50, 56–88; primary and secondary, 60–67, 132, 267; primary, 60, 61, 86, 117, 158; secondary, 51, 60, 62, 64, 65, 69, 70, 71, 117; sensible, 36, 41, 51, 60, 64, 66, 77, 116, 118, 134, 135, 139, 157, 158, 262, 272
Quine, W. V., 277, 278

Rask, Rasmus, 274
rationalism, 219, 222, 225
rationality, 165, 251, 259, 269
reason, 48, 149, 152, 154, 164, 165, 166, 167, 172, 179, 184, 190, 192, 193, 194, 198, 202, 209, 212, 216, 217, 218, 219, 222, 252, 257, 261, 266, 268
Reasonableness of Christianity, The, 2, 3, 20, 185, 192, 217, 257
reflection, 36
Reformation, 166
Reid, Thomas, 26, 30, 32, 106, 109
relation, 38, 50
religion, 166, 168, 172–98, 208, 210, 223, 238, 254, 283; epistemology of,

religion, *(cont.)*
    see epistemology of religion; natural,
    172, 175; philosophy of, *see* philoso-
    phy of religion; revealed, 172, 174,
    175
representation, 49–54, 123, 124, 187
representative, 229, 231, 232, 237
resemblance, 50, 63, 64, 116
resistance, 226, 227, 230, 231, 233, 234,
    235, 250, 251
responsibility, 172, 183, 187, 194, 196,
    259; *see also* obligation
Restoration, 7, 254
revelation, 166, 167, 189, 190, 191, 192,
    193, 195, 196, 202, 212, 217, 258, 261
revolution, 13, 234, 250
Revolution, Glorious, 14, 244, 251
reward, 181, 199, 201, 202, 204, 212,
    215
right, 165, 200, 205, 206, 209, 210, 213,
    214, 228–51; divine, 229, 254; natural,
    235, 242, 243, 244, 250
Roger, Jacques, 267
Royal Society, 9, 155, 162, 165, 254
rule, *see* law
ruler, 229, 230, 234, 235, 240
Russell, Bertrand, 261
Ryle, Gilbert, 26, 27, 114

Sanderson, Robert, 209
Saunderson, Nicholas, 268, 283
Schneewind, J. B., 224, 225
Scholasticism, 57, 58, 59, 76, 85, 122,
    144, 159, 162, 164
Schøsler, Jorn, 265
science, 65, 66, 72, 75, 116, 136, 156,
    162, 163, 164, 169, 171, 173, 219;
    moral, *see* morality, science of; natu-
    ral, 3, 6, 8, 9, 25, 58, 59, 67, 68, 70,
    130, 155, 156, 157, 161, 162, 163, 164,
    165, 169, 196, 197, 254, 255, 261, 264
scientia, *see* science
Scriptures, 166, 167, 185, 242, 243, 254,
    258, 261, 283
self, 262
self-consciousness, 105
self-interest, 209, 212, 216, 228
sensation, 28, 36, 44, 60, 66, 72, 91, 99,
    100, 152, 273
sense perception, *see* perception
senses, 148, 149, 154, 266, 268, 270

Sergeant, John, 26, 35
Sextus Empiricus, 146, 166
Shaftesbury, Anthony Ashley Cooper,
    Lord, 8, 9, 11, 13, 25, 250
Shapiro, B. J., 155
signification, *see* meaning
similarity, 117, 128, 129, 133, 134, 136,
    137, 145
Simms, J. G., 266
sin, 201, 202, 204, 206; original, 257
skepticism, 31, 54, 120, 121, 146, 147,
    168, 170, 208, 210, 219, 220, 266
Skinner, Quentin, 251
society, 203, 208, 209, 210, 216, 223,
    229–51, 257
Socinianism, 22, 23, 87, 185, 258, 261,
    284
solidity, 56, 57, 60, 61, 65, 73, 74, 80,
    87, 88, 99, 169
sort, 54, 77, 105, 106, 112, 113, 117,
    129, 130, 132, 133, 156, 159; *see also*
    species
soul, *see* mind
space, 57, 60, 112
species, 117–45, 157; *see also* sort
Spellman, W. M., 3
Spinoza, Baruch de, 265
spirit, 80, 81, 90; *see also* substance, im-
    material
Sprat, Thomas, 254
state of nature, 238, 240, 241, 242, 245,
    246, 247, 248, 250, 257
Stephen, Leslie, 252, 280
Sterne, Laurence, 253, 255
Stewart, Dugald, 252
Stillingfleet, Edward, 15, 21, 26, 27, 74,
    76, 78, 79, 82, 87, 98, 189, 261, 262,
    263, 283
Strauss, Leo, 247
Suárez, Francisco, 209, 214
subsistence, 242, 243, 244, 245, 246,
    250
substance, 38, 50, 51, 76–86, 87, 88, 98,
    99, 106, 107, 130, 132, 138, 139, 141,
    142, 156, 157, 158, 160, 161, 163, 204,
    262; immaterial, 74, 88, 98, 107, 108,
    111, 264; material, 42, 56, 61, 62, 73,
    87, 88, 98, 107, 111, 169
substantial form, 82, 117, 118, 159, 162
substratum, 51, 76–86, 87, 88; *see also*
    substance

Tarcov, Nathan, 3
taxes, 236, 237, 251
Taylor, Jeremy, 209
teleology, 103, 104
term, general, 126–30, 131–45; see also
    generality
testimony, 155, 184, 195, 196
theology, 3, 7, 23, 185, 187, 256, 257,
    261, 283
thinking matter, 69, 73, 76, 80, 98–104,
    169, 208, 263–66
Thomism, 209
thought, 27–35, 69, 74, 80, 88, 90–94,
    99, 101, 105, 107, 112, 114, 152, 169
time, 104, 105, 108, 112, 113, 114
Toinard, Nicolas, 274
Toland, John, 22, 265
toleration, 3, 16, 223
Tooke, John Horne, 277, 278
tradition, 173, 174, 198, 252
travel literature, 238, 258
truth, 146, 148, 152, 167, 178, 179, 182,
    191, 224
Tully, James, 225, 251
Turgot, Anne-Robert-Jacques, 273, 274
Two Treatises of Government, 1, 2, 14,
    17, 25, 216–17, 226–51, 257
tyrannicide, 227, 230
tyranny, 227, 228, 230, 231, 232, 233,
    234, 235, 250, 251
tyrant, 207, 211, 214, 225, 228, 230
Tyrrell, James, 15, 174, 222

understanding, 27, 129, 146, 148, 149,
    163, 164, 165, 167; conduct of, 173,
    179, 196

uneasiness, 94, 95, 96, 97, 203, 204, 208
universal, see generality
Utilitarianism, 278, 279

Van Leeuwen, H. G., 170
vice, see virtue
virtue, 200, 203
volition, 74, 88, 94–98, 104
Voltaire [François-Marie Arouet], 252,
    255, 264, 265, 267
voluntarism, 206, 211, 221, 222, 225
von Leyden, W., 25, 223, 225

Wainwright, Arthur W., 3
war, 230, 234
Webb, Thomas, 279
Whewell, William, 279
Whigs, 13, 14, 238, 250
will, 94, 181, 203, 204, 206, 208, 211,
    214, 221, 222, 228, 229, 239
Willis, Thomas, 8
Wills, Garry, 284
Wilson, Margaret D., 67, 70, 71
Wittgenstein, Ludwig, 30, 197, 275
Woolhouse, R. S. [Roger Woolhouse],
    145, 170, 171
Wootton, David, 284
word, see language
wrong, see right

Yolton, Jean S., and John W. Yolton, 3, 4,
    283
Yolton, John W., 32, 33, 88, 152, 170,
    264, 265, 279, 282

INDEX OF PASSAGES CITED

B MS Locke c.28: 114: von Leyden
  1954: 72–73 225
B MS Locke c.28: Laslett 1967:
  366n 237
B MS Locke c.34 15
B MS Locke f.2: 46 170
B MS Locke f.2: 92–93 170
B MS Locke f.2: 126 147
Deus: L II: 133–39 166
Draft A 43: D I: 74–75 149
Draft A 43: D I: 75 152
E Epis: 7 174
E Epis: 8 260
E Epis: 9 162
E Epis: 9–10 59
E Epis: 13 115
E I.i.2: 43 . . . .100, 146, 154, 260
E I.i.2: 44 162
E I.i.4: 44–45 148
E I.i.5: 45 . . . . 147, 169, 170
E I.i.5: 45–46 264
E I.i.5–6: 45–46 206
E I.i.6: 46 . . . . 147, 148, 264
E I.i.7: 47 . . . . 146, 147, 148
E I.i.8: 47 . . . . 27, 35, 152
E I.ii.1: 48 . . . . . 111, 149
E I.ii.2: 49 111
E I.ii.4: 49 149
E I.ii.5: 49 90
E I.ii.11: 52–53 150
E I.ii.15: 55 48
E I.ii.17: 56 . . . . . 150, 153
E I.ii.18–21: 57–60 151
E I.iii.1–2: 65–66 200
E I.iii.1, 4: 65–66, 68 166
E I.iii.1: 66 151

E I.iii.2: 66 151
E I.iii.3: 67 111
E I.iii.4: 68 200
E I.iii.6: 69 . . . . . 200, 225
E I.iii.6–8, 11: 69–70, 72–73 . . . 224
E I.iii.8: 70 200
E I.iii.9–13: 70–75 200
E I.iii.12: 73 149
E I.iii.12: 74 . . . . . 181, 201
E I.iii.13: 75 201
E I.iii.14–19: 76–80 201
E I.iii.22: 81 151
E I.iii.25: 82 151
E I.iv.8: 87 224
E I.iv.8: 87–88 201
E I.iv.9: 89 . . . . . 188, 256
E I.iv.12: 91 202
E I.iv.16: 94–95 187
E I.iv.20: 96–97 47
E I.iv.21: 98–99 256
E I.iv.22: 99 167
E I.iv.24: 101–2 202
E II.i.1: 104 36
E II.i.2: 104 . . . . . 148, 152
E II.i.3: 105 . . . . . 36, 152
E II.i.4: 105 36
E II.i.5: 106 33
E II.i.8: 107 48
E II.i.9: 108 . . . . . 28, 112
E II.i.10: 108 113
E II.i.11: 109–10 90
E II.i.11: 110 109
E II.i.15: 112–23 114
E II.i.22: 117 152
E II.i.23: 117 100
E II.i.24: 118 152

E II.i.25: 118.   .   .   .   .   .   37, 148
E II.ii.1: 119 36
E II.vi.2: 128.   91
E II.vii.1: 128   37
E II.vii.1 and 9: 128 and 131   .   .   . 36
E II.vii.2 and 7: 128 and 131   .   .   . 37
E II.vii.8: 131   90
E II.viii: 132–43   117
E II.viii.8: 134   .   .   .   . 27, 28, 123
E II.viii.9: 134–35   61
E II.viii.9: 135   88
E II.viii.10: 135.   60
E II.viii.11: 135–36   87
E II.viii.14: 137.   63
E II.viii.15: 137.   63
E II.viii.22: 140.   88
E II.ix.1: 143.   28
E II.ix.8: 145.   266
E II.ix.8: 145–46   20
E II.ix.8: 146.   266
E II.ix.11: 147–48   104
E II.x.2: 150 .   .   . 33, 43, 47, 53, 91, 93
E II.x.5: 151–52.   114
E II.x.5: 152 101
E II.xi.9: 159.   .   .   .   .   .   . 39, 40
E II.xii.1: 163   .   .   .   .   . 37, 38, 39
E II.xii.5: 165   223
E II.xii.6: 165   132
E II.xiii.19: 175 .   .   .   .   .   . 78, 84
E II.xiii.20: 175 78
E II.xx.1: 229   180
E II.xx.2: 229   .   .   .   . 180, 202
E II.xx.3: 229   91
E II.xx.6: 230–31   96
E II.xx.13: 231   97
E II.xx.15: 232   180
E II.xxi.4: 235   .   .   .   .   . 90, 215
E II.xxi.5: 236   203
E II.xxi.5–6: 236   91
E II.xxi.8–14: 237–40   203
E II.xxi.21–28: 244–48   203
E II.xxi.29 [1st ed]: 251n 114
E II.xxi.30: 250–51.   95
E II.xxi.31–32: 250–51   96
E II.xxi.31–38: 250–56   204
E II.xxi.31: 251 96
E II.xxi.33: 252 96
E II.xxi.33 [1st ed]: 256n 114
E II.xxi.35: 252–54.   96
E II.xxi.35: 253 97

E II.xxi.39: 257 96
E II.xxi.41–42: 258–59   203
E II.xxi.55: 269–70.   204
E II.xxi.56: 270 97
E II.xxi.58–70: 272–82   94
E II.xxii.1: 288   213
E II.xxii.1, 2, 5: 288–89, 290.   .   .   . 160
E II.xxii.4: 290   161
E II.xxii.6: 290–91   274
E II.xxiii.1: 295.   77
E II.xxiii.2: 295–96.   78
E II.xxiii.3: 296.   .   .   .   .   . 51, 106
E II.xxiii.6: 298.   106
E II.xxiii.12: 302   206
E II.xxiii.12: 302–3   264
E II.xxiii.15: 305   90
E II.xxiii.17: 306   88
E II.xxiii.23: 308   169
E II.xxiii.30: 313   88
E II.xxiii.32: 314   99
E II.xxiii.33: 314   165
E II.xxvii.3: 330   113
E II.xxvii.4: 331   113
E II.xxvii.5: 331   113
E II.xxvii.9: 335   .   .   .   . 105, 113
E II.xxvii.9–29: 335–48 104
E II.xxvii.10: 336   .   .   .   . 113, 262
E II.xxvii.12: 337   .   .   .   . 107, 108
E II.xxvii.14: 338   110
E II.xxvii.16: 340   .   .   .   . 109, 110
E II.xxvii.17: 341   110
E II.xxvii.24: 345   110
E II.xxvii.25: 345   107
E II.xxvii.25: 345–46   113
E II.xxvii.26: 347   110
E II.xxvii.27: 347   101
E II.xxvii.29: 348   113
E II.xxviii.2: 349   224
E II.xxviii.3: 350   224
E II.xxviii.4–5: 350–51 180
E II.xxviii.5: 351   .   .   . 181, 202
E II.xxviii.7: 352   .   .   . 181, 202
E II.xxviii.8: 352   .   . 165, 166, 167,
                                 181, 203, 214
E II.xxviii.8–10: 352–54 203
E II.xxviii.14: 358   204
E II.xxix.5: 364 34
E II.xxx.1: 372   .   .   .   .   . 49, 52
E II.xxx.2: 372–73   51
E II.xxx.2: 373   53

E II.xxx.3–4: 373–74 204
E II.xxx.4: 373 . . . . . . .38, 50
E II.xxx.5: 374 51
E II.xxxi.1: 375 49
E II.xxxi.2: 375 51
E II.xxxi.3–4: 376–77 204
E II.xxxi.3: 376 50
E II.xxxi.3: 377 50
E II.xxxi.6: 378–80. 161
E II.xxxi.8: 381 51
E II.xxxi.10–11: 382 160
E II.xxxi.13: 383 52
E II.xxxii.1: 384 33
E II.xxxii.4: 385 50
E II.xxxii.8: 386 48
E II.xxxii.15: 389 100
E II.xxxiii.5: 395 269
E II.xxxiii.6: 396 269
E III.i.2: 402 119
E III.i.5: 403 272
E III.ii.1: 405 . . .118, 119, 120, 257
E III.ii.2: 405 119
E III.ii.4–5: 406–7 125
E III.ii.8: 408 . . . . . .257, 275
E III.iii.1: 409 126
E III.iii.2: 409 127
E III.iii.3: 410 127
E III.iii.4: 410 127
E III.iii.6: 410 40
E III.iii.6: 410–11 127
E III.iii.6: 411 41
E III.iii.7: 411 . . . . 39, 41, 42, 128
E III.iii.9: 412 128
E III.iii.11: 414 . . . . 126, 129, 272
E III.iii.12: 414 . . . . . . 129, 130
E III.iii.12: 415 129
E III.iii.13: 415 . . . . . .117, 129
E III.iii.15: 417 . . . . . .131, 156
E III.iii.17: 417–18 159
E III.iii.17: 418 . . . . 117, 131, 159
E III.iii.18: 418 . . . . . .160, 205
E III.iii.18: 419 132
E III.iv.4: 421 36
E III.iv.7: 422 141
E III.iv.11: 425 270
E III.v.8: 432–33 274
E III.v.8, 10: 433, 434 160
E III.v.13: 436 161
E III.v.14: 436–37 157
E III.v.16: 437 271

E III.vi.2: 439 . . . . . .156, 157
E III.vi.3: 440 . . . . . .157, 158
E III.vi.6: 442 . . . . . .133, 145
E III.vi.10: 445 117
E III.vi.14: 448 134
E III.vi.15: 448 135
E III.vi.16: 448 135
E III.vi.17: 448–49 135
E III.vi.18: 449 135
E III.vi.19: 449 135
E III.vi.22: 450 135
E III.vi.23: 451 135
E III.vi.24: 452 . . . . . .118, 135
E III.vi.25: 452 118
E III.vi.25: 453 272
E III.vi.28: 455 139
E III.vi.30: 457–58 275
E III.vi.31: 458–59 142
E III.vi.39: 463–64 137
E III.vi.39: 464 138
E III.vi.44–51: 466–71. 257
E III.vi.51: 470–71 142
E III.ix.1: 475–76 125
E III.ix.3–4: 476–77 126
E III.ix.5: 477 206
E III.ix.6: 478 141
E III.ix.7: 478–79 275
E III.ix.7: 479 141
E III.ix.8: 479 143
E III.ix.10: 481 275
E III.ix.11: 481 206
E III.ix.12: 482 158
E III.ix.13: 482 139
E III.ix.13: 482–83 142
E III.ix.18: 486–87 141
E III.ix.22: 489 . . . . . .223, 275
E III.ix.23: 490 167
E III.x.15: 498 87
E III.x.18: 500 139
E III.x.20: 501–2 140
E III.x.21: 502 135
E III.x.22: 503–4 115
E III.x.23: 504 121
E III.xi.2: 509 272
E III.xi.9: 513 206
E III.xi.11: 514 143
E III.xi.12: 515 143
E III.xi.15: 516 205
E III.xi.17–18: 516–17 205
E III.xi.24: 521 143

E III.xi.27: 524 144
E IV.i.1: 525 176
E IV.i.2: 525 . . . . . . .152, 269
E IV.i.3: 525 154
E IV.ii.1: 530–31 153
E IV.ii.2: 532 153
E IV.ii.7: 533–34 178
E IV.ii.9: 534 165
E IV.ii.11: 536 100
E IV.ii.14: 537 . . . . . .168, 169
E IV.ii.14: 537–38 153
E IV.iii.6: 539–43 . . 99, 208, 263, 264
E IV.iii.6: 540 . . . . . .169, 263
E IV.iii.6: 540–41 . . . . 69, 100
E IV.iii.6: 541 . . . . .70, 101, 263
E IV.iii.6: 541–42 264
E IV.iii.6: 542 99
E IV.iii.11: 544 65
E IV.iii.13: 545 70
E IV.iii.18: 549 . . . . .165, 205
E IV.iii.20–21: 552–53 206
E IV.iii.25: 555 158
E IV.iii.28: 558 . . . . .154, 155
E IV.iii.28: 558–59 71
E IV.iii.28: 559 169
E IV.iii.29: 559 . . . 155, 161, 164
E IV.iii.29: 559–60 71
E IV.iii.29: 560 . . . 67, 75, 165, 170
E IV.iv.3: 563 123
E IV.iv.4: 563–64 123
E IV.iv.7–10: 565–68 206
E IV.v.2: 574 92
E IV.v.6: 576 92
E IV.vi.1: 579 271
E IV.vi.7: 582 165
E IV.vi.11: 585 164
E IV.vii.9: 596 44
E IV.vii.11: 598 269
E IV.viii.8: 614 163
E IV.x.1: 619 . . . . . .165, 187
E IV.x.1–5: 619–21 166
E IV.x.1–19: 619–30 101
E IV.x.2: 619 188
E IV.x.3: 620 188
E IV.x.3–5: 620–21 207
E IV.x.5: 620–21 . . . . 74, 189
E IV.x.5–6: 620–21 114
E IV.x.6: 621 . . . 187, 189, 207
E IV.x.7: 622 165
E IV.x.10: 623–24 . . . .101, 114

E IV.x.16: 627 101
E IV.x.16–17: 627–28 114
E IV.x.17: 627 102
E IV.xi.1: 630 168
E IV.xi.2: 630 168
E IV.xi.2–3: 631 168
E IV.xi.3: 631 169
E IV.xii.8: 643 . . . . .161, 205
E IV.xii.9: 644 . . . 155, 162, 170
E IV.xii.10: 645 . . . 156, 161, 169
E IV.xii.11: 646 . . . . .170, 259
E IV.xii.12: 647 148
E IV.xiii.3: 651 . . .165, 205, 223, 224
E IV.xv.3: 655 . . . . . 92, 154
E IV.xv.4: 656 184
E IV.xv.5: 656 182
E IV.xvi.6: 661 155
E IV.xvi.9: 663 . . . . . 93, 155
E IV.xvi.14: 667–68 193
E IV.xvii.24 182
E IV.xvii.24: 687–88 180
E IV.xviii.2: 689 189
E IV.xviii.3: 690 190
E IV.xviii.4–5 191
E IV.xviii.4: 690–91 . . 167, 191, 195
E IV.xviii.4: 691 167
E IV.xviii.5: 691–92 192
E IV.xviii.5: 692 167
E IV.xviii.6: 693 190
E IV.xviii.7: 694 167
E IV.xviii.8: 694 193
E IV.xviii.10: 695 . . . .167, 191
E IV.xix.3: 698 168
E IV.xix.5: 699 . . . . .193, 194
E IV.xix.6: 699 194
E IV.xix.7: 699 193
E IV.xix.10: 702 195
E IV.xix.11: 702 195
E IV.xix.14: 704 194
E IV.xix.15: 705 195
E IV.xix.16: 705 193
E IV.xx.3: 708 183
E IV.xx.11: 714 224
E IV.xx.15: 716 103
E IV.xx.17: 718–19 167
E IV.xxi.2–3: 720 2
E IV.xxi.3: 720 203
E IV.xxi.4: 720–21 2
E IV.xxi.4: 721 123
EL I: 117; QL I: 113 213

EL IV: 153; QL V: 161 216
EL IV: 153; QL V: 163 225
EL VI; QL VIII 213
EL VI: 181–83; QL VIII: 205 . . . 213
EL VI: 183; QL VIII: 205–7 . . . 214
EL VI: 185; QL VIII: 207 214
EL VI: 189; QL VIII: 213 214
Essay concerning Toleration (1667):
    Fox Bourne 1876: 1:174–94 . . . 25
Essay concerning Toleration (1667):
    B MS Locke c.28: Laslett 1967:
    366n 237
Journal 1677: B MS Locke f.2: 46 . 170
Journal 1677: B MS Locke f.2:
    92–93 170
Journal 1677: B MS Locke f.2: 126   147
Journal 1677: L I: 202 235
Letter 596: C II: 310 274
Letter 1309: C IV: 110–13 . . . 222
Letter 1309: C IV: 112–23 . . . 201
Letter 2059: C V: 595 166
Letter 2320: C VI: 215 235
Letter 3328: C VIII: 58 235
L I: 202 235
L I: 228–30 223
L II: 133–39 166
Locke 1894 281
Locke 1960 25
Locke 1967: 117–75 7
Locke 1967: 185–241 7
Locke 1971: 10 31
Locke 1977 7
Some Thoughts concerning Reading
    and Study for a Gentleman: W III:
    296 223
T I.ii.6: 162 229
T I.iv.40: 186–87 242
T I.iv.41: 187–88 243
T I.iv.41–42: 187–88 241
T I.iv.42: 188 243
T I.iv.43: 188–89 241
T I.vi.67: 208 239
T I.vii.74–77: 214–17 241
T I.ix.86: 222–23 242
T I.ix.87–92: 224–28 242
T I.ix.88–91: 224–27 243
T I.ix.92: 227–28 240
T I.ix.93: 228 243
T I.ix.97: 230–31 243
T I.ix.97–98: 230–31 241

T I.xi.126: 251 240
T II.ii.4–5: 287–89 239
T II.ii.5: 288 217
T II.ii.6: 288–89 . . . . . 239, 240
T II.ii.6–8: 288–90 239
T II.ii.7–8: 289–90 240
T II.ii.8: 290–91 239
T II.ii.9: 290–91 240
T II.ii.10–11: 291–92 240
T II.ii.11: 291–92 239
T II.ii.11–12: 291–93 240
T II.ii.15: 295–96 241
T II.v.25: 303–4 243
T II.v.26: 304–5 246
T II.v.27: 305–6 245
T II.v.28–30: 306–8 245
T II.v.30: 307–8 246
T II.v.31: 308 . . . . . . 245, 248
T II.v.32–33: 308–9 245
T II.v.34–36: 309–11 245
T II.v.36: 310–11 247
T II.v.37: 312–23 . . . . . 245, 247
T II.v.38: 313–14 247
T II.v.39: 314 . . . . . . 246, 248
T II.v.41: 314–15 . . . . . 246, 248
T II.v.43: 316–17 246
T II.v.45: 317 . . . 245, 247, 248
T II.v.46: 317–18 . . . . . 245, 246
T II.v.46–47: 317–19 247
T II.v.46–48: 317–19 247
T II.v.48–49: 319 246
T II.v.50: 319–20 247
T II.v.50: 320 237
T II.v.51: 320 . . . 245, 246, 248
T II.vi.75: 335–36 248
T II.vii.77: 336 216
T II.vii.94: 347–48 . . . . 232, 249
T II.viii.97: 350 232
T II.viii.102: 353 229
T II.viii.103: 354 235
T II.viii.105: 354–55 246
T II.viii.106: 355–56 229
T II.viii.107: 356–57 . . . . 248, 249
T II.viii.107–8: 356–58 248
T II.viii.108: 357–58 . . . . 246, 248
T II.viii.110–11: 359–61 216
T II.viii.111: 360–61 249
T II.viii.112: 361–62 229
T II.viii.120: 366 237
T II.ix.124: 368–69 238

T II.ix.124: 369 219
T II.xi.134: 373–74. . . . .232, 238
T II.xi.134–35: 373–76 240
T II.xi.135: 375–76. .237, 239, 240, 244
T II.xi.138: 378. 238
T II.xi.138: 378–79. . . . .228, 232
T II.xi.138–39: 378–80 236
T II.xi.140: 380. 236
T II.xi.142: 381 . . . . . .232, 237
T II.xii.143: 382 . . . . .228, 232
T II.xii.144: 382–83 233
T II.xii.147: 383–84 234
T II.xiii.149: 385 234
T II.xiii.151: 386 . . . . .229, 234
T II.xiii.151–53: 386–88 233
T II.xiii.153: 387 232
T II.xiii.153: 387–88 233
T II.xiii.154: 388 . . . . .232, 233
T II.xiii.155: 388 . . . . .233, 234
T II.xiii.155: 388–89 228
T II.xiii.156: 389–90 . . . .233, 234
T II.xiii.158: 391–92 233
T II.xiv.159: 392–93 . . . .232, 240
T II.xiv.159–60: 392–93 233
T II.xiv.161: 393 234
T II.xiv.162: 394 249
T II.xiv.163: 394 228
T II.xiv.163: 394–95 234
T II.xiv.164: 395 228
T II.xiv.166: 396 234
T II.xiv.167: 396 233
T II.xiv.167–68: 396–98 234
T II.xiv.168: 397–98 . . . .230, 233
T II.xv.171: 399–400 . . . .237, 240
T II.xv.173: 401. 237
T II.xvi.175: 402–3 229
T II.xvi.183: 408–9 . . . .240, 243
T II.xvi.186–87: 410–11 225
T II.xvi.190: 411–12 241
T II.xvi.192: 412 241
T II.xviii.199: 416 228
T II.xviii.199: 417 228
T II.xviii.200: 418 228
T II.xviii.202: 418–19 229
T II.xviii.208: 422 230
T II.xix.212: 425–26 232
T II.xix.213: 426 231
T II.xix.214: 426–27 234

T II.xix.215: 427 234
T II.xix.216: 427 234
T II.xix.217: 427–28 234
T II.xix.219: 429 234
T II.xix.222: 430–32 234
T II.xix.225: 433 235
T II.xix.227: 434 . . . . .229, 234
T II.xix.230: 435–36 . . . .234, 235
T II.xix.232: 437 . .226, 229, 230, 234
T II.xix.233: 438–39 230
T II.xix.241: 445 230
TE 186: 239 . . . . . .223, 235
Voluntas: B MS Locke c.28: 114:
    von Leyden 1954: 72–73 . . . 225
W III: 212 259
W III: 220 259
W III: 241 260
W III: 250 260
W III: 272 283
W III: 278 270
W III: 296 223
W IV: 8 and 449 82
W IV: 18 79
W IV: 19 87
W IV: 32 264
W IV: 33 . . . . 80, 264
W IV: 129–30 26
W IV: 130 27
W IV: 138–39 260
W IV: 146 190
W IV: [191] 263
W IV: 445–46 79
W IV: 446 79
W IV: 448 88
W IV: 467–68 73
W IV: 470–71 88
W VII: 9 258
W VII: 11. 252
W VII: 129 223
W VII: 133 218
W VII: 134 217
W VII: 135 196
W VII: 139 218
W VII: 140 166
W VII: 140–43 218
W VII: 146 218
W IX: 220 33
W IX: 250 33